Family Dynamics: Contemporary Issues in Family Law

Family Dynamics: Contemporary Issues in Family Law

edited by

Jane Scoular, LLB, LLM
Lecturer in Law, University of Strathclyde

Print on Demand Edition

Tottel
publishing

Published by
Tottel Publishing Ltd
Maxwelton House
41-43 Boltro Road
Haywards Heath
West Sussex
RH16 1BJ

Tottel Publishing Ltd
9-10 St Andrew Square
Edinburgh
EH2 2AF

ISBN 13: 978-1-84592-547-5
ISBN 10: 1-84592-547-5

First published 1996
Second edition 2002
Formerly published by LexisNexis Butterworths

Reprinted by Tottel Publishing Ltd 2007

British Library Cataloguing-in-Publication Data.
A catalogue record for this book is available from the British Library.

Typeset by Phoenix Photosetting, Chatham, Kent
Printed and bound in Great Britain by
CPI Antony Rowe, Eastbourne, East Sussex

Preface

Family law has developed beyond all recognition over the last thirty years. It is an increasingly complex and fascinating subject, demanding considerable application and ability from those specialising in the field. The very concept of 'family' has become broader and more inclusive, as the law has sought to reflect the changing views and customs of society.

This collection of essays offers a refreshingly modern, yet scholarly and philosophical approach to topics of current interest in family law. The status and attributes of traditional marriage; the rights and obligations of co-habitees, including same sex-couples; the increasingly broad definitions of 'parent' and 'parenthood' (including parenthood resulting from assisted reproduction); the need for protection of vulnerable family members; the philosophies underlying adoption procedures; the distinctive features of children's hearings and the advantages of mediation as opposed to traditional adversarial court procedure, are but a few of the subjects covered in these essays. Footnotes give useful references not only to case-law and legislation, but also to research work which might otherwise be difficult to trace. The authors and editor are to be congratulated on their achievement in gathering together such a wealth of material in such a readable form, and compiling a work which is both thought provoking and useful.

The Hon Lady Paton
The Court of Session
November 2001

Contents

List of Contributors

Alison Cleland is a Lecturer in Law at Napier University, Edinburgh.

Claire McDiarmid is a Lecturer in Law at the University of Strathclyde.

Elaine E Sutherland is a Senior Lecturer in Law at the University of Glasgow and Professor of Law at the Lewis and Clark Law School, Portland, Oregon.

Anne Griffiths is a Reader in Law at the University of Edinburgh.

Margaret Ross is a Senior Lecturer in Law at the University of Aberdeen.

Eric Clive is a Professor of Law at the University of Edinburgh.

Kenneth McK Norrie is a Professor of Law at the University of Strathclyde.

Clare Connelly is a Lecturer in Law at the University of Glasgow.

Jane Scoular is a Lecturer in Law at the University of Strathclyde.

Table of Statutes

Table of Cases

Table of Statutory Instruments

Table of European and International Materials

Introducing Family Dynamics: Contemporary Issues in Family Law

Jane Scoular

Family Dynamics is the first edited collection of essays on 'general' family law to emerge from Scotland[1]. It takes a distinctive approach in that its focus on 'the family' is influenced by Morgan's approach to family practices where individuals 'do' family[2] rather than 'passively residing within pre-given structures'[3]. In this way it is possible to consider the way in which families have adapted and transformed in light of, and have indeed contributed to, wider social trends, particularly emerging forms of citizenship, 'evolving employment patterns, shifting gender relations and increasing options in sexual relationships'[4]. Recognition of these dynamics requires a more complex understanding of the family as dynamic rather than as a pre-determined 'institution' separate from other social processes and in turn, such recognition demands a more nuanced approach to legal discourse. It is instructive, in this context, to consider the wider debate in law and society between an instrumental and a constitutive approach. Garth and Sarat outline the distinction:

> 'The basic question guiding the instrumental approach is what social results can be attributed to law or legal reforms . . . In framing these questions, law can be seen as an independent variable . . . something that is brought to an already constituted social situation'[5].

In contrast, a constitutive approach

> 'sees law more as a pervasive influence in structuring society than as a variable whose impact can be measured. Law is seen as a way of organizing the world into categories and concepts which, while providing spaces and opportunities, also constrains behavior and serves to legitimate authority'[6].

Thus law provides normative structures which can offer space and resources to increasingly diverse and democratic family relations while simultaneously

1 This is not to overlook the outstanding contribution made to the field by Alison Cleland and Elaine Sutherland's *Children's Rights in Scotland* (2nd edn 2001) W Green, Edinburgh. The focus of their collection, however, is the position and experience of children in a variety of legal contexts including family law.

2 D Morgan *Family Connections* (1996) Polity Press, Cambridge.

3 'The New Practices and Politics of Family Life' in E Silva and C Smart (eds) *The New Family* (1999) Sage, London.

4 *E Silva and C Smart* (eds) *The New Family* (1999) Sage, London p 1.

5 B Garth and A Sarat 'Studying How Law Matters' in B Garth and A Sarat *How Does Law Matter?* (1998) Northwestern University Press, Illinois.

6 A Sarat and T Kearns 'Beyond the Great Divide: Forms of Legal Scholarship and Everyday Life' in A Sarat and T Kearns (eds) *Law in Everyday Life* (1993) Univ of Michigan Press, Ann Arbor p 2.

increasing the province of governance[1] and constraining more radical elements of such projects.

Family law as a result 'must be seen as the outcome of social forces and as a force which in turn impinges on people in society, on their habits and their convictions'[2].

An appreciation of these dynamics inspires the title of this collection which explores the relationship between legal discourses and changing family forms, the dynamics of gender, sexuality and the increasing importance of children's rights.

Scots law informs many of the perspectives, but it is considered alongside comparative examples, anthropological and empirical work and the impact of policy and theoretical developments on this most vital area of law.

PART ONE: ENGAGING CHILDREN'S PERSPECTIVES IN FAMILY LAW

In Chapter 1, Alison Cleland begins by offering a conceptual history of 'childhood' as it has been constructed in society. This provides a framework from which to analyse the 'shift away from law's almost exclusive concentration on the protection of the individual child to a recognition of the interests, indeed rights of children as a class or group'[3] – a process very much accelerated by the recent constitutional recognition of children as rights-bearing citizens. In evaluating this transition, Cleland maps the various locations of decision-making in and about families and considers the effectiveness of mechanisms which facilitate the inclusion of children's voices. The various 'levels' of participation, from information to direct influence in a court case, are identified and measured against the UN Convention on the Rights of the Child and research on children's experiences in this field. Cleland's insightful conclusions aim to enhance the 'protected empowerment' of children in families and family law, brilliantly informs and invigorates the project for equivalent rights[4] of children in this context.

In Chapter 2 Claire McDiarmid offers an original perspective on the Scottish system of children's hearings. This chapter employs a feminist perspective[5] in theorising on the hearing process and its distinct approach to 'consensus, contextualisation and the recognition of the standpoint and accumulated knowledge of all contributors'[6]. Drawing on these themes. McDiarmid examines the issues raised in the previous chapter. She focuses in detail on the tensions between the paramountcy of the child's welfare and the increasing rights orientation in

---

1 M Foucault *The History of Sexuality, Volume One*, tr Robert, Hurley (1978) Vintage, New York. By bringing in sexualities previously outcast and reconstructing homosexuals as 'juridical subjects', the state is able to exert power in more diffuse ways through regulation and normalisation. Power in this sense is not negative but is productive: see C Smart *Feminism and the Power of Law* (1989) Routledge, London.

2 M Glendon *The Transformation of Family Law* (1996) University of Chicago Press, p 16, referring to the work of Otto Kahn-Freund.

3 A Bainham 'Children Law at the Millennium' in S Cretney and E Butler-Sloss (eds) *Family Law: Essays for the New Millennium* (2000) Family Law, Bristol p 113.

4 D Cornell *Beyond Accommodation* (1991) Routledge, New York.

5 K T Bartlett 'Feminist Legal Method' (1990) 103(4) *Harv LR*, p 829.

6 See C McDiarmid above, p 34.

child and family law. In considering the place of children's voices in the process[1] particular attention is paid to the issues raised by the child who is silent in a hearing. Both chapters can be seen to offer, not polar arguments but enriching perspectives which are equally concerned to promote and protect the agency and interests of children in family contexts.

PART TWO: CONFIGURING PARENTING

In Chapter 3, Elaine Sutherland provides an engaging analysis of the various constructions of 'parenthood' which are represented in legal discourse or indeed are excluded by its strictures. In contrast to historical approaches to the status of parent (which were influenced by 'patriarchal, marriage-oriented, adult-centric concepts'), this chapter presents 'parenthood' and 'parenting' as 'a fluid set of social practices and expectations that are historically and culturally situated, and its meaning is contingent upon broader social and political exigencies'[2]. This fluid concept is shown by Sutherland to reflect certain changes in 'political rhetoric, social policies, legal provisions, by innovations in biomedical technologies, and by new outlooks in social sciences'[3].

This analysis provides an excellent precursor to Chapter 4, where Anne Griffiths asks that we re-conceive our understandings of family away from a nuclear model towards a recognition of multiple parenthood – she argues cogently, that the dynamics of an 'individuals' life courses belie the salience of adhering to this type of paradigm when dealing with family relationships'[4]. Importantly both Sutherland's and Griffiths' approaches to the parenting issue recognise the importance of children's agency. Sutherland, as in her many contributions to this area, raises awareness of the interests and rights of children in any consideration of who may be, or what characteristics define, a parent. This is also the approach taken by Griffiths who refers to Carole Smart's empirical work on children's views of parenting and ways in which children negotiate their relationship with a variety of individuals who may perform this role. This work provides a vital perspective in an area that has traditionally been dominated by adult interests. Indeed this becomes the central focus for Margaret Ross's brilliant analysis of adoption law in Chapter 5. This chapter most directly takes on the themes of 'Family Dynamics' in vividly presenting the current legal process and meanings of adoption as a 'still-image' set against the moving picture of family life. Ross argues that the dramatic realignment of families which legal adoption performs does not reflect the dynamics of child-care and family life for those who experience this process. The renewed political support for adoption as a 'good thing for children' is questioned as, it is argued, security, in this context, is presented as only achievable by 'airbrushing' out 'difficult histories' and by configuring family boundaries which deny 'the subjective influences which constitute identity and completeness'[5].

1 C Hallett *et al The Evaluation of Children's Hearings in Scotland: Deciding in Children's Interests* (1988) Scottish Office CRU, Edinburgh.

2 S Sclater, A Bainham and M Richards *What is a Parent? A Socio-Legal Analysis* (1999) Hart Publishing, Oxford.

3 S Sclater, A Bainham and M Richards *What is a Parent? A Socio-Legal Analysis* (1999) Hart Publishing, Oxford p 1.

4 See A Griffiths above, p 101.

5 See M Ross above, p 128.

PART THREE: DEMOCRATISING INTIMATE PARTNERSHIPS

In Part Three contrasting perspectives are offered on the legal recognition and regulation of different family forms. Increasing pressure has been placed on law to reflect the wide-ranging ways in which individuals choose to form intimate relationships. Cohabiting relationships and same-sex partnerships are in particular attracting certain sporadic legal rights and obligations that were traditionally reserved for those who 'enjoyed' the privileged status of marriage.

In Chapter 6, the project to configure a modern civil code is used to inspire Eric Clive's exploration of the legal regulation of intimate partnerships. The opportunity to construct a new normative order brings with it the opportunity to consider the state's role in prescribing and regulating intimate relationships, a theme continued in the ensuing chapter. By reviewing the anomalous and discriminatory elements in current legal provision, Clive is able to restructure and propose a more inclusive and egalitarian model, which manages at the same time to be pragmatic in its approach.

In Chapter 7, Kenneth Norrie adopts an 'instrumental' approach in his exposition on same-sex relationships in family law. In outlining the changing social and legal perceptions of same-sex relationships, Norrie focuses in particular on the jettisoning of the 'moral' content of the concept of 'family' and consequent moves towards a functionalist approach which provide an opportunity for inclusion. Legal discourse, which has been instrumental in constructing homosexuality as criminal and dangerous and relationships as 'pretend families' is also able to provide resources and space in which minorities can mobilise, through the strategic use of rights and other concepts, in order to qualify for public resources and protection. Interestingly the distinct (yet overlapping) movements of contractualisation[1] and constitutionalism[2], which have recently impacted on family law, offer such a space. Yet Norrie warns that the legal norms of 'rights' or 'contract' are also able to 'constrain social change by constituting boundaries that circumscribe the more radical aspects of social action'[3]. Engagement in rights discourse is a useful way to appeal to law, which is only able to recognise and accommodate coherent identities. To prioritise 'rights' as a singular mode of political action, however, runs the risk of constituting identities in ways that fix sexuality as a historical fact[4] rather than the dynamic that it is[5]. Similarly the private contract model may also only offer recognition to those who fit within a heterosexist norm; that of the private, long-term, monogamous and economically independent unit[6]. Such projects carry with them the risk of assimilation rather than emancipation from fixed categories and notions.

1 J Dewar 'Family Law and its Discontents' *2000 Int J of Law, Politics and the Family* p 59. This describes the increasing recognition in legal discourse of marriage as agreement as opposed to status, cohabitation contracts and same-sex partnerships.

2 This describes the proliferation of Human Rights that we are currently experiencing in legal systems across Europe.

3 B Garth and A Sarat, 'Studying How Law Matters' in B Garth and A Sarat *How Does Law Matter?* (1998) Northwestern University Press, Illinois p 6.

4 See L Bower 'Queer Acts and the Politics of "Direct Abuse"' (1994) 28 *Law and Society Review* No 5, 1009. Bowers reviews the decision in *Bowers v Hardwick* 478 US 186, 92 L Ed 2d 140 (1986) which confined homosexuality to a fixed 'sodomitical essence' and gives the impression of homosexuals as a uniform group, which may be useful in terms of political mobilisation but is in no sense representative and may constrain other advancements.

5 J Butler *Gender Trouble: Feminism and the Subversion of Identity* (1990) Routledge, New York.

6 See Norrie, pp 28–29.

Liberal ideology casts the family in a private frame where its social function is to provide a financially autonomous, physically and emotionally fulfilling enclave for its members[1]. Work by 'moral campaigners' and feminists in particular has sought to raise awareness of the pervasiveness of violence in this sphere and set out to recast what has historically been considered 'a private issue' as a social problem, requiring legal and social intervention[2]. The formation of the Scottish Partnership on Domestic Abuse[3], and subsequent National Strategy to Address Domestic Abuse in Scotland[4] is testament to this progress. So too is the priority given to 'better protection for vulnerable partners' in the recent White Paper *Parents and Children*[5].

In Chapter 8, Clare Connelly strenuously challenges uncritical notions of the family as an enclave or '"safe" place in which care and nurture dominate over competition and danger'[6]. In reviewing the impact of research and policy on domestic abuse, she argues that a better understanding of the dynamics of abusive family relationships and the consequent effects on victims of violence, can inform not only criminal justice responses to this endemic problem but also decision-making in the family sphere where violence is too often a prevalent factor.

The theme of 'privatising the family' is often raised in relation to the increasing move towards informal methods of dispute resolution.

In Chapter 9, Jane Scoular considers the dynamics of power and gender in the context of family dispute processes, drawing particularly on the feminist critiques of the practice of mediation. At its most extreme, the problematisation of women's position in such processes warns that negotiation in cases involving domestic violence can further reify and privatise abuse[7]. Critiques have also examined women's bargaining power in informal settings more generally[8], a key theme being the ability of linguistic structures to reinforce women's apparent capacity for consensus[9]. More recent work has been informed by critiques of Gilligan's typology of care and rights[10] to produce a more sophisticated analysis,

---

1 A Diduck and F Kaganas *Family Law, Gender and the State* (1999) Hart Publishing, Oxford.

2 E Pizzey *Scream Quietly or the Neighbours Will Hear* (1974) Penguin, Harmondsworth.

3 The Scottish Partnership on Domestic Abuse (*http://www.scotland.gov.uk/library3/law/repo/00.asp*) was established in 1998 with a remit to recommend strategy on domestic abuse within the Government's overall policy on violence against women.

4 The National Strategy to Address Domestic Violence was published in 2000 (*http://www.scotland.gov.uk/library3/law/stra/00.asp*). It calls for the work on domestic violence to progress with the remit of a new national group to oversee work on violence against women. The national group will set up a number of issue–specific working groups which will facilitate the action plan which has identified the key objectives as provision, protection and prevention.

5 *http://www.scotland.gov.uk/justice/familylaw/pac-00.asp*.

6 A Diduck and F Kaganas *Family Law, Gender and the State* (1999) Hart Publishing, Oxford, p 11.

7 H Astor 'Feminist Issues in ADR' (1991) 65 *Law Institute Journal* (1991) 69-71; H Astor 'Domestic Violence and Mediation' (1990) *Australian Dispute Resolution Journal* 143; A Gagnon 'Ending Mandatory Mediation for Battered Women' (1992) *Harvard Women's Law Journal* 15 pp 272–294 at p 289.

8 T de Grillo 'The Mediation Alternative: Process Dangers for Women' (1990-1991) *Yale LJ* 100, 1545; A Bottomly 'What is Happening to Family Law: A Feminist critique of Conciliation' in C Smart and J Brophy (eds) *Women in Law*, (1985) Routledge and Kegan Paul, London.

9 S Cobb '"Theories of Responsibility": The Social Construction of Intentions in Mediation' (1994) 18 *Discourse Processes* 165–186 J Conley & W O'Barr *Just Words: Law, Language and Power* (1998) University of Chicago Press, Chicago & London.

10 C Gilligan *In A Different Voice, Psychological Theory and Women's Development* (1992) Harvard University Press, Cambridge, Mass.

which, by distinguishing caring 'for' and caring 'about', forms a necessary re-emphasis of the need to recognise the material outcomes of negotiated agreements[1]. The chapter aims not to counter these vital concerns but rather considers whether informal processes can sustain such a critique. The author argues that reflection on the ethical framework of mediation must focus on these recognised critiques and limitations, but can also offer new ways to conceptualise its potential to transform and empower[2].

The editor would like to thank her colleagues who contributed to this collection not only their ideas and enthusiasm for family law but also their vital encouragement and advice which helped sustain their rookie editor. This process was very much spurred on by a seminar in February 2001 at Strathclyde Law School where many of us (sadly not all) participated in an invigorating session, which very much helped shape the direction of this work. It is hoped that this is not the last of such congregations.

It is a happy coincidence that the commissioning editor at Butterworths, Jenny Blair, who helped get this project 'off the ground' will have a new addition to her own family when this book is published. The writers would like to thank her for her encouragement and commitment to the collection and this gratitude is extended to Carole Dalgleish and David Fleming who have adeptly managed the project to completion.

A final and important mark of thanks must also go to Lady Ann Paton, who so kindly agreed to write a preface for this collection.

1 C Smart 'The Legal and Moral Ordering of Child Custody' (1991) 18 *J Law & Soc*, No 4, p 485.

2 Although this is recognised to be much more circumscribed than many claims in this area would suggest.

1 Children's Voices

Alison Cleland

'The task is to open up a range of possibilities for children to receive information and to be consulted or represented, both inside and outside the family justice system'[1].

This chapter will consider the mechanisms by which children's voices – their views, feelings and opinions – can be heard and taken account of in family law decision-making processes. The conceptual framework around children's rights will first be examined, to ascertain why children's voices have been thought of as increasingly important parts of these processes. That examination will reveal the increasing prominence of a model of children's rights that will be termed 'protected empowerment'. Thereafter, the circumstances in which decisions about families are made will be mapped, to identify where children's voices may potentially be heard. Finally, the chapter will examine the mechanisms in place which are intended to allow children to express views, analysing how and to what extent children are able to influence family law decisions that affect their lives. That analysis will allow a judgment on whether Scots law can be regarded as having placed children in a state of 'protected empowerment' in family law decision-making.

CHILDREN'S RIGHTS: THE CONCEPTUAL FRAMEWORK

The development of the concept of children's rights must begin with the identification of children as a group in society, worthy of note and comment. This has not always been a given and indeed, in his philosophical discussion of the concepts of 'children' and of 'rights', Archard[2] begins with John Locke, noting that the philosopher, writing in the seventeenth century, regarded children as not yet fully rational human beings. The absence of rationality allowed Locke to conclude that children should be denied citizenship[3]. Locke wrote that it was only through education[4] that the child could be moulded into a person able to exercise reason.

1 C Piper 'Barriers to Seeing and Hearing Children in Private Law Proceedings' [1999] Fam Law 394 at p 398.
2 D Archard *Children: Rights & Childhood* (1993) Routledge, London.
3 D Archard *Children: Rights & Childhood* (1993) Routledge, London p 2.
4 See F W Garforth *Locke's Thoughts Concerning Education* (1964) Heinemann, London.

This was not, however, the only view of children in earlier centuries' writings. In his historical work on the family, sex and marriage, Lawrence Stone noted[1] that Christian, and particularly Calvinist, doctrine held that children were born into original sin and must therefore be subordinated to parents, who would repress their will.

The ways in which children have been viewed by society may account for the different approaches taken to 'childhood' throughout history. Many writers refer approvingly to Aries' work on childhood[2], in which he contends that in medieval society, the idea of childhood did not exist, with children being dressed and treated as adults from around age seven. Archard, however, states: 'Aries claims to disclose an absence in the past where he should only have found a dissimilar presence'[3]. Archard argues that what Aries regarded as a failure to recognise childhood as a concept in any real sense was simply a different understanding of the concept. The very useful distinction is drawn in his argument between a 'concept' and a 'conception' of childhood. Drawing on Rawls' writing on justice[4], it is argued that the concept of childhood requires that the child be distinguished from adults by some set of attributes and that the conception of childhood is the specification of those attributes. Since Aries himself admitted that adults were aware of differences between adults and children, Archard argues that there could have been a concept of childhood in medieval times, but the conception of it could have been significantly different from the modern conception of childhood. The distinction between concept and conception will be used throughout, to assess the 'conception' of childhood that may be influencing family law now.

What is the modern conception of childhood? Jean-Jacques Rousseau is regarded as the philosopher who first pioneered a modern view of childhood, in his educational treatise *Emile*, written in 1762[5]. The work, building on Rousseau's central theme that man is by nature good, suggested that children were moral innocents. As such, they were different from adults and, as a result of that different state, requiring special care and protection. The work of Aries illustrates how, during the sixteenth and seventeenth centuries, this awareness of difference led to children's gradual separation, by their clothes and by their activities, from adults.

Flekkøy and Kaufman[6] identify concern for protection and education of children in the nineteenth century as the basis for the concept of childhood as a state of vulnerability, separate from adults. Freeman[7] also identifies a protectionist view in the mid-nineteenth century, which was to be a time of child-saving and compulsory education. The legislation of the time reflected this protectionism. The Guardianship of Infants Act 1886, for example, required the court in custody disputes 'to make such order as it may think fit . . . having regard to the welfare of the infant . . .'[8].

---

1 L Stone *The Family, Sex and Marriage in England 1500–1800* (abridged edn, 1979) Penguin, Harmondsworth.

2 P Aries *Centuries of Childhood* (original translation, reprinted 1979) Peregrine Books, London.

3 D Archard *Children: Rights & Childhood* (1993) Routledge, London p 19.

4 J Rawls *A Theory of Justice* (1972) Oxford University Press, Oxford.

5 For an introduction to Rousseau's work, see R Grimsley *The Philosophy of Rousseau* (1973) Oxford.

6 M G Flekkøy and N H Kaufman *The Participation Rights of the Child* (1997) Jessica Kingsley, London; see especially ch 2.

7 M D A Freeman *The Rights and Wrongs of Children* (1983) Francis Pinter, London.

8 Discussed in A Cleland and E Sutherland (eds) *Children's Rights In Scotland* (2nd edn, 2001) W Green, Edinburgh, ch 2.

Hart, considering the historical development of children's rights, comes to the same conclusion. He states: 'gradually, children came to be considered as a special class and parents were increasingly expected to maintain, educate and protect them'[1]. It is perhaps fitting, given the importance of protection and welfare to the appreciation of children as a special group, that the origins of international statements on children's rights are to be found in the actions of Eglantyne Jebb, the founder of Save the Children. She campaigned for starving children in the defeated countries of Eastern Europe after World War I and drafted the first international statement of children's rights. This became the Declaration of the Rights of the Child, passed by the League of Nations in 1924.

Veerman[2] and Marshall[3] both analyse the importance of the 1924 Declaration and other international instruments in the formulation of a modern understanding of children's rights. They note that the original Declaration was concerned with the right to protection, as exemplified in the statement 'The child must be first to receive relief in times of distress'[4], and that the subsequent 1948 Declaration on the Rights of the Child was also overtly protective: 'The Child must be protected beyond and above all considerations of race, nationality or creed'[5].

Protection of children had long been an aim of legislation. Indeed, as early as the seventh century, the law for the protection of non-combatants extended to the protection of children until they were able to take up arms[6]. Welfare of children was familiar territory for the law in the early part of the twentieth century. Later, it moved to less familiar concepts as, according to Franklin:

> 'the notion of the "best interests of the child" increasingly came to be supplemented, if not superseded, by the principle that where appropriate the wishes of the child should inform legal decisions'[7].

The discussion of the nature of childhood and the idea of children's rights became more closely identified with notions of fundamental rights and freedoms, during the 1970s in particular, when several papers were written which have become known as the 'liberationist' arguments. Farson argued: 'The acceptance of the child's right to self-determination is fundamental to all the rights to which children are entitled'[8].

Farson and Holt[9] both argued that children were an oppressed group in society, and both discussed the importance of children being allowed to vote and to work. They saw children's exclusion from adult society as a means of holding them in a state of powerlessness. Such polemical arguments raised the question of the nature of 'rights' themselves and the capacity of children to exercise them. In relation to the nature of rights, Freeman's discussion of the different types of

1 S N Hart 'From property to person status: historical perspective on children's rights' 46 *American Psychologist* 1 , 53–59, at p 53.

2 P Veerman *The Rights of the Child and the Changing Image of Childhood* (1992) Martinus Nijhoff, London.

3 K Marshall *Children's Rights in the Balance* (1997) HMSO, Edinburgh.

4 League of Nations, Declaration of the Rights of the Child, 1924, art 3.

5 United Nations, Declaration on the Rights of the Child, 1948, art 1.

6 See K Marshall in A Cleland and E Sutherland (eds) *Children's Rights in Scotland* (2nd edn, 2001) W Green, Edinburgh.

7 B Franklin *The Handbook of Children's Rights* (1995) London, Routledge p 3.

8 R Farson *Birthrights* (1974) Collier Macmillan, London, p 11.

9 J Holt *Escape from Childhood* (1975) Penguin, Harmondsworth.

rights and their potential for exercise by children[1] is particularly useful. He notes that Hohfeld characterised some rights as privileges or freedoms, since they lacked correlative duties, and suggests that some children's 'rights', for example 'adequate nutrition' in the UN Declaration on the Rights of the Child, are in fact claims or privileges. Freeman identifies four categories of rights for children: welfare, protection, social justice and independence. Such analysis reinforces the importance of understanding when children may be regarded as able to claim or exercise rights on their own behalf.

Thus, the issue of child developmental psychology and the extent to which children could be regarded as holders of legal rights became important to the advancement of children's rights. That advancement was assisted, according to Flekkøy and Kaufman[2], by the increasing awareness of child development as a more visible social science. Freud had identified the period from age five or six to puberty as a time when children began to think differently about themselves and their world. Paiget, by studying children's conversations with each other and with adults, concluded that children's intellectual development progressed in predictable stages, including pure intellectual realism, at around age seven, and the stage of formal thought, at age eleven or twelve[3]. Discussion of children's evolving competencies paved the way for the suggestion that children's rights might include the right to participation.

It has been noted that the consideration of the nature of childhood allowed recognition of children as a special group in society and, from that recognition, concern for children's welfare and their need for protection were identified. It has also been noted that the emerging child 'liberation' arguments found some support in work on child development. The right of children to be active participants in decision-making alongside adults fitted well into discussions of human rights and the rights of citizenship, in the latter part of the twentieth century.

Marshall's analysis of the drafting of the UN Convention on the Rights of the Child[4] identifies this emerging emphasis on participation and citizenship. She notes that discussions concentrated initially on the welfare of children, but that as they continued, both France and Colombia argued for the child's right to be consulted, to be an active member of society in general and the family in particular. From these comments, the right of the child to be consulted in matters affecting him or her emerged[5]. Participation became an important focus for arguments about children's rights. In 1992, Hart produced his famous 'ladder of participation'[6], identifying different levels of children's participation in decision-making, from tokenism and decoration, up to child-initiated decisions made together with adults. It was argued that participation was appropriate not only because children deserved respect as human beings, but because it would assist them to function adequately as full members of society at a later date.

---

1 M D A Freeman *The Rights and Wrongs of Children* (1983) Francis Pinter, London ch 2.
2 M G Flekkøy and N H Kaufman *The Participation Rights of the Child* (1997) Jessica Kingsley, London p 18.
3 J Piaget *The Language and Thought of the Child* (3rd edn, 1959) Routledge & Kegan Paul, London.
4 K Marshall *Children's Rights in the Balance* (1997) HMSO, Edinburgh.
5 Now the UN Convention on the Rights of the Child 1989 art 12.
6 R A Hart *'Children's Participation: from Tokenism to citizenship'* (1992) (Innocenti essays No 4) UNICEF, Florence, Italy.

Twenty-first century conceptualisation of children's rights: protected empowerment?

Marshall[1] neatly encapsulates the essence of children's rights in the twenty-first century when she suggests that the drafters of the UN Convention on the Rights of the Child regarded ascertainment of children's views as a critical component of assessment of children's interests. The UN Convention on the Rights of the Child (hereafter 'the Convention'), ratified by the UK Government in 1991, states as one of its guiding principles:

> 'In all actions concerning children, whether undertaken by public or private social welfare institutions, courts of law, administrative authorities or legislative bodies, the best interests of the child shall be a primary consideration'[2].

However, the Convention also requires that:

> 'States Parties shall assure to the child who is capable of forming his or her own views the right to express those views freely in all matters affecting the child, the views of the child being given due weight in accordance with the age and maturity of the child'[3].

The Convention may be regarded as an influential document in relation to recognition of children's rights to protection from abuse and exploitation, and to their right to be heard. In 1992, the Scottish Law Commission *Report on Family Law*[4] cited several principles of the Convention in support of its proposed reforms. The Orkney Inquiry[5] drew on principles of the Convention, many of which had been mentioned by child care organisations in evidence to the Inquiry, in making recommendations for changes to child care law. The Government's White Paper on child care reform specifically referred to the child's right to be heard[6]. It might be argued that the process of consultation itself indicated the importance given to the child's right to participation, since the Government agreed to support and to publish details of a consultation with children and young people on the child care proposals[7]. The resulting legislation, the Children (Scotland) Act 1995, contains several important principles of the Convention[8].

In relation to family law, the relevant legislation is in the Children (Scotland) Act 1995 Part I and s 16. Part I governs private law family cases; s 16 is relevant where a children's hearing makes decisions affecting a family. Consideration of these reveals much about Scots law's approach to the conception of childhood and therefore of children's rights. The law begins[9] with a statement of parents' responsibilities towards their children, the first responsibility being 'to safeguard

1 K Marshall *Children's Rights in the Balance* (1997) HMSO, Edinburgh p 14.
2 UN Convention on the Rights of the Child 1989, art 3 (1).
3 UN Convention on the Rights of the Child 1989, art 12 (1).
4 Scot Law Com no 135.
5 *The Report of the Inquiry into the Removal of Children from Orkney in February 1991* (1992) HMSO, Edinburgh.
6 The Scottish Office Social Work Services Group *Scotland's Children: Proposals for Child Care Policy and Law* Cm 2286 (1993) HMSO, Edinburgh.
7 *Scotland's Children: Speaking Out, Young People's Views on Child Care in Scotland* (1995) HMSO, Edinburgh.
8 For a full analysis of the Children (Scotland) Act 1995 and the preceding Bill's passage through Parliament, see E K M Tisdall *The Children (Scotland) Act 1995: Developing Policy and Law for Scotland's Children* (1997) HMSO, Edinburgh.
9 Children (Scotland) Act 1995 s 1.

and promote the child's health, development and welfare'[1]. This reflects the welfare principle in art 3 of the Convention, and the child's need for protection[2] that was observed in earlier considerations of childhood and children's rights. Parents[3] are given rights under the Children (Scotland) Act 1995[4] in order that they may fulfil their responsibilities. Those who do not have parental responsibilities but who have care and control of children are placed under the responsibility to do what is reasonable in all the circumstances to safeguard the child's health, development and welfare[5].

The Children (Scotland) Act 1995 provides for the child's right to participation in family decisions in three ways. First, those reaching any major decision that involves fulfilling a parental responsibility or exercising a parental right shall:

> 'have regard so far as practicable to the views (if he wishes to express them) of the child concerned, taking account of the child's age and maturity . . . and without prejudice to the generality of this subsection a child twelve years of age or more shall be presumed to be of sufficient age and maturity to form a view'[6].

'Major decision' is not defined, although it is elsewhere provided that the appointment of a guardian would be regarded as such[7]. The Children (Scotland) Act 1995 thus makes a statement that it is expected that children will be consulted in decision-making within the family. Norrie has observed that there appears to be no sanction if this is not done and that the 'right' to be consulted is therefore 'symbolic and educative only'[8]. However, in Hohfeld's terms, the provision must surely be more than a claim, since there is a legal duty placed on those with parental responsibilities and rights to ascertain children's views.

Second, in considering whether to make any order relating to parental responsibilities or rights, guardianship of children or administration of children's property, the court:

> 'taking account of the child's age and maturity, shall so far as practicable –
>
> (i) give him an opportunity to indicate whether he wishes to express his views;
> (ii) if he does so wish, give him an opportunity to express them; and
> (iii) have regard to such views as he may express'[9].

Again, it is provided that a child of twelve years of age or more shall be presumed to be of sufficient age and maturity to form a view[10].

Third, the duty placed on the court in private law matters is placed, in the same terms, on a children's hearing making or reviewing a supervision requirement[11].

These provisions all require that children will be consulted. They include a presumption of maturity at age 12 and are qualified by the words 'so far as

---

1 Children (Scotland) Act 1995, s 1(1)(a).
2 UN Conventions on the Rights of a Child 1989, art 19 provides that states should take all appropriate steps to protect the child from abuse, neglect and exploitation.
3 Not all parents are given parental rights. Children (Scotland) Act 1995 s 3 provides that all mothers and fathers married to the child's mother will have these rights.
4 Children (Scotland) Act 1995, s 2.
5 Children (Scotland) Act 1995, s 5.
6 Children (Scotland) Act 1995, s 6.
7 Children (Scotland) Act 1995, s 7(6).
8 Kenneth McK Norrie *Greens Annotated Acts, Children (Scotland) Act 1995* (revised edn, 1998) W Green, Edinburgh, p 20.
9 Children (Scotland) Act 1995, s 11(7)(b).
10 Children (Scotland) Act 1995, s 11(10).
11 Children (Scotland) Act 1995, s 16(2).

practicable'. The only difference is the requirement in relation to the court and children's hearing that the child be given 'an opportunity' to express the views. That provision is clearly necessary, since mechanisms are required for any position to be put before a court or hearing, whereas presentation of a view in a family setting should be a relatively simple matter.

What do these provisions tell us about Scots law's conception of childhood? Archard[1] indicates that conceptions of childhood may differ in three respects: in boundaries, in dimensions and in divisions. The boundary of childhood is where it ends and Scots law's ambivalence to this is immediately apparent. Parental rights cease when the child reaches 16[2], the age of legal capacity in Scots law[3]. However, the age of majority is 18[4] and the parental responsibility to provide guidance continues until the child is 18[5]. The law clearly envisages a continuing protective role for parents as the child moves into adulthood.

The dimensions of childhood are explained as being the diverse vantage points from which to detect differences between children and adults. Archard gives examples of such vantage points: juridical, biological and epistemological. From the juridical perspective, children are judged as incapable of being legally responsible for their actions until they are eight years old[6] and there is a suggestion that the age of criminal responsibility should be raised further, to age 12[7]. Since, however, Scots law does have a relatively low age of criminal responsibility[8], and since very young children have been held contributorily negligent[9], the juridical perspective may not be the most significant in terms of childhood dimensions.

From the biological perspective, the crucial difference between adults and children has centred on the child's inability to reproduce. Scots law has, historically, seen the onset of puberty as significant. Until reform in 1991[10], children's legal status in civil proceedings was governed by whether they were pupils (below the age of puberty) or minors (had reached puberty). The common law position was that pupils had no ability to act for themselves, whereas minors could initiate or defend court proceedings, with or without a curator[11]. As a result of this biological perspective on childhood, it was not unheard of for children to be represented in court actions in the nineteenth century[12]. This may explain why, in the twenty-first century, Scots law appears more willing to grant children their place in legal proceedings than has been the case, for example, in England[13].

1 D Archard *Children: Rights & Childhood* (1993) Routledge, London p 24.
2 Children (Scotland) Act 1995, s 2(7).
3 Age of Legal Capacity (Scotland) Act 1991, s 1(1).
4 Age of Majority (Scotland) Act 1969, s 1(1).
5 Children (Scotland) Act 1995, s 1(2)(b).
6 Criminal Procedure (Scotland) Act 1995, s 41.
7 The Scottish Executive *Report of Advisory Group on Youth Crime* (2000) HMSO, Edinburgh, also available at www.scotland.gov.uk.
8 The age of criminal responsibility in Norway is 15 and in Belgium it is 18. For comparative analysis of juvenile justice systems, see McCarney (ed) *Juvenile Delinquents and Young People in Danger in an Open Society* (1996) Waterside Press, Winchester.
9 See, for example, *Banner's Tutor v Kennedy's Trs* 1978 SLT (Notes) 83; *Harvey v Cairns* 1989 SLT 107.
10 Under the Age of Legal Capacity (Scotland) Act 1991.
11 For more detailed discussion of the previous law see P Fraser *A Treatise on the Law of Scotland relative to Parent and Child* (2nd edn, 1866), especially pp 149–163 (pupils) and 376–389.
12 *Harvey v Harvey* (1860) 22 D 1198.
13 For contrast between the Scottish and English approaches to children's representation, see Cleland 'A Tale of Two Systems' [2001] 3 *Irish Journal of Family Law* p 18.

It is the epistemological perspective that seems most relevant to the current legal position. That the law has identified children as lacking adult reason and knowledge is clear from its careful imposition of duties on parents to provide to their children *in a manner appropriate to the stage of development of the child* [emphasis added] 'direction and guidance'[1]. That the law recognises the need for children to grow towards such knowledge and reason is equally clear, with the inclusion of the presumption of maturity at age 12. Age 12 must have been regarded as epistemologically, rather than biologically, significant, since law reform abolished all references to 'pupil'[2], which was a concept based on puberty, operating differently for boys and girls. There is additional evidence of the importance of the concept of maturity and reasoning: children of any age may consent to medical procedures and treatment under Scots law, if the doctor is satisfied they are 'capable of understanding the nature and possible consequences of the procedure or treatment'[3].

Having considered the boundaries and three dimensions identified in Archard's analysis, the divisions will now be considered. The divisions are the identified stages of a human being's early years. Under Roman law, four such stages were recognised[4] and Scots common law adopted a similar approach, recognising three stages: pupillarity, minority and majority. Archard suggests that a key period for the modern conception of childhood is 'adolescence', the time from age 12 until adulthood, whenever that may begin. Current Scots law clearly attaches significance to the adolescent or older child, by presuming that children aged 12 or over will have the maturity to form views on private and public law matters and on issues such as guardianship and making a will[5].

From the foregoing analysis, it is suggested that Scots law's conception of childhood is one where the boundary with adulthood is blurred, hovering somewhere around age 16 and 18. That conception regards the protection of children and the promotion of their welfare as crucial, and places that responsibility primarily on parents. It encompasses an understanding that children should grow towards maturity, placing significance on older children's views in decisions affecting them.

This conception of childhood allows for the operation of children's rights in a way that may be called 'protected empowerment'. All decision-makers, whether parents, courts or children's hearings, must regard the welfare of the child as the paramount consideration[6]. Protection of children's welfare is given the highest priority. This may mean refusing to follow a child's wishes, where those wishes conflict with perceived best interests. However, primary legislation, supported by court and children's hearings rules[7], provides that where children wish to be heard, their views must be taken into account. That places them in the same position as any adult coming before a court or hearing. To this extent, the law's insistence on the importance of children's views may be regarded as potentially empowering. An analysis of children's involvement in processes and the

1 Children (Scotland) Act 1995, s 1(1)(b).
2 Age of Legal Capacity (Scotland) Act 1991, s 1(2).
3 Age of Legal Capacity (Scotland) Act 1991, s 2(4).
4 Wilkinson & Norrie, *Parent and Child* (2nd edn, 1999) W Green, Edinburgh ch 2.
5 Age of Legal Capacity (Scotland) Act 1991, s 2(2).
6 Children (Scotland) Act 1995, ss 11(7)(a), 16(1).
7 OCR and Children's Hearings (Scotland) Rules 1996, SI 1996/3261.

effectiveness of mechanisms to facilitate such involvement will allow a judgment on whether Scots law can be regarded as having placed children in a state of 'protected empowerment'.

MAPPING DECISION-MAKING[1]

Informal decision-making within the family

Many decisions affecting children's lives will be made by children and their carers, without recourse to any outside process. Such decisions could relate to holidays, friends, bedtimes, food, and leisure activities. It has been noted that Scots law requires those exercising parental responsibilities and rights to have regard, so far as practicable, to the views of the child concerned and there is a presumption that children aged 12 or over will have the maturity to express views[2].

Marshall notes[3] that some other countries take a similar approach: in Sweden, custodians are required to make increasing allowance for children's views and wishes; in Denmark, parents are to involve children and give weight to their views in personal matters relating to the children.

In its Report recommending the imposition of the duty on parents to consult with their children, the Scottish Law Commission stated that one of the reasons it favoured the duty was to prevent parents from assuming that their children were too immature to consult[4]. The law was therefore intended to be persuasive, rather than prescriptive.

Unless many children were routinely to sue parents for failure to consult on issues of importance to them, case law will not assist us in forming a view of the extent to which children are being consulted. It may be noted in passing that it has been suggested that any decision of a parent remains valid despite a failure to consult[5], and therefore the enforcement of the provision remains problematic.

Informal decision-making outwith the family

A decision affecting family members may be taken in a setting such as mediation, in an attempt to resolve disputes without going to court. It is not usual for children to be involved in the mediation process, as research has shown[6], although a few projects do have a worker for children[7].

In addition to mediation, children may be involved in decision-making by instructing a solicitor to negotiate the terms of a minute of agreement, to avoid the need for court proceedings. Again, there are no indications of the extent to which this is happening. Is it accurate, in any event, to refer to minute of agreement negotiations as 'informal'? On the one hand, they are likely to take place in

1 The mapping approach owes much to the writing of K Marshall, in *Children's Rights in the Balance* (1997) HMSO, Edinburgh.
2 Children (Scotland) Act 1995, s 6(1)(b).
3 K Marshall *Childrens Rights in the Balance* (1997) HMSO, Edinburgh p 35.
4 *Report on Family Law* (Scot Law Com no 135) (1992) para 2.62.
5 Wilkinson & Norrie *Parent and Child* (2nd edn, 1999) W Green, Edinburgh at p 226.
6 *Giving Children a Voice in Mediation; A Study of Mediation Practice* (1994) National Family Mediation in conjunction with the Gulbenkian Foundation.
7 Eg Highland Family Mediation.

the shadow of ongoing court actions and to this extent are certainly linked to the formal processes. On the other hand, the practical mechanisms for reaching decisions – discussions with solicitors, exchange of correspondence – are more akin to mediation than to contested proceedings in court.

It may be suggested that the involvement of children's voices in negotiations among solicitors will depend on two things. First, children must be aware of their right to consult solicitors and feel able to do so. Second, solicitors must respond appropriately to the needs of young clients. These matters will be considered below.

Another type of 'informal' process is the decision-making taken at social work reviews or at other meetings between children, their families and social workers supporting them while the children are 'looked after'[1]. We are considering decision-making affecting families and, in such processes, decisions will often be taken about rehabilitating a child with his or her family, and about the level of contact that should take place between a looked-after child and siblings or parents. The law provides that before taking any decision with respect to a looked-after child, a local authority has a duty to ascertain and have regard to the child's views[2].

Formal decision-making about the family

Decisions about where children are to live and with whom they should have contact may arise in a divorce action. Sheriff courts and the Court of Session have jurisdiction to deal with divorce actions[3]. The sheriff court may deal with 'family actions'[4], which include actions of separation, declarator of parentage and any application for an order relating to parental responsibilities and rights. There is little research evidence about the effects on children of direct involvement in family court cases. This may be because until fairly recently, their involvement was minimal. There is, however, ample research evidence showing the negative effects of parental conflict and divorce itself on children[5]. Given the known negative effects on children's self-esteem, and on their ability to form relationships, studies of children's involvement in family cases are urgently required.

Decisions about where children are to live and whom they will see may be taken by children's hearings, rather than by sheriff courts, where the children are thought to be in need of compulsory measures of supervision[6]. Children have rights to attend their own children's hearing[7] and also a right to appeal against the decision of the hearing[8]. It will be necessary to consider children's involvement in both the hearings and the sheriff court at appeal stage, to analyse the extent to which the children's voices are heard in these processes.

---

1 A child is 'looked after', inter alia, if provided with accommodation by the local authority or placed on a supervision requirement by a children's hearing Children (Scotland) Act 1995, s 17(6).

2 Children (Scotland) Act 1995, s 17(3), (4).

3 Domicile and Matrimonial Proceedings Act 1973.

4 OCR r 33.1(1) gives full definition of 'family action'.

5 See, for example, P R Amato 'Children's adjustment to divorce: theories, hypotheses and empirical support' (1993) *Journal of Marriage and the Family* 55 at 23–38; B J Elliot and M P M Richards 'Children and Divorce: educational performance and behaviour, before and after parental separation' (1991) *International Journal of Law and the Family* 5 at 258–278.

6 Children (Scotland) Act 1995, s 56(6).

7 Children (Scotland) Act 1995, s 45 (1)(a).

8 Children (Scotland) Act 1995, s 51(1)(a).

PARTICIPATION IN DECISION-MAKING

Information on processes

The first thing that anyone requires, before forming and expressing a view on a matter, is information. In relation to family decisions, children will need to know about their rights to be consulted, and will require explanations of any formal or informal processes where the decisions will be made.

Children spend over 30 hours per week, for at least 11 years of their lives, in school. The education system is, therefore, a crucial source of information to them. There is no statutory curriculum in Scottish schools[1] and, in an overcrowded timetable, children are unlikely to be given much information about their rights and responsibilities. There is certainly no protected place in the timetable for such discussions and it appears to be up to individual teachers with an interest to insert relevant information into classes on personal and social education or development.

There are few public sources of information for children about their rights. The only national organisation with an advice service dedicated to child law and children's rights is the Scottish Child Law Centre[2]. The Centre has a freephone number for young people. However, the accessibility of the service to children is limited, since resources do not yet allow the advice line to run outwith school hours and the service is not widely advertised.

In relation to information for children on parental separation, the then Scottish Office (now Scottish Executive) commissioned the Scottish Child Law Centre to produce a magazine called *You Matter*, giving information about the law and court processes when parents separate. Information on the magazine's distribution, and children's views on its usefulness, are not available.

Since children are rarely involved in mediation, it is perhaps not surprising that there appears to be very little child-friendly information on the process[3] but, given the concerns that children have in relation to separation, as evidenced by research, explanations to allay children's fears would be valuable.

How do children who are looked after find out about their rights to express views in reviews? In areas where there are children's rights officers[4], leaflets and other child-friendly information on such rights are often available and distributed to children and young people in residential care. However, there has always been a perceived problem in making such information available to those on home supervision and in foster care, where carers' sensibilities may be a barrier to effective communication with the children.

In order to express a view in a family court action, children would have to be aware that the action was taking place. The court rules attempt to deal with this by requiring that where an order under the Children (Scotland) Act 1995, s 11 is sought, there should be intimation of the writ on the child[5] and that intimation must be in Form F9[6]. The Form F9 attempts to explain, in non-legal language,

1 Guidelines are produced by the Scottish Consultative Council on the Curriculum, eg *Curriculum Design for the Secondary Stage* (1999).

2 The Scottish Child Law Centre is a company limited by guarantee, and a registered Scottish charity, providing advice, information and training on children's rights and on child law, to children and those working with them.

3 Family Mediation Scotland does have two leaflets for children, explaining the process.

4 For example, City of Edinburgh Council and South Lanarkshire Council.

5 OCR r 33.7(1)(h).

6 The equivalent form in the Court of Session is Form 49.8N: RCS 1994 r 49.20.

how children may express views. It tells them that they can write to the court and suggests adults to whom the child might talk. It also gives the Scottish Child Law Centre's advice line number.

A pursuer may crave that intimation on the child be dispensed with. This information is available in court records. A pilot study for the Scottish Executive, which examined 502 court processes[1], found that in 34 per cent of all cases (ie divorce and non-divorce cases) intimation to the child was craved and in 35 per cent of cases dispensation was craved. The study noted that the older the children, the higher the percentage of intimation[2]. In relation to those cases where the court dispensed with the need for service on the child, it is not clear how a child would obtain information that there was a court case ongoing, and how they would know the mechanisms for expressing views in that case.

The study of court records also noted that in 26 per cent of cases where there was intimation to the child, a Form F9 was attached to the court process[3]. Where the Form F9 has been returned, this gives some indication that children have received information and been able to act on it. There is no guarantee, however, that the information on the form has been placed there by the child without undue pressure having been brought to bear by the parent with whom the child lives.

It is also easy to envisage a situation where a parent, having been made aware by a solicitor that the child would receive notification of the court case, would judge it appropriate to intercept the notification, perhaps believing the child would be upset or confused by the official information. In that situation, the child would be in the same uninformed position as the child in respect of whom intimation was dispensed with.

Involvement of children in informal processes

In relation to informal decisions within families, children who participated in a Madrid conference[4] considered topics that included 'the practice of civil consciousness within the family' and 'task-sharing within the family'. The children felt that lack of understanding between generations and excessive protectiveness by parents hampered their participation in family decision-making; they also indicated that they had a lack of information about their own rights[5].

To get an idea of how children may be expressing views, and with what success within their families, consideration is required of the research on family decision-making and assumption of roles. Fortin, summarising research on younger children[6], notes that there appear to be significant differences between children

1 'Monitoring the Children (Scotland) Act 1995: Pilot Study' (2000) SECRU.

2 'Monitoring the Children (Scotland) Act 1995: Pilot Study' (2000) SECRU para 4.9.3–4: 84% of 10–11-year-olds, 87% of 12–14-year-olds and 93% of 15–16-year-olds were to have intimation served on them.

3 'Monitoring the Children (Scotland) Act 1995: Pilot Study' (2000) SECRU para 4.9.5.

4 F Casas 'Policies for Children in Spain in Council of Europe' Evolution of the Role of Children in Family Life: Participation and Negotiation, Conference Proceedings, Ministerio de Asuntos Sociales, Madrid, (1994), discussed in M G Flekkøy and N H Kaufman *The Participation Rights of the Child* (1997) Jessica Kingsley, London p 104.

5 For further information on the points raised, see discussion paper by Mrs Esperanza Ochaita 'The participation of children in the Conference of Madrid; an analysis of the children's conclusions', reproduced in 'Children's rights and childhood policies in Europe; new approaches?' proceedings of Closing Conference of the Childhood Policies Project, Leipzig, 30 May–1 June 1996 (1996) Council of Europe Publishing.

6 See J Fortin *Children's Rights and the Developing Law* (1998) Butterworths ch 3.

up to around age 11 or 12, and those from that age up to age 18[1]. We might expect to see older children taking more active roles in family decision-making.

Flekkøy and Kaufman note that parental attitudes to participation of children are closely connected with attitudes to upbringing and that parental style may develop or reduce the capacity of children to participate. A study in Spain[2] indicated that in decisions about matters solely affecting the children, 88 per cent of those decisions involved the children in the family. There is a pressing need for research in Scotland into the decision-making processes within families, and into attitudes of parents to their children's participation.

While there is little research into decision-making in general within families, there is some information from research on decision-making in the context of parental separation and divorce. Scottish research[3] showed that parents assumed that they knew how their children felt about separation and divorce and did not take steps to test their assumptions. Other research[4] showed that children's experiences of parental separation were made more painful by the fact that they did not receive information from their parents. Fortin suggests[5] that it is reasonable to assume that while the research concerned divorcing couples, non-married parents would be likely to behave similarly, failing to involve children in these important decisions.

Given the lack of research information on family decision-making, views expressed by children in consultations with the Children's Rights Development Unit[6] in the United Kingdom are instructive. The Unit's former Director has summed up the message from young people, regarding the extent to which they are consulted about matters affecting them, thus:

> 'The theme which emerged from *every* group of young people without exception was that they felt that adults did not listen to them, did not respect them, did not take them seriously, did not value what they had to say. They felt this in respect of their personal relationships with parents, in school, in foster and residential care, at a wider level with regard to the media, politicians and policy-makers'[7].

There is a significant lack of information about children's involvement in informal family decision-making, but the available testimony from young people does not give grounds for optimism that when decisions are to be reached affecting children, parents and carers will think to consult them.

It has been noted that children are rarely involved in mediation[8]. Even in those

---

1 For details, see L Mann, R Harmoni and C Power 'Adolescent decision-making: the development of competence' (1989) 12 *Journal of Adolescence* 265.

2 F Casas (1994) 'Policies for Children in Spain in Council of Europe' Evolution of the Role of Children in Family Life: Participation and Negotiation, Conference Proceedings, Ministerio de Asuntos Sociales, Madrid, discussed in M G Flekkøy and N H Kaufman *The Participation Rights of the Child* (1997) Jessica Kingsley, London at p 104.

3 A Mitchell *Children in the Middle: Living Through Divorce* (1985) Tavistock Publications, especially ch 4.

4 J Wallerstein and J Kelly *Surviving the Breakup: How Children and Parents Cope with Divorce* (1980) Grant McIntyre.

5 J Fortin *Children's Rights and the Developing Law* (1998) Butterworths p 162.

6 The Children's Rights Development Unit was a non-governmental organisation set up to monitor and promote the UN Convention on the Rights of the Child in the UK. Its work continued for three years, culminating in the publication of *The UK Agenda for Children* (1994) CRDU, London, which analysed the extent to which law, policy and practice in the UK complied with the UN Convention on the Rights of the Child.

7 G Lansdown 'The Children's Rights Development Unit' in B Franklin *The Handbook of Childrens Rights* (1995) Routledge, London at p 113.

8 For detailed discussion of mediation, see ch 9 below.

mediation processes that do involve children, there is no evaluation of how and to what extent the children's voices are allowed to influence the processes. A study comparing the practice of solicitors, solicitor-mediators and all-issues family mediators in Scotland in assisting divorcing couples[1] noted that all three groups were reluctant to have direct contact with children. Solicitors' reasons related to potential conflicts of interest. The other two groups stressed the need for parents themselves to identify and respond to the children's needs. In England, there is a direct link between divorce, the courts and family mediation[2]. Court welfare officers are responsible for in-court mediation services and the concern, in relation to the child's right to be heard, is that research shows these officers rarely consult children[3].

The issue of informal decision-making processes outwith the family is discussed by Gomes[4], who considers initiatives in Greater Manchester to assist children in care. She notes the importance of accessible information for children on the new advocacy service, and that children's rights officers could support young people to express their points of view to social work officials on a range of issues. Such services were needed to allow children to participate in these informal processes because:

> 'the reality for the young people is that they feel that the workers go through the motions of appearing to involve them in the process, but often the decisions are being made elsewhere'[5].

Research on children's participation in child care reviews is not encouraging. Stein and Ellis[6], having spoken to young people about their experiences, concluded: '. . . how children and young people experience reviews is very much a lottery'[7]. These researchers, and others[8], identified support for young people as the most important factor in facilitating active participation. Children's rights officers who accompany children to reviews, or social workers who take a child-focused approach, can allow the young people to feel able to make a contribution to the process. One young person, writing of her experience of such support, said:

> 'We discussed what I wanted and explored options on how this could be met. This also gave me an opportunity to look at the reports written and comment on them. I then prepared a short report which included how I felt, what I wanted and why. This was so helpful in the review because when I became nervous or agitated I had something to refer to'[9].

1 F Myers and F Wasoff *Meeting in the middle: a study of solicitors' and mediators' divorce practice* (1999) HMSO SECRU.

2 Family Law Act 1996, s 13 allows the court to order parties to attend an information meeting about mediation.

3 M Hester, C Pearson and L Radford 'Domestic Violence: A national survey of court welfare and voluntary sector mediation practice' (1997) The Policy Press, p 30.

4 J Gomes 'An Overview of Advocacy' in J Dalrymple and J Hough *Having a Voice: An Exploration of Children's Rights and Advocacy* (1995) Venture Press, Birmingham.

5 J Gomes 'An Overview of Advocacy' in J Dalrymple and J Hough *Having a Voice: An Exploration of Children's Rights and Advocacy* (1995) Venture Press, Birmingham at p 25.

6 M Stein and S Ellis *Gizza Say* (1982) National Association of Young People in Care.

7 M Stein and S Ellis *Gizza Say* (1982) National Association of Young People in Care p 8.

8 For example Barclay Report *Social Workers – Their Role and Tasks* (1982) National Institute of Social Work.

9 S Patel 'Advocacy Through the Eyes of a Young Person', in 'An Overview of Advocacy' in J Dalrymple and J Hough *Having a Voice: An Exploration of Children's Rights and Advocacy* (1995) Venture Press, Birmingham at p11.

Again, there is a pressing need for research into the mechanisms available to assist young people in preparing for and participating in reviews. The work of social workers and children's rights officers in this area has not been studied.

Involvement of children in formal processes

By their nature, formal court and children's hearing processes may be monitored and researched more easily than informal settings and this section will consider how children's voices are being heard in family court cases and in children's hearings.

(1) Family actions

To exercise the right to separate representation in family proceedings, a child must first be able to instruct a solicitor. There is a preliminary point about the accessibility of the legal profession to young people. While there is little research on the issue, it seems unlikely that children and young people will think of solicitors' offices as welcoming or young person-friendly. This lack of accessibility is an issue to which the Law Society of Scotland requires to give priority[1].

Scots law makes it clear that the judging of a child's capacity to instruct a solicitor is a matter for the solicitor alone. Legislation provides that a child under 16 'shall have legal capacity to instruct a solicitor, in connection with any civil matter, where that person has a general understanding of what it means to do so'[2]. The presumption of maturity at age twelve applies[3]. This has meant that the courts have been unable to intervene to stop the separate representation of a child, once the child has been sisted as a third party. In *Henderson v Henderson*[4], the sheriff was very unhappy that a ten-year-old child was a third party to a divorce action, in which her father was seeking access to her, and said as much in his judgment[5]. However, he did not see it as the court's place to attempt to second guess the solicitor, or to take a view on the child's capacity to instruct: 'I was not happy with the situation, but it seemed to me that it would be wrong for me to do anything other than treat [the child] as any other child witness in any case'[6].

The importance of the Scottish approach to the promotion of children's rights to participation becomes clear when it is compared with equivalent provisions in England. Under English law, the general principle is that a child requires an adult to act with him or her, either a next friend (who will take their instructions and help them initiate proceedings) or a guardian *ad litem* (with whom they may defend proceedings)[7].

The Children Act 1989 directs the court to consider whether a child has sufficient understanding to apply for an order (orders relating to parental responsibilities and rights)[8]. Court rules support this by providing that a minor may initiate proceedings without a next friend or guardian *ad litem* where leave of the

1 The author is aware that work is proceeding to ensure that the Law Society of Scotland's website is accessible and user-friendly for young people.
2 Age of Legal Capacity (Scotland) Act 1991, s 2(4A).
3 Age of Legal Capacity (Scotland) Act 1991, s 2(4A), Children (Scotland) Act 1995, s 11(10).
4 1997 Fam LR 120.
5 *Henderson v Henderson* 1997 Fam LR 120 at 125, para 22–42.
6 *Henderson v Henderson* 1997 Fam LR 120 at 123, para 22–25.
7 Family Proceedings Rules 1991, r 9.2.
8 Children Act 1989, s 10(6).

court is obtained[1], or where a solicitor considers, having regard to understanding, that the child is able to give instructions in relation to the proceedings[2].

The Childrens Act 1989 and English court rules both refer to the child's 'understanding', to apply for a court order and to instruct a solicitor. The English courts have taken a cautious view of the understanding required. First, the more complex the proceedings, the less likely it is that the court will allow the child to have separate representation. In *Re S (A Minor) (Independent Representation)*[3] an 11-year-old child wished to be heard without a guardian *ad litem* in an extremely acrimonious and long-running custody battle. The court held that this was not appropriate, given the emotionally complex and highly fraught nature of the proceedings.

Second, the courts have taken it upon themselves to decide whether a child has sufficient understanding to instruct a solicitor, despite the fact that the rule refers only to the *solicitor* considering whether the child has that understanding. In *Re CT (A Minor) (Wardship: Representation)*[4] it was stated that the court was the final arbiter on the child's ability to instruct a solicitor. In *Re H (A Minor) (Guardian ad Litem: requirement)*[5] Booth J indicated that a great deal was expected of a child who wished to be directly involved in a court action. The child should be able to give instructions on many different matters as the case proceeds through court and make decisions as need arises.

The difference in approach leads to the following conclusions. Children in Scotland have a right to separate representation in family actions, subject only to two limitations. First, they must demonstrate to their solicitor a general understanding of what it means to instruct; and second the court must not refuse their minute to be sisted as a third party to the action. Both limitations are essential and would apply to any adult seeking to enter a family action as a third party. A solicitor cannot act for a client from whom he or she cannot take instructions, and a court must be able to consider the reasonableness of a person's application to become involved in any court action. Acceding to the request may affect the rights of the existing parties and result in further expense for all concerned.

By contrast, children in England do not have a right to separate representation in family actions, since the courts hearing such cases may simply override the children's instructions to solicitors, leaving them with no direct voice in the proceedings.

To obtain legal representation in court processes, children must be eligible for legal aid. Since April 1990 in Scotland, children under the age of 16 have been able to apply on their own behalf for advice and assistance under the civil legal aid scheme and have been assessed on their own resources[6].

The Scottish Office commissioned some research into the uptake of civil legal aid by children[7]. The research indicated that the number of applications by children doubled from 1995–96 to 1996–97, although those applications still accounted for only 3 per cent of total applications, that is, 844 applications[8]. The

1 Family Proceedings Rules 1991, r 9.2A(1)(a).
2 Family Proceedings Rules 1991, r 9.2A(1)(b).
3 *Re S (A Minor) (Independent Representation)* [1993] 3 All ER 36.
4 *Re CT (A Minor) (Wardship: Representation)* [1993] 2 FLR 278.
5 *Re H (A Minor) (Guardian ad Litem: requirement)* [1994] 4 All ER 762.
6 Legal Aid (Scotland) Act 1986, as amended by the Children (Scotland) Act 1995, s 92.
7 F Kean 'Research into the Uptake of Civil Legal Aid by Children under 16 and its Implications for Solicitors', unpublished report for Scottish Office: Legal Studies Research Branch.
8 F Kean 'Research into the Uptake of Civil Legal Aid by Children under 16 and its Implications for Solicitors', unpublished report for Scottish Office: Legal Studies Research Branch' p 6.

increase in applications is important, in that more children are taking advantage of mechanisms available to them to allow their voices to be heard in family actions.

There is no research presently available to indicate the rate of refusal of legal aid applications by children in Scotland or England, but a Legal Aid Board decision in England raised important matters in this regard. In *W v Legal Services Commission*[1], the Court of Appeal dealt with an application to set aside a Legal Aid Board decision to refuse to allow legal aid in proceedings to terminate contact between the child and the parent. The Court of Appeal accepted that the Board had discretion in the matter and refused to uphold the child's applications, since it was clear that to do so would result in delay while the decision was reconsidered, which would be incompatible with the welfare of the child. However, Dame Butler-Sloss stated that the decision in this particular case was not to be taken as a precedent for further refusal of legal aid; she noted that a child litigant should not be deprived of the legal representation that she ought to receive[2].

The basis of the Legal Aid Board decision to refuse was discussed in the case. It was noted that there was a focus on multiple representation and the potential waste of public money. Reasons given by the Scottish Legal Aid Board for refusing some children's applications in Scotland often state that there is no need for separate representation because the child could speak to the sheriff or to a reporter or curator, or state that the child wishes the same outcome as one of the adult parties. This is effectively the same approach as the Legal Aid Board, concerned about potential waste of public funds.

Both Legal Aid Boards' positions appear to breach the European Convention on the Rights of the Child, which states:

> 'In the determination of his civil rights and obligations . . . everyone is entitled to a fair and public hearing within a reasonable time by an independent and impartial tribunal established by law'[3].

Case law on this point discusses the issue of equality of arms. In *Dombo Beheer BV v Netherlands*[4] it was held that each party to a civil action should be able to present his case, including the evidence, in a manner which does not put him at a disadvantage as regards his opponent. A child cannot be left to rely on the possibility that a sheriff or justice *may* consent to speak with him or her. Neither the sheriff in Scotland, nor the justice in England, is under any obligation to do so and may refuse, ironically because of concerns that such an action may breach an adult party's right to due process[5]. Similarly, it is wholly inadequate to ask the child to rely on the reporter, curator or welfare officer to present her case. Those asked to prepare reports for the court have an obligation to do nothing other than advise the court of the child's views and may, in some cases, advocate against those views.

Representation by a solicitor will not be a viable option for every child who is the subject of a family action. The solicitor may take the view that the child is unable to give instructions. The child may be too intimidated or otherwise reluc-

---

1 *W v Legal Services Commission* [2000] 2 FLR 821.
2 *W v Legal Services Commission* [2000] 2 FLR 821.
3 European Convention on Human Rights, art 6.1.
4 *Dombo Beheer BV v Netherlands* (1994) 18 EHRR 213.
5 Particularly as the European Convention on Human Rights has now been incorporated into the law of both jurisdictions.

tant to speak to a solicitor. Or the child may simply have no idea that he could express a view on the matters in the case. In cases where the child is not separately represented, the sheriff may appoint a reporter[1] or curator *ad litem* to investigate and report on the child's circumstances, including the child's views.

Research has indicated that a reporter was appointed in 10 per cent of cases in the sample[2]. The curator's role, like that of the safeguarder in children's hearings, may be contrasted sharply with that of a legal representative. The curator is appointed by the court, is an officer of the court, and is not bound to take instructions from the child or to advocate the child's wishes. While a child's voice may be heard through the report, the influence of that voice on the final outcome may be limited.

Where a child expresses a view in the court process, it must be recorded in a prescribed way[3]. Thereafter, the sheriff may decide that the views should be kept confidential. If this is done, arrangements may be made for the views to be placed in a sealed envelope, marked 'confidential – views of the child' and seen only by the sheriff[4]. There are no figures for the frequency with which this is done, although the fact that there have been several reported cases on the matter indicates that it may be fairly high.

The sheriff may decide to discharge the duty to take account of the child's views by speaking directly to the child in chambers. Informal discussions with sheriffs indicate that some will not do this, feeling unequal to the task or being concerned that the information obtained is evidence which has not been heard by the adult parties and therefore liable to give grounds for appeal[5].

(2) Children's hearings

Children's hearings are intended to be child-centred[6]. The need for children to attend their hearings may be dispensed with[7], but since children have rights to attend their own hearings[8], they cannot be excluded from the proceedings if they wish to attend. The children's hearings rules[9] provide for a variety of methods by which children may attempt to influence hearings' decisions, including through a representative, by writing their own reports or through audio or video recordings[10]. However, despite this, research into the hearing system in 1998[11] suggested that children are rarely involved in the decision-making process. It indicated that in 70 per cent of cases, the child expressed no view or made a monosyllabic response to questions posed[12].

In order to form a view on what is being proposed before a hearing, children would require to have knowledge of what was contained in the reports about

1 OCR r 33.21.
2 'Monitoring The Children (Scotland) Act 1995: Pilot Study' (2000) SECRU, para 4.9.6.
3 OCR r 33.20(2).
4 OCR r 33.20 (2)(a) and (c).
5 Such a concern is likely to be more widespread with the incorporation of the UN Convention on the Rights of the Child into Scots law.
6 For detailed discussion of perspectives on the children's hearing system, see ch 2 below.
7 Children (Scotland) Act 1995, s 45(2).
8 Children (Scotland) Act 1995, s 45(1)(a).
9 Children's Hearings (Scotland) Rules 1996, SI 1996/3261.
10 SI 1996/3261, r 15(4).
11 C Hallet and N Hazel 'The Evaluation of Children's Hearing in Scotland' (1998) SOCRU vol 1.
12 C Hallet and N Hazel 'The Evaluation of Children's Hearing in Scotland' (1998) SOCRU vol 1 at p 47.

them made available to the hearings. Following *McMichael v UK*[1], reports were made available to 'relevant persons' (usually parents) attending hearings[2], but not to children. However, this is set to change, following the case of *S v Miller*[3]. It had originally been argued in this case that the failure to make reports available to children was a violation of the European Convention on Human Rights, art 6. The Reporter to the Children's Panel conceded the point[4] and advised the court of draft guidance for Reporters[5] that would recommend access to the reports for children in most cases. It is important that the child's right to crucial information on which a decision may be based has been recognised. However, it is a matter of regret that there appear to be no proposals to ensure that someone within the social work department, or other relevant office, has the responsibility of taking a child through the reports and explaining them.

The rules provide that where a child comes before a hearing, he or she may be accompanied by one person for the purposes of assisting the child[6]. Legal aid is presently not available for solicitors to attend hearings to assist children, but that may change as a result of *S v Miller*[7]. In that case, a bench of three judges in the Inner House decided that failure to make legal aid available for children's hearings – at least in a case where the child had been referred to the hearing as a result of an alleged offence – was a violation of the European Convention on Human Rights, art 6[8]. It would be difficult for the government to sustain an argument that legal aid should be made available to some children going to hearings, but not to others. The judgments in the case stressed the role of the solicitor in helping a child to understand the proceedings, and that role clearly applied whatever the ground of referral.

Historically, there has been resistance to the idea of increased attendance by solicitors at children's hearings. It has been feared that such attendance would undermine the informality of the hearing, which is seen as a particular strength of the process. However, in terms of children's empowerment, the availability of legal aid and the likely increase in solicitors' involvement are to be welcomed. Hearings make far-reaching decisions about children's futures, including whether contact should take place between them and members of their families. Legal advice before and during hearings will assist children in feeling able to contribute to discussions and to challenge adults' views of what is best for them.

In addition to having a representative at the hearing, a child might advise a hearing of his or her views through a safeguarder. A children's hearing, and a sheriff considering a matter referred from a hearing, is under an obligation in every case to consider whether a person should be appointed to safeguard the child's interests[9]. Safeguarders may be (but are not always) solicitors, but their role is entirely different from that of a solicitor for a child. They are not appointed by the child, cannot be dismissed by the child, and are under no obligation to advocate the child's views.

1 1995 ECHR (24 Feb, unreported).
2 SI 1996/3261, r 5(3).
3 *S v Miller* 2001 SLT 531.
4 *S v Miller* 2001 SLT 531 at p 542.
5 From Scottish Children's Reporters Association.
6 Children's Hearings (Scotland) Rules 1996 SI 1996/3261, r 11(1).
7 *S v Miller* 2001 SLT 531.
8 *S v Miller* 2001 SLT 531 at p 545 and pp 561–562.
9 Children (Scotland) Act 1995, s 41(1).

INFLUENCING DECISION-MAKING

To influence decisions, children must be involved. In relation to informal decision-making in and outwith families, it has been noted that there is a lack of information to tell children about their rights to express views and have those views taken into account. The solution to this may be seen as child advocacy in the widest sense. A useful definition of advocacy has been given by Melton:

> 'Child advocacy attempts to empower children, enabling them to make use of societal resources. Child advocates endeavour to raise the status of children and increase the responsiveness and accountability of institutions affecting them'[1].

More scrutiny of informal procedures is required, to identify what mechanisms are needed to allow children's voices to influence the decision-making.

In relation to formal decision-making about families, we have seen that the legal provisions ensure that, in principle at least, children's views must be sought before the courts or hearings reach a conclusion. The question is: how far are children being allowed to influence those conclusions? The answer lies in the responses of the solicitors and courts to children's participation.

To respond appropriately to the needs of young clients, solicitors must appreciate that children's needs as clients may differ from those of adults. Liddle[2] outlines the importance of taking an interview at a child's pace, being ready to explain in age-appropriate language about the case, and having the skills to put the child at ease without being patronising or clumsy. King and Young[3] suggest detailed preparation may be required before meeting a child client, to ensure an understanding of the child's family and his place in it.

The Law Society of Scotland introduced child law as an area of specialism. This is effectively meaningless, however, since there is no requirement that an applicant has any training or experience in working and communicating with children and young people. It is essential that the legal profession imposes high standards on all those in its ranks who offer services to children. There are models which Scotland could use, such as those in the United States of America[4] and in Australia[5].

The Scottish courts' response is best analysed by comparison with English cases. The English courts have allowed the need to protect a child to override the child's right to participate in proceedings. In *Re S (A Minor) (Independent Representation)*[6], for example, an 11-year-old child who wished to be heard without a guardian *ad litem* in an extremely acrimonious custody case was refused by the court. There were worries about the effect on the child of involvement in what was a very bitter court battle and these concerns, arising from the adults' failure to deal with matters appropriately, were allowed to override the child's clearly expressed wish to be heard in the case.

---

1 G Melton 'Children, politics and morality: The ethics of child advocacy' (1987) 16 *Journal of Clinical Psychology*, 4, pp 357–67, at pp 357–58.

2 Liddle 'Acting for Children' *Handbook for Solicitors and Guardians* Ad Litem *Working with Children* (1992) Law Society of Scotland, Edinburgh.

3 King and Young *The Child As Client: A Handbook for Solicitors Who Represent Children* (1992) especially chs 4–6.

4 'Recommendations of the Conference on Ethical Issues in the Legal Representation of Children' (1996) *Fordham Law Review* 1301.

5 Australian Law Reform Commission *Seen and Heard: priority of children in the legal process* ALRC 84 (1997) Commonwealth of Australia.

6 *Re S (A Minor) (Independent Representation)* [1993] 2 FLR 437.

The Scottish judiciary has also indicated concern about children's direct involvement in cases. In *Henderson v Henderson*[1] the sheriff was clearly concerned about the effect on the ten-year-old child who was a third party to the dispute about contact. He stated:

> 'I do not regard the fact that the child entered the process as a party as of assistance. She was therefore entitled to remain while all the evidence, some of which would have been distressing to her, was heard. In fact, she chose not to do so, but I would have had some difficulty in excluding her'[2].

That concern for welfare has not been allowed to override the child's right to due process. Sheriffs cannot override the judgment of the solicitor as to the child's capacity to instruct and, once the child is a third party, he or she has a right to be heard at all stages of the proceedings. In *Henderson v Henderson*[3], the sheriff described how, having accepted that the child had to be allowed to remain in the court, he removed his wig and gown and sat with the parties and their solicitors round the table.

Fourman v Fourman[4] concerned an opposed application by the mother of three children for a specific issue order, to allow her to take the children abroad to live with her. The eldest child, aged 14 at the time of the proof, wished to be heard in the process and was sisted as a third party to the action. The sheriff viewed that process as useful and allowed the child to give evidence by way of affidavit, to prevent the need for her to be heard in open court.

Both cases illustrate the operation of children's rights in a way that may be called 'protected empowerment'. Children are given their place in the decision-making forum, but adjustments are made to promote their welfare. A consideration of the cases on confidentiality of children's views illustrates this even more clearly. In *Dosoo v Dosoo (No 1)*[5] two children aged 14 and 12 were interviewed by a Reporter. They requested confidentiality and their views were placed in a sealed envelope. The defender sought disclosure, arguing that refusal would be a breach of the European Convention on Human Rights, arts 6 and 8. The views were not disclosed and the court observed that for a child to feel able to express his views freely he had to feel confident in privacy if he wished, which the court should respect except in compelling circumstances.

The opposite view was taken in *McGrath v McGrath*[6], where it was stated that the welfare principle did not apply to the question of whether a child's view should be kept confidential. It was a fundamental principle that a party was entitled to disclosure of all materials, although a court could take into account whether disclosure would involve a real possibility of significant harm to the child. In *Grant v Grant*[7], the court reserved its opinion as to whether the Children (Scotland) Act 1995 created a right of confidentiality for a child, but did refuse to accept that there had been a breach of natural justice, since the information in the curator's report had been explored at proof.

These cases clearly show the operation of 'protected empowerment'. If the child were to be treated like an adult, there would be no question of confidential-

1 *Henderson v Henderson* 1997 Fam LR 120.
2 *Henderson v Henderson* 1997 Fam LR 120, per Sheriff Bell at 125.
3 *Henderson v Henderson* 1997 Fam LR 120.
4 *Fourman v Fourman* 1998 Fam LR 98.
5 *Dosoo v Dosoo (No 1)* 1999 GWD 13-586.
6 *McGrath v McGrath* 1999 GWD 20-915.
7 *Grant v Grant* 2000 GWD 5-177.

ity of views; the requirement of due process would prevail. However, the courts appreciate that children's circumstances may be particularly difficult and have tried to protect the child's confidentiality, even in the face of adult rights. It seems likely that an authoritative decision may have to take the view that, in most cases, children cannot expect confidentiality, but the courts' approach has to date been child-centred and empowering of children.

CONCLUSION

An analysis of Scots law reveals a conception of childhood which accords children's welfare and the need to protect them the highest priority. Parents, courts and children's hearings are all under a duty to promote children's welfare as their paramount consideration. That conception of childhood also places significance on the epistemological view of children, as individuals who grow towards maturity, gaining knowledge and experience which will allow them to take part in decision-making. The most visible indicator of this approach is the presumption of maturity at age 12 and the recognition that children of any age, if judged capable, may consent to medical treatment and instruct solicitors.

Analysis of rules and case law reveals a procedural and judicial attitude which places children in a state of 'protected empowerment'. Courts and children's hearings must give children opportunities to express views if they wish to do so, and must take account of the views so expressed. Courts may not second guess a solicitor's judgment that a child is able to instruct him or her and neither they nor children's hearings may exclude a child who wishes to attend proceedings. Legal aid is available to children on their own resources in respect of family actions, and is likely to be made available for children's hearings. All this points to the empowerment of children, as a group able to stand before proceedings on an equal footing with the adults in the cases.

Family law cases reveal attempts to allow children's voices to be heard, while protecting them from potentially damaging situations. Children have been allowed to give evidence by way of affidavit, formalities have been relaxed during proofs and there has been a reluctance to disclose children's views, where such disclosure could place them in an invidious position in respect of their parents.

It seems that if children manage to get to the courts, they can have a reasonable expectation that their voices will be heard. The most persistent obstacles to the hearing of their voices remain the lack of information for children about their rights and the accessibility to an appropriately trained legal profession to help them exercise those rights.

2 Perspectives on the Children's Hearings System

Claire McDiarmid

INTRODUCTION

Since its inception in 1971, the Scottish children's hearings system has been the subject of research and analysis from a number of perspectives: comparative[1], procedural[2], empirical[3] and theoretical[4]. Whilst not all conclusions drawn have been entirely favourable, the distinctiveness of the system appears to be acknowledged universally and its embodiment of the welfare principle – that all intervention should be in the child's best interests – has been of considerable interest to juvenile justice theorists.

This chapter aims to contribute further to the theoretical side of the debate. It will examine the children's hearing as a form of legal process, considering it particularly as an example of a feminist legal method in practice. It will then go on to consider how well, as a process, it approaches two specific issues which are of particular relevance in the current human rights-orientated climate. These are, first, the possible conflict between the welfare principle and of the European Convention on Human Rights[5] art 8 and, second, the position of the child who remains silent at a hearing.

It is important to clarify at the outset that the chapter is written from the perspective of a member of the children's panel and its content is necessarily informed by the writer's personal experience in that role. This adds a practical dimension to the piece; however it is recognised that certain of the conclusions to which it leads must remain tentative, given that they arise from personal observation[6] rather than forming part of any formal research project.

---

1 S Asquith *Children and Justice: Decision-Making in Children's Hearings and Juvenile Courts* (1983) Edinburgh University Press, Edinburgh.

2 B Kearney *Children's Hearings and the Sheriff Court* (2nd edn, 2000) Butterworths, London; K Norrie *Children's Hearings in Scotland* (1997) W Green, Edinburgh.

3 C Hallett et al *The Evaluation of Children's Hearings in Scotland,* (vol 1), *Deciding in Children's Interests* (1998) Scottish Office Central Research Unit, Edinburgh; L Waterhouse et al *The Evaluation of Children's Hearings in Scotland,* (vol 3), *Children in Focus* (2000) Scottish Office Central Research Unit, Edinburgh; A Griffiths and R F Kandel 'Hearing Children in Children's Hearings' (2000) CFLQ 283.

4 A Morris and H Giller (eds) *Providing Criminal Justice for Children* (1983) Arnold, London; A Lockyer and F Stone (eds) *Juvenile Justice in Scotland: Twenty-Five Years of the Welfare Approach* (1998) T & T Clark, Edinburgh.

5 As incorporated into domestic law by the Human Rights Act 1998.

6 The writer has been a member of the City of Glasgow Children's Panel since 1996 and has attended in excess of 200 individual hearings.

THE CHILDREN'S HEARING AS A LEGAL PROCESS

The children's hearings system constitutes a legal process set up under the auspices of the Scottish legal system, specifically to adjudicate on the needs of children. It is interesting, therefore, to consider how best to characterise it *as* a legal process, before going on to demonstrate the value in viewing this from a feminist perspective.

As the name implies, a children's hearing is a forum which exists for the hearing and determination of issues arising directly either from the actions of a child or from the actions of another party towards, or in relation to, a child[1]. The only issue the determination of which is excluded from the remit of all hearings, is the establishment or rebuttal of the factual basis of the grounds for referral[2]. It is a basic principle of the system that adjudication of the facts is completely separate from the disposal of the case, the former being dealt with either by the acceptance of the child and any relevant person of the grounds[3] or, otherwise[4], by the decision of a sheriff after hearing evidence on the facts[5].

Once established by whichever mechanism, the grounds for referral, together with all other available information concerning the child, are presented to the panel as the material on the basis of which their decision is to be reached. As will be discussed more fully in the course of this chapter, panel members embrace a broad range of information in each individual case in reaching their decision, which is, initially, as to whether compulsory measures of supervision are necessary[6]. They are constrained only by general principles such as the need to operate within the legal framework for children's hearings, the paucity of possible decisions open to them and the 'overarching principles' which must be considered in reaching any decision.

Two of these (three) overarching principles[7] are that the child's welfare throughout his/her childhood is the hearing's paramount consideration, and the need to take cognisance of the child's views. Child-centredness, then, is at the heart of the process[8] and this concentration on the rights, interests (in both senses of that word)[9] and views of one participant (the child for whom the hearing has been called) over all the others, constitutes the first distinction between these proceedings and more traditional court processes[10]. Such processes seek ultimately to attribute remedies or sentences equitably, following determination of the facts (which is, in itself, often the major element of the proceedings). Thus the

---

1 Or, in certain circumstances, towards another child of whose household he/she is, or is likely to become, a member: Children (Scotland) Act 1995, s 52(2).
2 Children (Scotland) Act 1995, s 65(7).
3 Children (Scotland) Act 1995, s 65(5) and (6).
4 Ie if the grounds are denied by the child and/or the relevant person(s) or not understood by the child. Children (Scotland) Act 1995, s 65(7) and (9).
5 Children (Scotland) Act 1995, s 65(7). The children's hearing also has an option under that subsection to discharge the referral completely, as does the sheriff if an application is made to him/her in terms of the Children (Scotland) Act 1995 s 68(9).
6 Children (Scotland) Act 1995, s 69(1).
7 Listed in Children (Scotland) Act 1995, s 16(1), (2) and (3).
8 Scottish Child Law Centre *Children and Young People's Voices: The Law, Legal Services, Systems and Processes in Scotland* (1999) HMSO, Edinburgh p 50.
9 Ie interests in terms of matters and pastimes in which the child is interested, such as football or religion, and interests in terms of ends the pursuit of which will be beneficial to the child, such as security and stability in family life.
10 By which is meant a criminal trial or the hearing of a civil action.

emphasis at the decision stage is on awarding 'just desert'. Children's hearings, on the other hand, are concerned primarily with the child's needs and not at all with what he/she deserves, certainly in the form of punishment.

The second important distinction between the two forms of process lies in the aim pursued. Traditional court processes seek initially and, arguably, as their primary objective to ascertain 'what happened' or to establish the relative truth of competing claims. It is only once this has been achieved that consideration is given to the legal consequences of those findings. The children's hearings system, on the other hand, is concerned solely with moving the child forward from 'what happened'[1]. In strict law, the aim of the process is to decide whether or not to impose a supervision requirement on the child[2]. The only further guidance which the Children (Scotland) Act 1995 gives on this point is that '"supervision" ... may include measures taken for the protection, guidance, treatment or control of the child'[3]. In practice, and because it is more descriptive of the process in which they are involved, panel members themselves hold to the concept of deciding what is 'in the child's best interests'. It is a particularly interesting facet of the system that this concept of 'pure' welfare[4] remains at the heart of individual hearings, certainly in panel members' own understanding of their role.

Overall, then, these two matters – the elevated status of the child in the proceedings and the specialised purpose which the hearing serves – mean that the children's hearing does not fit comfortably into the traditional binary classification of legal processes as either adversarial or inquisitorial. Adversarial proceedings involve two competing sides in a metaphorical 'battle' to convince a relatively passive judge that one version of events is better substantiated than the other. Inquisitorial proceedings, on the other hand, are an attempt by an interventionist judge to ascertain the 'truth'. Neither describes fully the process at a children's hearing, with its concentration on the child's needs and views and its focus on outcome over events[5].

This is not to say that elements of adversarialism are never discernible in children's hearings. For example, where there is conflict between a family and another participant such as a social worker, it is sometimes difficult to facilitate the presentation of their polarised views to the hearing in a non-adversarial way. Equally, where the panel members generate much of the discussion in the form of questions, the hearing may take on an inquisitorial tone.

The important point is, however, that neither of these elements is a given in any hearing; nor, indeed, is any other aspect of the way in which discussion is invoked and conducted. This illustrates what is often regarded as the hallmark of

1 Ie the established grounds for referral.

2 Children (Scotland) Act 1995, ss 69(1) and 70.

3 Children (Scotland) Act 1995, s 52(3).

4 Most juvenile justice systems involve some mixture of 'welfare' and 'justice', the latter being concerned with issues such as the child's due process rights and 'just desert' in relation to 'sentencing' for offences. Taken as a whole, the Scottish system does incorporate elements of both branches of juvenile justice theory, in that children who commit serious offences can be referred to the justice-orientated adult courts. The children's hearings system, however, places the concept of welfare at the centre of all its decision-making. The only exception sometimes cited is found in the Children (Scotland) Act 1995, s 16(5) and authorises a children's hearing to allow protection of the public from serious harm to prevail over the paramountcy of the child's welfare.

5 Clearly, the sentencing process in a criminal trial or the decision as to remedy in a civil case may be closer to the process employed at a children's hearing. However even these processes operate within the adversarial or inquisitorial context.

the hearings system: its informality. Panel members attempt to ascertain, and to have regard to, the views of the child, as well as to ensure that all those present contribute to, and are included in, the discussion, but there are no specific rules as to how this drawing out process should be conducted. In fact, in that this function is specifically entrusted to lay people[1], it is bound to vary widely as each brings to the process his/her own skills and personality traits.

It is, however, also important not to lose sight of the fact that a children's hearing is a *legal* process. Once a children's hearing has been called, the attendance of the family is in no sense voluntary and the child's attendance can be compelled by the issue of a warrant to apprehend[2]. Although the manner in which discussion is conducted is relatively free and non-prescriptive, other aspects of the process are set down clearly as legal requirements. Those commentators who identify the process as a hybrid of the formal and the informal, then, represent that aspect of it best[3].

Why a *feminist* perspective?

If it is accepted that the process at a children's hearing conforms poorly to both the adversarial and the inquisitorial models, then it is important to look beyond these categories in attempting to classify it more accurately. In this regard, it is submitted that a children's hearing exemplifies in practice one particular strand of feminist legal theory – feminist practical reasoning. Before examining this legal method in detail, however, it is necessary to consider the appropriateness in general of any attempt to apply to children feminist theory, which is, by definition, concerned primarily with women[4].

Feminist theory has its origins in the experience of women and feminist *legal* theory has been particularly concerned with the elucidation of the fact that the seemingly value-neutral norms around which law is constructed are often, in fact, male norms[5]. Feminist scholars have considered this in relation to specific issues such as the law on self-defence[6] and the traditional 'reasonable man' test in the law of delict[7].

Feminism can also be said to serve a political as well as a purely theoretical purpose[8]. In that political context, it seeks to lay bare the inequalities between men and women and to redress, to some extent, the balance of benefit in favour of women. In law, this is often accomplished through the process of revelation of the invisible norm as male-orientated. One danger, however, of attempting to

1 See *Lockyer and Shore* at pp 41–47.

2 Children (Scotland) Act 1995, s 45(5).

3 See J Rose 'Procedure in Children's Hearings' 1994 SLT (News) 137 for a discussion of the distinction between 'the relative informality of the setting of hearings and the procedures which must be followed' (p 137).

4 There is also a growing body of feminist work looking at the social construction of male identity and coming under the broad heading of 'masculinities'. See, for example, R Collier *Masculinities, Crime and Criminology: Men, Heterosexuality and the Criminal(ised) Other* (1998) Sage, London; A Mark Liddle 'States, Masculinities and Law: Some Comments on Gender and English State Formation' (1996) *BrJ Crim* 401.

5 In the context of children's hearings, it is also important to note that these norms are adult *male* norms. See C McDiarmid 'A Feminist Perspective on Children Who Kill' (1996) *Res Publica* 3.

6 See K O'Donovan 'Defences for Battered Women Who Kill' (1991) *J Law & Soc* 219.

7 R Martin 'A Feminist View of the Reasonable Man: An Alternative Approach to Liability in Negligence for Personal Injury' (1994) *Anglo-Am LR* 334.

8 See J Conaghan 'Reassessing the Feminist Theoretical Project in Law' (2000) *J Law & Soc* 351.

extrapolate principles from the body of feminist work for application to another societal group (children) is that this may be seen to weaken that political message. In other words, if feminism is purely a theory, similar to, for example, utilitarianism, which can be drawn on in other contexts, then its political claim on behalf of women loses some of its strength.

Also, feminism has uncovered a historical tendency to treat women *as* children[1], which has contributed both to women's invisibility in traditional accounts of history[2] and to their economic effacement. There is, therefore, perhaps a heightened danger that using the same theoretical principles in relation to both women and children may amplify this tendency.

It is clearly important to be aware of both of these potential objections. Nonetheless, it is submitted that, if feminist theory is sufficiently cohesive and dynamic to be capable of application in other contexts, this is a strength of the discipline. Also, it is clear that there are some similarities in the positions occupied by women and children within contemporary society.

First, it is certainly true that power has, traditionally, been concentrated outwith the hands of children in much the same way as was the case for women. This may be justified, to an extent, in relation to children because, by definition, they lack maturity, mentally, emotionally and morally as well as physically. There is, however, some debate as to the extent of the disability to which immaturity, per se, should subject children[3]. In general, then, since one of the aims of feminism is to challenge the disempowerment of women, the methods which it uses to do this should be capable, at least to a limited extent, of extension to other disempowered groups including children[4]. This view has been recognised and pursued in detail by, in particular, Leena Alanen, who concluded that it is possible to 'identif[y] the present state of childhood studies with the first stage of feminist research two decades ago'[5]. Also, feminist analysis of specific issues such as the public/private distinction[6] could clearly impact on children in that both groups are, traditionally, situated together in the private domain.

Feminist practical reasoning

If this, then, explains why it is appropriate, in general, to apply feminist theory to children, it is necessary now to look specifically at feminist practical reasoning

1 This was noted as early as 1792 by Mary Wollstonecraft in *A Vindication of the Rights of Women* (1975) Penguin, Harmondsworth ch 2.

2 See eg A Summers 'Hidden From History: Woman Victims of Crime' in SK Mukherjee and J A Scott (eds) *Woman and Crime* (1981) Allen & Unwin, Sydney at p 22.

3 This view is taken to the extreme by the 'child liberationists'. See, for example, J Holt *Escape from Childhood: The Needs and Rights of Children* (1975) Penguin, Harmondsworth. For a more balanced view, see M Minow 'Children's Rights for The Next Generation: A Feminist Approach to Children's Rights' 1986 *Harv Women's LJ* 1.

4 For a discussion of the similar crossover between race and gender see D H Broom 'Another Tribe: Gender and Inequality' in C Jennett and R G Stewart (eds) *Three Worlds of Inequality: Race, Class and Gender* (1987) MacMillan, Melbourne, especially pp 264–267. It is important to note, however, that there are certain dangers inherent in utilising one narrative of inequality and discrimination as the basis for explanation of the position of another disempowered group within society. With regard to the race/gender crossover, for example, it is possible that some of the race literature may still incorporate a concealed male norm. For this reason, it is important to exercise caution and to be clear about the unique characteristics of both groups when seeking to apply feminist theory to children.

5 L Alanen *Modern Childhood? Exploring the 'Child Question' in Sociology* (1992) Institute for Educational Research, Jyväskylä p 24.

6 See, for example, R Gavison 'Feminism and the Public/Private Distinction' (1992) *Stan LR* 1.

and its applicability to the children's hearing system. This is a useful exercise because formal decision-making in the legal context operates at such a level of abstraction that the facts and issues which are decisive of the final outcome may be far removed from the reality of the lives of those whom the decision affects. This is especially the case where those people are women and children as the operation of the 'male norm' may erase from consideration completely those matters, and those specificities of their lives, which are, in their own opinions, decisive of their cases. Feminist practical reasoning facilitates full consideration of all elements of a case and particularly allows for the voices of the less powerful to be heard within the decision-making process.

The theory of feminist practical reasoning is fully expounded by Kathleen T Bartlett[1] and, as stated before, is an example of a feminist method for informing formal legal decisions. It exists, therefore, primarily as an alternative to, or, more exactly, a broadening out of, the theory of deductive reasoning employed by courts in applying the doctrine of precedent. A children's hearing, clearly, is not overtly constrained in its decision-making, and the way in which its panel members reason, by the principles of *stare decisis*. The hearing's status as a form of *legal* process has already been emphasised however and, therefore, it is appropriate to apply to it this form of legal methodology.

Also, the *feminist* element of this type of practical reasoning seeks to ensure particularly that the voices of women involved in the problem to be resolved are heard and their standpoints brought to bear. The process at a children's hearing has a similar aim but in relation not principally to women's voices but primarily to that of the child. Indeed, because the hearing is set up to provide an opportunity, first and foremost, for full participation by the child, but also, importantly, by his/her family and/or representatives, it can be characterised as particularly inclusive. Equally, because it seeks to obtain as much information as possible about the child's situation[2], it is a very good example of the principle of contextualising the relevant issues in order to reach a decision. This fits well with one of the justifications given by Bartlett for advocating the use of feminist practical reasoning, namely that 'reasoning from context allows a greater respect for difference and for the perspectives of the powerless'[3]. In that the children's hearings system strives to treat all families, and particularly children, with dignity and respect and to ensure that its decisions are informed by their views, a theory which also takes these objectives as a starting point is apposite.

In fact, this principle of looking widely at the available information has been pressed strongly by feminists in several legal spheres, particularly as a means of ensuring more just outcomes for battered women who kill, in relation to the criminal law on provocation and self-defence[4]. The fundamental idea, in that context, is that it is impossible to determine fairly whether the accused truly bears the moral and legal responsibility for the death of another merely by deciding whether the narrow legal definition of provocation is satisfied. This is particularly the case in

1 K T Bartlett 'Feminist Legal Methods' (1990) *Harv LR* 829, pp 849–863.

2 As a minimum, the hearing will have a social background report prepared by a social worker (Children (Scotland) Act 1995, ss 56(7) and 69(1)). It may also have reports from the child's school or nursery as well as psychological or medical reports. One of the hearing's strengths is, however, that it will also actively seek information and opinion from the child and the family before reaching a decision.

3 K T Bartlett 'Feminist Legal Methods' (1990) *Harv LR* 829, p 849.

4 See, for example, C Boyle 'The Battered Wife Syndrome and Self-Defence: *Lavallee v R*' (1990) 4 *Can J of Fam L* 171.

that the standard which the law uses to determine whether the accused was provoked, or indeed, whether he or she acted in self-defence, has been revealed to be predicated on the response expected from an adult *male* to a violent attack or outburst by another adult *male* of similar size and strength[1]. Women, on the other hand – and particularly women who have been subjected to sustained abuse by their partners over a long period – are likely to respond differently and to be moved to extreme violence by the cumulative effect of a number of acts of violence over that period rather than to lose control as a response to a single act. Unless the law takes account of the context in which such offences are committed, and the reality of the life of the accused prior to the killing, it can therefore be criticised for discriminating against women[2]. The limited information which the rules of evidence and precedent permit to establish this point is simply insufficient. The argument is that contextualising the offence, and allowing other details of the accused's life prior to the death to be brought to bear, makes for a fairer assessment of his or her responsibility. Thus, contextualisation serves to promote justice.

The children's hearing process is seeking to establish what constitutes the child's best interests. This is, and requires to be, a highly individualised decision which can only be taken by examining the grounds for referral in the context of the child's life as a whole. Consistency and conformity of individual decisions with each other is unimportant; evaluating all information presented in trying to determine how best to assist the child is crucial. Contextualisation, then, is key to the process. This is a further reason for regarding feminist practical reasoning as an illuminating lens through which to examine the children's hearings system.

How, then, does feminist practical reasoning operate in practice? Clearly, a basic tenet is this need for contextualisation in decision-making or, more precisely, the need to accept, at the outset, that all information available may be of relevance to the decision-making process. It is not appropriate, as the traditional process of 'distinguishing' cases demands, to seek from the beginning to pare away aspects of the case which fit poorly with previous decisions until all that is left are facts to which pre-existing legal principles can be neatly applied.

Thus, practical reasoning requires its exponents to look anew at every situation brought before them, instead of considering it in the light of previous similar cases. All aspects of the matter are brought to the decision-maker somewhat jumbled together and it is for him or her to disentangle them. He or she must decide how to characterise the problem and, indeed, what constitutes 'problem' in the first place as opposed to the means to resolve it. The decision-maker must then indicate exactly why he or she has made the decision he or she did together with the information upon which he or she relied in doing so. There is, therefore, considerably more room for the specificities of individual lives to be brought to bear on the decision.

This view of both decision-making and justification fits well with the process at a children's hearing where facts which are peripheral in other legal decision-making forums are accorded significance. For example, the fact that the child enjoys playing football may inform the decision ultimately reached since the hearing has the power to attach any condition to a supervision requirement, provided it requires compliance by the child[3]. Thus, a supervision requirement could

1 See O'Donovan 'Defences for Battered Women Who Kill' (1991) *J Law & Soc* 219 at p 221.

2 See D Nicolson and R Sanghvi 'Battered Women and Provocation: The Implications of *R v Ahluwalia* [1993] *Crim LR* 728.

3 Children (Scotland) Act 1995, s 70(3)(b).

stipulate, for example, that the child is to attend football training three nights a week, if this is considered to meet his or her needs, for example by minimising his or her opportunity to become involved in offending. Again, in justifying its decisions, a children's hearing cannot hide behind legal or social principles and generalisations. Parental drug use, for example, which is perceived generally as particularly adverse to the child's interests may not, in a specific case, impact upon the child as negatively as his or her own school- or peer-group-related difficulties. In all cases, panel members are required to tease out the elements of the problem, to weigh these carefully in relation to each other and to explain fully and clearly, by reference to these elements, the decision reached. In line with feminist practical reasoning, then, panel members' decision-making 'focus[es] on the specific, real-life dilemmas posed by human conflict – dilemmas that more abstract forms of legal reasoning often tend to gloss over'[1].

Children's hearings' use of the broadest range of information available in decision-making has been endorsed by the Court of Session in *O v Rae*[2]. The case turned on the children's hearing's consideration of an allegation of sexual abuse made by his eldest daughter against the father of five children[3]. This allegation had originally formed part of the grounds for referral in relation to the four younger children but had been deleted by the reporter at the proof hearing before the sheriff. The narrow question was whether a children's hearing could consider unestablished grounds in reaching its decision. The court decided that it could and partly justified its decision in the following terms:

> 'the children's hearings have wide powers of investigation.... [T]hey are not just a disposing body, and their powers are not to be seen as confined within narrow limits determined by the grounds for the referral. They are entitled to ask for and to consider information across a wide range and to obtain the views of various people, including social workers and any safeguarder as to what would be in the best interests of the child.'[4]

This is reinforced by the Children (Scotland) Act 1995, s 69(1) and the Children's Hearings (Scotland) Rules 1996, r 20(3)(a)[5], both of which specify a range of information which children's hearings are to consider, including 'any other relevant information available to them'. It is arguable therefore that children's hearings are not only authorised, but also required in law, to take on board as much information as is available[6].

This broad examination of the facts and fresh treatment of each individual case also serves to insulate the hearings system against a criticism which has been levelled against judicial application of the welfare principle: that the assimilation of the principle of the paramountcy of the child's welfare with the doctrine of precedent may result in the elevation of questionable assumptions about what constitutes a good for children in general, to the status of legal principles. In this regard, with reference specifically to English law, Helen Reece[7] has argued that

1 K T Bartlett 'Feminist Legal Methods' (1990) *Harv LR* 829 at p 850.
2 *O v Rae* 1993 SLT 570.
3 She was already on a supervision requirement and, therefore, not involved in the hearing concerning the other four children.
4 *O v Rae* 1993 SLT 570 at 574.
5 SI 1996/3261.
6 For an examination of the possible effect of the Human Rights Act 1998 on the decision in *O v Rae* 1993 SLT 570, see *S v Miller* 2001 SLT 531 at 542.
7 H Reece 'The Paramountcy Principle: Consensus or Construct' (1996) *Current Legal Problems* 267.

the acceptance as a precedent for application in future cases of the decision in the case of *C v C (A Minor) (Custody Appeal)*[1] that the mother's lesbian relationship was definitive of the case against her in a custody dispute, has formed the basis for a presumption, in other cases, in favour of heterosexual parenting, which a gay parent requires to rebut[2]. In Scotland, the case of *Brixey v Lynas (No 1)*[3] illustrates how a similarly discriminatory assumption – in this case that mothers are always more appropriate carers than fathers for very young children – can become a legal principle simply by being iterated by the House of Lords[4]. Whilst a children's hearing could reach a similarly discriminatory decision if at least two of its members made such assumptions about the best interests of the child, the system's strength, in this context, is that no future hearing would be required to follow that view. Also, because its focus is on the particular circumstances of the individual child, it is less likely to make reference to any view of what constititutes a general good for children as a generic group.

All of this might tend to suggest that panel members' decision-making is not directed at all by rules. In fact, and perhaps particularly because children's hearings take legal decisions, it would be impossible for them to operate completely outwith the framework which some adherence to rules provides. According to Bartlett, in relation to feminist practical reasoning, '[a]long the specificity-generality continuum of rules, [practical reasoning] tends to favor less specific rules or "standards" because of the greater leeway for individualized analysis that standards allow'[5]. Again, this is helpful in the analysis of the operation of the children's hearing in that rules tend to underlie rather than actually direct the manner in which decisions are taken.

The hybrid nature of the system, in terms of its mix of legal requirement and informality, has already been noted. The Children (Scotland) Act 1995, supplemented by the Children's Hearings (Scotland) Rules 1996[6], sets down a legal framework within which each children's hearing is required to operate. These rules can be said to shape the process, giving it definition and outline, by requiring certain procedural matters to be dealt with at specific points in the hearing. For example, an obligation is imposed on the chairman[7] of the hearing to explain the purpose of the hearing to the family before the hearing proceeds[8]. Similarly, the end of the hearing is characterised by a requirement that the chairman inform the family of the hearing's decision, the reasons for that decision and the rights of appeal[9]. Rules of this nature, then, are relatively mechanical[10] and could be characterised as lying more towards the 'specificity' end of the rule continuum.

There are other rules, however, which sit closer to the 'generality' end of the spectrum and which are more integral to panel members' reasoning and

1 *C v C (A Minor) (Custody Appeal)* [1991] 1 FLR 223.
2 H Reece 'The Paramountcy Principle: Consensus or Construct' (1996) *Current Legal Problems* 267 at 1 p 287.
3 *Brixey v Lynas (No 1)* 1996 SLT 908.
4 See E E Sutherland 'The Maternal Preference: Neither a Presumption Nor a Principle?' (1996) *JR* 414 for a critique of the decision.
5 K T Bartlett 'Feminist Legal Methods' (1990) *Harv LR* 829 at p 852.
6 Children's Hearings (Scotland) Rules 1996, SI 1996/3261.
7 The gender-specific term 'chairman' is used throughout the Children (Scotland) Act 1995 and Children's Hearings (Scotland) Rules 1996, SI 1996/3261.
8 Children's Hearings (Scotland) Rules 1996, SI 1996/3261, r 20(2).
9 Children's Hearings (Scotland) Rules 1996, SI 1996/3261, r 20(5).
10 Although, clearly, they do not, nor could they, attempt to advise the chairman how to carry out these obligations.

decision-making processes. *Primus inter pares* of these are the three overarching principles set out in the Children (Scotland) Act 1995, s 16. These are: the paramountcy of the child's welfare throughout his or her childhood, the need to have regard to the child's views, and the idea that an order should only be imposed where it is better to do so for the child, than not to do so. Each principle is a factor to which panel members make conscious reference in deciding cases although they are also stated broadly within the legislation and therefore operate as 'standards' rather than as detailed 'rules'. Similarly, the paucity of decisions available to the panel – effectively either to impose a supervision requirement[1] or to discharge the grounds[2] – is a legal constraint on the use which it can make of the information presented[3].

Bartlett's model of feminist practical reasoning, then, explains well the use made of rules in the children's hearings process, and, overall, its concentration on contextualisation and justifying decisions in real terms is particularly enlightening in this context.

Having looked, thus, at the process in a children's hearing as an example of the praxis of feminist practical reasoning, it is now necessary to consider the children's hearings system's response, as a process, to the two specific issues outlined in the introduction: the potential conflict between the welfare principle and the rights of parents under the European Convention on Human Rights, art 8, and the position of the child who remains silent in the hearing.

These two issues have been chosen because they illustrate well the particular attributes of the children's hearings process which the foregoing discussion has highlighted. The overt concentration on the *child* which is the cornerstone of the system might give rise to the challenge that the role and empowerment of *parents* within the hearing is limited. The first section aims to contest this view. It argues that, even in the context of the Human Rights Act 1998, where positions are routinely polarised by a legal process which *can* only concern itself with one perspective[4], the inclusionism which the hearing practises, and its recognition of the child's position as the centre of a set of familial (and other) relationships, allows it to resist such a challenge both legally and practically.

The second section concentrates more on the hearing's ability to attune itself to the perspective of the child and to respect, in its decision-making, his or her choice to remain silent. It draws on the perceived strength of the system that part of its process involves collating and evaluating the broadest range of information available and it argues that the space created for children to remain silent if they wish is, in fact, a positive attribute.

THE WELFARE PRINCIPLE AND THE RIGHTS OF PARENTS

The UN Convention on the Rights of the Child enshrines the principle that

> '[i]n all actions concerning children, whether undertaken by public or private social welfare institutions, courts of law, administrative authorities or legislative bodies, the best interests of the child shall be a *primary* consideration [emphasis added]'[5].

---

1 Children (Scotland) Act 1995, s 70(1).

2 Children (Scotland) Act 1995, s 69(12).

3 This is tempered to an extent by the ability to attach conditions to supervision requirements: Children (Scotland) Act 1995, s 70(3).

4 That of the person alleging a violation of his or her rights.

5 Art 3(1).

Commentators[1] have noted that Scots law goes further than this by requiring that 'the welfare of th[e] child throughout his childhood shall be [a children's hearing's] *paramount* consideration [emphasis added]'[2].

In order to meet this standard, then, it is appropriate for the hearing to prioritise the child's interests over those of all other participants.

Hitherto, partly because of the strength with which these legislative provisions are expressed, but also as a result of panel members' desire to benefit children, and the social acceptability of this, there has been no particular problem practically, politically or legally in attaching such importance to the child's position. The Human Rights Act 1998, however, has created a potential ripple in this apparently clear water. In giving effect, in UK domestic law, to the European Convention on Human Rights, the 1998 Act confers rights on 'everyone'[3] – ie on all individuals equally. Children, as human beings, are clearly covered by its provisions; however, in contrast to the position under the Scottish domestic legislation, their rights are neither especially safeguarded nor given precedence over those of adults. Thus, a decision of a children's hearing which has taken the child's welfare as its paramount consideration, in accordance with the Children (Scotland) Act 1995, might still fall foul of the Human Rights Act 1998 if it appears that, in reaching its decision, the hearing has failed fully to recognise a parent's Convention right. This situation is most likely to arise in terms of art 8 of the Convention which confers on everyone (ie a child and his or her parents alike) 'the right to respect for his private and family life'. The decision of a children's hearing that a child should be looked after and accommodated by the local authority[4], which is taken by reference primarily to the child's interests, might therefore violate the *parent's* art 8 rights.

The unfettered right to respect for family life is limited by art 8(2) which allows interference with the basic right

> 'by a public authority . . . [where this] is in accordance with the law and is necessary in a democratic society in the interests of national security, public safety or the economic well-being of the country, for the prevention of disorder or crime, for the protection of health or morals, or for the protection of the rights and freedoms of others.'

It is apparent, then, that the article envisages that the need for some balancing of rights will arise in its application. In this balancing process, the jurisprudence of the European Court seems to suggest that it is legitimate to act definitively in the child's best interests provided, first, that this is justified by one of the exceptions to the basic right set out in art 8(2) and, second, that the parents (or anyone else with a right)[5] have participated fully and meaningfully in the decision-making process. It is also necessary that they should have been fully informed of

1 Eg J P Grant and E E Sutherland 'Scots Law and International Conventions' in A Cleland and E E Sutherland (eds) *Children's Rights in Scotland* (2nd edn, 2001) W Green, Edinburgh para 3.33.

2 Children (Scotland) Act 1995, s 16(1).

3 Many of the articles commence with the phrase 'everyone has a right to . . .' or similar formulations. See for example European Convention on Human Rights, arts 5, 8, 9 and 10.

4 Children (Scotland) Act 1995, s 70(3)(a) allows a children's hearing to attach a condition to a supervision requirement requiring the child 'to reside at any place . . . specified in the requirement.'

5 The definition of 'relevant person' under the Children (Scotland) Act 1995, s 93(2)(b) is sufficiently broad to include someone with the day-to-day care of the child who is not, in fact, his or her parent.

their 'due process' rights to appeal[1] and to call for a review[2] of the children's hearing's decision.

This was made clear in the case of *W v United Kingdom*[3] which has resonance in the children's hearings context, although it was specifically concerned with a decision taken by an English local authority to allow the adoption of W's child. In reaching its conclusion that there had been a violation of art 8, the court examined a series of decisions taken by the authority where the parents had either not been informed and involved or else had apparently been under a misapprehension as to the likelihood that their child would be returned to their care. According to the court:

> '[t]he relevant considerations to be weighed ... must perforce include the views and interests of the natural parents. The decision-making process must therefore, in the Court's view, be such as to secure that their views and interests are made known ... and duly taken into account ... and that they are able to exercise in due time any remedies available to them[4].'

A clutch of cases decided on the same day as *W v United Kingdom*[5] reached identical conclusions to the extent of adopting expressly the reasoning in that case on the procedures necessary to ensure compliance on this point with art 8[6]. *R v United Kingdom*[7] was concerned with a decision by a local authority to assume the applicant's parental rights in relation to two of her children, and to terminate her access to them after they had been looked after several times by foster parents, under the auspices of the local authority, due partly to the applicant's partner's drinking and her own difficulties in securing suitable accommodation. The local authority's failure to keep her properly informed and its exclusion of her from certain key discussions were sufficient to amount to a breach of art 8. *O v United Kingdom*[8] related to the restriction and termination of the applicant's access to his children, who had been placed with foster parents after the applicant assaulted one of them. The court decided that art 8 had not, in fact, been breached. Although the case is not explicit on this point, this may have been because the applicant had the benefit of legal assistance and representation in challenging some of the decisions taken by the authority. In *B v United Kingdom*[9] the applicant, who had attended a school for the mentally abnormal, was neither consulted nor given an opportunity to attend meetings at which decisions which resulted in the adoption of her son were taken. The applicant's father was similarly excluded from the decision-making process. This was sufficient to establish a breach of art 8.

This line of decisions makes it clear that, assuming there is justification for the action taken in terms of art 8(2), the informed involvement of parents in the decision-making process validates action taken in relation to children which

1 Children's Hearings (Scotland) Rules 1996, SI 1996/3261, r 20(5)(c) requires the chairman of the hearing to inform the child and relevant person(s) of their right to appeal under the Children (Scotland) Act 1995, s 51.

2 Rights to call for a review are set down in the Children (Scotland) Act 1995, s 73.

3 *W v United Kingdom* (1988) 10 EHRR 29.

4 *W v United Kingdom* (1988) 10 EHRR 29 at 49–50 para 63.

5 *W v United Kingdom* (1988) 10 EHRR 29.

6 For a discussion of the principle see Lord Reed 'The European Human Rights Dimension' (1999) *Scottish Journal of Criminal Justice Studies* 21 at pp 30–34.

7 *R v United Kingdom* (1988) 10 EHRR 74.

8 *O v United Kingdom* (1988) 10 EHRR 82.

9 *B v United Kingdom* (1988) 10 EHRR 87.

would otherwise constitute a breach of the right to respect for private and family life[1]. It is important now to look at the hearings system's ability to respond appropriately to this principle. As discussed above, in reaching any decision, and particularly a decision as serious and emotive as an issue of a child's residence and/or contact with parents, a children's hearing will make use of a wide range of material. This includes material delivered verbally at a hearing by family members, to which considerable importance is attached. The key role played by parents is set out by Janice McGhee and Lorraine Waterhouse. They state that children's hearings 'aim [...] to work in partnership with parents to identify needs and solutions in the best interests of the child, assuming most parents will want the best for their children'[2]. This view of the hearing as a process for family- rather than solely child-centred decision-making is also taken by the Principal Reporter to the Scottish Children's Reporter Administration, Alan Miller[3].

Indeed, the close involvement of parents in the decision-making process is mandated by the legislative framework on which the system rests. In terms of the Children's Hearings (Scotland) Rules 1996, r 20(4)[4], the hearing chairman is required to

> 'inform the child *and any relevant person*[5] of the substance of any reports [etc] ... if it appears to him that this is material to the manner in which the case of the child should be disposed of and that its disclosure would not be detrimental to the interests of the child'.

Perhaps more significantly, r 20(3)(c) imposes an obligation to 'discuss the case with the child, *any relevant person*[6], any safeguarder and representative if attending the hearing'.

Thus, if the hearing does not afford to the parents the same opportunity as it offers to the child to discuss the relevant issues, this constitutes a ground of appeal against its decision. In fact, children's hearings usually adhere both to the letter and to the spirit of these provisions, striving to achieve consensus[7] by drawing all participants into the process[8]. It appears then that, both in theory and in practice, the operation of the children's hearings system satisfies the basic requirements of art 8, even where the decision ultimately taken is clearly in the child's, and not necessarily the parents', interests.

---

1 This general principle of informed involvement has been affirmed more recently in a different context in *Z v Finland* (1998) 25 EHRR 371. The case concerned the seizing, and possible future publicisation, of Z's medical records in relation to the criminal trial of her husband for manslaughter. Z objected to this, partly under art 8. The court, however, took the view that, because all steps had been taken by her and her medical advisers to indicate her objections, 'the decision-making process leading to the measures in question was such as to take her views sufficiently into account for the purposes of Article 8' (at 407).

2 J McGhee and L Waterhouse 'Justice and Welfare: Has the Children (Scotland) Act 1995 Shifted the Balance?' 1998 *Journal of Social Welfare and Family Law* 49, p 50.

3 A Miller 'The Children's Hearings System and the European Convention' 2000 *JLSS* 25 at p 27.

4 Children's Hearings (Scotland) Rules 1996, SI 1996/3261.

5 Emphasis added.

6 Emphasis added.

7 Lord Reed 'The European Human Rights Dimensia' (1999) *SC J of Crim Justice Studies* 21 at p 28.

8 C Hallett et al The Evaluation of Children's Hearings in Scotland (Vol 1) Deciding in Children's Interests (1998) Scottish Office Research Unit, Edinburgh at p 50. L Waterhouse et al *The Evaluation of Childen's Hearing in Scotland* (Vol 3) *Children in Focus* (2000) Scottish Office Central Research Unit, Edinburgh noted that 'both parents and children ... felt that their views were listened to ... at the hearing': p 109.

This is, of course, quite a mechanistic approach to the operation of art 8. An alternative is to examine the welfare principle itself to ascertain whether it can be interpreted so as to pre-empt any conflict with the Human Rights Act 1998 in the first place. This has been attempted by Jonathan Herring in relation to the English courts' interpretation of the principle as set down in the Children Act 1989[1], and its potential conflict with the Human Rights Act 1998. Herring notes that:

> '. . . the present law's understanding of the welfare principle is individualistic. By this is meant that the child and his or her welfare are viewed without regard for the welfare of the rest of his or her family, friends and community. The claims of other members of the family and of the community are only relevant to the extent they directly affect the child's welfare'[2].

Herring's objective is to find a mechanism for balancing parents and children's rights, within the English court structure, in such a way that both the welfare principle and rights under the Human Rights Act 1998 are properly respected. He argues that previous attempts to do this are flawed because they examine the issue as a clash between two competing sets of rights one of which must predominate, thereby forcing the other set into subservience. In his view, this is unhelpful when the rights in question all arise within a family relationship and most families would not view themselves as battling internally in this way[3]. He proposes instead what he terms

> 'relationship-based welfare . . . the effect of which is to move away from conceiving of problems as a clash between parents' and children's rights and towards seeing what is a proper parent–child relationship. The child's welfare is promoted when he or she lives in a fair and just relationship with each parent, preserving the rights of each, but with the child's welfare at the forefront of the family's concern'[4].

Herring is suggesting that viewing the child and his or her interests in isolation is not, in fact, the best way to maximise his or her welfare. Instead, examination of all the relationships within the family of which he or she is an integral part is required, in an attempt to strengthen those ties so that all family members have their rights respected, but the child's interests are primary. In this way, he diminishes the concentration on the child alone but by requiring that he or she is viewed, arguably more realistically, as only one player – albeit the central one – in his or her family unit. If the welfare principle is interpreted in this way then conflict with the Human Rights Act 1998 is obviated because the principle itself takes on board parents' rights as a facet of the child's best interests.

Because a children's hearing is a family forum, it is arguable that this attempt to disentangle the family relationship and make legal orders in the interests of improving its operation is, in fact, exactly what it does. Although any order made can only impose obligations on the child, it is quite usual for some of the discussion at the hearing to centre on issues concerning parents, such as, for example, managing and reducing drug use or assistance which might be available with depression. This is not regarded as a departure from the welfare philosophy

1 The Children Act 1989, s 1(1) contains a provision as to the paramountcy of the child's welfare which is similar to that in the Children (Scotland) Act 1995, s 16(1).

2 J Herring 'The Human Rights Act and the Welfare Principle in Family Law – Conflicting or Complementary?' (1999) *CFLQ* 223 at p 225.

3 J Herring 'The Human Rights Act and the Welfare Principle in Family Law – Conflicting or Complementary?' (1999) *CFLQ* 223 at pp 232–233.

4 J Herring 'The Human Rights Act and the Welfare Principle in Family Law – Conflicting or Complementary?' (1999) *CFLQ* 223 at pp 232–233.

because improvement in these areas for the child's primary care-giver is almost certain to impact positively on the child's life also. The hearing's contextualisation of the child's position – considering him or her at the centre of the matrix of his or her own individual family and social ties – also satisfies Herring's definition of relationship-based welfare. Herring's argument may lose some of its cogency where the children's hearing's decision is to impose a condition of residence outwith the family home although, if one of the reasons for this is that the parent–child relationship has broken down, his view remains valid.

Overall, however, whether or not it is necessary to redefine the welfare principle in this way, it certainly appears that a cogent argument against a challenge by a parent under art 8 can be made, on the basis of the current theory and practice at a children's hearing.

THE SILENT CHILD

It is clear therefore that, as a forum, the children's hearing seeks to involve all participants in decision-making. It remains the case, however, that the views of the child are accorded particular importance. In order to be able to formulate a view on the subject matter of the hearing, clearly the child needs to have an understanding of the grounds for referral, the nature and purpose of the hearing and the prominent role which he or she is permitted and encouraged to play.

In this regard, the recent case of *S v Miller*[1], which considered a number of challenges to the children's hearings system arising under the European Convention on Human Rights, arts 5 and 6, specifically examined the issue of *legal* representation of children at children's hearings. The author welcomes the opinion expressed by all three judges that, in complicated cases, or in cases where a child might have a defence to a criminal charge which would not necessarily be evident either to him or her or to the lay panel members, free legal representation might well be required to ensure that the child's right to a fair trial under art 6 is not violated[2]. The judgments indicate respect for the informal, non-adversarial nature of the proceedings at a children's hearing while at the same time recognising that not

> 'all the children appearing before a hearing [will] be able to understand, far less to criticise or to elucidate, all the reports and other documents and all the factors which the hearing may be called upon to consider when deciding what measures are most appropriate to deal with their case'[3].

It is submitted that legal representation, confined to those cases where the child cannot adequately comprehend and assimilate the documentation and the applicable law without assistance, is likely to enhance his or her ability to express views or to have these represented to the hearing on his or her behalf[4]. As a caveat, however, it is vital that solicitors undertaking such work for young clients are fully briefed in, and respectful of, the unique process utilised by children's

1 *S v Miller* 2001 SLT 531.
2 *S v Miller* 2001 SLT 531 at 544–546, 560–563 and 577–579.
3 *S v Miller* 2001 SLT 531 at 544 per Lord Rodger.
4 At the same time, however, the need to preserve the informal character of the proceedings and to prevent the encroachment of adversarialism is recognised.

hearings. Legal representation should guide the child through complex legal issues and facilitate his or her own participation in the hearing. Much of the perceived benefit will be lost if, instead, solicitors seek to monopolise the hearing's time with obtruse legal argument and generally to treat the hearing as identical to a court.

Even if legal representation of the highest and most sensitive quality is made available in complicated cases, however, this will not detract from the need to match up other innovative mechanisms for hearing the child's voice in the hearings context with the child's own, individualised personality traits and skills[1]. It is with this point, in relation primarily to the child who remains silent in his or her hearing, that this part of the chapter is primarily concerned.

This follows the UN Convention on the Rights of the Child, art 12 which states:

> '1. States Parties shall assure to the child who is capable of forming his or her own views the right to express those views freely in all matters affecting the child, the views of the child being given due weight in accordance with the age and maturity of the child.
>
> 2. For this purpose, the child shall in particular be provided the opportunity to be heard in any judicial and administrative proceeding affecting the child, either directly, or through a representative or an appropriate body, in a manner consistent with the procedural rules of national law.'

This principle is echoed by the Children (Scotland) Act 1995, which, in addition, makes the presumption that a child aged 12 or more is 'of sufficient age and maturity to form a view'[2], and requires a children's hearing 'to have regard to such views as [the child] may express'[3].

It is apparent from the legislative background, then, that the views of the child are of very considerable importance. Also, one of the *raisons d'être* of the children's hearings system is to provide a forum where the child (and his or her family) are treated with dignity and respect in the discussion of their case. This is a point to which considerable emphasis is given in the training of panel members and it is clearly crucial to its application in practice that the child's voice is heard and given due weight. It is particularly important bearing in mind the general disempowerment of children within society and the difficulty which many of them will experience in all circumstances in articulating their position to adults[4]. It is taken as a given, then, in this chapter, that the views of the child are crucial in the children's hearings context. It must also be noted that some children contribute fully in the hearing setting[5] and it is reasonable to interpret this as a sign that the atmosphere lends itself to this.

The point which this part of the chapter seeks to address, however, is the position of the child who remains silent while actually attending his or her hearing. According to Hallett et al, in the hearings which they observed for their research, '[v]ery few children and young people asked questions or initiated discussion'

1 Especially in that none of the three judges recommended the provision of blanket legal aid for all hearings.

2 Children (Scotland) Act 1995, s 16(2). This is reiterated in the Children's Hearings (Scotland) Rules 1996, SI 1996/3261, r 15(5).

3 Children (Scotland) Act 1995, s 16(2)(c).

4 See A Griffiths and R F Kandel 'Hearing Children in Children's Hearings' (2000) *CFLQ* 283, particularly at p 287.

5 C Hallet et al *The Evaluation of Children's Hearings in Scotland* (Vol 1) *Deciding in Children's Interests* (1998) Scottish Office Research Unit, Edinburgh, p 47.

and their contributions to the ongoing discussion 'were frequently monosyllabic or single line contributions'[1]. This is despite the fact that 'there is no doubt that panel members tried often and hard, even in the face of difficult topics and angry or withdrawn participants'[2] to elicit views. These observations are borne out in other hearings[3]. At first glance then, this does appear to be a failing of the system, a tenet of which is facilitating the participation of children in a manner not open to the courts.

It is submitted, however, that provided, as would appear to be the case, the *opportunity* for participation is made available, the actual fact of a child remaining – and being permitted to remain – silent at his or her hearing, may be, in some ways, a strength of the system in that it is simply one facet of the general principle of respect for children and families which is at the heart of the system[4].

First, the nature of the matters under discussion at a hearing is always personal and often extremely painful. While some children may feel more comfortable discussing these with strangers, the Scottish Child Law Centre's recent research gives some support to the view that a larger proportion would prefer to speak to someone they know and trust[5]. In addition, the children's hearings format is designed for maximum openness for, and amongst, the whole family so that the child is actually being asked to give his or her views to three people he or she does not know at all (the panel members), but in the presence of those closest to him or her (his or her family)[6]. It would be extremely difficult for most adults to find an appropriate way of responding in such circumstances.

As a hearing progresses, panel members will observe, and be sensitive to, the effect that any line of discussion appears to be having on a child. The child's interests are not served by sustained pressure to answer questions which clearly cause distress or which lead to him or her effectively withdrawing from all further participation in the hearing. In such circumstances, the child's attentive silence may be preferable.

The general difficulties which are apparent in this area were articulated, albeit anecdotally, in relation to her own role in court proceedings by a curator *ad litem*, in the course of the Scottish Child Law Centre's research into hearing children's voices. She said:

> 'I often think that you're wading in there, and you hope you're doing the right thing; but really you could be doing some dreadful damage. . . . There are times when I think "I'm sure that child is itching to tell me something, but they're just not ready to do it"; and I'm never sure whether to play softly softly and to back off from putting any pressure on the child, and just don't know what the best way is to make them respond'[7].

---

1 C Hallet et al *The Evaluation of Children's Hearings in Scotland* (Vol 1) *Deciding in Children's Interests* (1998) Scottish Office Research Unit, Edinburgh, p 47.

2 C Hallet et al *The Evaluation of Children's Hearings in Scotland* (Vol 1) *Deciding in Children's Interests* (1998) Scottish Office Research Unit, Edinburgh, p 50.

3 From the writer's personal observation as a member of the children's panel.

4 In this respect, then, it is submitted that it is overstating the case to suggest that the child who remains silent in a hearing is not involved in the decision-making process. See ch 1.

5 Scottish Child Law Centre *Children and Young People's Voices: The Law, Legal Services, Systems and Processes in Scotland* (1999) p 10. Although this was specifically in relation to obtaining legal advice, information and representation in the first place.

6 See A Griffiths and R F Kandel 'Hearing Children in Children's Hearings' (2000) *CFLQ* 283 at pp 292–293.

7 Scottish Child Law Centre *Children and Young People's Voices: The Law, Legal Services, Systems and Processes in Scotland* (1999) p 69.

If the child is being asked for a view on his or her residence, and that view is a preference for accommodation outwith the family home, the child may experience guilt in giving voice to it in front of his or her parents[1]. Again, he or she may fear repercussions at home from an abusive parent in relation to disclosure of the abuse made at a hearing[2]. Although it is possible to exclude a relevant person from part of the hearing to assist in obtaining the child's views[3], the obligation to inform that person of 'the substance of what has taken place in his absence'[4] means that the child cannot be offered confidentiality for what he or she says. This is clearly not conducive to the frightened child's expression of his or her opinions. All of these are good reasons for respecting a child's decision, or indeed need, to remain silent in the hearing.

The Children's Hearings (Scotland) Rules 1996 themselves can be construed as an acknowledgment of the fact that children may prefer not to express their views within the hearing itself. Rule 15(1)[5] states:

> 'The children's hearing, taking account of the age and maturity of the child whose case has been referred to the hearing ... shall so far as practicable give the child an opportunity to indicate whether he wishes to express his views.'

This rule could have been expressed more strongly by the omission of the words 'to indicate whether he wishes to'. Even in its implementation of the UN Convention on the Rights of the Child, then, the Scottish legislation has been drafted so as not to pressurise children into expressing views.

The second point which is of importance in this context is that the nature of the child's silence may, in itself, convey information to the panel. The relatively unconstrained nature of panel members' decision-making and the breadth of the information on which it relies has already been discussed. Provided that it is explained at the hearing itself, and properly documented in the panel's reasons for decision, it is acceptable for a panel decision to take into account non-verbal cues given by the child[6]. Such indicators are likely to be taken on board both subconsciously and consciously by panel members and it is submitted that this is appropriate in a system staffed by lay people where each panel member will bring his or her own unique perspective to the decision-making process. Part of the purpose of giving the child both a right and an obligation to attend his or her own hearing[7] is to allow panel members to fit the individual into the context of the reports provided concerning him or her.

It is accepted, however, that non-verbal cues will only ever form part of the basis of decision and that, in some circumstances, they are liable to be misconstrued. A child's refusal to sit next to her mother, for example, may indicate anything from an expression of independence, to irritation over a minor issue, to fear. Panel members obviously require to exercise caution in interpretation. The

1 J Thomson 'The Welfare Principle – Under Attack or Strengthened' 1996 SLT (News) 115 at p 117, makes a similar point about requiring children to express a view in custody disputes as to their preference for residing with one parent as against the other.
2 A Griffiths and R F Kandel 'Hearing Children in Children's Hearings' (2000) *CFLQ* 283 at p 292.
3 Children (Scotland) Act 1995, s 46(1)(a). A relevant person can also be excluded if his/her presence is likely to cause significant distress to the child (s 46(1)(b)).
4 Children (Scotland) Act 1995, s 46(2).
5 Children's Hearings (Scotland) Rules 1996, SI 1996/3261.
6 Training in this area was, in fact, recently offered to City of Glasgow panel members.
7 Children (Scotland) Act 1995, s 45(1).

point is simply that it would be wrong to suggest that the child who remains silent contributes nothing to the hearing.

Of course, this defence of the hearing's approach to the silent child takes no account of the more deep-seated criticism that, if children are not participating in hearings in an informed and enthusiastic fashion, the hearings system is failing in one of its primary aims. It is clear from the research conducted by Rosemary Gallagher on behalf of the Scottish Child Law Centre that there is a need to prepare children better for hearings and to educate them both in the nature of the proceedings themselves and in their own rights[1]. This would assist the child who is overawed and, by clarifying in advance the importance of the child's views, might encourage all children to express these.

Also, it is already accepted that children may find the verbal expression of their views daunting. For this reason, the Children's Hearings (Scotland) Rules 1996 recognise a number of alternative means by which the child's position on the matters under discussion may be brought to the attention of the hearing[2]. First, the child's representative may appear at the hearing for this purpose and may present the child's views either together with the child, where appropriate, or else on the child's behalf. Second, the child may convey views in writing or on audio or video tape or through an interpreter. Finally, a safeguarder may fulfil this function[3].

These are clearly useful methods of bringing the child's views to the attention of the panel, yet they are underutilised. Indeed, Griffiths and Kandel discovered that some children were not even aware of their right to bring a representative to the hearing[4], nor is the diversity of this option clear. A child can select anyone as his or her representative, including another child. It is evident from the research of both Griffiths and Kandel and the Scottish Child Law Centre that there is a need to provide much more information to children about children's hearings and to prepare them more thoroughly as to the way in which the hearing will proceed[5]. While it is hoped that this in itself will assist children in managing to speak out at the hearing, it would also be helpful in making these other methods of presenting views apparent to them. The potential conflict between the child's view – what he or she wants to happen – and his or her welfare – what is deemed to be in his or her best interests – has been noted by many commentators. The best person to represent the child's views is the child him or herself but requiring him or her to articulate these verbally within the children's hearing is not always possible, sensible or useful. Using other methods, in those cases where it is appropriate, such as those already provided for in the legislation, and outlined above, is particularly in keeping with the children's hearings' philosophy of treating every child as an individual.

1 Scottish Child Law Centre *Children and Young People's Voices: The Law, Legal Services, Systems and Processes in Scotland* (1999), pp 99–101.

2 Children's Hearings (Scotland) Rules 1996, SI 1996/3261, r 15(4).

3 See ch 1 for a discussion of the safeguarder's role and the difference between safeguarding the child's interests (the purpose for which safeguarders are appointed in terms of the Children (Scotland) Act 1995, s 41(1)(a)) and advocating for the child's views.

4 A Griffiths and R F Kandel 'Hearing Children in Children's Hearings' (2000) *CFLQ* 283 at p 298.

5 This point is made strongly in ch 1 above. See particularly under the heading 'Participation in Decision-Making: Information on Processes' and at pages [31] and [32].

CONCLUSION

Despite sustained criticism over a number of years, the welfare principle has remained the bedrock of the children's hearings system and has allowed children in trouble to be dealt with, for the most part, in a humane and understanding way. Indeed, given that there are indications – the media response to the murder of James Bulger being one – that society has moved on from a generalised, liberal acceptance of the need to protect and nurture all children, including those who offend, towards a more edgy and uncertain discussion of the current nature and status of childhood itself[1], it is submitted that the welfare principle now has particular importance. This is because it places children, a societal group which is traditionally disempowered and lacking in advocates, at the forefront of decision-making directly concerning them.

Feminist practical reasoning, with its concentration on hearing the voices of the disempowered, provides a particularly useful perspective on the hearings system, giving insights on the need for contextualisation, and on the use of rules, which are highly relevant in this context. Feminist advocates of this method suggest that its use can promote justice for women. Since the children's hearings system already puts many of the method's precepts into practice, it is not unreasonable to consider that, in so doing, it produces well-mediated outcomes for children.

The Human Rights Act 1998 has already given rise to a number of challenges to the children's hearings system in the case of *S v Miller*[1]. The European Convention on Human Rights, art 8 is perhaps the most likely to present a direct challenge to the welfare principle and this chapter has sought to argue that current practice at children's hearings is sufficiently robust and inclusive to withstand this.

Finally, the current, welcome concentration on the rights of children places considerable emphasis on the need to obtain their views, in reaching decisions on their welfare. Although accepting fully the great importance of this, and welcoming the decision in the *S v Miller*[2] case that, in certain circumstances, free legal representation of children and their parents might be appropriate, this chapter has sought to argue for the need to respect a child's decision to remain silent within a children's hearing. This in no sense downgrades the significance to be attached to the child's views in the decision-making process. It merely requires that appropriately individualised and child-centred mechanisms for obtaining such views are utilised where the child, for whatever reason, is unwilling or unable to vocalise these in the hearing itself.

---

1 See, for example, A James and A Prout (eds) *Constructing and Reconstructing Childhood: Contemporary Issues in the Sociological Study of Childhood* (1990) The Falmer Press, London.
2 *S v Miller* 2001 SLT 531.

3 Parentage and Parenting

Elaine E Sutherland

'School Abolishes Mother's Day' announced a recent newspaper headline[1]. The story which followed reported that a school in New York had decided to stop celebrating Mother's Day and Father's Day in order to avoid offending same-sex couples. What does this story tell us about parentage and parenting? It was clear from the, sometimes outraged, comments in the reports that 'motherhood' and 'fatherhood' are concepts to which adults have considerable attachment and which elicit emotional responses. That the issue arose at all suggests that traditional concepts employed when discussing family relationships are sometimes inadequate in the light of the very diverse family arrangements prevailing today. Perhaps what is most interesting of all is the fact that the discussion was so adult-centred. No mention was made of upsetting the *children* of same-sex couples.

Nor was there discussion of other children living in what are sometimes described as 'non-traditional relationships': the many children who do not live in a single household with their married parents. As birth outside marriage increases, fewer children are born to married parents[2]. Significant numbers of unmarried parents are living together when the child is born and continue to do so after the birth[3]. Separation and divorce mean that, for many children who do start out living with both parents, the situation is temporary. Parental cohabitation with, or remarriage to, a non-parent results in yet more permutations, with the blended family becoming far from rare. 'Non-traditional relationships' are rapidly becoming commonplace.

This chapter explores some of the issues surrounding parenthood and, as the very vast literature[4] on the subject suggests, there is no shortage of controversy. It

1 *Times*, 9 May 2001 p 17. See also, W Neuman 'Critics Strike The "Mother" Lode – Rip Into School For Banning Mom's Day' *New York Post*, 9 May 2001.

2 43% of children born in Scotland in 2000 were to unmarried parents: Registrar General for Scotland *Annual Report 2000* (General Register Office for Scotland, 2001) Table 3.1.

3 83% of the births were registered jointly by the child's parents and 74% of these parents were living at the same address: Register General for Scotland *Annual Report 2000*, (General Register Office of Scotland, 2001) Table 3.3.

4 The following is a small sample of the books available: A Bainham, S D Sclater and M Richards (eds) *What is a Parent?* (1999) Hart, Oxford; C Barton and G Douglas *Law and Parenthood* (1995) Butterworths, London; D Blankenhorn *Fatherless America* (1995) Basic Books, New York; A Burgess *Fatherhood Reclaimed: The Making of Modern Fathers* (1997) Vermillion, London; E Bartholet *Family Bonds: Adoption, Infertility and the New World of Child Production* (1999) Beacon Press, Boston; N Dowd *Redefining Fatherhood* (2000) New York University Press, New York; J Eekelaar and J Sarcevic (eds) *Parenthood in Modern Society: Legal and Social Issues for the Twenty-First Century* (1993) Martinus Nijhoff, Nordrecht and Boston; M A Fineman *The Neutered Mother, the Sexual Family, and Other*

may be helpful at the outset, if the terms being used here are clarified. This chapter will focus on two concepts: parentage and parenting. Broadly, 'parentage' will be used to explore what the legal system recognises as the child-parent link. In this context 'genetic parent' will be used to denote a person with whom the child has a genetic link, while 'social parent' will be used when referring to a person who has fulfilled some parenting function. Of course, for many children, the same individuals will often be both genetic and social parents. However, as we shall see, there are cases where this is not so and it is often these cases which pose the greatest difficulty for the legal system. 'Parenting' will be used to explore which persons are permitted or required by the legal system to carry out some or all of the functions of a parent[1]. It is, perhaps, inevitable that these two distinct facets of parenthood should overlap, since the issue of parentage usually arises, in a legal context, either in the attaching of responsibilities to an individual or where a person is seeking the opportunity to engage in parenting.

There are a number of parties with an interest in how we address the issues of parentage and parenting. The central character in all of this is, of course, the child and he or she clearly has an interest. Genetic parents may have an interest, as do social parents and other persons, sometimes described as 'third parties'. What of the state and society as a whole? Again, there is an interest there, not least because the state bears the ultimate responsibility for ensuring that children's rights and interests are protected[2]. In our exploration of parenthood, our primary focus will be the law in the UK and the US.

PARENTAGE

What is parentage? It is tempting to offer the rather circular answer that parentage is the connection between two persons as child and parent. At its simplest, parentage is the genetic link between a child and the people who contributed to his or her genetic make-up. Presently, we will move on to consider the wider notion of parenting, that is, who may be given the opportunity to fulfil some parental role in respect of a particular child and why. For now, we are concerned with what parentage means and upon whom recognition as a parent will be bestowed by a given legal system. That is to ask the question from a relatively 'adult' perspective. In the course of examining these issues, it will become apparent that there is a child-centred perspective which must be addressed as well and that other questions emerge as a consequence.

Twentieth Century Tragedies (1995) Routledge, New York; U Narayan and J J Bartkowiak *Having and Raising Children: Unconventional Families, Hard Choices and the Social Good* (1999) Pennsylvania University Press, Philadelphia. In addition, there is an abundance of journal articles, beyond those cited herein, addressing aspects of parenthood.

1 Separate questions surround the opportunities for individuals to become parents in the first place and the restrictions which may be placed on that by law and other factors, like economics. Sadly, discussion of such matters as eugenics, access to assisted reproduction, and the classic 'hard case' of future use of frozen embryos in cases of dispute are beyond the scope of this chapter. Nonetheless, it is worth noting that these issues raise similar questions about children's rights, adult rights and the role of the state.

2 That the state has an obligation to protect the rights and interests of the child is fundamental to the UN Convention on the Rights of the Child and the European Convention on Human Rights. While the Constitution of the USA approaches the issue differently, it acknowledges that children have certain rights.

Origins and identity

Precisely which factors contribute to an individual's sense of identity, and how that identity develops over time, are complex and controversial questions[1]. It has been described as 'a complex mix of factors including nature and nurture contributing to a sense of self-knowledge, self-awareness and self-esteem'[2]. One part of an individual's identity is his or her genetic origins. However, there is more to identity than simple genetics, as the United Nations Convention on the Rights of the Child ('the Convention') recognises in arts 7 and 8. While it acknowledges name, nationality and family relations as being part of identity, it is certainly arguable that race, religion, culture and language are also relevant[3].

At the outset, a further, perhaps obvious, point should be noted. In order for an individual to seek information about his or her origins and identity, that individual must know that there is something to be sought beyond what is immediately apparent. So, for example, if a child grows up believing that his or her social parents are also the genetic parents, when this is not the case, he or she will not know that there is any further information to be found. It is quite possible that he or she may never know the truth. This raises the whole question of disclosure and there is a strong case to be made for honesty rather than deception. That view is already widely accepted in the UK in respect of adopted children[4] and more recent work suggests it is also true for children who result from the use of techniques involving donors[5]. This is hardly surprising, not least because the truth has an invidious way of creeping out in families, and sometimes in the worst possible circumstances. Where deception has centred on something so fundamental, the damage to trust within a relationship may be considerable. In addition, where something has been kept secret, there is the implication that it is somehow shameful.

While the desire to know about one's genetic origins may stem from a need to 'complete the picture', it should not be dismissed as idle curiosity, since it is through that knowledge that the individual may gain indications of other issues surrounding identity. In some cases, the quest for information may be prompted by more pragmatic considerations, like the individual's own need for information about his or her medical history. This flags up one of the key dilemmas faced by the legal system. Is it enough that the individual receives non-identifying information (ie information that indicates racial, religious and other background factors, possibly including elements of medical history) or should he or she have access to details which may lead to the identification of a genetic parent? We will return to this question presently. First, we must consider how legal systems approach the issue of identifying origins.

1 See J Goldstein, A J Solnit and A Freud *Beyond the Best Interests of the Child* (2nd edn, 1979) Free Press, New York; J M Masson and C Harrison 'Identity: Mapping the Frontiers' in N V Lowe and G Douglas (eds) *Families Across Frontiers* (1996) Martinus Nijhoff, The Hague; J Triseliotis *In Search of Origins* (1973) Routledge and Kegan Paul, London.

2 A Bissett-Johnston 'The Child's Identity' in A Cleland and E E Sutherland (eds) *Children's Rights in Scotland* (2nd edn, 2001) W Green, Edinburgh at para 5.1.

3 Stewart 'Interpreting the Child's Right to Identity in the UN Convention on the Rights of the Child' (1992) 26 Fam LQ 221.

4 J Triseliotis *In Search of Origins* (1973) Routledge and Kegan Paul, The Hague; J Triseliotis, J Shireman and M Hundleby *Adoption: Theory, Policy and Practice* (1997) Cassell, Edinburgh pp 36–41, and the materials cited therein. See further, pp 56–58 below.

5 A McWhinnie 'Should Offspring From Donated Gametes Continue to be Denied Knowledge of Their Origins and Antecedents?' (2001) 16 *Human Reproduction* 807. See further, pp 60–62 below.

Law and parentage

There is historical precedent for young children being stolen from parents and spirited away to a new family, with the intention that the truth about their origins would never become known. Where a practice of this kind is widespread and systematic, it is generally associated with a totalitarian regime. One example can be found in the 'Germanisation' programme undertaken by the Nazis under which as many as 200,000 children may have been removed from their 'non-Aryan' parents in occupied Europe, given false birth certificates, and adopted by German couples[1]. More recently, during the 'dirty war' in Argentina in the 1970s and 1980s, it appears that children were kidnapped or deceived about their origins and adopted by 'suitable' families, usually those of police or army officers[2]. DNA testing has made possible the identification of some of the children but it should be noted that not all of the children want to explore the truth about their origins[3]. This gives us the first hint of yet another dilemma. What of the children, many of whom are now adults, who do not want to know of their genetic origins? Do they have a right to have their wishes respected? What of members of the birth family, like the grandmothers in Argentina who wanted to trace and meet their grandchildren? Do they have any rights? Of course, there is widespread condemnation of children being denied information about their origins for political reasons[4], but how do we reconcile the competing interests?

---

1 Gitta Sereny gives a moving account of her work as a child welfare officer with the United Nations Relief and Rehabilitation Administration (UNRRA) in the 1940s which attempted to trace and return the children to their birth parents. About 20,000 Polish children were returned home after the war. In a chilling reminder that governments are capable of incredible double-standards, Sereny notes that, as East-West relations worsened in the aftermath of the war, stories began to circulate among UNRRA workers that 'Washington was considering issuing a fanatically anti-Soviet order (and seeking agreement to it in Britain) to resettle all children of Russian origin . . . in the US, Australia and Canada, instead of returning them to their homes and life under the Soviets'. See Gitta Sereny 'Stolen Children' *Talk* November 1999 104.

2 The details came to light largely as a result of the efforts of the Mothers of the Plaza de Mayo. Despite the general amnesty for crimes committed during that time, kidnapping of children was not included and a number of politicians and naval and military officers have been arrested. See G Van Bueren *The International Law on the Rights of the Child* (1995) Martinus Nijhoff, Dordrecht, pp 118–120 and the footnotes cited therein.

3 See, for example, C Lamb 'Give me back my past' *Sunday Telegraph*, 17 September 2000, which reports a 22-year-old woman's dilemma when confronted with the possibility that the man she regards as her father may have been involved in the death of her parents, albeit he denies any involvement. She has engaged a lawyer, declined to have a DNA test, and refused to meet the women who believe themselves to be her grandmothers.

4 It is interesting that it was the Argentinian delegation that was the prime mover behind the UN Convention on the Rights of the Child, art 8: see G Van Bueren The International Law on the Rights of the Child (1995) Martinus Nijhoff, Dordrecht pp 118–119. Examples can be found of a child's identity being changed and concealed where the justification advanced by the authorities is that it is in the child's best interests. Thus, in the US, children are sometimes taken onto the Witness Protection Program, along with a parent, and both of them are given new identities. Where only one parent enters the Program along with the child, this can result in interference with the child's relationship with a parent who is not participating in the Program. See, for example, *Ruffalo v United States* 539 F Supp 949 (W D Mo 1982), affirmed and remanded 702 F 2d 710 (8th Cir 1983), where a mother who had custody of her son was unsuccessful when she sued to prevent the child's inclusion in the Program along with the boy's father. She later succeeded in securing semi-annual visitation (565 F Supp 34 (W D Mo 1983)) and damages from the federal government for interference with her right to visitation and communication with her son (590 F Supp 706 (W D Mo 1984)). See also *Franz v United States* 707 F 2d 582 (D C Cir 1983) and *Politte v Politte* 727 S W 2d 198 (Mo Ct App 1987).

Thankfully, these are unusual cases. What of the more ordinary cases? Do legal systems make it possible for children to have accurate information about their genetic origins? It is simplest to approach this question from the starting point of conception achieved by ordinary intercourse without donor assistance[1] and a pregnancy which does not involve the use of a surrogate. How does the legal system approach the issue of recognising parentage? Acknowledging the importance of recording the fact of a child's birth and the salient surrounding details, legal systems provide for the registration of birth. For example, in Scotland, the function is undertaken by the Registrar General for Scotland[2] and, in the USA, a similar function is carried out by the various Vital Records Offices throughout the country[3]. Where the child's parents are married to each other, the procedure for registration is relatively straightforward. Where the parents are not married at all, but are in agreement as to paternity, registration is, again, fairly simple. Problems begin to arise where the mother is married to someone other than the father of the child, due largely to the presumptions which surround paternity, and this is where we can begin to see radically different approaches being taken by different legal systems.

Legal systems have long confronted disputes over parentage and, in particular, disputes over paternity[4]. Usually, the dispute requires resolution at an early stage and, traditionally, the child's mother often sought to establish paternity in order to obtain financial support from the father of the child. However, as we have seen, the child may have personal and pecuniary reasons for wishing to establish paternity and, of course, the father may wish to establish his own paternity, and third parties, like grandparents or siblings, may have an interest.

One technique which legal systems have found useful in dealing with cases of disputed paternity is the development and application of presumptions. In Scotland, for example, a man is presumed to be the father of a child: if he was married to the child's mother at the time of conception or subsequently; failing such a marriage, if he and the mother acknowledge that he is the child's father and register the child accordingly; or where a court has declared him to be the child's father[5]. Each of these presumptions can be rebutted by proof on the balance of probabilities[6] and, in practice, DNA profiling has made the process reasonably simple. It is worth noting that the marriage-centred presumption can be rebutted in the same way as the others. Thus, where the father of a married woman's child is someone other than her husband, the truth of the matter can be established in court and the records amended accordingly, provided that the

1 The same rules would apply where conception has been effected with assistance, provided that the couple's gametes were the only ones used in the process. For an excellent discussion of infertility in men and women and the treatment options, see J K Mason *Medico-Legal Aspects of Reproduction and Parenthood* (2nd edn, 1998) Ashgate, Aldershot chs 8 and 9.

2 Information on the Office of the Registrar General can be found at: http://wood.ccta.gov.uk/grosweb/grosweb.nsf.

3 Information on Vital Records Office can be found at: http://vitalrec.com.

4 In the past, disputes over maternity were virtually unknown; *cf Douglas v Duke of Hamilton* (1789) 2 Pat 143. Surrogacy has opened up the whole question, as have other aspects of assisted reproduction, including theft of, or error in placing, genetic material. In addition, there are occasional cases where a baby is given to the wrong parents in the hospital shortly after birth: see *Twigg v Mays* (18 August 1993) and *Mays v Twigg* 543 So 2d 241 (Fla, 1989). See further E E Sutherland *Child and Family Law* (1999) T & T Clark, Edinburgh, paras 4.4–4.6 and 4.69–4.70.

5 Law Reform (Parent and Child) (Scotland) Act 1986, s 5(1). The presumption in respect of husbands is similar in England and Wales.

6 Law Reform (Parent and Child) (Scotland) Act 1986, s 5(4).

adults involved wish that to happen[1]. Where the adults or, at least, some of them would prefer to deceive the child about his or her genetic origins, the rules on who may give consent to the testing of the child, assuming the child is too young to do so[2], can help them[3].

In the US, states again employ presumptions in establishing paternity. While the Uniform Parentage Act[4] applies presumptions similar to those found in Scots law, in a number of states the marriage-centred presumption is *irrebuttable*[5]. Thus, in Oregon, for example, it is *conclusively presumed* that the father of a married woman's child is her husband, where the couple were cohabiting at the time of conception and the husband was neither sterile nor impotent[6]. The marriage-centred presumption probably accords with reality more often than not[7], but why create a legal provision which is incapable of reflecting the truth for all cases? In legal terms, the answer lies in the decision of the US Supreme Court in *Michael H v Gerald D*[8], where a man who was almost certainly the genetic father of a married woman's child, Victoria, sought to establish his paternity of the child and to be granted visitation rights. In so doing, he challenged the conclusive presumption, contained in the California statute and identical in its terms to the Oregon provision, on the basis that it violated his due process rights. That case, and the approach of lower courts and

1 See, for example, *Russell v Wood* 1987 SCLR 207, where a woman sought to establish that her daughter was the child of the man with whom she had been living, prior to his death, and not her husband, in order that the child could benefit under a trust. Indeed, the practice of the registration authority in Scotland accommodates a married woman registering a man other than her husband as the father of her child, provided that the named man and the husband both accept the truth of her assertion.

2 A child can consent to a medical procedure if, in the opinion of the treating physician, he or she understands the nature and possible consequences of the procedure: Age of Legal Capacity (Scotland) Act 1991, s 2(4).

3 As a general rule, an adult cannot be compelled to give a sample of blood or genetic material, albeit the court may draw a contrary inference from refusal: *Whitehall v Whitehall* 1958 SC 252 and Law Reform (Miscellaneous Provisions) (Scotland) Act 1990, s 70. Where the child does not have capacity to consent to testing, any person with parental responsibilities or rights or who has care and control of the child can consent on the child's behalf and the court may only give its consent where no one is entitled to give consent or where a person is unwilling to take the responsibility of giving consent: Law Reform (Parent and Child) (Scotland) Act 1986, s 6. In *Smith v Greenhill* 1993 SCLR 776, for example, a court refused to order testing when a man, with whom the (married) mother had had intercourse, sought to establish paternity. For a discussion of how these rules can operate, see E E Sutherland *Child and Family Law* (1999) T & T Clark, Edinburgh paras 4.20–4.27.

4 (1973) 9B ULA 287 (1987). The Uniform Parentage Act is currently being revised and the new version is due to have its final reading in August 2001. It is envisaged that it will incorporate the Uniform Putative and Unknown Fathers Act 1989 and the Uniform Status of Children of Assisted Conception Act 1989. Uniform statutes are produced by the National Conference of Commissioners on Uniform State Laws and provide blueprints for legislation which states can adopt, in whole or in part, as they wish. Individual states may choose to draft legislation of their own and thus, uniform statutes are to be contrasted with federal statutes which do apply across the whole country.

5 It should be noted that the Uniform Parentage Act, in its original form and as revised, allows for rebuttal of the presumption.

6 Oregon Revised Statutes (hereinafter 'ORS') 1999, s 109.070(1)(a). Where the spouses are not cohabiting, the presumption is disputable: ORS, s 109.107(1)(b).

7 There are no accurate statistics for the number of children born to a married woman where her husband is not the child's father since, in most families, no tests are carried out. McWhinnie 'Should Offspring From Donated Gametes Continue to be Denied Knowledge of Their Origins and Antecedents' (2001) 16 *Human Reproduction* 807 at 814 cites a research study from the London School of Economics and reported in the *Sunday Times* on 23 January 2000, suggesting the figure may be as high as one in seven children.

8 491 US 110 (1989).

legislatures in other US jurisdictions[1], is discussed at length elsewhere in this volume[2]. However, for our purpose, the significance of the decision was the court's rejection of his claim. This proceeded on the basis of the protection afforded to the traditional, marital, family unit. In respect of Victoria's claim to have her relationship with both men protected, the court adhered firmly to the 'either or' notion that having more than one father was simply not a possibility.

What is the policy behind such an approach? The fact that Victoria and her mother were again living in a family setting, with the mother's husband, undoubtedly made it easier for the court to justify its decision on the basis of regard for the established family unit and the institution of marriage, with the latter viewed as serving the interests of the married woman. Supporting the established family unit can be argued to serve the child's interests as well, although, as we shall see, other mechanisms could have achieved the same end. The rights of the husband were given precedence over those of the non-marital putative father. What happens when it is the husband who is seeking to have the genetic truth established or upheld, often to avoid financial responsibilities to the child? Arguably, in such circumstances, his rights are not being respected by clinging to the pretence of 'husband as father'. While some states do permit such a husband to seek to rebut the presumption, others have used the principle of estoppel (personal bar[3]) to prevent such action[4]. Certainly, it cannot be argued that Victoria was being protected from knowledge of her mother's adultery, since she was aware of the existence of both men. It would have been quite possible to recognise that both men had a link with this child, and to reach the decision on visitation on other criteria.

'Secrets and lies'[5]

As the presumption attaching to the paternity of a married woman's child in some US jurisdictions demonstrates, legal systems are quite capable of pretending that the facts are other than they are. Even in Scotland, where the law can accommodate honesty, the procedures are such that there may be little protection against deception. Another legal technique for bending the truth is the use of 'legal fictions'. The difference between the law simply condoning lying or closing its eyes to the truth and the creation of a legal fiction is that, when the latter is employed, the law acknowledges that it is fabricating. As we shall see, it will often use phrases indicating that an individual will be 'treated as the child of' a

1 The equal protection argument was not addressed by the Supreme Court but it has been raised in other cases. See, for example, *A v X, Y, and Z* 641 P2d 1222 (Wyo, 1982), cert denied 459 US 1021 (1982) and *Re Paternity of CAS* 468 NW2d 719 (Wis, 1991).

2 See ch 4 below.

3 The argument that a mother was personally barred from seeking aliment for a child because she had failed to use contraception, as the father allegedly believed she was, has been rejected in Scotland: *Bell v McCurdie* 1981 SC 64. A person who has 'accepted' a child into his or her family can thereby acquire the obligation to aliment the child: Family Law (Scotland) Act 1985, s 1(1)(d). There is some doubt that a person can have 'accepted' a child into the family where the conduct is based on an erroneous assumption. In any event, the concept of acceptance applies only to the question of aliment and does not apply to other matters, like succession.

4 *Miscovich v Miscovich* 688 A2d 726 (Pa, 1997), affirmed 720 A2d 764 (Pa, 1998) and *BEB v RLB* 979 P2d 514 (Alaska, 1999).

5 The title of this section owes its inspiration to LS McGough and A Peltier-Falahahwazi 'Secrets and Lies: A Model Statute for Co-operative Adoption' 60 *La LRev* 13 (1999).

particular person or 'treated in law' as the parent of a particular child, when it is accommodating situations where that is not so in the genetic sense. When the law does this, at least it is flagging up that it is engaged in deception and, indeed, may be recognising social parenting. We will explore some examples of where legal fictions are employed in the context of parenthood before moving on to examine a further, equally important, issue. When a legal fiction is used, what opportunity is there for the child and perhaps others to get to the underlying reality? To put the question another way: when a legal fiction is created, to what extent does the law also try to wipe out the truth altogether?

Adoption

Adoption is the process whereby the child–parent relationship is created by order of the court. Beginning in the 1850s, various states in the US introduced adoption legislation[1]. While it was known to Roman law, adoption was not one of the concepts received into Scots law initially, with adoption only being recognised in 1930[2], four years after it was accepted in England and Wales[3]. As a general rule, the law employs the technique of providing that the child will be treated as the child of the adopter or adopters[4], albeit there are exceptions to this general rule[5]. A host of fascinating questions surround adoption, not least whether the concept is necessary at all and whose interests it serves[6]. Should single people be permitted to adopt a child? If couples are allowed to adopt children, should couples who are cohabiting outside marriage and same-sex couples be included?[7] For our present purpose we are concerned primarily with the facts about the child's genetic origins and this, in turn, leads on to two questions. Does the legal system ensure that the child is informed, at some stage, *that* he or she is adopted? What, if any, further information is given to the child? Does this include information which will enable the child to trace a birth parent? We will return to the issue of what, if any, opportunity there is for contact between the birth parent(s) and the child during the latter's childhood when we consider parenting.

In the United Kingdom, it would be very difficult to hide the fact of adoption from a child, at least once the child got to the stage of having access to his or her

1 Massachusetts is generally credited as having been the first state to do so, in 1851. However, Zainaldin gives the credit to Alabama, in 1850: J Zainaldin 'The Emergence of a Modern American Family Law: Child Custody, Adoption and the Courts, 1796–1851' (1979) 73 *Nw ULRev 1038*. Prior to legislation being passed, individual adoptions were sometimes effected by legislative acts.

2 Adoption (Scotland) Act 1930.

3 Adoption Act 1926.

4 Historically, in Scotland, since the mother of a child born outwith marriage was not the child's legal guardian, some single women did adopt their own children. In addition, at one time, where a step-parent wanted to adopt his or her partner's child, the birth parent also had to adopt the child. Thankfully, the need for these absurd legal contortions has been removed. A special expedited adoption procedure remains, however, where a child has resulted from a surrogacy arrangement using the genetic material of one of the proposed adopters: see n 7 p 60, below.

5 For example, in Scotland, adoption does not alter the relationship between the child and birth relatives for the purpose of the prohibited degrees of marriage or the criminal law on incest, nor does it deprive a child who is a UK citizen of his or her nationality: Adoption (Scotland) Act 1978, s 41. That old British chestnut 'succession to titles, honours and coats of arms', which remains of importance to the non-marital child and also features in the context of assisted reproduction, is also an exception to the general effect of adoption: Succession (Scotland) Act 1964, s 37(1)(a).

6 These questions are addressed in ch 5 below.

7 See ch 7 below.

birth certificate, since that certificate indicates that the information contained therein is derived from the Adopted Children Register. Essentially, this means that, while adopters can delay telling a child that he or she is adopted, the truth will become known eventually. Thus, there is every incentive for openness about the fact of adoption[1]. In addition, and from the outset, Scots law gave the adopted person the right to gain access to his or her birth records on reaching a specified age, that age currently being set at 16 years old[2]. An adopted person who indicates that he or she wishes to exercise this right must be advised that counselling is available, although accepting counselling is not a prerequisite of access to the records[3]. It was not until 1975 that England and Wales embraced this right of access to adoption records[4]. Thus, the adopted person is often able to trace at least some birth relatives and sometimes one or both birth parents. It should be noted that this access to identifying information is a one-way street. The genetic parents cannot gain access to information which would enable them to trace the child, although in England and Wales there is provision for an Adoption Contact Register, which enables adoptees and birth parents to indicate that they would welcome contact[5].

The whole issue of openness about adoption and access to records has a very different, and highly controversial, history in the US. While the earliest adoption statutes did not provide for sealing of adoption records, by the middle of the twentieth century most states had opted for sealed records and secrecy, with a new birth certificate being issued, indicating the adopters as the child's parents[6]. Arguably, this was done to protect the child's interests, most notably from the stigma of illegitimacy, to ensure the child's integration into the adopted family, and to secure the privacy of the new family unit. It also served the interests of birth mothers in starting a new life, free from what was, at the time, the shame of non-marital motherhood. By the latter part of the twentieth century, this approach began to be challenged, largely by adoptees who wanted to know more about their genetic origins and their birth parents, but also by birth mothers. The majority of states now provide for disclosure of non-identifying information, while a number make the disclosure of identifying information a possibility in certain circumstances. Essentially, four models have emerged for disclosing identifying information: 'good cause' statutes, mutual consent registries, search and consent or veto provisions, and open records statutes. It is the

1 This makes the maverick decision in *C Petrs (Parent and Child: Adoption)* 1993 SLT (Sh Ct) 8 all the more absurd. There, the court participated in the decision of the mother and her husband to deceive the child on the issue of paternity. See E E Sutherland 'Adoption: The Child's View' 1994 SLT (News) 37. For a similar case in England over deception as to maternity, see *Re S (A Minor) (Adoption)* [1988] 1 FLR 418.

2 Adoption (Scotland) Act 1978, s 45(5). The age at which a person can gain access to his or her own adoption records was reduced from 17 to 16 by the Children (Scotland) Act 1995, Sch 2, para 22; A(S)A 1978, s 45(6).

3 Local authorities and approved adoption societies are obliged to provide counselling: A(S)A 1978, s 45(6A) and (6B).

4 Children Act 1975.

5 Adoption Act 1976, s 51A, added by the Children Act 1989, Sch 10, para 21.

6 For very full discussion of the history of adoption and the thinking behind sealed records and secrecy, see H Hildebrand 'Because They Want To Know: An Examination of the Legal Rights of Adoptees and Their Parents' 24 *SIll ULJ* 515 (2000); R-A W Howe 'Adoption Laws and Practice in 2000: Serving Whose Interests?' 33 *Fam LQ* 677 (1999); J Kuhns 'The Sealed Adoption Records Controversy: Breaking Down the Walls of Secrecy' (1994) 24 *Golden Gate UL Rev* 259.

open records statutes which have provoked most controversy[1], since they do not allow the birth parent to prevent disclosure, and the road to them has been hard fought. In Oregon, for example, the open records provision, which permits any adopted person, aged 21 or over, to gain access to his or her sealed adoption records, began life as a ballot initiative[2], passed by the voters in 1998. Enforcement of the initiative was stayed when six women, who had surrendered their children for adoption years before, challenged the statute as violating their constitutional rights in terms of both privacy and their reasonable contractual expectations. They were unsuccessful[3], but the debate surrounding both the ballot measure and the litigation revealed competing interests.

What are the competing interests in open adoption today? It is clear from the action taken by the Oregon mothers that some genetic parents – and it will almost always be the mothers – want secrecy to be retained, most probably because they have not told spouses, children and friends, of the child they had many years before. Some adopters may feel that allowing the adoptee access to identifying information will lead to contact with birth mothers which will somehow threaten the adopted family. What is the threat here? Will a strong relationship between an adoptee and his or her adoptive parents be diminished simply because the adoptee forms a link with another person? That is rather like suggesting that individuals have only a limited amount of friendship and love to distribute. What of the adoptees themselves? There is always the possibility that an adoptee will face rejection or some unpleasant reality if he or she traces a birth parent, but these people are adults and, with adequate provision for counselling, they should be entering their inquiry prepared for such a possibility. That, it is submitted, is the real point. That the adoption took place was a result of choices made by the adopters and, often, the birth parents[4]. If an adoptee seeks to open records, he or she is making a choice at that stage and the fact that he or she is doing so suggests a need to establish further details of his or her identity. If competing interests have to be prioritised, the case for those of the adoptee prevailing is strong. Certainly, for future adoptions, the case appears unanswerable. For birth mothers who were promised anonymity, it is a matter of moving the goalposts, something that usually appears inequitable. However, if legal systems are to develop along with changing social conditions, goalposts sometimes have to be moved. Given the very different attitude to

1 Contrast the views expressed in H Hildebrand 'Because They Want to Know: An Examination of the Legal Rights of Adoptees and Their Parents' (2000) 24 SIll ULJ 515, with those expressed in F Hunsaker 'Oregon's Ballot Measure 58: A Grossly Unfair and State-Sanctioned Betrayal of Birth Mothers' 39 *Fam & Conciliation Courts Rev* 75 (2001) and C R Reiss 'The Fear of Opening Pandora's Box: The Need to Restore Birth Parents' Privacy Rights in the Adoption Process' 28 *Sw ULRev* 133 (1998). A middle course is argued for in B S Silverman 'The Winds of Change in Adoption Law: Should Adoptees have Access to Birth Records' 39 *Fam & Conciliation Courts Rev* 85 (2001).

2 A ballot initiative allows the electorate in the state to vote on a proposal for law reform and, if the initiative passes, the legislature is then obliged to give effect to it. Ballot Measure 58 owed much to the efforts of Bastard Nation, a national organisation which seeks to have adoption records opened up across the US.

3 *Does 1–7 v State of Oregon* 993 P2d 822 (Or, 1999), *Does 1–7 v State of Oregon* 330 Or 138 (2000). The women were joined in their action by National Council for Adoption. See F Hunsaker 'Oregon's Ballot Measure 58: A Grossly Unfair and State-Sanctioned Betrayal of Birth Mothers' 39 *Fam & Conciliation Courts Rev* 75 (2001).

4 Given the pressures faced by single mothers in the past, their decision to place the child for adoption was often not a 'free choice' in any real sense. In addition, even today, a court can authorise adoption in the face of parental opposition, usually as the 'end point' in the child protection process.

non-marital motherhood prevailing today, any stigma they may now face is so reduced that a case can be made.

Assisted reproduction

The development, and wide use, of techniques involving a third party to assist in reproduction is of relatively recent origin[1]. Broadly, they include conception resulting from the use of gametes donated by a third party, surrogacy and germline genetic modification[2]. Limits of space preclude a discussion of the techniques themselves and they are described fully elsewhere[3]. The use of these techniques raises a host of fascinating questions. Opinions range from the view that any interference with the 'natural' method of reproduction is wrong, and the techniques should not be used at all, to the belief that, if we can assist individuals who require help to have a child, we should do so[4]. Of course, all points in between have their adherents and there is extensive debate about the persons to whom the techniques should be available[5]. For our present purpose, we must confine our inquiry to questions similar to those we explored in relation to adoption.

How does the legal system deal with the attribution of parenthood in the context of assisted reproduction? In the UK, the Human Fertilisation and Embryology Act 1990 provides a number of simple rules, albeit these rules do not preclude the possibility of disputes over who is permitted to be involved in the child's life. The woman who gives birth to the child, and no other woman, is treated as the mother of the child[6]. Provided that married partners are treated together in a licensed facility, the husband, and no other man, is treated as the father of the child borne by his wife, unless he can show that he did not consent to the treatment[7]. If that rule on paternity does not apply, a similar rule applies to the male partner of the woman who bears the child, again, provided they are treated together at a licensed facility[8]. A host of shortcomings in these, apparently simple, rules are obvious, not least in their failure to accommodate same-sex couples. Heterosexual couples, where they achieve pregnancy other than

1 While there are Talmudic and biblical examples of donor insemination and what might, very loosely, be described as 'surrogacy', it was only in the latter part of the 20th century that the techniques became widely available. For historical perspective, see D J Cusine *New Reproductive Techniques: A Legal Perspective* (1988) Gower, Dartmouth ch 3.

2 While the prospect of it becoming a reality increases by the day, the cloning of human beings is beyond the scope of this chapter. In its simplest form, cloning would result in the child having only one genetic parent.

3 See J K Mason *Medico-Legal Aspects of Reproduction and Parenthood* (2nd edn, 1998) Ashgate, Aldershot; E E Sutherland Child and Family Law (1999) T & T Clark, Edinburgh paras 4.28–4.73.

4 The *Report of the Committee of Inquiry into Human Fertilisation and Embryology* (Cmnd 9314, 1984) marked the first systematic attempt in the UK to address what were then seen as the fundamental issues. Such was the controversy even then that the Report contains three separate expressions of dissent. The Report formed the basis of UK legislation and further inquires have been conducted into various aspects of assisted reproduction: see *Review of the Consent Provisions of the Human Fertilisation and Embryology Act 1990* (Department of Health, 1997) and *Surrogacy Review for Health Ministers of Current Arrangements for Payments and Regulation* (Cm 4068, 1998).

5 Whether there should be an upper age limit for recipients, and particularly female recipients, of treatment is highly contentious. Whether the techniques should be available to same-sex couples generates further controversy.

6 Human Fertilisation and Embryology Act 1990, s 27(1).

7 Human Fertilisation and Embryology Act 1990, s 28(2).

8 Human Fertilisation and Embryology Act 1990, s 28(3).

through the use of a licensed facility, are thrown back on the presumptions discussed earlier on parentage.

Despite the shortcomings, the system in the UK has been viewed with approval from the US where no such blanket system applies[1]. At present, issues of parentage are resolved on the basis of non-uniform state statutes or by the courts applying common law principles. Inevitably, the decisions are varied and inconsistent, resulting in voluminous literature[2]. Various models based on theories of privacy[3], property[4], contract and estoppel[5] have been advocated or applied, with most cases arising from disputes over the opportunity to engage in parenting.

Assisted reproduction provides enormous opportunities for concealing the truth about a child's biological origins, particularly where the gametes used were donated anonymously. Where a married woman has a child as a result of anonymous donor insemination, nothing prevents the couple from registering the husband as the child's father[6]. The concept of confidentiality precludes the medical profession if, indeed, its members have been involved, from flagging up the truth. Where donated gametes have been used to enable a woman to carry a foetus to term, again, provided donation is anonymous, nothing prevents her from asserting that she is the child's mother. Surrogacy provides less opportunity for deception, since it may be rather more difficult, although not impossible, to explain to friends and family how a woman who never appeared to be pregnant now has a babe in arms[7]. As the cases illustrate, fabrications are more likely to unravel where the donor and recipient know each other's identity and problems are magnified when there is some element of continuing relationship[8]. Other scenarios for the truth leaking out present themselves. A man may seek to avoid paying child support on the basis that he is not the genetic father of his wife's child. A woman may meet a claim for contact or visitation with a child by disclosing that the claimant is not a genetic parent. The child's need for medical treatment, or simple curiosity about physical resemblance, may flag up to him or her that matters are not as they have seemed. Nonetheless, the fundamental point about many cases of assisted reproduction is that the child may never

1 The Uniform Status of Children of Assisted Conception Act 1989 has not been adopted widely, although a number of states have regulated aspects of assisted reproduction: see K E Koehler 'Artificial Insemination: In The Child's Best Interests?' 5 *Alb LJ Sci & Tech* 321 (1996).

2 See, for example, M Garrrison 'Law Making for Baby Making: An Interpretive Approach to the Determination of Legal Parentage' 113 *Harv LRev* 835 (2000); A E King 'Solomon Revisited: Assigning Parenthood in the Context of Collaborative Reproduction' 5 *UCLA Women's LJ* (1995); M Z Pelias and M M DeAngelis 'The New Genetic Technologies: New Options, New Hope and New Challenges' 45 *Loyola LRev* 287 (1999).

3 R Rao 'Reconceiving Privacy: Relationships and Reproductive Technology' 45 *UCLA LR.* 1077 (1998).

4 *Johnson v Calvert* 851 P2d 776; K Roosevelt III 'The Newest Property: Reproductive Technologies and the Concept of Parenthood' 39 *Santa Clara LRev* 79 (1998). See also S L Gillers 'A Labor Theory of Parenthood' (2001) 110 *Yale LJ* 691

5 *Re Buzzanca* 72 Cal Rep 2d 280 (1998).

6 Research suggests that many parents had not told their children that they were conceived as a result of donor insemination: see C Gottleib, O Lalos and F Lindblad 'Disclosure of Donor Insemination to the Child' (2000) 15 *Human Reproduction* 52.

7 In the UK, where a surrogate has been involved, it is possible for the 'commissioning couple' to adopt the child, with an expedited form of adoption being available where one of the prospective adopters has contributed genetic material: Human Fertilisation and Embryology Act 1990, s 30.

8 See, for example, *Jhordan C v Mary K* 179 Cal App 3d 386 (1986) and *Thomas S v Robin Y* 209 A2d 298 (NYS, 1994).

know that he or she was conceived in this way. If the child does not have this information, then he or she is in no position to request further details.

Assuming that the child knows that a donor or surrogate was involved in his or her birth, what further information is available to the child? In the UK, there is provision for only limited, largely non-identifying, information about any donor to be given to the individual who resulted from assisted reproduction, once he or she reaches adulthood[1]. The possibility of greater openness is being considered in the UK and the likelihood of a challenge under the European Convention on Human Rights, art 8[2] may encourage change. There is no blanket provision in the US but, in one case, donor anonymity was lifted to enable a deposition to be taken from the donor in an action by his daughter against the sperm bank for negligence[3]. Identifying information about donors was first made available to children in Sweden in 1984. Austria, Switzerland and two Australian jurisdictions have now followed suit and other jurisdictions are considering doing so[4].

In the light of the arguments in favour of disclosure of identifying information to adoptees, it is difficult to see why children who result from assisted reproductive technology should be treated any differently. What additional considerations apply? Certainly, donors may have been promised anonymity at the time of donation and, again, we must confront the issue of moving the goalposts. However, donors could be given protection from financial liability and, in any event, if the information is made available to their offspring only once they have reached adulthood, that issue is unlikely to arise. Donors would seem to have less need for protection than birth mothers who have surrendered children for adoption, since no stigma attaches to donation. There is the possibility that, were donor anonymity to be removed, fewer donors would come forward and the opportunity for people to have children in this way would be reduced. In Sweden, which has the longest history of openness, both the number of donors and the demand for donor insemination fell immediately after the law was changed, but that trend has now reversed[5]. It is sometimes argued that secrecy surrounding the whole issue of assisted reproduction is, in part, an attempt to protect the social parent from 'the shame of infertility'. Whether such a problem exists at all depends on the extent to which society attaches special importance to the ability to procreate. Certainly, it can be argued that it is no more shameful to be unable to breed than it is shameful to be unable to do a host of other things, like swimming or explaining Einstein's theory of relativity.

What of the child's rights? Exploring the case for disclosure, McWhinnie examines various studies of donor insemination children: those concerned with child development and those examining the quality of interpersonal family relation-

---

1 Human Fertilisation and Embryology Act 1990, s 31.

2 It has been reported that a test case will be brought by a brother and sister born as a result of donor insemination: C Dyer 'Offspring from Artificial Insemination Demand Father's Details' (2000) 312 *BMJ* 654.

3 *Johnson v California Cryobank* (2000) 95 Cal Rep 2d 864. The sperm bank had failed to disclose that the sperm sold to the daughter's mother and her husband came from a donor with family history of autosomal dominant polycystic kidney disease, a condition the child had inherited.

4 See L Frith 'Gamete donation and anonymity' (2001) 16 *Human Reproduction* 818 for details of the various provisions.

5 K Daniels and O Lalos 'The Swedish Insemination Act and the availability of donors' (1995) 7 *Human Reproduction* 1871.

ships[1]. These tend to support disclosure. In the few studies of donor-assisted children who had reached adulthood and discovered the facts about their conception, they expressed distress at the delay in disclosure and the lack of information available to them: in one child's words, 'Even their birth certificate was a lie'[2].

PARENTING

As we have seen, the legal construct of parentage is founded on presumptions, sometimes recognising genetic reality, or legal fictions. What is 'parenting'? We are not concerned, at this stage, with the important question of 'good' or 'bad' or even 'good enough' parenting. Rather, the term 'parenting' is being used here to denote the opportunity to fulfil some of the responsibilities or exercise some of the rights traditionally associated with parents. Who is permitted to decide where the child lives or to spend time with the child? Who has a right to participate in important decisions, like where the child goes to school or whether the child will have a particular course of medical treatment? It is apparent, from the outset, that, for many adults and children, the law is a practical irrelevance. The fact that a person is involved in a child's life may mean the adult is, in practice, doing some or all of these things. Thus, for example, a step-parent may live with the child or a grandparent may see the child frequently and play a big part in decision-making. Nonetheless, here we are concerned with the people clothed by the law with the right to do these things, since it is the legal position that matters when disputes or crises arise. Thus, we must consider the opportunity that the various persons who do not have a vested legal right to parent have to gain that legal recognition. Here, we are moving well beyond the narrow ambit of genetic and presumed parents and those treated as such. In all of this, we must not lose sight of the central character: the child. What role does he or she have in participating in decision-making or instigating litigation[3]? In examining the question of who is permitted to engage in parenting, we start at the beginning, by examining who is clothed with the parenting function from the outset. We will then consider whether 'others' and, if so, which others, may be allowed to participate and the criteria applied in allowing them to do so.

From the beginning

As a general rule, recognition of parentage, whether through the implicit or actual operation of presumptions, is the ticket to the automatic right to participate in parenting. The, very significant, exception to the general rule is the non-marital father, to whom we will return presently. That case aside, the recognition of a person as the mother or 'married father'[4] of the child allows him or her to fulfil the parenting role. Thus, in Scotland, mothers and married fathers

1 A McWhinnie 'Should Offspring from Donated Gametes Continue to be Denied Knowledge of Their Origins and Antecedents?' (2001) 16 *Human Reproduction* 807 at pp 808–811.

2 A McWhinnie 'Should Offspring from Donated Gametes Continue to be Denied Knowledge of Their Origins and Antecedents?' (2001) 16 *Human Reproduction* 807 at p 812.

3 The role of the child is discussed fully in ch 1 above.

4 This term is being used to denote the father married to the child's mother. A father married to someone other than the child's mother is a non-marital father, in this context, and suffers the same discrimination.

acquire responsibilities and rights automatically[1] and similar rules operate in US jurisdictions. Automatic acquisition of parental responsibilities and parental rights from the moment of the child's birth is not subject to any test of merit, although the opportunity to exercise them can be seriously restricted from the outset, where there is cause for concern over the child's welfare[2]. At a later stage in a child's life, parenting may be restricted or removed by a court in the context of, for example, divorce proceedings or at the instance of the authorities charged with child protection.

What of the non-marital father? Historically, he is both a demonised and a tragic figure. While most legal systems have sought a more inclusive approach to him, he remains something of an outsider, with his genetic link to the child being less recognised than that of other genetic parents. Legal systems have no difficulty in attaching financial responsibility to non-marital fathers. In the late twentieth century, the increase in the number of children being born outside marriage, concern over rising benefits bills, and something of a crusade against 'deadbeat dads', all contributed to broadly contemporaneous action along remarkably similar lines in a number of countries[3]. Essentially, these provide for centralised government-run systems for the collection of child support. It is not suggested that there should be a straight correlation between supporting a child financially and gaining access to the right to parent. Children are not a commodity in which a stake can be bought. Nonetheless, the ability of legal systems to recognise and, where necessary, to seek out the non-marital father is significant.

In Scotland, the non-marital father does not acquire parental responsibilities and rights automatically[4]. Where the child's mother agrees, and this is entirely at her discretion, he can acquire them by registering a standard-form written agreement[5]. Failing this, the only way for him to gain any legal right to engage in parenting is by applying to a court. There have long been calls for reform of the law[6] and the latest proposal on the table is to permit the non-marital father equality with other genetic parents, where he has been registered as the father at the time of the child's birth; something which, again, is at the discretion of the child's mother[7]. The non-marital father suffers similar discrimination in England and

1 Children (Scotland) Act 1995, s 3(1).

2 See, for example, *A v Kennedy* 1993 SLT 1188, where child protection proceedings were taken in respect of a baby because she was about to become part of the same household where an older sibling had died as a result of being assaulted. A similar line was taken in *D (A Minor) v Berkshire County Council* [1987] 1 All ER 20, where the mother had continued to use heroin during the antenatal period.

3 In Australia, the process began with the Child Support (Assessment) Act 1989. In the UK, it began with the Child Support Act 1991 and the latest amendment thereto is currently the Child Support Pensions and Social Security Act 2000. Similar developments have taken place in the US: see T Graves 'Comparing Child Support Guidelines' 34 *Fam LQ* 149 (2000) and L J Harris 'The Proposed ALI Child Support Principles' 35 *Willamette LR* 717 (1999). The Supreme Court of Wisconsin upheld the Constitutionality of the sentence imposed by a lower court on a father who was convicted of intentionally refusing to pay child support. The eight year prison sentence was suspended but the father was subject to five years probation, a condition of which was that he would not have another child unless he could show he was able to support that child and his existing children; *Wisconsin v Oakley* 629 NW 2d 200 (2001).

4 Children (Scotland) Act 1995, s 3(1)(b).

5 C(S)A 1995, s 4.

6 Scottish Law Commission *Report on Family Law* (Scot Law Com no 125, 1992) paras 2.36–2.50. See also E E Sutherland *Child and Family Law* (1999) T & T Clark, Edinburgh, paras 5.44–5.67.

7 *Parents and Children: A White Paper on Scottish Family Law* (Scottish Executive, 2000) paras 2.12–2.14 and Proposal 1.

Wales[1], with the law being subject to the same criticisms[2]. There, law reform is underway at the time of writing[3]. Nonetheless, the non-marital father's right to seek judicial permission to engage in parenting in the UK is clear, as witnessed by the large body of cases proceeding through the courts. In the US, the general position is that the 'mere existence of the biological link' does not guarantee him constitutional protection equivalent to the mother or married father[4]. He must show interest in, or willingness to assume responsibilities in respect of, the child, or an established relationship, before the fact of parentage entitles him to seek recognition of his right to parent[5].

Where a person is treated as a parent by the operation of legal fictions, again, he or she is charged with the function of parenting. Thus, once a child has been adopted, the adopter or adopters are endowed with much the same responsibilities and rights as mothers and married fathers. There is the possibility of a genetic parent continuing involvement in the child's life, through the mechanism of open adoption[6], but the adopters are nonetheless central to parenting.

Where a child has resulted from assisted reproductive techniques using donated gametes, the law again clothes the person treated as the parent with the opportunity to parent. In the UK, provided that the Human Fertilisation and Embryology Act 1990 applies, the woman who bears the child is treated as the mother and she is the person who has parental responsibilities and rights, irrespective of the fact that her genetic material may not have been used at all. Similarly, the husband of a woman who bears the child is treated as the father and he will, again, be permitted to parent. Where an unmarried woman is treated along with her partner, while he will be treated as the child's father, this simply confers on him the status of a non-marital father and he will be subject to the same discrimination. Where assisted reproduction falls outwith the ambit of the 1990 Act, the questions surrounding both parentage and parenting fall to be resolved under other legal principles, which opens the door to genetic parents entering the picture and, quite possibly, being given some opportunity to parent. In the US, the Uniform Status of Children of Assisted Conception Act sought to achieve similar regulation but it has not been adopted widely, with states either enacting their own legislation or leaving resolution to the courts.

Where parentage, of whatever hue, leads to parenting, it can be seen as creating a simple starting point, serving the interests of the child, the parents and the

1 Children Act 1989, ss 2(2) and 4(1)(b).

2 A Bainham 'When is a parent not a parent: reflections on the unmarried father and his child in English Law' (1989) 3 *Int J of Law and the Family* 208 and N Lowe 'The Meaning and Allocation of Parental Responsibility: A Common Lawyers Perspective' (1997) 11 *Int J of Law, Policy and the Family* 192.

3 The Adoption and Children Bill 2001, cl 91, provides for the automatic acquisition of parental responsibilities and parental rights by the non-marital father on birth registration. For the background to this proposal, see Lord Chancellor's Dept *The Law on Parental Responsibility for Unmarried Fathers* (1998) HMSO.

4 *Lehr v Robertson* 463 US 248 (1983).

5 *Stanley v Illinois* 405 US 645 (1969); *Caban v Mohammed* 441 US 380 (1979).

6 The courts in England and Wales have been more willing than those in Scotland to use the legislation allowing for conditions to be attached to granting the adoption petition to permit post-adoptive contact between a birth parent or other birth relative and the adoptee: *Re C (A Minor) (Adoption Order: Conditions)* [1989] AC 1. See A B Wilkinson and K McK Norrie *The Law of Parent and Child in Scotland* (2nd edn, 1999) W Green, Edinburgh at paras 4.77–4.80. In the US, agreements between adopters and birth parents sometimes permit such contact in a number of states: M M Mahoney 'Open Adoption in Context: The Wisdom and Enforceability of Visitation Orders for Former Parents under the Uniform Adoption Act' 51 *Fla LRev* 89 (1999).

state in allocating responsibility for children. It will frequently accord with the reality of who is actually parenting. However, when that starting point excludes a parent, like the non-marital father, the interests of the child and the father may be taking second place to other considerations. Whose interests are prevailing? The old spectre of the child of rape or incest is frequently produced as the justification for protecting both the child and the mother from the unworthy father. We have no figures to tell us how many such fathers are out there but the number must be small. Undoubtedly, protection from them may be necessary, assuming, of course, they are aware of the child's existence and have any desire for contact. Then there is the otherwise 'unworthy' father, who seeks to be involved in parenting out of spite or in order to persecute, or further persecute, the child's mother. What of the spiteful, unworthy mother, who seeks to deny the father any role in the child's life for reasons wholly unconnected with the child's welfare? Should a legal system simply deny that she exists? Such an approach fails to take account of the fact that courts feel able to deal with such ghastly parents when the dispute arises in the context of marital breakdown. Where the legal system denies the father the opportunity to get through the door of the court, his sincerity, and what he has to offer the child, cannot be tested. How many children lose valuable parenting input as a result? What of the birth parents and donors who are similarly denied the opportunity to demonstrate that they have something to offer the child? Does this have similar results of denying children opportunities as well?

Parenting and agreements

There is considerable scope for the relevant adults to reach agreement over legal recognition of parenting, with or without the assistance of mediation[1]. As we have seen, in the UK there is the possibility of agreements between mothers and non-marital fathers, allowing the father the opportunity to parent. There is a proposal to create a similar type of agreement to enable step-parents to acquire parental responsibilities and rights without the need to go to court[2]. Some birth parents and other relatives reach agreement on a degree of involvement in the child's life after adoption.

Clearly, there is a strong societal interest in parties reaching agreement and resolving disputes without using litigation, not least in terms of court and other costs. For many of the individuals involved, the opportunity to give legal effect to what is happening in practice, offers security at less economic cost than would attach to court proceedings. Where there has been dispute initially, resolution by agreement can empower the individuals and enable them to avoid the acrimony, delay and cost associated with litigation. This assumes that, in reality, there has been uncoerced agreement. Some commentators express concern over mediation, in this respect[3]. The real danger with agreements is that they may be made for the convenience of the adults involved, without the child being given any

1 See ch 9 below for further discussion.

2 *Parents and Children: A White Paper on Scottish Family Law* (Scottish Executive, 2000) paras 2.25–2.45 and Proposal 2. In England and Wales, the Adoption and Children Bill 2001, cl 92 provides for such agreements.

3 Much of the literature here raises the concern that women can be manipulated or oppressed by the mediation process. See, for example, T Grillo 'The Mediation Alternative: Process Dangers for Women' 100 *Yale LJ* 1545 (1991); D Majury 'Unconscionability in an Equality Context' 7 *Fam LQ* 123 (1991).

opportunity to participate in the decision[1]. In some cases, like agreement between unmarried birth parents, the child will be too young to participate in the decision-making process. However, agreements between divorcing parents, parents and step-parents, and in respect of open adoption, may all concern an older child. It is essential that we provide real mechanisms to ensure that such children are given a meaningful opportunity to participate.

Parenting in cases of dispute

Where a dispute arises between two or more people who already have the right to parent, litigation presents a means of resolution. Legal systems have long experience of adjudicating disputes between, for example, separating and divorcing parents and, of course, litigation is the only route open to many non-marital fathers. What criteria courts apply will be considered presently. First, however, we must consider the position of persons who have no established legal right to parent, but who wish to seek such a right. A whole range of people, including step-parents[2] and grandparents, may have had considerable involvement in the child's life or, in the case of a young child, they may want to do so. Can they seek the assistance of the court in gaining legal recognition? Remember, they may be seeking extensive involvement, including the right to have the child live with them or to participate in important decisions, or they may simply be seeking the right to contact or visitation. Again, we find a good example of considerable divergence between legal systems in approaching this issue, by studying Scotland and the US.

Scotland offers maximum openness in allowing interested parties to get through the door of the court and make a case for their opportunity to parent. Any person who 'claims an interest' may apply to the court for an order relating to parental responsibilities and rights, unless the person falls within the excluded categories[3]. The provision has been used by grandparents[4], step-parents[5] and others who have had some involvement with a child. Thus, a woman was able to apply for contact with her former partner's child after the couple's same-sex relationship had come to an end[6].

Similar provisions operated in many jurisdictions in the US[7] until the recent decision in *Troxel v Granville*[8], where the US Supreme Court struck down a Washington state statute which allowed grandparents to apply to a court for vis-

1 See *Alternative Dispute Resolution in Scotland* (Central Research Unit, 1996); *Giving Children a Voice in Family Mediation* (National Family Mediation and the Gulbenkian Foundation, 1994); C Bruch 'And how are the children? The effect of ideology and mediation on child custody and children's well-being in the United States' (1995) *Int J of Law and Fam* 106.

2 Here, the term 'step-parent' is used to mean not only the spouse of a parent but also a cohabitant, irrespective of gender.

3 Children (Scotland) Act 1995, s 11(3)(a). A person falls within the excluded categories if his or her parental responsibilities or rights have been extinguished by an adoption order (including expedited adoption proceedings applicable to surrogacy) or transferred to an adoption agency or a local authority: Children (Scotland) Act 1995, s 11(3) and (4).

4 See, for example, *Senna-Cheribbo v Wood* 1999 SC 328.

5 See, for example, *Robertson v Robertson* (OH, 7 December 1999, unreported), where, in addition to seeking residence of one child and contact with two others, a man sought parental responsibilities and rights in respect of his stepdaughter.

6 The case *R v F* which was heard in Dunfermline Sheriff Court is unreported, but an account of it can be found in J Fotheringham 'Parental Responsibilities and Rights as for Homosexual Couples' 1999 SLT (News) 337.

7 For a pre-*Troxel* discussion, see G A Holmes 'The Tie That Binds: The Constitutional Right of Children to Maintain Relationships with Parent-Like Individuals' 53 *Md LR* 358 (1994).

8 *Troxel v Granville* 120 S Ct 2054 (2000).

itation rights. There, a dispute arose between the mother of two girls and their paternal grandparents, with whom the children had an established relationship, over the amount of visitation the grandparents could enjoy with the girls. The children's parents had never been married and, after they separated, the father went to live with his parents and took the girls to their home during his own regular visitation. After the father committed suicide, the grandparents initially continued to see the children regularly. Six months later, the girls' mother indicated to the grandparents that she proposed to limit visitation to one short visit per month. The grandparents petitioned for more extensive visitation under the relevant Washington state statute which allowed 'any person' to petition and directed the court to apply a 'best interests' test in reaching its decision[1]. Thus began six-and-a-half years of litigation, during which time the girls' mother had married and her husband had adopted the children. The Supreme Court's decision is less helpful than it might have been, not least because it is a plurality decision[2] and is narrowly tailored to the facts of the particular case[3]. Essentially, it found that the Washington statute, as applied in the particular case, violated the substantive due process rights of a fit parent to decide whom her children should see and when. The court indicated that there is a presumption that a fit parent will act in the best interests of her children and that, in such circumstances, the state is not justified in intruding on private (parental) decision-making within the family. All but one of the justices, quite astonishingly, failed to discuss the case from a children's rights perspective[4]. The plurality opinion was critical of a decision being taken solely on the basis of a judicially determined 'best interests' test[5]. Quite what the impact of that decision will be is a matter of some debate, but it has already had the effect of limiting the rights of grandparents[6] and others[7].

1 Wash Rev Code ss 26.10.160(3).

2 Three justices joined Justice O'Connor in the plurality opinion, two other filed decisions concurring in the result but for their own reasons, and three justices dissented. A 4–1–1–3 decision is open to varying interpretations. A majority decision would have provided clearer guidance.

3 Justice O'Connor struck down the Washington statute 'as applied' in this particular case. While the judgment gives some indication of why this was done and thus, by implication, what is unacceptable about the statute, it does not address the general question of whether such a statute would always fail to pass constitutional muster.

4 Justice Stevens (dissenting) in *Troxel v Granville* at 120 S Ct 2054 (2000), p 2072 observed: 'The constitutional protection against arbitrary state interference with parental rights should not be extended to prevent the States from protecting children against the arbitrary exercise of parental authority that is not in fact motivated by an interest in the welfare of the child.'

5 Justice O'Connor observed: 'The Washington nonparental visitation statute is breathtakingly broad . . . [I]n the state of Washington a court can disregard and overturn any decision by a fit custodial parent concerning visitation whenever a third party affected by the decision files a visitation petition, based solely on the judge's determination of the child's best interests' (*Troxel v Granville* 120 S Ct 2054 (2000) at p 2061).

6 See, for example, *Brice v Brice* 752 A 2d 1132 (2000, Md); *Belair v Drew* 2000 Fla LEXIS 1980, 5 October 2000; *Lulay v Lulay* 2000 Ill LEXIS 1694, 26 October 2000; *Richardson v Richardson* 766 So 2d 1036 (2000, Fla); *Newton v Thomas* 2001 Wh 1338379 (Or, 2001).

7 Already, one court has followed *Troxel v Granville* 120 Sct 2054 (2000) in denying visitation rights to former foster carers: *Re Richardson* 2000 WL 869450, 23 June 2000, Circuit Court of Virginia. In one case where a same-sex former partner was successful, the decision was essentially procedural and related to jurisdiction: *Gestl v Frederick* 754 A 2d 1087 (2000, Md). The former partner of a deceased mother who was initially successful in applying for visitation with the children lost the right when the children's father appealed: *Harrington v Daum* 18 p 3d 456 (Or, 2001). Furthermore, the parent's right to determine what should happen to the child would appear to extend to deciding which third party should have custody (residence) where the parent was not choosing to exercise this herself: *Lawrence v Lawrence* 713 NYS 2d 418 (2000). Oregon is one of a number of states to have amended the statute allowing for grandparent and 'psychological parent' visitation; ORS 109.119 (2001 edition).

Whose interests are being given precedence in the very different approaches of Scots law and the Supreme Court in *Troxel v Granville*? The latter has, to some extent, the benefit of certainty or, at least, it will have once its full implications become clear. Certainty reduces litigation and, thus, may serve the state's economic interest. In protecting the parent's right to due process and privacy, the court was giving precedence to the position of those with a vested right to parent as opposed to third parties. While this can be seen as supporting the established family unit, it should not be forgotten that the children in *Troxel* already had an established relationship with their grandparents. Of greatest concern was the virtual absence of any discussion of the rights or interests of the children in the case. That is not to say that the Scottish approach is without its problems. The opportunity for a whole range of people to seek redress in the courts can pose a threat to the security parents might feel in respect of the raising of their children[1]. The role of the child in the decision-making process is far from being well supported and the extent to which courts receive accurate and meaningful information on the child's views presents problems[2]. A further difficulty arises in this 'open' system of access to courts over parenting – the criteria to be applied.

Where a court is asked to decide on parenting issues, a standard test has long been that the best interests of the child should prevail. This continues to be the standard applied in the UK and many jurisdictions in the US, and accords with the UN Convention on the Rights of the Child[3]. The operation of the 'best interests' standard has long been criticised as vague and arbitrary[4], sexist[5] and in need of replacement[6]. In Scotland[7], unlike many other jurisdictions[8], there is no statutory checklist of factors to guide the court on what will contribute to, or detract from, the child's welfare. However, when one notes that virtually every checklist has the final criterion of 'all the circumstances of the case', it becomes apparent

1 The prospect of a successful challenge to the current position by applying the privacy argument and the European Convention on Human Rights, art 8 is, it is submitted, unlikely, not least because the European Court has expressly recognised the importance of the relationship between grandchildren and grandparents and, indeed, the child and other relatives.

2 The role of the child is discussed fully in ch 1 above.

3 UN Convention on the Rights of the Child, art 3.

4 The literature here is vast but R H Mnookin 'Child Custody Adjudication: Judicial Functions in the Face of Indeterminacy' 39 Law and Contemporary Probs 227 (1975), is often regarded as the seminal article. Despite its shortcomings, the welfare principle at least claims to be child-centred: B B Woodhouse 'Child Custody in the Age of Children's Rights: The Search for a Just and Workable Standard' 33 *Fam LQ* 815 (1999).

5 F Olsen 'The Politics of Family Law' 2 *Law and Inequ* 1 (1984); M A Fineman *The Illusion of Equality: The Rhetoric and Reality of Divorce Reform* (1991); J C Murphy 'Legal Images of Motherhood: Conflicting Definitions from Welfare "Reform", Family, and Criminal Law' 83 *Cornell L Rev* 688 (1998).

6 M S Melli 'Towards a Restructuring of Custody Decision-making at Divorce: an Alternative Approach to the Best Interests of the Child' in J Eekelaar and P Sarcevic *Parenthood in Modern Society* (1993) Martinus Nijhoff, where the author prefers the 'primary caregiver ' standard. That standard has, in turn, been criticised as a thinly disguised version of the maternal preference: R Neely 'The Primary Caretaker Parent Rule: Child Custody and the Dynamics of Greed' 3 *Yale Law and Pol'y Rev* 167 (1984).

7 After consideration, the Scottish Law Commission rejected a statutory checklist of factors which the court would be required to consider in assessing welfare, on the basis that such a checklist would be necessarily incomplete, might divert attention from other factors which ought to be considered, and might result in judges taking a mechanical approach to decision-making: *Report on Family Law*, paras 5.20–5.23. That the opposite view was taken by the Law Commission in England and Wales is demonstrated by the list found in the Children Act 1989, s 1(3) and (4): see *Report on Guardianship and Custody* (Law Com no 172, 1988) paras 3.17–3.21.

8 In England and Wales, for example, see the Children Act 1989, s 1(3) and in Oregon, see ORS ss 107.137.

that the presence or absence of a checklist probably makes little difference. The fact remains, however, that difficulty in finding the perfect standards to apply to parenting decisions does not free the courts from having to do so. Certainly, the elusive nature of such a standard is no argument at all for arbitrary rules on who can get into court in the first place.

CONCLUDING THOUGHTS

To return to the newspaper headline cited at the beginning of this chapter, do Mother's Day and Father's Day matter? Perhaps that is a personal question, particularly for every adult child who has ever forgotten either. For legal systems there are more pressing issues. How do legal systems approach legal recognition of parentage and to whom should opportunities for parenting be extended? It is submitted that these are separate, if not wholly separable, questions.

Knowledge of genetic parentage clearly matters for a host of reasons and, as adoptees have long demonstrated, many individuals seek further information about their wider genetic heritage. Legal systems have shown themselves to be equivocal over honesty on this issue. In so far as the presumptions surrounding parentage enable legal recognition of the truth, more often than not, they may be a benign way of helping a legal system to operate efficiently and cheaply and with minimal interference in the lives of individuals. However, where they create absolute rules which may or may not reflect reality, their continued existence must be questioned. Of course, we could require DNA testing of everyone before parentage was accepted[1], but this might involve wasteful expense and undue intrusion. It is when the legal system sets out to create parentage through the use of fictions that it is incumbent on it not to block an individual's access to his or her identity. Meaningful access requires a number of changes in existing provision. First, meticulous records must be kept of birth parents and donors, and it has to be acknowledged that some jurisdictions are improving in this respect. Second, children or certainly young adults must know when adoption or assisted reproductive techniques are part of their background. By ensuring that adults become aware of the fact of adoption through birth certificates, there is a strong incentive for adoptive parents in the UK to address the issue of disclosure at an earlier stage. The inclusion of similar information on the birth certificates of children of assisted reproductive techniques would, again, encourage early disclosure[2]. Third, full access to identifying birth or donor information must be available to the children who want it. That would leave them the choice about what, if any, further steps they take. That brings us to the final issue surrounding parentage. Should identifying information be a two-way, rather than a one-way, street? Should birth parents and donors be able to trace the children, at some future stage? It is submitted that, if we are to give primacy to the child's rights, a blanket provision to this effect is undesirable. The now-adult children may not want contact and, in that, their privacy must surely be respected. It must be remembered that it was not the children who made the choices here. Donors, adopters, those who have used assisted reproductive techniques and, in some

1 There are reports of men obtaining do-it-yourself DNA testing kits by mail and having their children and themselves tested secretly: 'Check your Paternity by Post' *Times*, 1 June 2001, s 2, p 4.

2 The Warnock Committeee thought this idea worthy of consideration in the future: *Report of the Committee of Inquiry Into Human Fertilisation and Embryology* (Cmnd 9314, 1984) para 4.25.

cases, birth parents, were given the chance to choose. The ultimate choice on contact must be left to the children.

What of parenting? It is not suggested here that a genetic or social link between an adult and a child should necessarily result in the adult being given legal recognition of some right to parent. Rather, it is suggested that the chance for a child to benefit from the input of the various individuals should be maximised. Where agreements can be reached between adults, this frequently happens, in fact, and sometimes in law. Legal systems should, however, be wary of an over-eagerness to save on court costs by allowing the adults to reach legally binding agreements without any scrutiny of these agreements. Courts already have in place a system for reaching decisions in disputed cases. While that system is imperfect, the goal should be to improve it by, for example, finding *fora* where the child who wants to can have a meaningful opportunity to participate in the decision-making process. Such a forum should then be available on an inclusive, rather than narrowly limited, basis. In short, adult notions of privacy must not be allowed to take precedence over children's rights.

4 Reconceiving Families and the Ties that Bind: A More Inclusive Approach?

Anne Griffiths*

CHANGING FAMILY FORMS

Contemporary family life covers a wide array of de facto familial forms including lone-parent households, cohabiting heterosexual and same-sex couples, as well as marital relationships. Not only is there diversity in the types of family that exist in Scotland today but individuals may enter into a number of these forms in their lifetime as they move from marriage to lone parenthood on to a cohabiting relationship, or from cohabitation to marriage[1]. As a result of this diversity and the changing nature of familial relationships it is estimated that one in eight children will form part of a lone-parent household at some point in their lives before they reach the age of 16. Such diversity raises questions about the types of relationships that Scots law should recognise as 'family' relationships that are worthy of protection and promotion given that individuals may form part of more than one family unit at any one point in time[2]. Thus, where a husband and wife who have children are divorced and re-partner, their children not only continue to form part of a family unit with respect to them, but may also form part of a new family unit comprising their parent's new partner, and possibly that partner's children, together with any children resulting from the new union. In this situation, where multiple ties exist, how far are legal and social constructions of family life and parenthood in tune with one another when it comes to handling disputes over the child's welfare and the issue of legal rights?

How far does marriage continue to define the legal relationship between parent and child and what impact does this have on an unmarried father's

* The author would like to thank John J Sampson, Beth Youngdale, Randy Kandel, David Nichols, Stephen Tierney, Keith Taylor, Bren Neale and Kenneth Norrie for their invaluable comments on a draft version of this chapter. The text as it stands however, is the author's sole responsibility.

1 According to *Social Trends 2001*, No 31, the proportion of non-married women aged under sixty almost doubled between 1986 and 1998–99 from 13% to 25% (p 41). According to the Registrar General for Scotland, *Annual Report 1999*, the number of marriages taking place in Scotland was one of the lowest since 1895 (at p 127). 41% of live births were to unmarried parents but over 60% of these were jointly registered by parents living at the same address (p 31); 51% of children who were adopted were adopted by a step-parent or relative of the child (p 145). Results from the General Household Survey 1998–99 show that step-families (married and cohabiting) accounted for about 6% of all families with dependent children in Great Britain: see *Social Trends 2001* (p 53). Single-parent households account for 60% of those households that were surveyed in Scotland: see *Scotland's People: Results from the 1999 Household Survey*.

2 See A Bissett-Johnson and C Barton, 'The similarities and differences in Scottish and English family law in dealing with changing family patterns', (1999) *Journal of Social Welfare and Family Law*, Vol 21 (1), pp 1–21.

relationship with his child? This question is a pertinent one, given that the European Convention on Human Rights has recently been partially incorporated into UK law by the Human Rights Act 1998. Of particular interest is art 8, which guarantees the 'right to family life' which according to the jurisprudence of the European Court of Human Rights is not restricted to marital families but extends to de facto family relationships[1]. How are the rights and interests of various family members to be accommodated in promoting the welfare of the child while upholding an individual's human rights? A comparative analysis of another jurisdiction's handling of these issues may be instructive. This chapter will pursue the issue of contact between parent and child in the context of two cases from the USA, one involving a US Supreme Court decision in *Michael H and Victoria D, Appellants v Gerald D*[2], and the other, a decision of the Supreme Court of Texas, *Re JWT, A Minor Child*[3]. It will then examine the position under Scots law and explore the implications that these two different legal systems have for individuals' claims to visitation and contact.

In both jurisdictions it is clear that women and men are treated differently. Women acquire the status of a parent together with full parental responsibilities and rights on the birth of their child (regardless of their marital status). Men, however, do not acquire such legal status or responsibilities and rights through a mere biological connection to the child. They must either (a) have been married to the mother at the time of conception or birth, or, where unmarried, (b) have acted in some way – through cohabitation with mother and child in a family unit, or through support and contact – to establish a familial bond with the child. In cases of dispute, both jurisdictions invoke presumptions of paternity, rules relating to parental responsibilities and rights and to the interests and welfare of the child in regulating conflict, although the scope and application of the law varies as the case law from both jurisdictions will demonstrate.

MICHAEL H AND VICTORIA D APPELLANTS v GERALD D[4]

Carole married Gerald in 1976. While married, she had an affair with a neighbour, Michael H, and had a child, Victoria, in 1980. Gerald was listed as the father on the birth certificate and always held Victoria out to the world as his daughter, but Carole informed Michael that she believed that he was the father and subsequent blood tests showed that there was a 98.07% probability that Michael was Victoria's father. Between 1981 and 1984 Victoria lived with Carole but found herself in a variety of 'quasi-family units' moving back and forth between living with Michael, Gerald, and another man, Scott K. During the three- and eight-month periods when Michael lived with Carole and Victoria he treated Victoria, and held her out to others, as his child. In November 1982, rebuffed in his attempts to visit Victoria, Michael filed a filiation action in the California Superior Court to establish his paternity and right to visitation.

The court appointed an attorney and guardian *ad litem* to represent Victoria's interests. On behalf of Victoria he filed a cross-complaint asserting that if she had more than one psychological or de facto father, she was entitled to maintain her filial relationship with both. In May 1983, Carole contested Michael's suit while

1 *Marckx v Belgium* (1979–80) 2 EHRR 330.
2 *Michael H and Victoria D, Appellants v Gerald D* 491 US 110.
3 *Re JWT, A Minor Child* 872 SW2d 189.
4 *Michael H and Victoria D, Appellants v Gerald D* 491 US 110.

living with Gerald in New York. In August 1983, however, she took up with Michael again in California and withdrew her motion. In April 1984, Carole and Michael signed a stipulation that Michael was Victoria's natural father but this was never filed because Carole left Michael the following month to return to Gerald with whom she subsequently had two children. In May 1984, Michael and Victoria, through her guardian *ad litem*, sought visitation rights for Michael *pendente lite*.

To determine if visitation would be in Victoria's best interests, the Superior Court appointed a psychologist to evaluate Victoria, Gerald, Michael, and Carole. The psychologist recommended that Carole retain sole custody, but that Michael be allowed continued contact with Victoria pursuant to a restricted visitation schedule. The court granted an order to this effect but Gerald, who had intervened in the action, moved to have the action dismissed on the ground that under the California Evidence Code, § 621 there were no triable issues of fact as to Victoria's paternity, as under that section he was conclusively presumed to be her father. This section provides that 'the issue of a wife cohabiting with her husband, who is not impotent or sterile, is conclusively presumed to be a child of the marriage'[1]. The presumption may be rebutted, but only in limited circumstances, by blood tests, and only if a motion for such tests is made within two years from the date of the child's birth, either by the husband, or, if the natural father has filed an affidavit acknowledging paternity, by the wife[2].

The Superior Court upheld Gerald's motion on the basis that as he was cohabiting with his wife at the date of Victoria's conception and birth, and as he was neither impotent or sterile, he was conclusively presumed to be Victoria's father. In doing so, the court rejected Michael and Victoria's arguments as to the constitutionality of § 621 and also denied their motions for continued visitation pending the appeal under the California Civil Code, § 4601, which provides that a court may, in its discretion, grant 'reasonable visitation rights . . . to any person having an interest in the welfare of the child.' It denied visitation rights on the basis that to allow them would 'violat[e] the intention of the Legislature by impugning the integrity of the family unit[3].' Both Michael and Victoria appealed but the California Court of Appeal affirmed the judgment of the Superior Court and denied their petitions for a rehearing. The case came before the US Supreme Court after the California Supreme Court denied discretionary review.

Structure of legal system in USA: claims pursued

It is important to note that within the structure of the American legal system the 50 individual states have rights to legislate on matters, such as family law, that fall within their own jurisdiction. However, such legislation must not fall foul of either state constitutions or the Federal Constitution which incorporates a Bill of Rights guaranteeing and upholding certain rights and freedoms with respect to individuals[4].

In this case Michael H challenged the constitutionality of the Californian Evidence Code, § 621 on the basis that:

1 Cal Evid Code Ann § 621(a) (West supp 1989).
2 See Cal Evid Code Ann §§ 621(c) and (d) (West Supp 1989).
3 Supp App to Juris Statement A-91.
4 For more detailed account see *Modern Constitutional Law: Cases and Notes* (6th edn) Ronald D Rotunda 2000 West Group.

(1) in being denied the opportunity to demonstrate his paternity in an evidentiary hearing his procedural due process rights as a putative natural father were being infringed; and
(2) that as a natural father he had a constitutionally protected 'liberty' interest in his relationship with his child which the provisions of the Californian Evidence Code, § 621 violated and thus denied his rights to substantive due process.

Out of the nine Supreme Court Justices, the plurality opinion written by Justice Scalia held that neither Michael's procedural nor substantive rights to due process had been infringed, although their findings were not at one with one[1]. Four Justices dissented from the plurality's judgment. In the plurality's opinion, the terms of § 621, while framed in terms of a presumption, were viewed as expressing and implementing a substantive rule of law which represented the state legislature's determination, that as a matter of overriding social policy 'the husband should be held responsible for the child and that the integrity and privacy of the family unit should not be impugned'[2]. In other words, it was accepted that in these circumstances the state had legitimate interests in denying putative natural fathers a right to an evidentiary hearing on paternity[3]. This was because 'if Michael were successful in being declared the father, other rights would follow – most importantly, the right to be considered as the parent who should have custody'[4].

On the issue of substantive due process Michael argued that he had a constitutionally protected 'liberty' interest in the parental relationship he had established with Victoria and that protection of the marital union represented an insufficient interest on the part of the state in terminating the parent/child relationship. According to Justice Scalia, in order to establish such an interest it must be one that is 'traditionally protected by our society' that is 'so rooted in the traditions and conscience of our people as to be ranked as fundamental'[5]. In his view, such protection is accorded to relationships that develop within the 'unitary family' which 'is typified, of course, by the marital family, but also includes the household of unmarried parents, and their children'[6]. On this basis Scalia argues that the legal issue in this case is whether or not the relationship put forward by Michael between himself and Victoria 'has been treated as a protected family unit under the historic practices of our society, or whether on any other basis it has been accorded special protection'[7]. He answers this question in the negative,

1 The Supreme Court's decision in this case may be contrasted with that of the European Court of Human Rights in *Kroon v Netherlands* (1995) 19 EHRR 263 where it held that Dutch law, which made it impossible for a biological father to gain recognition of his paternity where the mother was married to another man unless the husband denied paternity, was in breach of the European Convention on Human Rights, art 8.

2 *Michael H and Victoria D, Appellants v Gerald D* 491 US 110 at 119–120.

3 Note that Justice Scalia argued that because the statute categorically denies all men an opportunity to establish paternity, the challenge could not accurately be viewed as a procedural one (491 US 110, at 111), but five other justices were of the view that the flaw inhering in a conclusive presumption that terminates a constitutionally protected interest *without any hearing whatsoever* (emphasis added) is a procedural one.

4 *Michael H and Victoria D, Appellants v Gerald D* 491 US 110 at 118.

5 *Michael H and Victoria D, Appellants v Gerald D* 491 US 110 at 122. See *Snyder v Massachusetts* 291 US 97, 105; 54 SCt 330, 332; 78 LEd 674 (1934) (Cardozo, J).

6 *Michael H and Victoria D, Appellants v Gerald D* 491 US 110 at 124, n 3.

7 *Michael H and Victoria D, Appellants v Gerald D* 491 US 110 at 124.

asserting that 'to the contrary, our traditions have protected the marital family (Gerald, Carole and the child they acknowledge to be theirs) against the sort of claim Michael asserts'[1].

However, while concurring with Justice Scalia's judgment as a whole, Justices O'Connor and Kennedy dissented from the mode of historical analysis that Scalia adopts when identifying liberty interests protected by the Due Process Clause of the Fourteenth Amendment which they found to be 'somewhat inconsistent with our past decisions in this area'[2]. Not only that, but as Justice Brennan observes in his dissenting judgment,

> 'Five Members of the Court refuse to foreclose "the possibility that a natural father might ever have a constitutionally protected interest in his relationship with a child whose mother was married to, and cohabiting with, another man at the time of the child's conception and birth'[3].

Thus Justice Stevens framed the issue in terms of whether or not the California statute denied the appellants 'a fair opportunity to prove that Victoria's interests would be served by granting Michael visitation rights'[4] and, in doing so, was prepared to recognise 'that enduring "family" relationships may develop in unconventional settings'[5]. Nonetheless, at the end of the day, he found that the California statute was not unconstitutional because the California Civil Code, § 4601 provided Michael with an opportunity to persuade the court that as an 'other person having an interest in the welfare of the child'[6] reasonable visitation rights should be granted. The court's decision declining to grant such rights was not unjust, because given the stable and harmonious family home in which Victoria eventually ended up,

> 'I find nothing fundamentally unfair about the exercise of a judge's discretion that, in the end, allows the mother to decide whether her child's best interests would be served by allowing the natural father visitation privileges'[7].

Dissenting judgments

Substantive due process

Three dissenting justices, in a judgment written by Justice Brennan, took issue with applying the concept of tradition to limit the remit of a 'liberty' interest. While noting the plurality's concern with limiting the scope 'for judges to substitute their own preferences for those of elected officials'[8], they nonetheless rejected tradition as a means of limiting the scope of due process because what constitutes tradition is always open to interpretation and because it operates in favour of the status quo in ways which make it hard to 'recognize that times change' and that 'sometimes a practice or rule outlives its foundations'[9]. Not only that, but the plurality construes tradition in very specific forms that go beyond

1 *Michael H and Victoria D, Appellants v Gerald D* 491 US 110 at 124.
2 *Michael H and Victoria D, Appellants v Gerald D* 491 US 110 at 132.
3 *Michael H and Victoria D, Appellants v Gerald D* 491 US 110 at 136.
4 *Michael H and Victoria D, Appellants v Gerald D* 491 US 110 at 132.
5 *Michael H and Victoria D, Appellants v Gerald D* 491 US 110 at 133.
6 *Michael H and Victoria D, Appellants v Gerald D* 491 US 110 at 133.
7 *Michael H and Victoria D, Appellants v Gerald D* 491 US 110 at 136.
8 *Michael H and Victoria D, Appellants v Gerald D* 491 US 110 at 137.
9 *Michael H and Victoria D, Appellants v Gerald D* 491 US 110 at 141.

the general interests, such as 'freedom from physical constraint, marriage, child-bearing and others . . . [that] form the core of our definition of 'liberty'[1]. Thus the plurality, according to Justice Brennan,

> 'does not ask whether parenthood is an interest that historically has received our attention and protection . . . Instead, the plurality asks whether the specific variety of parenthood under consideration – a natural father's relationship with a child whose mother is married to another man – has enjoyed such protection'[2].

The dissenting justices view the plurality's interpretative approach as inappropriate because:

(a) It is inconsistent with past case law. They observe that cases such as *Eisenstadt v Baird*[3] and *Griswold v Connecticut*[4] would have reached a different result, for if the question had been raised 'whether the specific interest under consideration had been traditionally protected', the answer would have been a resounding 'no'[5].
(b) It is unnecessary, as this case does not present a 'new' interest for consideration, because where 'the interest under consideration is a parent-child relationship, we need not ask, over and over again, whether that interest is one that society traditionally protects'[6].
(c) It leads to a misinterpretation of previous Supreme Court cases involving unwed fathers[7], for while the plurality claim the intent of these cases was to protect the 'unitary family', the dissenting justices maintain that

> 'Though different in factual and legal circumstances, these cases have produced a unifying theme: although an unwed father's biological link to his child does not, in and of itself, guarantee him a constitutional stake in his relationship with that child, such a link combined with a substantial parent–child relationship will do'[8].

The dissenting justices criticise the plurality's definition of the 'unitary' family, observing that despite ' paying lipservice to the fact that marriage is not the crucial fact in denying constitutional protection to the relationship between Michael and Victoria'[9], it is, in fact, a determining factor enabling Gerald, Carole and Victoria to be viewed as a unitary family, while denying this status to Michael, Victoria and Carole when the 'only difference between these two sets of relationships is the fact of marriage'[10]. They view the plurality's 'exclusive rather than inclusive definition' of the 'unitary family' as being 'out of step with other decisions' and amounting to a 'pinched conception of the 'family'[11]. They assert that 'In a community such as ours, 'liberty' must include the freedom not to conform', yet the plurality 'squashed this freedom by requiring specific approval from history before protecting anything in the name of liberty'[12].

1 *Michael H and Victoria D, Appellants v Gerald D* 491 US 110 at 139.
2 *Michael H and Victoria D, Appellants v Gerald D* 491 US 110 at 139.
3 *Eisenstadt v Baird* 405 US 438.
4 *Griswold v Conneticut* 381 US 479.
5 *Michael H and Victoria D, Appellants v Gerald D* 491 US 110 at 140.
6 *Michael H and Victoria D, Appellants v Gerald D* 491 US 110 at 142.
7 See *Stanley* v *Illinois* 405 US 645 (1972); *Quilloin* v *Walcott* 434 US 246 (1978); *Caban* v *Mohammed* 441 US 380 (1979); and *Lehr* v *Robertson* 463 US 248 (1983).
8 *Michael H and Victoria D, Appellants v Gerald D* 491 US 110 at 142.
9 *Michael H and Victoria D, Appellants v Gerald D* 491 US 110 at 143.
10 *Michael H and Victoria D, Appellants v Gerald D* 491 US 110 at 144.
11 *Michael H and Victoria D, Appellants v Gerald D* 491 US 110 at 145.
12 *Michael H and Victoria D, Appellants v Gerald D* 491 US 110 at 141.

They are also critical of the way in which the plurality's focus on the 'unitary family' conflates the question whether a liberty interest exists 'with the question what procedures may be used to terminate or curtail it'[1]. Thus the plurality fail to 'first ask whether the person claiming constitutional protection has an interest that the Constitution recognizes' before going on to consider whether or not the state may legitimately implement 'procedures that will attend the deprivation of that interest'[2]. By conflating these two considerations and taking the state's interests into account in defining whether or not a liberty interest exists the plurality fail to protect those important interests or statutes 'whose situations do not fit the government's narrow view of family life'[3]. Thus the 'premature consideration of California's interests'[4] gives rise to a situation in which the liberty interest varies with the state's interest in recognising that interest 'instead of focusing on Michael and Victoria's interest in their relationship with one another'[5]. Such an approach represents 'a bad day for due process when the state's interest in terminating a parent–child relationship is reason to conclude that that relationship is not part of the "liberty" protected by the Fourteenth Amendment'[6].

Procedural due process

The dissenting justices also challenge the plurality's judgment that Michael's right to procedural due process had not been infringed. They dispute the view that what matters is not the father's ability to claim paternity, but his ability to obtain 'substantive parental rights'[7]. They observe that the 'point of procedural due process is to give the litigant a fair chance of prevailing, not to ensure a particular substantive outcome'[8]. They argue that the effect of the Californian Evidence Code § 621 is to deprive Michael of the opportunity to establish that he is Victoria's father with the result that he is unable 'to take advantage of the best-interest standard embodied in § 4601 of California's Civil Code which directs that a parent be given visitation rights unless the visitation rights would be detrimental to the best interests of the child'[9]. Thus Michael is not only deprived of the benefits of the best-interest standard, but also of any chance of maintaining his relationship with Victoria because California case law is such that 'When, as a result of § 621, a putative father may not establish his paternity, neither may he obtain discretionary rights as a 'nonparent' under § 4601'[10]. In reaching this conclusion they dismiss Justice Stevens' interpretation of case law as upholding individualised assessment when it comes to granting visitation rights in these circumstances as 'wishful thinking'[11].

Finally, they answer the question 'whether California has an interest so powerful that it justifies granting Michael no hearing before terminating his parental rights'[12] in the negative, arguing that it is not § 621 that protects a stable marital

1 *Michael H and Victoria D, Appellants v Gerald D* 491 US 110 at 145.
2 *Michael H and Victoria D, Appellants v Gerald D* 491 US 110 at 145.
3 *Michael H and Victoria D, Appellants v Gerald D* 491 US 110 at 145.
4 *Michael H and Victoria D, Appellants v Gerald D* 491 US 110 at 146.
5 *Michael H and Victoria D, Appellants v Gerald D* 491 US 110 at 146.
6 *Michael H and Victoria D, Appellants v Gerald D* 491 US 110 at 146–147.
7 *Michael H and Victoria D, Appellants v Gerald D* 491 US 110 at 147.
8 *Michael H and Victoria D, Appellants v Gerald D* 491 US 110 at 147.
9 *Michael H and Victoria D, Appellants v Gerald D* 491 US 110 at 148.
10 *Michael H and Victoria D, Appellants v Gerald D* 491 US 110 at 149.
11 *Michael H and Victoria D, Appellants v Gerald D* 491 US 110 at 149.
12 *Michael H and Victoria D, Appellants v Gerald D* 491 US 110 at 154.

relationship and maintains the relationship between the child and presumed father, 'but the best-interest principle'[1]. Of the objectives put forward for the justification of the section, on the grounds that it protects the integrity and privacy of the matrimonial family, 'only the preservation of privacy is promoted by the refusal to hold a hearing itself'[2]. As the dissenting justices observe, to allow such a hearing in no way determines the issue as Michael 'first must convince a court that he is Victoria's father' and then, 'even if he is able to do this, he will be denied visitation rights if that would be in Victoria's best interests'[3].

In his separate dissenting judgment Justice White asserts that 'Michael more than meets the mark in establishing the constitutionally protected liberty interest discussed in *Lehr*[4] and recognized in *Stanley v Illinois*[5] and *Caban v Mohammed*'[6,7] which entitles him to protection under the Due Process Clause of the Fourteenth Amendment. He opines that both procedural and substantive due process are denied Michael under the California statute in question because 'he is foreclosed from establishing his paternity and is ultimately precluded by the State, from developing his relationship with his child'[8].

RE JWT, [A MINOR CHILD][9]

In the Texas case *Re JWT, A Minor Child.* the facts seem nearly identical. In fact there were several distinctions that make the biological father's claims slightly stronger. First, the wife planned to divorce her husband and marry the child's father, Larry G, who was involved in arranging for her ante-natal care and made several payments for her obstetric treatment. The woman and her husband, however, reconciled and dismissed their divorce action. Before the child's birth Larry G brought an action under the Texas Family Code alleging that he was the father of JWT, acknowledging responsibility for child support payments, and requesting a judicial declaration of paternity and recognition of his visitation rights. Finally, after the child's birth he unsuccessfully attempted to maintain contact with JWT. Under a court order blood tests were carried out which showed a 99.41% probability that Larry G was JWT's biological father and excluded the husband's possibility of paternity.

Under the Texas Family Code of the time several provisions operated in tandem to prevent a man claiming to be a child's biological father from suing either to rebut the marital presumption or to claim parental rights by establishing paternity[10]. In these circumstances, the Supreme Court of Texas held that the statutory scheme depriving a man who claims to be a child's biological father of standing

1 *Michael H and Victoria D, Appellants v Gerald D* 491 US 110 at 154.
2 *Michael H and Victoria D, Appellants v Gerald D* 491 US 110 at 154.
3 *Michael H and Victoria D, Appellants v Gerald D* 491 US 110 at 156.
4 *Lehr v Robertson* 463 US 248 (1983).
5 *Stanley v Illinois* 405 US 645 (1972).
6 *Caban v Mohammed* 441 US 380 (1979).
7 *Michael H and Victoria D, Appellants v Gerald D* 491 US 110 at 160.
8 *Michael H and Victoria D, Appellants v Gerald D* 491 US 110 at 163.
9 *Re JWT, A Minor Child* 872 SW2d 189.
10 Thus the marital presumption with respect to paternity may not be challenged by any party outside the marriage except a government entity, see TexFamCode §§ 12.02(a), 12.06(a). A biological father only has standing to sue under the Family Code if the child he claims has no presumed father: see TexFamCode § 11.03(a)(7). He may only lodge a paternity suit under Ch 13, which is limited to children who have no presumed father.

either to rebut the marital presumption or to claim parental rights by establishing his paternity, violates the due course of law guarantee of the State Constitution. Of the nine justices, six concurred with Justice Doggett's judgment and two dissented. It is important to note that in this case the due course of law guarantee 'has independent vitality, separate and distinct from the due process clause of the Fourteenth Amendment to the U.S. Constitution'[1]. On the other hand, in contrast to *Michael H and Victoria D, Appellants v Gerald D,* Larry G had no opportunity to establish a relationship with the child after JWT's birth.

While recognising that the 'State has a legitimate interest in minimizing familial disruptions that are harmful to the child'[2], the plurality endorsed the Court of Appeal's observation that 'this marital unit was clearly disrupted'[3] before Larry G ever filed suit. They also endorsed the Court of Appeal's view that

> '[Resolution of these difficulties by the husband and wife] does not, we feel, give license to the state to perpetuate the myth of "presumption of paternity" so as to deprive the biological father of at least a chance of being able to exercise those rights, duties, privileges, and responsibilities that all civilized societies have recognized to be fundamentally ingrained in the concept of parenthood'[4].

The plurality took account of the fact that paternity today can be established with 'near certainty' and formed the view that the focus should 'be directed toward what is best for the child – it may be in the best interest of the child to allow development of a relationship with the natural father and it may not'[5]. They refused to accept the dissenting justices' proposition that the determination of best interest and the definition of family should be left 'exclusively to the biological mother'[6]. However, Justice Hecht opined:

> 'I agree with the Court that in determining what rights a biological father may have in his child, the best interest of the child must be considered. I do not agree with the implication in the Court's opinion . . . that the best interest of the child is the only, or always the paramount, consideration. The interests of the mother and her husband in preserving their family unit exclusive of the biological father are equal in dignity to the biological father's interest and entitled to equal consideration. Such interests are especially important when the best interest of the child is unclear. For example, when it appears that a child would do as well or better with his biological father as with his mother and her husband, should the biological father be allowed visitation if his continued presence in the child's life would almost certainly imperil the stability of the mother's marriage'[7].

Dissenting judgments

Among the dissenting justices, Justice Enoch took the view that a

> 'putative biological father who claims parental rights to a child and who is also a stranger to the marriage into which the child is born does not have a common law, statutory, or constitutional interest that is protected by the Texas Constitution'[8].

1 *Re JWT, A Minor Child* 872 SW2d at 197.
2 *Re JWT, A Minor Child* 872 SW2d at 197.
3 *Re JWT, A Minor Child* 872 SW2d at 197.
4 *Re JWT, A Minor Child* 815 SW2d at 869.
5 *Re JWT, A Minor Child* 872 SW2d at 197.
6 *Re JWT, A Minor Child* 872 SW2d at 197.
7 *Re JWT, A Minor Child* 872 SW2d at 199.
8 *Re JWT, A Minor Child* 872 SW2d at 200.

While accepting that *Michael H and Victoria D, Appellants v Gerald D* is not binding on the court, he finds it 'instructive and persuasive'[1]. Although he views *Stanley v Illinois*[2] as affording constitutional recognition and due process protection to a putative biological father, this was only 'absent a powerful countervailing interest'[3], which in this case is provided by

> 'an interest which promotes the marital relationship, preserves intact and protects an existing family from disruption and interference by external forces, and protects the child from confusion, torn affection, and the stigma of illegitimacy'[4].

His colleague, Justice Cornyn, takes issue with the plurality who merely find the Supreme Court case to be 'useful in understanding' what he considers to be 'our essentially identical due process clause'[5]. He is also critical of the court for adopting Justice Brennan's dissenting opinion in that case (together with an opinion by the Louisiana Supreme Court[6]) 'as its lodestar'[7]. His analysis would require a court in determining the importance of a putative father's right to take account of the following factors:

> '(1) the presence of a biological connection, (2) the duration and quality of the relationship that has actually developed, [fn 15][8] (3) the putative father's efforts to fulfill the obligations of fatherhood, and (4) the presence of countervailing family interests, particularly when the child is born to a traditional family'[9].

On this basis, while meeting the requirements of (1) and (3), 'these factors are offset by what I hold are the 'more substantial' countervailing due process rights of the family'[10]. In these circumstances, in his view, the putative father 'is entitled to no scrutiny more searching than the rational basis test'[11]. Thus, if the state interests are legitimate and the statute is related to them in a rational manner, 'the statute is constitutionally valid'[12]. In finding this to be the case, he maintains that, even 'if the court is correct' that the putative father 'has a Texas constitutional right entitled to recognition, the state has legitimate and significant reasons to prohibit paternity lawsuits altogether when a marital family is involved'[13].

In response to this case, the Texas legislature added § 160.110 to the Texas Family Code to allow putative biological fathers access to the court to determine paternity under certain circumstances.

THE CHILD'S PERSPECTIVE

Our discussion, so far, has ignored the child's perspective and right to constitutional protection to maintain the parent–child relationship as a person in his or

1 *Re JWT, A Minor Child* 872 SW2d 189 at 201.
2 *Stanley v Illinois* 405 US 645.
3 *Re JWT, A Minor Child* 872 SW2d 189 at 201, quoting from *Stanley* 405 US 645 at 651.
4 *Re JWT, A Minor Child* 872 SW2d 189 at 201.
5 *Re JWT, A Minor Child* 872 SW2d 189 at 208.
6 *Re Adoption of BGS*, 556 So.2cd at 549–50 n.2.
7 *Re JWT, A Minor Child* 872 SW2d 189 at 208.
8 Justice Coryn cites *Lehr v Robertson* 463 US 248 at 261; 103 SCt at 2993: 'The difference between the developed parent-child relationship that was implicated in *Stanley* and *Caban*, and the potential relationship involved in *Quilloin* and this case, is both clear and significant.'
9 *Re JWT, A Minor Child* 872 SW2d 189 at 214.
10 *Re JWT, A Minor Child* 872 SW2d 189 at 214.
11 *Re JWT, A Minor Child* 872 SW2d 189 at 214.
12 *Re JWT, A Minor Child* 872 SW2d 189 at 214.
13 *Re JWT, A Minor Child* 872 SW2d 189 at 214.

her own right[1]. The issue was not touched on in *Re JWT [A Minor Child]*[2] but in *Michael H and Victoria D, Appellants v Gerald D*[3], the child Victoria was a party to the action and argued that:

(1) her rights to due process to maintain a filial relationship with both her putative natural father and her mother's husband had been infringed; and
(2) her rights to equal protection had been infringed, because unlike her mother and presumed father, she had no opportunity to rebut the presumption of her legitimacy[4].

With respect to her first claim, the plurality held that her constitutional rights to due process had not been infringed. They reached this decision because her claim

> 'is not that California has erred in preventing her from establishing that Michael, not Gerald, should stand as her natural father. Rather, she claims a due process right to maintain her filial relationships with both Michael and Gerald'[5].

According to Justice Scalia, despite the guardian *ad litem*'s belief 'that such an arrangement can be of great psychological benefit to the child'[6], he dismissed 'the claim that a state must recognize multiple fatherhood' because it 'has no support in the history or traditions of this country'[7]. For 'California law, like nature itself, makes no provision for dual fatherhood'[8]. On the other hand, in considering whether 'she has a liberty interest in maintaining a filial relationship with her natural father', Justice Scalia asserts 'we find that, at best, her claim is the obverse of Michael's and fails for the same reasons'[9].

The plurality also rejected Victoria's claims that her right to equal protection had been violated 'because unlike her mother and presumed father, she had no opportunity to rebut the presumption of her legitimacy'[10]. In reaching this decision they applied the ordinary 'rational relationship' test to the Californian Evidence Code § 621. They refused to apply a strict scrutiny standard because they rejected her argument 'that in denying her the right to maintain a filial relationship with Michael, the State is discriminating against her on the basis of her illegitimacy'[11]. They maintained that Victoria is a legitimate child under California law, and as such 'she is treated in the same manner as all other legitimate children: she is entitled to maintain a filial relationship with her *legal* [emphasis added] parents'.

They held that § 621 meets the rational relationship test because California's decision to treat Victoria differently from her parents, Carole and Gerald, pursues the legitimate end of preventing the disruption of an otherwise peaceful union by

1 For discussion on legal systems' tendencies to endorse adult- rather than child-centered perspectives on the parent-child relationship see ch 3, E Sutherland, 'Parentage and Parenting' in *Child and Family Law* (1999) T & T Clark, Edinburgh.
2 *Re JWT, A Minor Child* 872 SW2d at 189.
3 *Michael H and Victoria D, Appellants v Gerald D* 491 US 110.
4 Note that Michael also raised an equal protection claim but the Supreme Court did not deal with it as it had not been raised or deliberated upon in the lower courts: see *Michael H and Victoria D, Appellants v Gerald D* 491 US 110 at 117.
5 *Michael H and Victoria D, Appellants v Gerald D* 491 US 110 at 131.
6 *Michael H and Victoria D, Appellants v Gerald D* 491 US 110 at 131.
7 *Michael H and Victoria D, Appellants v Gerald D* 491 US 110 at 131.
8 *Michael H and Victoria D, Appellants v Gerald D* 491 US 110 at 117.
9 *Michael H and Victoria D, Appellants v Gerald D* 491 US 110 at 131.
10 *Michael H and Victoria D, Appellants v Gerald D* 491 US 110 at 131.
11 *Michael H and Victoria D, Appellants v Gerald D* 491 US 110 at 131.

the rational means of not allowing anyone but the husband or wife to contest legitimacy.

These cases highlight the difficulties surrounding definitions of family and parenthood. While marriage need not be a defining factor, as demonstrated by the case of *Re JWT*, it clearly operated as a determining one in the interpretation of the Californian Evidence Code § 621 in the *Michael H* case. In that case the court refused to countenance the notion of 'multiple' or 'dual' fatherhood, thus denying Victoria the right to maintain her relationship with Michael, whom blood tests showed to a 98% probability to be her father, while insisting on maintaining the fiction that Gerald was her father. It did so on the basis that in law there could only be one father and that father was Gerald. Yet Victoria viewed both men as her 'father', a position that was willing to accommodate both the social and biological aspects of parenthood. While these aspects are often combined in the same person, they need not be, as for example in the case of a child who is conceived through artificial insemination by donor. How then are we to construct 'parenthood' and what implications does this have for the recognition of familial relationships and legal rights that accompany them?[1] This is important, especially given the increasing numbers of children who are living in households with an adult who is not their biological mother or father. Such children may view these adults as 'mum' and 'dad' because they fulfill the social role of a parent but in the absence of a biological connection, to what extent is this parent-child relationship recognised in law?[2] Or, put another way, to what extent should a biological connection determine a parent–child relationship? The American cases discussed above represent some attempts to grapple with these issues which we will now examine in the context of Scots law.

THE SCOTTISH PERSPECTIVE

Under the Children (Scotland) Act 1995, which governs the parent–child relationship in Scots law, emphasis is placed on parental responsibilities which are attached to parental rights. Thus rights are not treated as freestanding legal powers that vest in a parent who may exercise them as he or she pleases, that is, without regard for the child's best interests or welfare, but are recognised only in so far as they exist to enable parents to fulfil their responsibilities towards their children[3]. As with other jurisdictions, Scots law upholds certain presumptions with respect to paternity, including the presumption that a man is the father of a child if he was married to the mother of the child at any time between the child's conception and birth[4]. Unmarried fathers can also benefit from a presumption of paternity but only where both he and the mother have acknowledged that he is the father of the child and where he has been registered in the appropriate register as the child's father[5]. Thus the woman's co-operation and registration are

1 In the case of a child conceived through artificial insemination by a donor it is the husband of the woman giving birth who is recognised in law as the father and not the sperm donor. See the Human Fertilisation and Embryology Act 1990, s 28(2).

2 For this reason the Scottish Executive is reviewing the position of step-parents and discussing the circumstances under which they might acquire parental responsibilities and rights: see *Parents and Children: The Scottish Executive's proposals for Improving Scottish Family Law* (2000) Crown Copyright.

3 See Lord Scarman in *Gillick v West Norfolk and Wisbech Area Health Authority* [1986] AC 112 at p 184.

4 See the Law Reform (Parent and Child) (Scotland) Act 1986, s 5(1)(a).

5 See the Law Reform (Parent and Child) (Scotland) Act 1986, s 5(1)(b).

essential as both requirements must be met before the presumption will apply. While some authorities have taken the view that where the woman is married, this presumption cannot apply[1], Norrie argues that it is better to interpret the legislation in terms of the man's rather than the woman's marital status[2]. Thus, in his view, an unmarried man could avail himself of the presumption even where the woman was married to another man. This would not have assisted Michael or the putative father of JWT, the unmarried fathers in the American cases discussed above, as the women in these cases were unwilling to co-operate with them. Presumptions, however, can be rebutted on 'a balance of probabilities'[3].

The difficulty that Michael faced, and that the putative father of JWT initially confronted, was that they were pre-empted from establishing parentage on the basis of a conclusive presumption that they were not permitted to challenge. While it has been argued that, at common law, only proof of impotence or non-access could rebut the presumption that the husband is the father of his wife's child, Norrie observes:

> 'Whatever the historic position may have been, it is now clear in relation to the statutory presumption that not only impotence and non-access . . . but all other facts and circumstances relevant to infer non-parentage may be invoked to rebut the presumption in section 5(1)(a)'[4].

Thus, according to Scots law, Michael and JWT's putative father could have challenged the presumption by raising an action for declarator of parentage[5]. Once again, the standard of proof is on a balance of probabilities whether or not it is a presumption that is being challenged. Scottish case law reveals that any person with a legally enforceable interest that turns on parentage or non-parentage of a child has title to sue for declarator. Such persons include parents (whether presumed, putative or actual) and the child. Thus Victoria, the child in the *Michael H* case, would have been entitled to raise an action of declarator of non-parentage with respect to Gerald or a declarator of parentage with respect to Michael. What must be established in such actions is that a genetic link exists between alleged parent and child. Where scientific evidence, such as DNA profiling, is available, the court will take cognisance of this in its findings. If Michael and JWT's putative father had been subject to Scottish jurisdiction they would have encountered no difficulty in establishing their claim to parentage.

But they would have gained little advantage from this, as having the status of a parent in Scots law would not have automatically accorded them parental responsibilities and rights. This is because a declarator of parentage does not confer parental responsibilities and rights in and of itself. In *Michael H* the plurality of the court were concerned that if Michael were given the opportunity to establish his paternity this would result in his acquiring the full panoply of parental rights that extend well beyond visitation. In Scots law, merely establishing paternity does not in itself establish a full parent-child relationship. While parental

1 See Commentary on s 5(1)(b) of the Law Reform (Parent and Child) (Scotland) Act 1986 of the Current Law Statutes Annotated 1986, Vol 1, (1987) W Green, Sweet & Maxwell Ltd and Stevens and Sons Ltd.

2 See K Mck Norrie and AB Wilkinson *Law Relating to Parient and Child in Scotland* (1999) Scottish Universities Law Institute Ltd and W Green, Edinburgh at 89.

3 See the Law Reform (Parent and Child) (Scotland) Act 1986, s 5(4).

4 K Mck Norrie and AB Wilkinson *Law Relating to Parent and Child in Scotland* (1999) Scottish Universities Law Institute Ltd and W Green, Edinburgh at 87.

5 Under the Law Reform (Parent and Child) (Scotland) Act 1986, s 7.

responsibilities and rights vest in a child's mother on birth, they only vest in the father if he is 'married to the child's mother at the time of the child's conception or subsequently'[1] or if he has registered an agreement made with the mother in terms of the Children (Scotland) Act 1995, s 4, or if he acquires such rights by court order. In order to acquire such rights in Scotland, both Michael and the putative father of JWT would have had to apply for a court order, in their case for a contact order[2] (which is the Scottish equivalent of a visitation order), to accompany the declarator of parentage. While the blood link between parent and child is a significant factor[3], it is not conclusive when it comes to determining what is in a child's best interests having regard to the actual relationship that exists between the child and disputing adults. It is important to note that even where parents have parental responsibilities and rights, their application is always subject to the welfare test in a dispute before the court, that is, of being exercised in the best interests of the child.

Thus, a child's welfare prevails over parental responsibilities and rights, a fact which is made clear by the terms of the Children (Scotland) Act 1995 which provide that a court order relating to a child can only be granted if the requirements of s 11(7) are met. These are that:

(1) the welfare of the child throughout his or her childhood shall be [the court's] paramount consideration[4];
(2) children must be given the opportunity to express their views and have them taken into account where sufficiently mature[5]. There is a presumption in favour of children aged 12 or over having such maturity[6];
(3) there should be minimum intervention, that is, a court should only make an order if it is better for the child to make such an order than to make no order at all[7].

These provisions reflect overriding principles which apply to children more generally under the Children (Scotland) Act 1995. They represent an attempt to bring the Scottish legal system into line with the UN Convention on the Rights of the Child in its dealings with children[8], especially arts 3 and 12, as well as with the European Convention on the Exercise of Children's Rights. The court's powers under the 1995 Act, s 11 are wide ranging and cover all aspects of the parent-child relationship, including residence, removal of parental responsibilities and rights, and a specific issue order which permits the court to make an order regulating 'any specific question' which has arisen in relation to parental

1 See the Children (Scotland) Act 1995, s 3(1)(b).
2 Children (Scotland) Act 1995, s 11(2)(d).
3 *Sanderson v MacManus* 1997 SC (HL) 55; *Osborne v Matthan (No 3)* 1998 SC 682.
4 Children (Scotland) Act 1995, s 11(7)(a).
5 Children (Scotland) Act 1995, s 11(7)(b).
6 Children (Scotland) Act 1995, s 11(10).
7 Children (Scotland) Act 1995, s 11(7)(a). But note that where it is deemed to be in the child's best interests that an order be made this does not mean that the intervention must be kept to a minimum. The test is rather what would be better for the child as against no order being made at all.
8 For details see K Marshall, 'The History and Philosophy of Children's Rights in Scotland' in A Cleland and E Sutherland (eds) *Children's Rights in Scotland: Scots Law Analysed in the Light of the UN Convention on the Rights of the Child* (1996) W Green, Edinburgh pp 1–19 at 18; K Mck Norrie and AB Wilkinson *Law Relating to Parent and Child in Scotland* (1999) Scottish Universities Law Institute Ltd and W Green, Edinburgh at pp 1–2, n 8; E Sutherland *Child and Family Law* (1999) T & T Clark, Edinburgh at pp 86–90, n 18.

responsibilities or rights, or guardianship, or the administration of the child's property[1]. Michael and the putative father of JWT would have had no difficulty in acquiring access to a hearing in Scotland as the court is empowered to entertain applications from a person who 'not having, and never having had, parental responsibilities or parental rights in relations to the child claims an interest'[2]. 'Person' is very broadly construed and include unmarried fathers, grandparents, step-parents, siblings or other relatives and anyone else with a connection to or legitimate concern for the welfare of the child, for example, foster carers. It is also open to a child to make an application as he or she qualifies as a person having an interest[3]. This means that the child Victoria, in the *Michael H* case, would also have had title to raise an action on her own behalf to regulate contact with her natural father.

It is important to note that where an order regulating contact is made under the Children (Scotland) Act 1995, s 11(2)(d), the person benefiting from it does not thereby acquire parental responsibilities and rights (if he or she does not already possess such rights) entitling him or her, for example, to be consulted by a parent making major decisions relating to the child[4]. Thus the fears of the US Supreme Court in the *Michael H* case, that if Michael were allowed to establish parentage and granted visitation rights he might then pursue full parental rights which would prove disruptive to the marital family, would not arise in Scotland.

Having access to a hearing does not guarantee that a court will make an order as it must consider the factors set out in the Children (Scotland) Act 1995, s 11(7). However, these factors would have expressly afforded Victoria the opportunity to make her views known on contact. Although under the age of 12 and therefore unable to benefit from the presumption of maturity, this would not preclude her from expressing a view and having it taken into account if she was deemed sufficiently mature[5]. Thus Norrie is of the view that 'to deny a hearing to a child of sufficient understanding, even when under the age of 12, would amount to a failure to observe the duty laid upon the court by section 11(7) of the 1995 Act'[6]. This duty is further buttressed by the rules of court which prohibit the court from making any order where a child indicates that he or she wishes to express a view unless the court has given due weight to these views[7]. The wishes and views of a mature child must be given due weight but that does not mean that the court is obliged to act on them as it is the welfare of the child that is its 'paramount consideration'. The question then arises to what extent is maintaining a link with a blood parent presumed or assumed to be in a child's best interests, and what role, if any, does marital status have in these considerations?

1 Children (Scotland) Act 1995, s 11(2)(e).

2 Children (Scotland) Act 1995, s 11(3)(a)(i).

3 Children (Scotland) Act 1995, s 11(5).

4 Children (Scotland) Act 1995, s 6.

5 Children (Scotland) Act 1995, s 11(10) states that the presumption of mental capacity at age 12 is expressly 'without prejudice' to the generality of the obligation to have regard to the child's views taking account of his or her age and maturity.

6 K Mck Norrie and AB Wilkinson *Law Relating to Parent and Child in Scotland* (1999) Scottish Universities Law Institute Ltd and W Green, Edinburgh at p 349.

7 RCS 1994, r 49.30; OCR 1993, r 33.

WELFARE OF THE CHILD

In *Sanderson v McManus*[1], a case involving an unmarried father seeking access to his child[2], Lord McCluskey in the Inner House took the view that a father should not be under the onus of proving that access was positively beneficial to the child. He opined that 'the link between a child and each of its natural parents is so important in itself that, unless there are very strong reasons to the contrary, it should be preserved'[3].

His brethren, however, while noting the intrinsic value of the parent–child relationship is merely one factor to be taken into account in assessing the child's welfare, held that the court may not make an order 'unless it is satisfied that to do so would be in the best interests of the child'[4]. As the father was not married to the mother, and therefore had no parental rights, the onus was on him, in principle, to convince the court that an order should be made. When the case went to the House of Lords, Lord Hope endorsed their views noting that while 'the relationship between the natural father and the child can never be dismissed as irrelevant'[5],

> 'The more fundamental question is whether the natural link between the child and his parent is so important that the court must always seek to preserve it unless there are strong reasons to the contrary. Whatever may have been the position at common law the effect of s 3(2) of the Act of 1986 has been to remove any rule or principle to this effect'[6].

This approach may be contrasted with that of English case law which Norrie observes upholds 'a strong presumption in favour of contact between a child and his or her parents' whether married or unmarried[7]. In reaching his decision Lord Hope was influenced by Lord Dunpark's ruling in *Porchetta v Porchetta*[8] that a father with no statutory right to access can only acquire that right if the court is satisfied that it is in the best interests of the child. On the basis of this test the court in *Porchetta* held that the father, who was divorced from the mother and who had 'only seen the child twice for fleeting moments'[9], was not entitled to access. Under this test even a father with parental rights can be denied access to his child[10]. Thus Scottish cases uphold a view that biology on its own is insufficient to justify an order for access and that aspects of the social relationship between father and child are a relevant consideration, so that, as the sheriff prin-

1 *Sanderson v McManus* 1996 SLT 750.

2 Although this case arose prior to the 1995 Act coming into force, the Law Reform (Parent and Child) (Scotland) Act 1986, s 3 which was in force was framed in much the same terms, as the court had to have regard to the welfare of the child as the paramount consideration and could not make any order relating to parental rights unless to do so was in the interests of the child.

3 *Sanderson v McManus* 1996 SLT 750 at 752D.

4 *Sanderson v McManus* 1996 SLT 750 at 752H.

5 *Sanderson v McManus* 1997 SLT 629 at 635D.

6 *Sanderson v McManus* 1997 S.L,T, 629 at 634K.

7 K Mck Norrie and AB Wilkinson *Law Relating to Parent and Child in Scotland* (1999) Scottish Universities Law Institute Ltd and W Green, Edinburgh at p 329.

8 *Porchetta v Porchetta* 1986 SLT 105.

9 *Porchetta v Porchetta* 1986 SLT 105.

10 As was the father in *White v White* (2000) *Current Law Digest* at 485. See also *Russell v Russell* 1991 SCLR 429 at 431 where the judge held that merely stating that the father had affection for the child and desired to maintain a link was insufficient as these statements amounted to no more than saying 'he is seeking access because he is the child's father'.

cipal observed in *Lamont v Lamont*[1], 'the question for the court is whether contact with the parent has something to offer which is likely to benefit the child's welfare. This question must be examined from the point of view of the child'. The sheriff principal goes on to opine: 'It may normally be assumed that the child will benefit from continuing contact with the natural parent. But there may be cases where it is plain on the evidence that it has nothing to offer at all.' Thus, as Lord Clyde observed in *Sanderson v McManus*: 'In many cases it may well be proper to regard it as a factor of the very greatest weight. On the other hand the unusual case cannot be excluded where in all circumstances it may be proper in the interests of the child to exclude access to a parent'[2].

Thus, overall, the Scottish courts take the view that maintaining the link between biological parent and child is an important but not an overriding consideration. While the onus may be on a father to establish that contact will be to the child's benefit, the court will take into account all the evidence so that 'The matter then becomes one of overall impression, balancing one consideration against another and having regard always to the consideration which has been stated to be paramount'[3]. How they balance such considerations in practice, however, has been the subject of some criticism[4]. Thus, Edwards[5] has taken the sheriff principal in *Lamont* to task for awarding a father access rights with little evidence of any positive benefits to the child 'and some clear evidence of adverse effect[6].' Although each case must be judged on its merits, what appears to be crucial is whether or not the circumstances of each particular case are interpreted as falling within the remit of normal or unusual cases. Consequently, the sheriff principal in *Lamont* held that as the case had 'no unusual features' he was 'satisfied that the circumstances do not justify the unusual course of refusing access at this stage'. On the other hand, Lord Clyde in *Sanderson v McManus* observes that

> 'where there has been the absolute commitment to a lasting relationship, as may be affirmed by a marriage, and where the mother has entered into a new partnership which is intended to be permanent and which can provide the child with a secure background, there may be circumstances where that unusual course of refusing access to the father may be justifiable in the interests of the child'[7].

Lord Clyde's observations were reiterated by the sheriff principal in *Lamont*[8]. Like Justice Stevens in *Michael H and Victoria D, Appellants v Gerald D*, these judges place a premium on the stable family environment in which mother and child currently find themselves, one which is evidenced by marriage. This may explain why in *Donnelly v Green*[9] an unmarried father was able to acquire access rights although the mother had established a cohabiting relationship with another man.

1 *Lamont v Lamont* 1998 Fam LR 62 at para 62-11.

2 1997 SC (HL) 55 at 65F, cited in *Lamont v Lamont* 1998 Fam LR 62 at para 62-11.

3 *Lamont v Lamont* 1998 Fam LR 62 at para 62-10.

4 See J Thomson 1999 SLG 130 who considers whether recent case law reveals an abuse of s 11 orders.

5 L Edwards 'Life After Sanderson v McManus: What Next?' 1998 SLT (News) 299.

6 L Edwards 'Life After Sanderson v McManus: What Next?' 1998 SLT (News) 1998 299 at 301. See also her criticism at 301of *Davidson v Smith* 1998 FamLR 21 where the court awarded a father access, although 'according to the *Sanderson* dicta, the father's only argument was the preservation of the 'natural link' and this would not do on its own to rebut the onus of proof.'

7 *Sanderson v McManus* 1997 SC (HL) 55 at 65.

8 *Lamont v Lamont* 1998 Fam LR 62 at para 62-12.

9 *Donnelly v Green* 1998 Fam LR 12.

Donnelly v Green[1]

In this case a married woman (the defender) had an affair with the pursuer, Donnelly. When the pursuer found out that she had had a child, James, he contacted her and she confirmed that she thought the child was his. After she separated from her husband in 1994 the defender and pursuer bought a flat together and the pursuer commuted to and from his work in London. When at home he treated James as his child and he and the defender socialised with the pursuer's parents and his extended family. In 1995, after an argument, the defender refused to let the pursuer have contact with James and went on to live with another man whom James began to call 'daddy'. After repeatedly unsuccessful attempts at maintaining contact the pursuer raised an action of paternity and access. In 1997 a DNA test was carried out which showed that the probability that the pursuer was James' father was 99.99%. At the date of proof James was four-and-a-half years old and had not been in contact with the pursuer for 18 months.

At first instance, the sheriff granted the pursuer a declarator of paternity but refused access on the basis that the difficulties that had occurred were due to the pursuer's behaviour and that access would not be in the child's best interests. On appeal, however, the sheriff principal found that the sheriff had incorrectly focused on 'the respective merits and demerits of the parents'[2] which were only 'peripherally related to the interests of the child', and that he had 'made no findings in fact in relation to the interests of the child'[3]. He rejected the psychologist's evidence that access would not work because of the defender's bad behaviour on the basis that 'If that [ie defender's] attitude is unjustifiable and persisted in for motives other than the interests of the child ... then the sooner it is corrected the better'[4].

This approach, which is in line with that of English courts who have resisted allowing the resident parent's hostility towards contact to amount to sufficient reason for denying contact[5], is out of line with other Scottish authorities where the courts have held that the child's interests are such that contact should be denied, even where this has nothing to do with the pursuer's behaviour but reflects tensions brought about through the resident parent's hostility to contact through that parent's obstruction of access or negative influence over the child's state of mind[6]. The sheriff principal also rejected the defender's argument that the status quo should be upheld given the lapse of time that had elapsed since the pursuer's last contact with James, on the basis that 'While that consideration is important it does not outweigh the desirability of some contact being established now at an early date'[7]. Comparing the facts of this case with Lord Clyde's observations in *Sanderson*, he found that

> 'it is in the interests of this child who has the name of a man who is not his father, who is living with his mother's third cohabitee, and who has no natural extended family other than that of the pursuer, that he grow up knowing the situation and his relatives rather than being faced with it out of the blue at some later date. That he must know

1 *Donnelly v Green* 1998 Fam LR 12.
2 *Donnelly v Green* 1998 Fam LR 12 at para 3-25.
3 *Donnelly v Green* 1998 Fam LR 12 at para 3-26.
4 *Donnelly v Green* 1998 Fam LR 12 at para 3-25.
5 *A v N (Committal: Refusal of Contact)* [1997] 1 FLR 533; *Re J (A Minor) (Contact)* [1994] 1 FLR 729.
6 *Russell v Russell* 1991 SCLR 429.
7 *Donnelly v Green* 1998 Fam LR 12 at para 3-25.

> at a later date was recognised by the defender. The evidence that he may well not even now have a stable home is clear from the attitude of the defender's current cohabitee who was not prepared to say in evidence that he intended to marry the defender. Accordingly there is no evidence that there is a new partnership which is intended to be permanent and can provide the child with a secure background'[1].

In these circumstances he considered that it was in the child's interests to maintain contact with the pursuer and his extended family.

Whether or not there is a stable family unit of which the child forms part is an important factor in decision-making about contact. In assessing the character of a new relationship marriage is viewed as a key element in establishing its stability and permanence although given divorce rates, especially for second marriages, such reliance on status may prove misplaced[2]. It would appear that if the mother in *Donnelly* had been married to her new partner the pursuer might well have failed in his bid for contact. In contrast with *Michael H*, Donnelly was in a better position to press his suit because the defender's marriage had broken down and was about to end in divorce, and her husband, who was registered as James' father, was only 'half hearted about James'[3]. While James might call his mother's new partner 'daddy' this was not deemed a significant factor as the new partner was not prepared to commit himself to marriage. However, even where the new partnership is viewed as stable and involves marriage it will not necessarily deprive an unmarried father from having contact, if he can establish that this would benefit the child[4].

Non-intervention principle and unmarried fathers

Although Donnelly was successful in pursuing his claim for contact he had to overcome a hurdle that faces all parents, namely, the 'no order' principle embodied in the Children (Scotland) Act 1995, s 11(7)(a). This provides that the court should only make an order if it is better for the child to make such an order than to make no order at all. The rationale for this provision was to promote private ordering, that is, to encourage parents to reach their own decisions about their children's welfare without resort to courts. But a consequence of its enactment has been to more firmly entrench the maintenance of the status quo. Academic commentators have observed how courts over the years have demanded good reasons for disturbing the status quo when called on to decide what a child's welfare requires[5]. Given that many young children remain in their mothers' care when relationships end[6], and judicial dicta to the effect that Scottish courts take account of the fact that very young children have a stronger need for their mother

1 *Donnelly v Green* 1998 Fam LR 12 at para 3-26.

2 Research has suggested that second marriages are significantly more unstable than first marriages: see C Gibson 'Contemporary Divorce and Changing Family Patterns' pp 9–38 in M Freeman (ed) *Divorce: Where Next?* (1996) Dartmouth, Hants, England and Vermont, USA. See also Registrar General for Scotland's *Annual Reports 1995 and 1996* which show that roughly 25% of marriages are second marriages and that second marriages have a high rate of breakdown.

3 *Donnelly v Green* 1998 Fam LR 12 at para 3-08.

4 See *Davidson v Smith* 1998 FamLR 21. See also Edwards' critique of the decision in this case cited at fn 106.

5 See L Edwards and A Griffiths *Family Law* (1997) W Green/Sweet and Maxwell, Edinburgh at p 208; E Sutherland *Child and Family Law* (1999) T & T Clark, Edinburgh at pp 228–229.

6 See *Social Trends 2001* no 31 at p 53.

than their father when it comes to custody[1], fathers (both married and unmarried) may well experience difficulties in pursuing claims for residence or contact.

However, the barriers that fathers face have been somewhat alleviated by a recent decision of the Inner House in *White v White*[2] where the court held that the wording of the 1995 Act is such that one can infer 'that Parliament has proceeded on the general principle that it conduces to the welfare of children if their absent parent maintains personal relations and direct contact with them on a regular basis'[3]. It does, however, recognise that there are limits to parental responsibilities so that parents need not act 'if it is impracticable[4], for instance, because they are working far from home'[5]. Similarly parents are not expected to fulfil their responsibilities where these 'would not in fact operate in the interests of the child'. The court held that the general principle of promoting contact was in line with the UN Convention on the Rights of the Child, art 9.3 which requires states to 'respect the right of the child who is separated from one or both parents to maintain personal relations and direct contact with both parents on a regular basis, except if it is contrary to the child's best interest'.

In reaching a decision about contact, the court declined to be bound by *Sanderson* (as the court in that case was not considering the effects of the 1995 legislation) or to accept the view that in actions of this nature the onus was on a father to establish that contact is positively in the child's interests. Instead, the court drew attention to the fact that the terms of the Children (Scotland) Act 1995, s 11 (which permit the court to make an order *ex proprio motu*) make it clear that the question of onus does not arise. Thus in all cases, whether or not an individual has made an application for contact to the court,

> 'The court must consider all the relevant material and decide what would be conducive to the child's welfare. That is the paramount consideration. In carrying out that exercise the court should have regard to the general principle that it is conducive to a child's welfare to maintain personal relations and direct contact with his absent parent. But the decision will depend on the facts of the particular case and, if there is nothing in the relevant material on which the court, applying that general principle, could properly take the view that it would be in the interests of the child for the order to be granted, then the application must fail'[6].

As Lord McCluskey observed in his judgment:

> 'All the authorities, however they phrase the matter, are agreed that the link between a child and the child's biological parents is a factor of some materiality in the making of that judgment. Different judges and authors have expressed themselves differently as to the weight to be accorded to maintaining such a link in the particular circumstances of each unique case. But no one has said that it is irrelevant; and no one could suggest that it should be left out of account . . . It follows that the possibility and the advantages of maintaining the link between the father and his daughter fall to be taken into account when the court comes to make the judgment required of it under the 1995 Act; but, however its importance may be assessed in the circumstances of any particular case, it is one factor among many. It may be determinative; it may not.

1 See Lord Morison in *Brixey v Lynas* (No 1) 1994 SLT 847 at 849 paras H-I where he also observed that although this preference should not be regarded as a presumption it was strengthened if preservation of the status quo also favoured the mother's case for custody.
2 *White v White* 2001 SLT 485.
3 *White v White* 2001 SLT 485 at 490G-H.
4 Children (Scotland) Act 1995, s 1(1).
5 *White v White* 2001 SLT 485 at 490I-J.
6 *White v White* 2001 SLT 485 at 491G-H.

> It must always be a matter of weighing all the material bearing upon welfare and the interests of the child. It would be impossible to list all the other matters that might be relevant, because life constantly throws up unprecedented circumstances; and the law has to be flexible enough to cope with the unforeseen'[1].

In upholding a general principle promoting contact the majority of the court were not, however, prepared to go as far as the sheriff in stating that where a parent has parental responsibilities and rights 'only the strongest competing disadvantages will be likely to prevail to establish that the welfare of the child would not be served by allowing contact with the parent'[2].

But even where parents in Scotland may benefit from a general principle promoting contact, the non-residential parent who needs to apply to the court to enable him to fulfil his parental responsibilities is still faced with overcoming the 'no order' principle, albeit that he or she no longer has to meet the requirements concerning the onus of proof[3]. The court's decision in *White* has clearly strengthened the position of the non-residential parent with regard to seeking contact but the no-order principle still exists and so, displacing the status quo (where this does not involve outright or blatant hostility or indifference to contact) may still prove problematic. However, the Inner House in *White* expressly recognised that such an order 'will be necessary where the parent with the sole parental right of residence either refuses to allow contact or is indifferent or uncooperative in ensuring that contact takes place'[4]. Thus, there is recognition that the hostile or un-cooperative parent should not determine what is in the child's interests by default, because of the difficulties that face the non-residential parent in overcoming the no-order principle. Starting from a general principle upholding contact strengthens the position of non-residential parents (namely fathers) because they can now proceed from a basis upon which their interests are clearly acknowledged rather than having to establish these interests *de novo*. Not only that, but in ruling that the provisions of the Children (Scotland) Act 1995 are in line with the European Convention on Human Rights, art 8, the court also acknowledges the need for 'the provision of an adjudicatory and enforcement machinery protecting individuals' rights'[5]. Although the court recognises that the obligation to facilitate contact is not absolute as 'the rights and freedoms of all must be taken into account'[6] it is sensitive to the fact that a fair balance must be struck 'between the competing interests of the individual and the community'[7]. In taking cognisance of European Court decisions, the Scottish courts will be obliged to take a more proactive role in providing an effective and enforceable remedy for a litigant where a human rights violation is raised[8], as the court did in this case.

In *White* the father had contact with both his daughters on divorce and hostility had only arisen between the mother and father when he moved away from Scotland and started a relationship with another woman. The sheriff held that it was in the younger daughter's interests to maintain contact with her father, even

1 *White v White* 2001 SLT 485 at 494A-G.
2 Quoted by the sheriff principal in *White v White* at 1999 SLT 106 at 109A.
3 For further discussion see K Norrie 'Whither the No-Order Principle' 2001 SLPQ Vol 6, pp 86–89.
4 *White v White* 2001 SLT 485 at 489C.
5 *White v White* 2001 SLT 485 at 492C.
6 *White v White* 2001 SLT 485 at 492D–E.
7 *White v White* 2001 SLT 485 at 492D.
8 See W Shehan 'Human Rights – Positive Obligations Imposed on Courts' (2001) 49 *Greens Fam Law* pp 2–4.

although, at age eight, she had expressed the view that she did not wish to have contact with him on several occasions. Although there was evidence that the daughter's asthma attacks 'were caused by discussion of the proceedings relating to contact and by the prospect of contact' the sheriff formed the view that this distress 'would be likely to disappear as she became familiar once more with her father'[1]. The Inner House upheld his findings, and on appeal from the sheriff principal, restored the sheriff's decree.

Although *White* dealt with a father who had parental responsibilities and rights by virtue of the Children (Scotland) Act 1995, s 3(1)(b), the question arises as to how far the court's analysis applies, more broadly, to fathers in general. In 1992 the Scottish Law Commission questioned whether the differential treatment accorded to fathers on the basis of marital status was in keeping with prevailing social attitudes given the increasing numbers of children born outside marriage[2]. Despite attempts to publicise agreements in terms of the Children (Scotland) Act 1995, s 4, there has been a very limited response. Between 1996 and 1998 only 322 such agreements were registered in a period 'when about 30,000 unmarried couples jointly registered their babies'[3]. This situation has prompted the Scottish Executive to consider reforming the law to allow unmarried fathers to acquire parental responsibilities and rights either automatically – the only criterion being biological parenthood – or on entry in the Register of Births[4]. The current position, however, raises questions about whether Scots law is infringing on individuals' human rights.

HUMAN RIGHTS DIMENSION

A Scottish perspective

It is clear that where contact is an issue unmarried fathers' due process rights are not infringed in Scotland as they are entitled to a hearing whether or not they have parental responsibilities and rights. However, this is not the case with adoption, where it is only those who qualify as a 'parent' whose consent is required before an adoption order can be made. In this situation, a parent is defined in both biological terms as well as a person with parental responsibilities and rights[5]. Thus, unmarried fathers who lack registered s 4 agreements, or court orders conferring such rights, have no right to participate in the adoption process

1 *White v White* 2001 SLT 485 at 488E.
2 *Report on Family Law* (Scot Law Com no 135, 1992) paras 2.36–2.51.
3 *Improving Scottish Family Law: A Consultation by the Scottish Office, Home Department* (1999) para 5.4.3.
4 This was suggested in *Improving Scottish Family Law: A Consultation by the Scottish Office, Home Department* (1999) para 5.5. However, in the subsequent *Parents and Children: a White Paper on Scottish Family Law* (2000) the Scottish Executive considered that to automatically award parental responsibilities and rights to biological fathers was going too far and that the best approach would be to confer them on those unmarried fathers who jointly register the birth of a child with the child's mother: see paras 2.12–2.14.
5 Adoption (Scotland) Act 1978, s 65(1) as amended by the Children (Scotland) 1995 Act, Sch 2, para 29(a)(v).

and their consent to adoption is not required[1]. They are treated in a different way from mothers and married fathers when it comes to parental rights because, as noted earlier, mothers acquire such rights on the child's birth and married men acquire them automatically by virtue of being married to the child's mother.

This legislative position was challenged in *McMichael v UK*[2] when an unmarried father took his case to the European Court of Human Rights on the basis that he had no domestic legal right to obtain custody of his son or to participate in care and adoption proceedings before a children's hearing involving him. He argued that this infringed his right to respect for 'family life' under the European Convention on Human Rights, art 8 in a discriminatory manner that was contrary to art 14. His action was unsuccessful. While the European Court in *Marckx v Belgium*[3] held that the notion of family life is not confined to marriage-based relationships but may encompass other de facto ties such as those between an unmarried mother and her child[4], it ruled that there had been no violation of arts 8 and 14 in McMichael's case. This was because the government was able to appeal to the proviso contained in art 8(2) which requires any interference with family life to be justified on the basis that it is in accordance with the law and necessary to achieve a legitimate aim in a democratic society. In taking account of this the European court has allowed a margin of appreciation to member states, taking on board the political climate at the given time.

The court accepted the government's explanation that the aim of the relevant legislation was to provide a mechanism for identifying 'meritorious' fathers who might be accorded parental rights, thereby protecting the interests of the child and the mother. For discrimination to occur under art 14 it must have 'no objective and reasonable justification', that is if it does not pursue a 'legitimate aim' or there is not a 'reasonable relationship of proportionality between the means employed and the aim sought to be realised'[5]. The court took cognisance of the Commission's[6] observation that:

> 'it is axiomatic that the nature of relationships of natural fathers with their children will inevitably vary, from ignorance and indifference at one end of the spectrum to a close stable relationship indistinguishable from the conventional matrimonial-based family unit at the other'[7].

The court ruled that in this case the government's aim was legitimate and that the conditions imposed on natural fathers for obtaining recognition of their parental

1 He may feature in the process if the sheriff considers that he falls within the category of persons entitled to notice because, for example, he has care and control of the child, provides maintenance, has applied for a residence or contact order, or is simply a person who 'ought to be served with notice of the hearing.' See Act of Sederunt (Child Care and Maintenance Rules) SI 1997/291, r 2.28(4). Such a decision, however, remains at the discretion of the sheriff and even where notice is served does not mean that the unmarried father's consent must be acquired before the adoption can be granted.

2 *McMichael v UK* (1995) 20 EHRR 205.

3 *Marckx v Belgium* (1979–80) 2 EHRR 330.

4 The complaint in this case was that the Belgian legal system did not make it possible for a legal filiation link to be established between an unmarried mother and her child from the moment of birth, or at least, not without suffering serious detriment with respect to inheritance rights.

5 See *Marckx v Belgium* (1979–80) 2 EHRR 330 at para 33.

6 Until its abolition by Protocol 11, cases brought to Strasbourg were of course considered initially by the European Commission of Human Rights.

7 Commission's Report, para 126.

role respected the principle of proportionality. There was thus an objective and reasonable justification for the difference of treatment complained of[1].

It is interesting to note that the European Court reached a different conclusion in the earlier case of *Keegan v Ireland*[2]. In this case the applicant and his girlfriend planned to have a child during the year that they were living together. They became engaged shortly before the girlfriend discovered that she was pregnant. The relationship ended shortly afterwards and the pregnant woman decided to give the child up for adoption. The father was not notified about or given the opportunity to participate in subsequent adoption proceedings. The court had to decide whether or not this case came within the ambit of 'family life' and in doing so it considered a number of factors, including the length of the relationship between the applicant and the child's mother, and the fact that the pregnancy had been planned. The court ruled that there was something amounting to family life in the form of a bond between applicant and child that came into existence when the child was born.

It may be that the differing rulings can be accounted for on the grounds put forward by one of the judges, Mr Loucaides, in *McMichael*, that in the Irish case the father had applied for guardianship, that there had been a 'serious' and 'genuine' dispute over the applicant's rights and that 'it had been established in the Irish courts that in such proceedings regard must be had to the wishes and desires of the natural father to enjoy the society of his child, subject to other overriding considerations'[3].

More recently, in *B v UK*[4] the court revisited the issue of whether unmarried fathers are discriminated against in the protection given to their relationships with their children by comparison with the protection given to married fathers under English law. In this case a child was born to unmarried parents in 1994. They separated soon after his birth but the father maintained regular contact with his child. In 1997 he applied for a parental responsibility order and various other orders including a prohibited steps order to prevent the mother taking the child to Italy. The mother took the child to Italy and the father sought ex parte orders for the child's return under the Hague Convention on the Civil Aspects of International Child Abduction 1980. The High Court held that the child's removal was not unlawful as the father did not have parental responsibility and it declined to grant an ex parte declaration in wardship because the child had always lived with the mother. The court deemed it inappropriate to demand that the mother return with the child so that the father could have contact. When the Court of Appeal dismissed his application for leave to appeal he complained to the European Court that his rights under the Hague Convention, arts 8 and 14 had been violated because he had not been afforded the same protection with respect to his relationship with his child as that accorded to married fathers.

He was unsuccessful in his claim. While the European Court acknowledged that under the Children Act 1989 married fathers acquire parental responsibility automatically, while unmarried fathers need to acquire it in accordance with the 1989 Act's provisions, this did not violate his rights, as, following on from *McMichael*, 'there exists an objective and reasonable justification for the difference in treatment between married and unmarried fathers with regard to the

1 See *McMichael v UK* (1995) 20 EHRR 205 at para 98.
2 *Keegan v Ireland* (1994) 18 EHRR 342.
3 *McMichael v UK* (1995) 20 EHRR 205 at 233.
4 *B v UK* [2000] 1 FLR 1.

automatic acquisition of parental rights'[1]. Thus, the court's refusal to treat persons like the applicant, who only have contact with their child, on an equal footing with persons who have the child in their care, such as those with custody, has an objective and reasonable justification lying in the different responsibilities involved in the two situations. It is important to note that when the court reached its decision the European Convention on Human Rights had not yet been incorporated into domestic law in the form of the Human Rights Act 1998. Thus a question remains as to whether incorporation will affect the margin of appreciation[2].

The difficulty in drawing conclusions about the scope of the Hague Convention, arts 8 and 14 has been commented on and attributed to the whole range of variables that may apply in any given situation together with questions about the margin of appreciation[3]. Nonetheless, scholars have observed a general trend in the case law upholding family life in all relationships concerning mothers and children (regardless of their marital status) and between children and married fathers[4]. This is so, even where divorce has intervened[5]. What is less clear are the circumstances in which an unmarried father will be successful in establishing that family life exists between him and his child. What emerges from the case law from Strasbourg is that a mere biological connection between an unmarried father and his child is insufficient to establish 'family life'. In *Soderback v Sweden*[6] the Commission found that a family tie existed between an unmarried father and his child in circumstances in which he had never had a steady relationship with the mother but had shown some commitment to contact with the child, although contact had been very limited, partly because of the mother's resistance to it. However, although the Commission upheld the unmarried father's claim – that his right to respect for family life had been violated through the adoption of his child by the mother's new husband which had taken place without his consent – the European Court held that there had been no breach of ECHR, art 8 because, unlike the *Johansen*[7] case on which the Commission based its decision, this case did not 'concern a parent who had custody of the child or who in any other capacity had assumed the care of the child'[8]. In other words, where unmarried fathers are concerned, something more than a blood link must be established. Thus case law takes account of whether or not the father lived with the mother, and whether or not the pregnancy was planned, and examines the nature of the relationship between mother and father and the degree of interest which the father has demonstrated in the child[9].

1 *B v UK* [2000] 1 FLR 1 at 5.
2 See L Edwards 'Life After Sanderson v McManus: What Next?' 1998 SLT (News) 299 at 304.
3 See Harris, O'Boyle and Warbrick *Law of the European Convention on Human Rights* (1995) Butterworths, Edinburgh, Dublin and London at p 303.
4 See W Sheehan and J Adams 'Human Rights and the Concept of 'Family Life' (2000) 47 Greens Fam Law pp 2–4; I Karsten 'Atypical Families and the Human Rights Act: The Rights of Unmarried Fathers, Same Sex Couples and Transexuals' 1999 EHRLR pp 195–207.
5 See *Berrehab v Netherlands* (1988) 11 EHRR 322.
6 *Soderback v Sweden* 1998 EHRLR 342.
7 *Johansen v Norway* (1997) 23 EHRR 33.
8 *Soderback v Sweden* (1998) Reports of Judgments and Decisions [of the European Court of Human Rights] 3086 at 3095.
9 See C Forder 'Article 8 ECHR: The Utter Limits of Family Life and the Law of Parenthood' (1997) 1(2) *Maastricht Jounral of European and Comparative Law* pp 125–142.

An American perspective

Similar concerns surface in American case law involving constitutional protection of the parent-child relationship. As we noted in earlier discussion of the *Michael H* and *JWT* cases (491 US 110 and 872 SW2d 189, respectively), such protection takes the form of claims under the due process or equal protection clauses of the Fourteenth Amendment to the US Constitution. It is well established that when a statutory classification significantly interferes with the exercise of a fundamental right it cannot be upheld unless it is supported by sufficiently important state interests and is closely tailored to effectuate only those interests[1]. The first case to uphold the constitutional relationship between an unmarried father and his children was *Stanley v Illinois*[2] Stanley lived with his children and their mother on an intermittent basis for 18 years. When the mother died, an Illinois law, which presumed that unwed fathers were unfit, required the state to take the children on as wards. While the statute provided a hearing to determine whether or not a parent was unfit, Stanley was denied the right to such a hearing because he did not fall within the state's definition of 'parent' which only encompassed mothers and married or divorced fathers. The US Supreme Court held that while the state's aims to protect children from neglect were legitimate, the means they employed to do so were too broadly drawn as they operated on the assumption that all unmarried fathers were unsuitable and neglectful parents. The state argued that most unmarried fathers in Illinois were unfit and so to require a hearing in every case was administratively inconvenient. However, the Supreme Court held that as the state's interest in caring for Stanley's children was minimal if he was in fact a fit parent, the advantage acquired through procedure by presumption was insufficient to justify refusing him a hearing. It therefore held that his right to due process had been infringed. It also held that the differential treatment accorded to him and all unmarried fathers as distinct from other parents was contrary to the equal protection clause.

In reaching its decision the court took account of the fact that Stanley was a biological and social father to his children. What was at issue post-*Stanley* was the degree to which biological paternity alone would trigger constitutional protection. In *Quilloin v Walcott*[3] a father questioned the constitutionality of a Georgia statute that accorded all unmarried mothers but only certain unmarried fathers the right to veto the adoption of their children. These included those who later married the mother and acknowledged the child as his own, or who obtained a court order declaring the child legitimate. In this case the child's mother and father had never lived together and the father had only provided irregular child support although he had visited the child regularly. The mother remarried when the child was three and the child's step-father sought to adopt him. Quilloin, the father, attempted to block the adoption and to secure visitation rights but he did not seek custody or object to the child's continuing to live with the mother. The child expressed a desire to be adopted by his stepfather but also wished to continue visitation with his natural father. The trial court determined that adoption was in the child's best interests. On appeal to the Supreme Court, Quilloin focused his equal protection claim solely on the disparate statutory treatment of his case and that of a married father.

---

1 *Zablocki v Redhail* 434 US 374 (1978).
2 *Stanley v Illinois* 405 US 645 (1972).
3 *Quilloin v Walcott* 434 US 246 (1978).

In this case the Supreme Court held that Quilloin did not have a constitutionally protected interest. His substantive rights under the due process clause were not violated by the application of a 'best interest of the child' standard. This was because he had not petitioned for legitimation at any time in the 11-year period between the child's birth and the filing for adoption. If he had done so he would have been entitled to veto the adoption. He did participate in a hearing but was only entitled to speak to the child's best interests. The court also held that equal protection principles did not require that Quilloin's authority to veto an adoption be measured by the same standard as is applied to the divorced father as his interests 'are readily distinguishable from those of a separated or divorced father'[1]. For 'legal custody of children is, of course, a central aspect of the marital relationship, and even a father whose marriage has broken apart will have borne full responsibility for the rearing of his children during the period of the marriage'. In contrast, compared with an unwed father who has never shouldered any significant responsibility for the child's rearing, 'Under any standard of review, the State was not foreclosed from recognizing this difference in the extent of commitment to the welfare of the child'[2]. This form of reasoning is very similar to that employed by the European Court in *B v UK*[3] where it held that the difference in treatment accorded to married and unmarried fathers under UK law, with regard to the automatic acquisition of parental rights, could be justified on the basis of their differing degrees of responsibility with respect to the child's care.

It is clear from *Quilloin* that the biological link between an unmarried father and child is insufficient in itself to trigger a constitutionally protected interest. This was further substantiated in *Caban v Mohammed*[4] where the court held that an unmarried father had a constitutionally protected interest where he had 'established a substantial relationship with the child and has admitted his paternity'[5]. In this case a step-father petitioned the New York Surrogate Court for adoption of his wife's children who were born out of wedlock. The New York statute at issue gave the unmarried mother, but not the unmarried father, the right to withhold consent to adoption. The natural father, Caban, had lived with the child's mother for five years. When they separated he continued to see his children frequently, to contribute to their support, and even at one point had actual custody of them. The Supreme Court held that the equal protection clause was violated by the sex-based distinction between unmarried mothers and unmarried fathers in New York domestic relations law which permitted an unmarried mother, but not an unmarried father, to block the adoption of their child simply by withholding consent.

The court rejected the state's asserted justification for the statute, that a mother has a closer relationship with her children and that the state has an interest in promoting the adoption of non-marital children. The court made it clear that 'In those cases where the father never has come forward to participate in the rearing of his child, nothing in the Equal Protection Clause precludes the State from withholding from him the privilege of vetoing the adoption of that child'[6].

1 *Quilloin v Walcott* 434 US 246 (1978) at 255.
2 *Quilloin v Walcott* 434 US 246 at 255.
3 *B v UK* [2000] 1 FLR 1.
4 *Caban v Mohammed* 1441 US 380 (1979).
5 *Caban v Mohammed* 1441 US 380 (1979), 392.
6 *Caban v Mohammed* 1441 US 380 (1979) at 392.

However, in the case where a father has established a substantial relationship with his child 'no showing has been made that the different treatment afforded unmarried fathers and unmarried mothers under [the statute] bears a substantial relationship to the proclaimed interest of the State in promoting the adoption of illegitimate children'[1]. What is key is the type of relationship that the father has established with his child. So, in *Lehr v Robertson*[2] the court held that an unmarried father, Lehr, was not entitled to notice of an adoption proceeding brought by his child's mother and her husband. The biological father, Lehr, argued that the court denied him due process and that the differential treatment in the statute denied him equal protection. The court rejected his claims, for although it recognised that an unmarried father may deserve protection in some cases, a mere biological connection did not establish legal paternity entitling him to notice and a hearing before the child could be adopted. The court observed that

> 'The significance of the biological connection is that it offers the natural father an opportunity that no other male possesses to develop a relationship with his offspring. If he grasps that opportunity and accepts some measure of responsibility for the child's future, he may enjoy the blessings of the parent-child relationship and make uniquely valuable contributions to the child's development. If he fails to do so, the Federal Constitution will not automatically compel a state to listen to his opinion of where the child's best interest lie'[3].

As Lehr had not assumed any responsibility for the care of his child his interest in maintaining a relationship with his child was not constitutionally protected. His equal protection argument also failed. As he had never established a substantial relationship with his child, while the mother had continuous custodial responsibility for the child, the New York statutes under which a putative father was not entitled to notice of adoption proceeding (unless he mailed a postcard to the putative father registry) did not deny him equal protection. This was because the statute did not distinguish between a mother and father who were similarly situated, for, unlike the mother, Lehr had never established a custodial, personal, or financial relationship with his child. The difficulty with the majority view is highlighted in Justice White's dissent, ie the position of the unmarried father who is prevented from establishing any social relationship with the child, not due to his own indifference or neglect, but because of the mother's behaviour. In this case the mother had concealed her whereabouts after the child's birth and had refused to let Lehr set up a trust fund to support his daughter. She had also threatened to have him arrested if he continued to persist in attempting to see his daughter. In these circumstances it is not surprising that Lehr failed to establish more than a biological connection with his daughter. However, the majority of justices in the Supreme Court in *Lehr* did not address the issue of the degree of constitutional protection to be afforded to an unmarried father where the mother is instrumental in preventing him from establishing a social relationship with his child[4].

---

1 *Caban v Mohammed* 1441 US 380 (1979) at 393.

2 *Lehr v Robertson* 463 US 248 (1983).

3 *Lehr v Robertson* 463 US 248 (1983) at 262.

4 Where hostility to contact on the part of the residential parent arises because of threatened or actual abuse this is an important consideration for courts. It is beyond the scope of this article to discuss it here but the Scottish Office, Home Department has raised the question of how presumptions about contact under the Children (Scotland) Act 1995 and the best interests of the child should be dealt with where there has been an issue of domestic violence or abuse in *Improving Scottish Family Law* (1999) paras 7.1–7.4. The Scottish Partnership on Domestic Violence are currently reviewing the whole question of abuse and how to tackle it in Scotland.

PERSPECTIVES IN COMMON

It is clear from both American and Scottish case law that where unmarried fathers are concerned a biological link with their children is insufficient to protect their interests in maintaining the parent-child relationship through contact or visitation rights. Fathers in this position must establish some form of social connection with the child. In this respect men are treated differently from unmarried women who acquire parental responsibilities and rights automatically on the birth of their child. As one commentator has observed, 'for mothers, biology ordains and constitutes a 'maternal' role and thus carries 'social significance'; for fathers it is simply a fact of 'nature' not necessarily connected in any way to social consequences'[1]. Thus men are required to do more than procreate in order to establish family ties with their children, for while 'Biology . . . gives men options' it 'inexorably makes women mothers'[2]. This view of the differences between biological maternity and paternity clearly influenced Justice Stevens who delivered the majority judgment in *Lehr v Robertson* 463 US 248 (1983) and who, in his dissenting judgment in *Caban v Mohammed* 1441 US 380 (1979), observed that there existed ' a symbiotic relationship between mother and child' that provided a 'physical and psychological bond' between the two, a bond not 'present between the infant and the father or any other person'[3]. A similar view was espoused by the Inner House in *Brixey v Lynas (No 1)* where the court declared that 'during her infancy the child's need for the mother is stronger than the need for the father'[4].

While married men are treated differently from unmarried men when it comes to parental responsibilities and rights, because marriage is deemed to accord social recognition of the parent–child relationship through the creation of a family unit, when it comes to contact or visitation all those seeking a court order must establish that it is in the child's interests. In Scotland, as discussion of the case law has demonstrated, consideration of the child's welfare is as pertinent to a married or divorced father's claim to contact as it is to that of an unmarried father. Furthermore, whether married or not, all men have to overcome the hurdle of the no-order principle (even if the onus of proof is no longer an issue post-*White*[5]). It is mainly men who find themselves in this position because the majority of parents with residence in Scotland (as in the USA) are women[6]. Although Scots law makes explicit provision for the child to make his or her views about contact known, if he or she so desires, such views must always be subject to the welfare test which is the court's paramount consideration. Even the

1 See J L Dolgin 'Just a Gene: Judicial Assumptions About Parenthood' (1993) 40 *UCLA LR* 637 at p 652 commenting on Chief Justice Berger's dissent in *Stanley v Illinois* 405 US 645 (1972) where he disavowed the significance of biological paternity as compared with biological maternity.

2 J L Dolgin 'Just a Gene: Judicial Assumptions About Parenthood' (1993) 40 *UCLA LR* 637 at p 661.

3 *Caban v Mohammed* 441 US 380 (1979) at 405 n 10.

4 *Brixey v Lynas (No 1)* 1994 SLT 847 at 849I. Although these views claim to be based on biological differences between men and women, they reflect cultural considerations which have been the subject of some critique. See E Sutherland 'Mother Knows Best' 1994 SLT (News) 375 and D L Chambers 'Rethinking the Substantive Rules for Custody Disputes in Divorce', (1984) *83 Mich LR* 477, 527–538.

5 *White v White* 2001 SLT 485.

6 Exceptions do exist as demonstrated by the case of *Osborne v Matthan (No 2)* 1998 SC 682 where a mother who had been in prison and who was about to be deported to Jamaica sought to regain custody of her daughter, aged four, who since the age of 18 months had been brought up by another woman who was not related to the family.

UN Convention on the Rights of the Child, art 9.3 which upholds the child's right to contact with a parent, provides a disclaimer where this would be contrary to the child's best interests.

Given the complexities of balancing individuals' rights in the context of family relationships which involve more than one person, it is not surprising that there is a need to adopt an overview and that the welfare test exists. What is more problematic is the way in which it has been applied by courts who continue to adhere to the paradigm of the nuclear family as constituted by a man and a woman. Marriage may or may not feature as part of the relationship but there can only be one parent of either sex[1]. Thus in *Michael H*, the focus on protection of the 'unitary' family in which there could only be one male parent led to a denial of Michael's visitation rights as he was excluded from the status of being Victoria's parent. The argument was that if his paternity was established he would acquire full parental responsibilities and rights and thus potentially disrupt the family unit in which Victoria was living through the exercise of these rights. The notion that Victoria might have two legal 'fathers' was dismissed outright by Justice Scalia[2]. Yet both men played a role in Victoria's life, and Michael in his application to the courts was not seeking to disrupt the marital family but only to maintain contact through visitation with Victoria. That this created tensions among other family members should not have operated in and of itself to deny either him or Victoria the opportunity to establish their interests in maintaining contact. Had he been married to and divorced from Victoria's mother, such a position would not have been tenable, even although the existence of another family unit comprising Victoria's mother and a new husband might have engendered just as much tension and potential disruption. Nor would the fathers in *Quilloin v Walcott*[3] or *Lehr v Robertson*[4] have lost their right to constitutional protection of the parent–child relationship if they had been married to their children's mothers.

One American scholar has argued that it is not the unmarried father's relationship with his children that is at stake here, but rather his relationship with their mother[5]. This is because

> 'A man becomes a father by relating to his child in the context of family. That context is prototypically created by the development of a spousal or spouse-like relationship between a father and his child's mother. Thus, in the end, the father is required to effect his relationship with his biological children through acts in the world in order to protect that relationship through resort to law. However, not any acts will do. The acts that make a biological father a social and legal father are familial acts, acts that socialize the 'natural' facts by inserting themselves in, and thus defining themselves through, a certain ordering of the relationship between the father and his child's mother'[6].

Looked at from another perspective the overriding concern in these cases involving unmarried fathers 'is the desirability of creating or legally endorsing a 'new'

1 For the difficulties that this causes gay, lesbian, or transsexual relationships involving children see *X, Y and Z v UK* (1997) 9 EHRR 56 and I Karsten, 'Atypical Families and the Human Rights Act: The rights of Unmarried Fathers, Same Sex couples and Transsexuals' 1999 EHRLR pp 195–207.

2 *Michael H and Victoria D, Appellants v Gerald D* 491 US 110 at 117.

3 *Quilloin v Walcott* 434 US 246 (1978).

4 *Lehr v Robertson* 463 US 248 (1983).

5 See J L Dolgin 'Just a Gene: Judicial Assumptions About Parenthood' 40 *UCLA LR* 637.

6 J L Dolgin 'Just a Gene: Judicial Assumptions About Parenthood' 40 *UCLA LR* 637 at p 672.

family unit, and of protecting it by excluding the old father, seen as a potentially destabilising influence'[1].

What is clear is that under Scots law a father in Michael H's position (and even the child Victoria herself) would have had access to a hearing in court for reasons discussed earlier. However, discussion of Scots case law and the legal provisions pertaining to an unmarried father's position in adoption proceedings also make it clear that the interests of the child may operate to deny a father contact with his child, especially where that child is living in another family unit. For these purposes another family unit is perceived to exist when the custodial parent enters into another cohabiting partnership that displays some signs of permanence with a person of the opposite sex. Thus we have Lord Clyde's observations in *Sanderson v McManus* that the child's interests may preclude contact where a mother has entered into a new partnership which is intended to be permanent and which provides the child with a secure background. In Lord Clyde's view such a partnership was clearly identified with marriage[2]. This perspective is shared by other judges, so that, in *Donnelly v Green* an unmarried father was able to succeed in this claim for contact because the sheriff principal did not consider the mother's new cohabiting relationship to be sufficiently secure to provide a stable environment for the child. In reaching his decision he was influenced, in part, by the fact that the mother's cohabitee was not prepared to get married at the date of the proof[3].

Moving beyond the nuclear family: towards a recognition of multiple parenthood?

Thus the judicial approach in both jurisdictions is geared towards maintaining the traditional nuclear family, preferably with marriage. Yet the diverse range of family forms outlined at the beginning of this chapter and their changing nature through individuals' life courses belie the salience of adhering to this type of paradigm when dealing with family relationships. Judicial recognition of such changes in parents and children's lives involves one family unit becoming substituted for another at the expense of those who cannot, or no longer, fit into the desired paradigm. So those who occupy parental roles as 'mothers' or 'fathers' in everyday life, whether it be a grandparent caring for his or her grandchildren, or a same-sex couple caring for their child born through artificial insemination by donor, or a step-parent, may well find themselves excluded from the legal definition of parenthood[4]. Social practice that allows for a degree of flexibility in accommodating parental roles may well be at odds with legal reality.

An example is provided by Carol Stack[5] who worked in 'The Flats', a poor high-rise area in a modern American city where the population were predominantly African–American and unemployed. In this environment many young women had children which they raised themselves. In this case the community

1 See A H Young 'Reconceiving the Family: Challenging the Paradigm of the Exclusive Family' (1998) *6 Am U J Gender & L* 505–555 at p 530.

2 *Sanderson v McManus* 1997 SC (HL) 55 at 65.

3 *Donnelly v Green* 1998 FamLR 12 at para 3-26.

4 For discussion of these issues see ch 3, E Sutherland 'Parentage and Parenting' in *Child and Family Law* (1999) T & T Clark, Edinburgh.

5 C Stack 'Personal Kindreds' in Martha Minow (ed) *Family Matters: Reading on Family Lives and the Law* (1993) The New Press, New York pp 23–31.

demonstrated flexibility in assigning parental roles, as who qualified as 'daddy' or 'mama' at any given moment in time depended on whom the community recognised as fulfilling the functions attached to a parental role and not on biological connections. Thus the biological mother might not qualify as 'mama' if she is unable to take care of her child. If this function is taken over by her mother or sister or some other female relative it is this person who becomes 'mama'. Similarly the biological father will only become a 'daddy' if he chooses to validate his claim through taking on the responsibilities associated with parenthood. Nonetheless, even in this system where a succession of persons slip in and out of parental roles, these roles remain fixed in an individual male and female.

But we have noted earlier that children may well assign these roles to more than one individual as Victoria did in *Michael H.* While the court in that case dismissed any notion of 'dual fatherhood' there are issues about the extent to which law should recognise that parenthood may involve more than one person of the male or female sex. The trial court refused to do this in *Michael H* on the basis that 'the existence of two fathers as male authority figures will confuse the child and be counterproductive to her best interests'[1]. This judgment was based on judicial assumption rather than on any concrete evidence. The assumption, which is predicated on an understanding of culture, is not something that should be treated as a given because there are social groups who have divided parenting responsibilities among several adults rather than allocate parental status to a child's two biological parents[2].

Leaving aside the question of social organisation in other societies, there is evidence that children both in the USA[3] and UK[4] regularly negotiate their relationships with two persons, most usually their biological and step-parents, whom they refer to as 'mum' or 'dad', without this necessarily causing them distress or confusion. There are those who argue that children should have more than one parent of each sex to provide them with more role models[5]. Rather than closing off family relationships, as the court did in *Michael H* and *Quilloin,* it may be more beneficial for children if the law were to adopt a more inclusive approach[6], rather than excluding persons that may be important to them, as the court did in these cases where it denied the natural fathers legal recognition of their paternity. In both these cases the children concerned wished to maintain a relationship with both fathers. While it has already been noted that under Scots

1 *Michael H and Victoria D, Appellants v Gerald D* 491 US 110 at 118.

2 Eg see L Lenero-Otero (ed) *Beyond the Nuclear Family Model: Cross-Cultural Perspectives* (1977).

3 See B Yngvesson 'Negotiating Motherhood: Identity and Difference in 'Open' Adoption *Law & Society Review,* Vol 31 (1) pp 31–80.

4 See V Morrow *Understanding Families: Children's Perspectives* (1998) National Children's Bureau supported by Joseph Rowntree Foundation, London; who found in her study that 'overall children appeared to have an accepting, inclusive view of what counts as family and their definitions did not centre around biological relatedness or the 'nuclear' norm. See also C Smail, B Neale and A Wade 'Children's Perspectives on Post Divorce Family Life'.*The Changing Experience of Childhood: Families and Divorce* (2001) Polity Press/Blackwell Publishers Ltd, Cambridge and Oxford.

5 See R Thamm *Beyond the Nuclear Family* (1975). See also A H Young 'Reconceiving the Family: Challenging the Paradigm of the Exclusive Family' (1998) *6 Am U J Gender & L* 505–555. See also ch 5 below.

6 Maintaining contact between birth families and those who adopt has been found to have positive consequences for both the children and their adoptive parents. See A R Appell, 'Blending Families through Adoption: Implications for Collaborative Adoption Law and Practice' (1995) *75 BU L Rev* 997–1061 at 1013.

law a natural father may apply to the court for contact, this is unlikely to be viable where, as in *Quilloin*, adoption is upheld by the court. Where a court holds that it is in a child's interests to be adopted it is unlikely to uphold a natural father's right to contact, at least while 'closed' adoptions remain the norm.

One response to this issue has been to argue that while social practices may embrace many forms of parenthood, the law cannot afford to do so. Where parties agree among themselves there may be no problems and the interests of all can be accommodated. However, where conflict arises and they are at odds with one another the law cannot be expected to deal with the complexities of rights in the context of multiple parenthood. There are two rejoinders to this argument. The first concerns the position of those parties who do support multiple parenthood[1]. For example, those who are committed to the concept of 'open' adoption, that is in continuing to include one or both birth parents in the child's life within his or her new adopted family, may wish to structure a legal agreement to this effect. Rather than relying on informal understandings they may wish to delineate the rights of both sets of parents. It is not clear, however, if such a contract would be enforceable in Scots law given the current legal approach to adoption that involves substituting one person's rights as a parent for those of another. The second rejoinder concerns the issue of legal complexity and extending the number of persons whose interests would have to be taken into consideration in cases of dispute. This is not as great a problem as is perceived because courts already have to deal with disputes between parents, they do so on the basis of the no-order principle, and in any event must operate in all cases on the basis of the child's welfare as their 'paramount consideration'. To extend the legal recognition of familial ties in the circumstances outlined in this chapter would surely benefit families in Scotland today given the diversity that they encompass and the range of relationships that they embrace.

1 For discussion of the issues concerning parenthood in the context of adoption see ch 5, M Ross 'Adoption in the 21st Century: Still Image Against A Moving Picture'.

5 Adoption in the 21st Century: Still Image Against a Moving Picture?

Margaret Ross

INTRODUCTION

The perspective

In this chapter the traditional, supportive approach to adoption is challenged, with the conclusion that adoption as we know and accept it has no place in a modern system of child and family law[1]. Viewed on a case by case basis, it is easy to rationalise that a child in respect of whom adoption is sought will benefit from the granting of that order. However, looking critically at the tests for adoption in the United Kingdom even as they exist at present, it would be possible, and it is argued here appropriate, to conclude that an order short of adoption should always be made. There will be some rare cases where a child is truly without any identifiable kin and where an order resembling adoption as traditionally understood appears to be the only humanitarian approach. However, how can one say that in the future it will not be possible to identify a biological link between that child and another individual or family who may be able to make a positive contribution to that child's future? It is submitted here that in *every* situation where a child's future is considered, the severance of a legal connection with the birth family is impossible to justify. The number of adoptions applied for now is small[2], and it might have been thought that adoption has, naturally, had its day. However there is pressure at government level to expand access to adoption as a means of accommodating children in long term care. In Scotland there have been

1 The author has acted as a curator and/or reporting officer in adoption applications since 1983 with almost invariable support for the granting of the individual application. Her unease about aspects of adoption law (but not with adoption per se) have been voiced in the past: see M Ross 'Parental Rights after adoption: a potential dilemma' (1993) 38 JLSS 301; M Ross 'Attitudes to Sexual Orientation in Adoption Law' (1997) 1 *Edin LR* 370; M Ross 'Step parent adoption', Dec 1995, 'Adoption Law', The Law Society of Scotland; M Ross 'Is the Child's Welfare Paramount?', Feb 1998, 'Adoption Law', The Law Society of Scotland. The author is grateful to Rosemary O'Neill LLB (Hons) for challenging discussions on the topic.

2 Averaging 450 per annum in Scotland over the period 1997–99: see www.scotland.gov.uk/stats/educ.htm, and 3,962 for England and Wales in 1999, falling from 4,387 in 1998: see www.statistics.gov.uk; 2,200 of the annual figure adopted in England and Wales during that period were looked-after children: see *Adoption, Prime Minister's Review* (Performance and Innovation Unit Report, July 2000) (hereafter 'PIU report') para 2.4.

calls for increased interest in adoption[1]. In England and Wales a target of 40% increase in adoptions of looked-after children by 2004–2005 has been set[2].

Adoption as generally experienced is a neat and tidy process of social regulation. It is one with which most who approach it as active participants feel happy and secure, and it is one widely advocated and rarely challenged even in current social policy. Executive statements abound declaring confidence in adoption and desire to widen access to it[3]; and legislative change proposed by the legislatures in both Parliaments in the United Kingdom aims for reinforcement and purification of the process. However nowhere has there been a truly critical evaluation of adoption per se within a strategy of child and family law. Can it be compared realistically rather than idealistically with the alternatives that exist for generating a secure, caring home environment for a child without detaching that child from birth identity[4]? There appears to be an unspoken reluctance to make such a challenge, and professional expression of unease about adoption[5] is usually coupled with a rationalised acceptance of the process[6].

Quality of parenting rather than parentage or parenthood is at the core of modern child care law and policy[7], yet adoption in concept presupposes that the former is necessary for the latter. The process of adoption involves a welfare test. In Scotland since 1996 the child's welfare has been paramount in the decision to grant an order[8], and it has been proposed that it become paramount in the adoption law of England and Wales[9], where at present it is given first consideration[10]. Additionally adoption should not be planned, or an order for it granted, unless consideration has been given to whether there is a better, practicable, and less radical alternative[11]. Severance of legal relationships with birth parents is a traditional feature of legal adoption, perceived to be a necessary step towards the

---

1 The Scottish Education Minister on 22 May 2001 called for more people to come forward to adopt children from care, SE Press Release 1309/2001, in response to the publication of halved adoption rates over the previous decade.

2 Department of Health *Adoption: A New Approach* (Cm 5017, Dec 2000) p 5 and paras 4.16–4.18. For criticism of a target-driven approach see C Barton 'Adoption – The Prime Minister's Review' [2000] Fam Law 731–735; C Ball 'The White Paper, Adoption: A New Approach, A "curate's egg"' (2001) 25(1) Ad & Fos 6 at 12.

3 Most prominently in the PIU report, in the Foreword to which the Prime Minister states 'We know that adoption works for children.' As C Barton 'Adoption – The Prime Minister's Review' [2000] Fam Law 731–735 points out, this statement is not supported in the PIU report itself. The Department of Health website at www.Department of Health.gov.uk/adoption/ extols the virtues of adoption.

4 A thorough review has been carried out recently by the New Zealand Law Commission, *Adoption and Its Alternatives: A Different Approach and a New Framework* (Report no 65, September 2000). This review was influenced by the current legislative regime in Scotland, and is a source of clear discussion of the place of adoption in a spectrum of child law.

5 As in G Schofield 'Parental responsibility and parenting – the needs of accommodated children in long-term foster-care' (2000) 12 CFLQ 345 at 360.

6 See for example M Hayes and C Williams *Family Law: Principles Practice and Policy* (2nd edn, 1999) Butterworths, London 330–344; Adoption Law Reform Group comments on adoption, summarised at www.baaf.org.uk/adreformsum.htm.

7 For a thought-provoking discussion of this see M Freeman 'The Next Children's Act' [1998] Fam Law 341.

8 Adoption (Scotland) Act 1978, s 6, as substituted by the Children (Scotland) Act 1995, s 95.

9 Department of Health, *Adoption: A New Approach* (Cm 5017, Dec 2000), para 4.14; Adoption and Children Bill, cl 1(2). The proposed provision is in the same terms as the existing Scottish test.

10 Adoption Act 1976, s 6.

11 Children Act 1975, s 53; Adoption (Scotland) Act 1978, s 6A as introduced by the Children (Scotland) Act 1995, s 96.

security that adoption offers for the child[1]. Can it not be argued equally strongly that the severance is static, unnecessary and patently denying of a key element, that is birth identity? It is adult-centred rather than child-centred. It does not reflect in law the actual need for the adopter to assume responsibility for the whole child[2] including the child's natural origins and kin[3].

Adoption seems ideal to satisfy both the need for permanency on the part of the child with the adopter's need to parent. The convenience of it is unquestionable, but it has lured us into repeatedly assuming that the model of adoption is a good one. We continually suppress unease arising from the simplistic visions of adoption which prevail[4] in society in general, amongst policy makers, amongst prospective adopters, amongst children adopted or about to be adopted, and in the practice of social work and law[5]. Those simplistic visions are nevertheless challengeable. Against an expanding background of experience and research in other jurisdictions into impacts of adoption and other models of permanency, perhaps the unease can be articulated and legitimated. At very least it can add a dimension to the anodyne treatment of adoption in the United Kingdom in recent years.

The context

Adoption has drawn extensive attention in the years leading up to this twenty-first century. There have been lurid press headlines about the purchase of babies via the internet; chat shows setting adopter against adopter against parent; and fly-on-the-wall documentaries about the joys and traumas of the adoption process[6]. This has taken place alongside increasing political interest and activity such as the setting of targets for matching willing adopters to looked-after children[7]. All have reinforced the image of the adoption process as it is commonly understood, namely a means of creating a permanent parent–child arrangement, emulating a blood tie, and erasing the legal ties with all blood relatives[8]. Can

1 On the other hand adoption-like processes in many indigenous cultures generally add the chosen adoptive relationship to the existing familial connections, seeing this as a positive contribution to the welfare of the child, and preservation of genealogical history and cultural heritage. See the review of adoption practices in Maori and South Pacific Island cultures in New Zealand Law Commission *Adoption and Its Alternatives: A Different Approach and a New Framework* (Report no 65, Sept 2000) ch 9 and App G.

2 Identity, linked to a need for completeness, is one of the key findings of the research undertaken by J Feast & D Howe *Adoption, Search and Reunion: The Long Term Experiences of Adopted Adults* (The Children's Society, March 2000); and see J Feast 'Comment: Adoption and Identity' [2000] Fam Law 287.

3 A Courtney 'Loss and Grief in Adoption: The Impact of Contact' [2000] 24(2) Ad & Fos 33.

4 H Argent, in a review of A Treacher and I Katz (eds) *The Dynamics of Adoption: Social and Personal Perspectives* (2000) at (2001) 25(1) Ad & Fos 79, notes that these are 'concerns and preoccupations of most people who have anything to do with adoption'.

5 Some of these are expressed in A Treacher and I Katz (eds) *The Dynamics of Adoption: Social and Personal Perspectives* (2000).

6 For example, First Frame for Channel 4 'The Fight for a Child' (Feb 2000), assisted by the British Agencies for Adoption and Fostering (hereafter 'BAAF'), BAAF Annual Review 1999/2000 pp 12–13.

7 Department of Health *Adoption: A New Approach* (Cm 5017, Dec 2000) p 5 and paras 4.16–4.18.

8 This has been the case even with adoption by step-parents, but in Scotland step-parents may now apply to become adopters without the birth parent having to be a co-applicant. The birth parent requires to agree to the adoption: Adoption (Scotland) Act 1978, s 15(1)(aa), inserted by the Children (Scotland) Act 1995, s 97(2).

adoption, which is seen in these still images, survive as an element of the moving picture of organic and dynamic family law? Thoughtful consideration of recent coverage of adoption in specialist media suggests that it cannot survive[1], or at least not in the case of adoption of children older than infants[2] who have some emotional tie to a birth family. However the popular perception appears to be that it must be uniquely protected from tinkering or tarnishment. Furthermore the clear message from political leaders is that adoption is good for children and must be encouraged. It may be said that the academic commentators simply cannot leave well alone, but on the other hand they, uniquely, can assess adoption from a position of detachment from individual case work, but of engagement with the patterns of child and family relationships as they are increasingly researched and understood.

It has been said that adoption is a social problem 'concerned not only with legal matters but also emotional, psychological, moral and educational aspects'[3]. It is certainly an area of law at the socio-legal interface. It is somewhat anachronistic to refer to it as a 'problem', and in this article the preferred term is 'remedy'. Its aim should be to make secure and promote the child's welfare, and the perception of problematics derives from the severance requirement and its static effect. This chapter is informed by studies in the social sciences[4], but its focus is the intensely legalistic nature of adoption. Those studies help to set the context in which adoption is now expected to operate, but invariably in such studies, academic materials and policy papers the legalistic nature and effect of adoption is accepted without question[5]. The legal effect of adoption is starkly obvious and reasonably well known within the population at large, but it assumes a stereotypical static family unit that increasingly fails to reflect the realities of family life[6]. This is surely a situation in which popular perceptions must be educated and stereotypical images should be capable of adjustment. However, to do so requires acceptance that (a) adoption is not a discrete process but an element of family dynamics, and (b) legal rights and duties do not themselves provide the key to positive experiences of family relationships[7].

There is a tension between the desire for legal certainty and the need for flexibility where family relationships are concerned. Sadly, the reforms currently advocated through the adoption reviews in England[8] will not address this

---

1 For example N Lowe 'The changing face of adoption – the gift/donation model versus the contract/services model' (1997) 9 CFLQ 371.

2 J Castle 'Infant adoption in England: a longitudinal account of social and cognitive progress' (2000) 24(3) Ad & Fos 26 reveals reasonable outcomes in infant adoption but not as overwhelming as popularly perceived.

3 'Opinion on Adoption' (92/C 287/08) Economic and Social Committee of the European Community, Official Journal no C 287/18 para 1.1.1.

4 Many of these are published by BAAF in their journal *Adoption & Fostering*, and in other publications such as their *Annual Review*; Ivaldi *Surveying Adoption, a comprehensive analysis of local authority adoptions 1998/99 – England* (2000) BAAF and the useful collection of material on adoption in Hill & Shaw (eds) *Signposts in Adoption* (1998) BAAF.

5 For example in S Mann 'Adoptive Parents: A Practice Perspective' (1998) 22(3) Ad & Fos 42.

6 Day S Sclater and C Piper 'Remoralising the family? – Family policy, family law and youth justice' (2000) 12 CFLQ 135–151 at 151.

7 On this in the context of parental responsibilities see J Eekelaar 'Rethinking Parental Responsibility' [2001] Fam Law 426 at 429–430.

8 The white paper published in 2000 was preceded not only by the PIU report (the focus of which is the adoption of looked-after children) but by *Review of Adoption Law: Report to Ministers of an Interdepartmental Working Group* (Oct 1992) Department of Health; *Adoption: The Future* (Cm 2288, Nov 1993); and *Adoption – A Service for Children* (Mar 1996) Department of Health.

tension at its fundamental level, and there is no reason to assume that the review in Scotland announced recently[1] will offer this challenge, since its remit is to '... review adoption law and practice in Scotland and *work to break down barriers to adoption*'[2] (emphasis added). The English review does to some extent resist the apparently incontrovertible attractions of adoption, by introducing an additional order short of adoption, named 'special guardianship', which is intended to give a greater degree of security than the orders currently available under the Children Act 1989[3].

It is clear, given the political messages emitted this century[4], that it is too much to expect that we will have *radical* re-examination of the inherent viability of adoption by legislatures in the United Kingdom as a result of the recent or current reviews[5]. However, when the next re-examination undoubtedly will occur, it requires to be more fully informed by the outcomes of empirical research[6] (preferably independent of the perceived shackles of public authority commissioning) and rigorous examination of adoption in a wider social and legal context. At this stage it is timely to draw together and focus on the themes of concern about adoption and to suggest that they are sufficient to sound its death knell. But first, what is the nature and purpose of adoption as it is known in the United Kingdom[7]?

THE NATURE OF ADOPTION

Semantics

The word 'adopt' derives from the Latin *(ad)optare* meaning 'to choose (for oneself)'. Used in any context, including the adoption of children, the word focuses

1 *Scottish Parliament Official Report* vol 11, no 11, cols 1185–1234, 4 April 2001. Adoption was considered in *The Future of Adoption Law in Scotland* (1993) SWSG. The *Review of Child Care Law in Scotland* (1990) HMSO had touched on adoption only briefly at paras 24.1–24.16. Scottish Office discussion papers were issued from 1990 to 1993, and for details see Sutherland *Child and Family Law* (1999) T&T Clark, Edinburgh para 8.3 n 10. Consequently a number of significant changes were made by the Children (Scotland) Act 1995, Pt III and Sch 2.

2 The debate surrounding its announcement revealed MSPs' very personal experiences of adoption and looked-after children, and notable consensual acceptance of adoption's 'goodness' although some expressed caution: see *Scottish Parliament Official Report* vol 11, no 11, per Cathy Jamieson MSP at cols 1205–1206 and Dr Richard Simpson MSP at cols 1210–1211.

3 Adoption and Children Bill, cl 94. For criticism of this see C Barton 'Adoption and Children Bill 2001 – Don't let them out of your sight' [2001] Fam Law 431 at 435. Professor Barton seems drawn to the notion of parenthood as a precursor to permanence, linked it would seem to his distrust of the similarity of special guardianship to custodianship, an order which was introduced by the Children Act 1975, rarely used and abandoned in 1989. See also C Barton 'Adoption – The Prime Minister's Review' [2000] Fam Law 731 at 735.

4 For an examination of the effect of such messages in the last few years of the 20th century see J Eekelaar 'Family law: Keeping us on message' [1999] 11 CFLQ 387. A Barlow and S Duncan 'Supporting families? New Labour's communitarianism and the 'rationality mistake', Part I' (2000) 22 JSWFL 23 provides an interesting dicussion of whether state-imposed policy can be effective in aligning families.

5 For a criticism of the English position see C Ball 'The White Paper, Adoption: A New Approach, A "curate's egg"' (2001) 25(1) Ad & Fos 6.

6 Some studies are carefully summarised and examined in B Lindley 'Open Adoption – Is the door ajar?' [1997] 9 CFLQ 115, but it is recognised there that there is a need for ongoing, extensive longitudinal studies.

7 The chapter will draw upon Scottish and English sources, which are similar, but not identical. The laws throughout the UK will be more similar if many of the provisions of the Adoption and Children Bill are enacted.

on selection, acceptance and assumption of responsibility. It follows from this that, linguistically, adoption puts the focus on the choice of the adoptive parent rather than on the interests of the child, although the latter will normally be the stated aim of the former. In terms it does not carry an implication that the choosing for oneself will obliterate the link with those from actual origins. Thus to adopt an idea, an argument, an animal does not in any way pretend that the adopter is not the true source. However in the adoption of children that pretence is integral to both cause and effect.

Definition

Adoption of a child can be variously described, for example, as a 'process by which the legal relationship between a child and his or her birth parents is severed and an analogous relationship between the child and the adoptive parents is established'[1] or 'radical divestiture of the responsibilities, rights, duties, powers, interests and obligations of the biological parents brought about by operation of law in favour of the adoptive parents'[2].

These definitional examples are wholly typical of the emphasis in child adoption on the issue of severance of the relationship of parentage and its resultant responsibilities and rights. That has been the hallmark of the process since the development of adoption laws in the United Kingdom[3], although loss of inheritance rights through the birth family was not a feature of the first wave of legislation[4]. In severance, the focus is on parents rather than the child, albeit that a welfare test must be met for the adoption order to be granted. The welfare test was a safeguard against unscrupulous adopters at first[5], the primary purpose of adoption being the recognition in law of the status of the substitute carer[6]. That carer's role was founded in contract, and adoption was described as a 'court ratified contract'[7]. The contractual process of realigning rights and responsibilities otherwise imposed by the law of persons developed naturally to reflect the choices and needs of individuals[8], before statute intervened to regulate or validate such contractual arrangements.

1 Interdepartmental Review of Adoption Law *The Nature and Effect of Adoption* (Discussion paper no 1, 1990) Department of Health, para 2.

2 A Wilkinson and K Norrie *The Law of Parent and Child in Scotland* (2nd edn, 1999) W Green, Edinburgh para 4.03.

3 It is how the process works chronologically. At least momentarily in adoption cases, but for up to a year in freeing for adoption orders, the child is parentless in legal terms, responsibilities after freeing being vested in local authority: Adoption (Scotland) Act 1978, s 18, Adoption Act 1976, s 18.

4 In Scotland the Succession (Scotland) Act 1964 and in England the Adoption of Children Act 1949.

5 See N Lowe 'The changing face of adoption – the gift/donation model versus the contract/services model' (1997) 9 CFLQ 371.

6 See N Lowe 'The changing face of adoption – the gift/donation model versus the contract/services model' (1997) 9 CFLQ 371.

7 S Cretney 'From Status to Contract' in F Rose (ed) *Consensus ad Idem: Essays in the Law of Contract in honour of Guenter Treitel* (1996) Sweet & Maxwell, London at p 256. The title of that essay derives from H Maine *Ancient Law* (10th edn, 1909) p 174.

8 H Maine *Ancient Law* (10th edn, 1909) at p 172 states 'The movement of progressive societies has been uniform in one respect. Through all its course it has been distinguished by the gradual dissolution of family dependency, and the growth of individual obligation in its place. . . . Nor is it difficult to see what is the tie between man and man which replaces by degrees those forms of reciprocity in rights and duties which have their origin in the Family. It is Contract.' This is explored in relation to adoption and division of property on divorce in S Cretney 'From Status to Contract' in F Rose (ed) *Consensus ad Idem: Essays in the Law of Contract in honour of Guenter Treitel* (1996) Sweet & Maxwell p 251.

Legislative recognition of adoption

Statute law on adoption is an invention of the twentieth century[1], there being no formal recognition of such a process until 1926 in England and 1930 in Scotland[2], albeit that adoption was an integral part of Roman law[3], which has had a lasting influence on the law of Scotland in many other respects. Its purpose in Roman law was to generate heirs, and it has been argued that this continued to be the covert purpose of the introduction of adoption laws in various jurisdictions[4]. Prior to the twentieth century, adoption had not featured in the laws of continental Europe[5]. In 1991–92 the Economic and Social Committee of the European Community carried out an investigation into the nature of adoption laws across the Community. In its 'Opinion on "Adoption"'[6] it differentiates between 'full adoption', defined as

> 'A legal act, which, after the abandonment of a child, substitutes "adoptive" affiliations for "biological" consanguinity, conferring on the adoptive parents full parental rights and obligations. Likewise, in its dealings with the adoptive parents, the adopted child has the duties and rights stemming from natural consanguinity. It loses all legal ties with its natural parents'

and 'simple adoption' is defined as

> 'A legal provision essentially applicable to intra-family situations. For example an uncle adopts his nephew without the latter losing his blood ties with his natural family. The uncle looks after and brings up his nephew who may take on the uncle's name and become his heir, with the same rights as a natural child. The child continues to maintain links with its biological heir'[7].

The opinion, in addition to synthesising data on adoption laws gathered from the member states, is paradigmatic of the superficial and praise-laden treatment of adoption that is iterated in domestic reviews of adoption, and for this alone it is worth dwelling on it for a moment. The committee notes that at the time of their review there were pressures on the traditional view of adoption deriving from (a) increasing attention to child welfare and rights, (b) rapid exchange of ideas and experience in the social, family and educational spheres, (c) freer movement of people and (d) the growth in international adoptions[8]. It describes adoption as 'a vexed issue, eliciting a range of responses from reproval to admiration'[9], and counsels against drawing general rules from the experience of individual cases.

1 For a review of the social concerns surrounding its introduction see J Tresiliotis 'Adoption – evolution or revolution' written in 1995 and reproduced in M Hill & M Shaw (eds) *Signposts in Adoption* (1998) BAAF, London.

2 Adoption of Children (Scotland) Act 1930, Adoption of Children Act 1926. For a review of its introduction in other jurisdictions see N Lowe *'English Adoption Law: Past, Present and Future'* in S Katz, J Eekelaar and M Maclean (eds) *Cross Currents* (2000) Oxford University Press at pp 308–309.

3 For a discussion of the history and character of adoption in Scotland see A Wilkinson and K Norrie *The Law of Parent and Child in Scotland* (2nd edn, 1999) W Green, Edinburgh paras 4.01–4.03.

4 Starkly described by Friedman in *A History of American Law* (2nd edn, 1985) Simon and Schuster, New York at 212 quoted by Sutherland *Child and Family Law* (1999) T &T Clark, Edinburgh at para 8.3 n8.

5 A Wilkinson & K Norrie, *The Law of Parent and Child in Scotland* (2nd edn, 1999) W Green, Edinburgh para 4.01.

6 *Official Journal* no C287/18. In the appendix to the opinion, C 287/23-26, there is a comparison of key features of adoption law in the member states.

7 *Official Journal* C287/18 Opinion on Adoption, preamble.

8 *Official Journal* C287/18 para 1.1.2. In this chapter it is argued that these pressures have reached a destructive level.

9 *Official Journal* C287/18 para 1.2.1.

However, it proceeds to focus on admiration of adoption and the facilitation of it as a means of ensuring a secure family life for a child. Some attention is paid to the interests of the child[1], acknowledging that this has developed as an important and latterly central factor in the philosophy of adoption laws and processes[2]. However, the bulk of the opinion focuses on the process of 'abandonment' by the biological parent and the needs of the adoptive parent to be respected, even to the extent of respecting the adopters' needs to justify inhibiting the child from learning of biological origins[3]. This ignores the need for a child to know about family background which is integral to the child's right to family life under the European Convention on Human Rights, art 8[4], and separately a right protected by the UN Convention on the Rights of the Child, arts 8 and 9[5].

In one brief section the committee notes that different forms of fostering are needed and should be encouraged[6] but does not link this to its acknowledgment of the 'sovereign right of a child to be able to live in a family where he is loved and can himself love and be happy and secure'[7]. It would appear to be assumed that *only* adoption can achieve that right; indeed the committee comments:

> '[A]ttempts are occasionally made to draw up priorities or reveal conflicts between the interests of the child and those of its adoptive parents. This is futile, not to say morally unjustifiable. The happy child is the child who is wanted and accepted, be he a biological or an adopted child'[8].

This quoted analysis makes two basic, unsupported assumptions. The first is that a child could not be happy and accepted in a family setting with which he or she has neither a biological nor an adoptive relationship. The second is that the relationships of biology and adoption can be equated. It can be argued, however, that they can be equated only by the legal fiction of adoption, and there is evidence that adoption is more effective if that difference is acknowledged[9]. The fiction of the law is not the reality. As Day, Sclater and & Piper observe[10], 'family law strategy becomes coercive rather than supportive if it merely reflects formalised norms of family relationships'. Before the openness that has become the evolving reality in the adoptions of older children, the fictions of replacement of and equation with biological parents drove the reality.

Adoption has lost the supportive function that it may have needed when it was first recognised in legislation. An extensive range of legal interventions falling short of adoption can support the permanence of a family setting. Its continuing legal denial of birth relationships is both out of step with the reality of many post-adoption informal links with birth families, and implicitly discouraging of such arrangements.

1 *Official Journal* C287/18 paras 1.4.1–1.4.6.3.
2 *Official Journal* C287/18 para 2.1.
3 *Official Journal* C287/18 paras 2.15 and 3.
4 *Gaskin v United Kingdom* (1990) 12 EHHR 36 at para 49.
5 UN Convention on the Rights of the Child, art 8 (preservation of identity), art 9 (protection from separation from parents). On this see A Cleland & E Sutherland (eds) *Children's Rights in Scotland* (1996) W Green, Edinburgh at paras 3.5–3.13 and 7.36–7.38. See also E Sutherland's commentary on this area in ch 3 above.
6 Paras 2.16 and 2.16.1.
7 Conclusion, para 3.
8 Para 1.4.3.
9 B Lindley 'Open Adoption – Is the door ajar?' (1997) 9 CFLQ 115 at 123. There she draws upon a review of research on experiences of post-adoption contact undertaken by Thoburn and Tresiliotis.
10 Day, Sclater and Piper 'Remoralising the family? – Family policy, family law and youth justice' (2000) 12 CFLQ 135–151 at 151.

Adoption can be contrasted sharply with the factual history of permanent caring for a child from outwith the family. The social tradition of bringing up a child as one's own is well recognised and documented[1]. There was no enforceable obligation imposed by these informal relationships, although Sutherland notes that parties and the court was using the term 'adoption' early in the twentieth century[2], to describe what were effectively private fostering arrangements[3]. The court in *Kerrigan v Hall*[4] rejects the notion of contractual alienation of property in a child although private fosterage agreements which did not alienate the child's biological connections were recognised[5], but the system of adoption laws that has developed in the twentieth century authorises such alienation when ordered by the court, having regard to the welfare test.

The move towards statutory force for the alienation of a child from one set of legal parents to another was pragmatic rather than philosophical or conceptual[6]. Reports of committees preceding the introduction of legislation in England and Wales recognised separately that it was legitimate for persons wishing to parent another person's child to seek a legally acknowledged and enforceable mechanism for so doing[7] and that the community should give some recognition to the factual relationship between adopter and child[8]. A welfare test would ensure that the child's interest would be protected in the process. This amalgam of satisfying the needs of adults to parent and endorsing an arrangement for a child under a welfare test is something that we have grown to know and expect of adoption. Some see it as a social panacea[9] whilst others comment that it is adoption's essential dilemma[10]. Whichever view one takes, adoption no longer operates in the way that was envisaged at the time of its statutory inception.

PURPOSES FOR ADOPTION IN THE TWENTY-FIRST CENTURY

The legal tests

The test for adoption in England is currently:

> 'In reaching any decision relating to the adoption of a child a court or adoption agency shall have regard to all the circumstances, first consideration being given to the need to safeguard and promote the welfare of the child throughout his childhood; and shall so far as practicable ascertain the wishes and feelings of the child regarding

1 See for example *Kerrigan v Hall* 1901 4F 10; *Report of the Departmental Committee on the Adoption of Children* ('The *Hurst Report*') (Cmd 9248, 1954) para 11; *Report of the Departmental Committee on the Adoption of Children* ('The *Houghton Report*') (Cmnd 5107, 1972) para 10.

2 E Sutherland *Child and Family Law* (1999) T&T Clark, Edinburgh paras 8.2 and 8.3, citing *Kerrigan v Hall* 1901 4F 10 and *Briggs v Mitchell* 1911 SC 705.

3 E Sutherland *Child and Family Law*, para 8.3.

4 *Kerrigan v Hall* 1901 4F 10.

5 E Sutherland *Child and Family Law* (1999) T&T Clark, Edinburgh, para 8.3.

6 In England the *Report of the Committee on Child Adoption* ('the *Hopkinson Report*') (Cmd 1254, 1921) and the *First Report of the Child Adoption Committee* ('the *Tomlin Report*') (Cmd 2401, 1924–25). For a discussion of their respective approaches see C Barton and G Douglas *Law and Parenthood* (1995) Butterworths, London at pp 73–75.

7 *Hopkinson Report* para 14.

8 *Tomlin Report* para 9.

9 This is the thrust of the PIU report: See also *Hopkinson Report* para 14.

10 C Barton and G Douglas *Law and Parenthood* (1995) Butterworths, London at 75.

the decision and give due consideration to them, having regard to age and understanding'[1].

In Scotland the corresponding provisions are

> '... in reaching any decision relating to the adoption of the child, a court or adoption agency shall have regard to all the circumstances but –
>
> (a) shall regard the need to safeguard and promote the welfare of the child concerned throughout his life as the paramount consideration; and
> (b) shall have regard so far as practicable –
>   (i) to his views (if he wishes to express them) taking account of his age and maturity; and
>   (ii) to his religious persuasion, racial origin and cultural and linguistic background'[2].

In complying with these duties an adoption agency in Scotland

> 'shall, before making any arrangements for the adoption of a child, consider whether adoption is likely to best meet the needs of that child or whether for him there is some better, practicable, alternative; and if it concludes that there is such an alternative it shall not proceed to make such arrangements'[3].

Usage of adoption

The numbers of adoptions have steadily declined since peaking in the 1960s[4]. Development and legalisation of biological interventions to prevent, terminate, manipulate or sustain the birth of children according to the desires of those who might be parents has, in many cases, provided the solution to those original underlying aims of adoption. With a few exceptions, instead of providing a means for creating parentage in a child already born where none existed or was wanted, the modern day adoption is used in two distinctly different ways. First, adoption by relatives (usually step-parents) is a means of repositioning a child's parentage whilst the child is within a private stable family setting. Second, adoption by strangers is usually undertaken in cases where the parenting arrangements for a child have broken down. Usually this occurs after some years of the child being looked after by his or her birth family, although occasionally babies are still given up for adoption at birth[5]. Adoption provides a means of permanently establishing a child within a new family as an alternative to other care orders available under the Children Acts in Scotland or in England which regulate the responsibilities of parenting but not parenthood.

These present day models of adoption in the United Kingdom resemble the simple and full adoptions referred to in the 1992 Opinion on 'Adoption' in the European Community, but the United Kingdom, unlike some member states, does not have a different procedure for dealing with them, except in the case of

1 Adoption Act 1976, s 6.
2 Adoption (Scotland) Act 1978, s 6.
3 Adoption (Scotland) Act 1978, s 6A.
4 Adoption trends are examined by Lowe in 'The changing face of adoption – the gift/donation model versus the contract/services model' (1997) 9 CFLQ 371, and 'English Adoption Law: Past, Present and Future' in S Katz, J Eekelaar and M Maclean (eds) *Cross Currents* (2000) Oxford University Press p 307.
5 J Castle 'Infant adoption in England: a longitudinal account of social and cognitive progress' (2000) 24(3) Ad & Fos 26.

step-parent adoptions, where it is now possible for the step-parent to adopt without interference with the natural legal relationship between the child and the step-parent's spouse[1].

It appears then that, given the changing profile of situations in which adoption proceeds, the underlying rationale has gone. However the 'legitimate' aims of providing children for childless couples and recognising long term care arrangements, as identified by the Hopkinson[2] and Tomlin Committees[3] respectively, are in fact still the principal reasons for selection of adoption as compared to another alternative. Certainly reviews in subsequent years recognise the continuing need for adoption[4], but apart from the increasing tendency to advocate openness in adoption, no reviews have challenged those long-recognised reasons for adoption. The question is whether those reasons can or should be sustained in the twenty-first century. If not, can they be replaced with sustainable aims that are legitimate now and able to justify adoption as a process for the new century?

Security

Adoption enables a child to experience a full legal relationship with a person who is exercising or willing to exercise the parenting role. The sole purpose appears to be to generate a sense of security on the part of child and adopter, by making the adoptive relationship unassailable from intrusions deriving from the child's birth origins. As currently drafted in Scotland the welfare test requires that the *child's* security is the paramount consideration and in England that the child's security is the first consideration, yet it is folly to pretend that the *adopter* is not equally drawn to that security. Those who now apply for adoption are, by so doing, revealing that they are not content with an informal arrangement or lesser order to reflect their parenting role. One has to question whether the availability of adoption as a means of generating security in fact reduces the level of security felt through the de facto arrangement or orders short of adoption. Could that level of security be enhanced by the absence of the adoption option?

The adopter's need to parent is frequently perceived to be altruistic. Altruism no doubt plays a part[5], but the adopter's need to help and to share are surely the underlying motivators. A childless couple may feel the need to express parenting desires and abilities. Existing parents, conscious of their abilities to parent, may respond positively to the 'Can you give a child a home?' adverts in the media, internet or adoption databases. It is desirable to recognise the adopter's motives, not in order to criticise or insult but in order to focus upon the notion of parenting rather than on the concept of parenthood or parentage. One of the hardest issues to weigh in the consideration of adoption is the effect that the adopters' need for security has on the child's feelings of security[6]. The adopters' needs are clearly

1 Adoption (Scotland) Act 1978, s 15(1)(aa), inserted by the Children (Scotland) Act 1995, s 97(2). The Adoption and Children Bill approaches the matter by making it easier for step-parents to acquire parental responsibility: cl 92.

2 Hopkinson *Report*, Pt I, which approached adoption in very positive terms, stressing the urgency of the need to introduce legally-recognised adoption.

3 Tomlin *Report*, para 9, although the contents of paras 4–9 and 11 show that the committee is far from convinced by many of the arguments in favour of the introduction of adoption laws.

4 *Hurst Report* (1954) para 23, *Houghton Report* (1972) paras 15–16.

5 In the Opinion on 'Adoption', *Official Journal* C287/18 at para 1.4.3 the Economic and Social Committee states that it is 'insulting to suspect that their generosity is self-centred and calculating'.

6 S Gair 'Adoptive mothers' attitudes to contact: Highlights from an Australian study' (1999) 23(3) Ad & Fos 38 provides some insight, but further studies in the United Kingdom are necessary.

acknowledged in the various committee reports on adoption[1]. However, the evidence increasingly available from qualitative studies of children cared for outwith the birth family requires us to face the issue of the adult needs in adoption[2].

Nowhere is the adult need for security more evident than in step-parent families. There, parenting already occurs and the motive for the application for adoption must be the desire for parenthood. The alternatives of caring for the child under informal arrangements or regulated by an order short of adoption could be valued more. If valued more by the parent, this would enhance the child's sense of security. However in seeking completeness of the 'family', particularly if there are birth children of the parent and step-parent, the order is sought in name of the security of the child; for example to make the child on equal terms with birth children or to legitimise a change of surname. These formalities could be achieved by testamentary provision, usage and statutory declaration respectively. Surely factors such as these are only pivotal to the child's sense of belonging if they are given that significance by adults. The formalising in law of secure parenting is an adult imperative. That imperative is shaped by laudable values, but they are the values which predicated the introduction of lawful adoption in the very different social climate of the 1920s and 1930s, fuelled by lack of information or cynicism regarding the existence, effectiveness and workability of lesser remedies.

Understanding alternatives

In the case of children looked after by a local authority, the security of adoption as craved by many stem from the reports of others as to what adoption would provide, and success stories of permanence associated with adoption. Children in such a situation are unlikely to be aware of success stories associated with fostering, since those remaining or returning to be looked after will be the counter-examples. They will be associated with the failures of birth parenting or fostering[3]. Children who are looked after, and in many instances their foster families, may crave freedom from the intrusion of local authority social workers and birth parents. Some find the converse, in that support, whether professional, financial or social, is not as accessible as they would want after adoption[4]. Management of the irritation of intrusion is not in itself a convincing reason for following the radical path of adoption. If adoption did not exist, more attention would no doubt have been given to the levels of intrusion, involvement or support that are required in long-term parenting. What is important is the effect that this has on the security of the relationship between the child and the person providing the parenting. Again, surely it is the reaction to the intrusion that causes insecurity and the adults in the child's life could lead by example in reducing the

1 This was openly acknowledged by the Hopkinson and Tomlin Committees, but the latter with some scepticism.

2 S Gair 'Adoptive mothers' attitudes to contact: Highlights from an Australian study' (1999) 23(3) Ad & Fos 38; C Piper 'Assumptions about children's best interest' (2000) 22 JSWFL 261.

3 In the debate on adoption review in the Scottish Parliament Dorothy Grace Elder MSP vividly recounts failure stories involving looked-after children '. . . with their noses pressed to the windows . . .' from this '. . . age in which a feckless parent can still stop a child from being liberated into adoption by someone who would really care for them': *Scottish Parliament Official Report* vol 11, no 11, cols 1222–1224, 4 April 2001.

4 M Ryburn 'Welfare and Justice in Post-Adoption Contact' [1997] Fam Law 28; K Challand 'Calling for post-adoption monitoring and support: a personal statement' (2000) 24(4) Ad & Fos 29.

sense of insecurity or impermanence. Crucially, would they be more willing to feel secure with a less radical order if indeed there was no adoption available in the range of possibilities for care planning?

The following quotation from the Department of Health website on adoption gives a somewhat incomplete summary of the law to the person interested in adoption:

> 'It is the fundamental right of every child to belong to a family; this principle underpins the 1989 United Nations Convention on the Rights of the Child . . . Where children cannot live with their birth families, for whatever reason, society has a duty to provide them with a fresh start and where appropriate a permanent alternative home. Adoption is one means of giving children the opportunity to start again . . . Adoption is not an option of last resort; to regard it as such is a failure to understand the nature of adoption and its advantages for a child unable to live with his own family'[1].

As discussed in the previous section, positive non-critical images and messages about adoption are spread and flourish despite their clear conflict with the reality of today's family relationships, and with domestic law and international convention which does place adoption as a remedy of last resort.

In the present legislative regime in the United Kingdom adoption should not be applied for until alternatives which would be better for the child and less interventionist have been explored. In that exploration of alternatives, how reflective are those adults of actual needs as assessed against the advantages and disadvantages of all possible options? Is long-term fostering considered seriously in placement of children from the care system? Could more security be built into the fostering arrangements[2], or a full range of other orders be explored?[3] Research studies show that children have a greater concern about the continuity of parenting than about the legal status of a carer[4]. Reviews to date fail to argue convincingly that adoption should command such a position based on its internal integrity or on its external effect on the desirability of alternative orders. If the person exercising this parenting role did so under some authority short of adoption such as guardianship or an order for parental responsibilities and rights, this authority would co-exist with the remaining responsibilities of the birth parent curtailed as those are by the positive effects of the authority of the de facto 'parent'. This is the situation under the child legislation currently applying in Scotland and in England, which is permissive and inclusive. However, the permissiveness of the law is not echoed by the attitudes of the persons who steer the decisions made about children, nor indeed is it shared by children themselves. The leading arguments against lesser orders which retain links with birth families are that they will cause confusion for the child, and will involve organisational difficulties in making decisions about care of the child. However these are

1 www.doh.gov.uk/adoption/.

2 Even the Economic and Social Committee advocated this in 1992: *Official Journal*, C287/18 at para 2.16.1. See also S McCracken and I Reilly 'The systemic family approach to foster care assessment' (1998) 22(3) Ad & Fos 16.

3 Custodianship introduced by the Children Act 1975 (effective in 1985) was not a popular process, as it was considered to be 'the poor man's adoption': see C Barton 'Adoption – The Prime Minister's Review' [2000] Fam Law 731 at 735 and C Barton 'Adoption and Children Bill 2001 – Don't let them out of your sight' [2001] Fam Law 431 at 435, where he notes that the process was 'abrogated by the 1989 Act, mainly on the basis of its uncertainty and capacity for conflict'. It could only be so considered against the traditional favouring of adoption.

4 J Feast and D Howe *Adoption, Search and Reunion: The Long Term Experiences of Adopted Adults* (March 2000) The Children's Society.

practical factors which up to a third of children cope with at present as a result of family breakdown and family reordering by remarriage or cohabitation[1].

Extended orders to secure continuity and security of parenting were advocated in the recent white paper on adoption in England, and a form of special guardianship appears in the Adoption and Children Bill[2] which was presented to Parliament in January 2001 but not enacted before Parliament was dissolved for the general election of May 2001. The attempt to create flexibility in the system so that the range of child care orders is expanded has been criticised by some[3], but welcomed by others[4]. None have considered how such orders might work if there was no choice of adoption.

The child's views

Decisions concerning children should not be made without the child being offered the opportunity to express a view[5]. This is enshrined in the UN Convention on the Rights of the Child[6] and in domestic legislation there has been an effort to reinforce the importance of this as a real and recognisable right[7]. In Scotland the right is reflected in the Children (Scotland) Act 1995[8] and in rules of civil procedure[9]. In Scotland a child of 12 or above is required to consent to adoption before the order can be made[10], but is not a party to the proceedings. In England the child's views should be obtained before an order is made, but there is no formal process for obtaining consent[11].

In the white paper of December 2000 there are frequent quotes from children about wanting to be adopted[12]. Ahmed: 'I felt like my life was starting again.' Zoe: 'I felt safer.' There is no doubt these are sincerely held views, but if one were to unpack the adult influences on which those views were predicated, and to educate fully about alternatives and the security that they could provide, would these views be so strong? Jason: 'Try to listen to what we want instead of guessing. You don't know us.' Darren: 'I would have liked to have understood more.' Tellingly, Clare states: 'I wait, I wait, I wait, I wait . . . no news . . . not for five years.' Is it not the case that what these quotes disclose is a lack of communication, education and understanding by adults? As stated above, adoption is well understood in

1 Many also cope in the context of open adoption: see M Sykes 'Adoption with contact: a study of adoptive parents and the impact of continuing contact with the family of origin' (2000) 24(2) Ad & Fos 20.

2 Adoption and Children Bill, cl 94.

3 C Barton 'Adoption and Children Bill 2001 – Don't let them out of your sight' [2001] Fam Law 431 at 435.

4 C Ball 'The White Paper, Adoption: A New Approach, A "curate's egg"' (2001) 25(1) Ad & Fos 6.

5 On this subject generally, see ch 1 above.

6 UN Convention on the Rights of the Child, art 12.

7 C Sawyer 'One step forward, two steps back – the European Convention on the Exercise of Children's Rights' (1999) 11 CFLQ 151.

8 Children (Scotland) Act 1995, s 6 and, re adoption, Adoption (Scotland) Act 1978, s 6(1)(b) & (2) as amended by the Children (Scotland) Act 1995, s 95.

9 For a discussion of the Scottish procedures see M Ross 'Reforms in Family Proceedings in the sheriff court: raising conflicts in civil justice' (1998) 3 *Contemporary Issues in Law* 1.

10 Adoption (Scotland) Act 1978, s 12(8).

11 For interesting discussions on the weight to be given to the views of the child, see M Hayes and C Williams *Family Law: Principles Practice and Policy* (2nd edn 1999) Butterworths, London pp 318–322; Sawyer 'Conflicting rights for children: Implementing welfare, autonomy and justice within family proceedings' (1999) 21 JSWFL 99.

12 Department of Health *Adoption: A New Approach* (Cm 5017, Dec 2000) p 8.

comparison to more permissive and inclusive alternatives. Its tidiness and finality are understandably attractive to a child who has been looked after by the local authority after parenting by birth parents has failed, and fostering arrangements have been unsatisfactory. However, instead of directing efforts to the expansion of adoption, should those efforts not be directed to better inform, to support birth families, to enhance fostering arrangements and expand access to orders short of adoption?

Permanency throughout life

Adoption legislation centres the process upon the welfare of the child. Adoption uniquely creates permanency because it deletes the birth family from the equation. Permanency in care-planning of children came to prominence in the 1980s as a result of the work of certain researchers and commentators on fostering[1], but was overtaken in the 1990s by increasing focus on non-intervention and promoting adult acceptance of responsibilities towards children rather than rights in or to them. Children are now given more details of birth families, particularly when the child is older when adopted, but without contact arrangements or goodwill on the part of adoptive parents there is no legal route for tracing birth family until the adoptive child is an adult. In fact, increasingly there is openness and contact with birth relatives after adoption[2]. The permanence of parenting comes from the adopters but the permanence of identity emanates from birth origins[3]. Is it necessary or indeed reasonable to erase the legal traces of that birth identity?

The starkest example of the tension between permanence, legal parenthood and parenting capacity lies in the Scottish provision prohibiting birth parents after adoption or complete removal of parental responsibilities from seeking any order for parental responsibilities. Until 1995 it was provided by the Law Reform (Parent and Child)(Scotland) Act 1986 that 'any person claiming interest' could seek an order in relation to parental rights in respect of a child[4]. In *D v Grampian Regional Council*[5] a birth mother whose children had been looked after and then freed for adoption applied under that provision for contact with the children. The question of whether it was competent for a person who had had a parental interest erased by freeing for adoption to claim interest under this provision was one which proceeded to the House of Lords. The decision there was that to interpret the provision as broadly as it read would cut across adoption law, and since nothing in the 1986 Act was to have that effect[6] the provision had to be read narrowly, to exclude the birth mother[7]. Parliament resolved any legislative conflict by

1 For example J Tresiliotis 'Identity and security in adoption and long-term fostering' (1983) 7 Ad & Fos 22, J Rowe et al *Long Term Foster Care* (1984) BAAF, London.

2 M Ryburn 'Welfare and Justice in Post-Adoption Contact' [1997] Fam Law 28; M Sykes 'Adoption with contact: a study of adoptive parents and the impact of continuing contact with the family of origin' (2000) 24(2) Ad & Fos 20; Casey and Gibberd 'Adoption and Contact' [2001] Fam Law 39.

3 J Feast and D Howe *Adoption, Search and Reunion: The Long Term Experiences of Adopted Adults* (March 2000) The Children's Society; and see J Feast 'Comment: Adoption and Identity' [2000] Fam Law 287.

4 Law Reform (Parent and Child) (Scotland) Act 1986, s 3(1).

5 *D v Grampian* RC 1995 SCLR 516.

6 Law Reform (Parent and Child) (Scotland) Act 1986, s 9(1).

7 Lord Jauncey opined that an exceptional situation affecting the welfare of a child after adoption could be put to the *nobile officium* of the Court of Session, a power to facilitate an equitable process not otherwise permitted by law. It is questionable whether it could now be used in a situation expressly precluded by law.

providing expressly in the Children (Scotland) Act 1995[1] that a person whose parental responsibilities and rights have been extinguished by adoption[2], or transferred to a relevant agency by a freeing order or a parental responsibility order, is excluded from the range of persons who may seek an order in relation to the child. Accordingly, even if, after adoption, the birth parent has a role in the child's life during childhood, that person is deprived by law of the right to seek an order for parental responsibilities and rights in relation to the child. This is a position unique to a previous parent, although a complete stranger who may have an interest in claiming such parental responsibilities and rights has the competence to apply, and so too has a birth parent who did not previously have parental responsibilities and rights[3]. How can it be justified, applying a dynamic model of child care and family life, that at all times after adoption, any other person claiming an interest will have more legal potential for an award of some form of parental responsibility in respect of the child than the person who was that child's birth parent? This ignores the reality that the birth parent moves on. A parent who was unable due to youth, addiction, or undue influence to provide for the child's needs at a point in the life of child and parent when the adoption-driving still photograph was taken, will be deemed unable to contribute in any way before the child reaches adulthood. This is to compound one legal fiction with another, and in the terms of the legislation itself to ignore the paramountcy of the child's welfare.

Furthermore, this is perversely discriminatory against birth mothers. Much has been written about the discrimination against birth fathers in having no automatic parental responsibilities and rights[4]. This provision has the unexpected effect that if a birth father takes no steps to have responsibilities vested in him by agreement or court order, he retains an interest to seek an order after extinguishment or transfer of the rights of the birth mother. A birth mother who invariably has automatic parental responsibilities will not have this option. It could be argued that this is a reasonable procedural safeguard for the birth father who did not have an automatic right of intimation in adoption proceedings, but equally it could give rise to a situation more perverse than that which the House of Lords had to consider when interpreting the earlier statutory conflict.

Domestic permanence, an unrealistic benchmark when applied to many family situations, is assumed to be created by the legal permanence of adoption. Neither is more than an ideal in today's family dynamics; but does the law of adoption follow or attempt to set that dynamic? It may not seem unreasonable to use adoption to aim for the ideal; however the problem appears to lie in the fact that one assumes that the ideal justifies the legal severance from birth identity. Rather, as the preceding discussion demonstrates, the ideal and the preference for severance should be tested against the evidence and ethics of the new century.

1 Children (Scotland) Act 1995, s 11(3)(a)(iii) and (4).
2 Or an order under the Human Fertilisation and Embryology Act 1990: 1995 Act, s 11(4)(c).
3 Children (Scotland) Act 1995, s 11(3)(a)(i).
4 A recent example is J Eekelaar 'Rethinking Parental Responsibility' [2001] Fam Law 427. In Scotland see E Sutherland 'Parental responsibilities and rights agreements: better half a loaf than none at all?' 1998 SPLQ 3(4) 265–277; and see generally ch 4 above.

EVIDENCE AND ETHICS

Quantitative and qualitative evidence

The numbers of adoptions sought are not large. They have fallen in the latter part of the twentieth century but appear to have levelled out in recent years[1]. Traditionally the reasons given are that there are fewer unwanted pregnancies, that there is better support for single parents and the increased availability of assisted reproduction for childless couples. Elevating the welfare of the child to paramount rather than first consideration, and principles of minimum intervention, do not appear to have had a significant effect in themselves, since there is no significant difference in numbers following their introduction in Scotland.

It is not likely that the numbers of adoptions will continue to decline to the extent that the process becomes totally moribund, particularly when at the turn of this new century adoption achieved an injection of interest. This can be seen in terms of media coverage and policy initiatives – all geared towards preserving the integrity of adoption, and reinforcing its quality as an option for care planning. In its study of adoption in 2000 the Performance and Innovation Unit of the Cabinet Office had been asked by the Prime Minister 'to address whether there should be more use of adoption as an option for looked after children'. In the report that followed, the Unit noted, albeit after a survey that they described as 'impressionistic', that, particularly in the 1980s, adoption was not used as widely as it might have been as an option for permanence for a child being looked after by a care agency[2]. The Unit highlighted policy incentives to adoption in the form of the 'Quality Protects' programme with its 'aim of returning adoption to the mainstream of children's services, maximising its use while minimising delay', increased investment in local authorities providing care, and a local authority circular entitled 'Achieving the Right Balance' on adoption practice[3]. The Unit's report contains statistical data surrounding the use of adoption, and its timing for children in relation to periods of being looked after and ages when placed for adoption. Such data is gathered systematically and is easily presented in a discussion of this sort. Presented in the context of this idealistic report it paints a picture of delay for the child before adoption is considered or arranged. This is presented as a bad aspect of care planning, proceeding on the assumption that adoption should not be a course of last resort[4]. Data about social and educational development of looked-after children as compared to adopted children is often produced to encourage adoption[5] but if adoption was not available, instead would there be greater investment in ensuring that children have a better experience than at present while looked after or in fostering?

Qualitative data is much more scarce than the quantitative. The Performance and Innovation Unit report points to a number of publications in which adoption

1 Averaging 450 per annum in Scotland over the period 1997–99 (see www.scotland.gov.uk/stats/educ.htm) and 3,962 for England and Wales in 1999, falling from 4,387 in 1998 (see www.statistics.gov.uk.) 2,200 of the annual figures adopted in England and Wales during that period were adopted from care: see PIU report, para 2.4.

2 PIU Report, para 2.12.

3 (1998) 20.

4 www.doh.gov.uk/adoption/intro.htm.

5 Scottish Parliament Official Report vol 11, no 11, cols 1185–1234, 4 April 2001; PIU report, ch 2; *Adoption: A New Approach* (Cm 5017, Dec 2000) ch 2.

is considered in comparison to reintegration with the birth family[1]. It does not point to any data about the use of adoption in comparison to other options for caring outwith the birth family. Surveys are carried out into experiences of adoption and experiences of foster or residential care, but the respective outcomes are not compared. Even less available or viable is the comparison of outcomes linked to individual cases, since each child is different even among sibling groups. It is understandable that for an individual child the respective options cannot be assessed directly, and that decisions about an individual child cannot be altered because of adverse research findings, but such findings are vital nonetheless to dynamic planning of child care strategies and laws.

Recently there have been valuable publications following upon some qualitative analysis of the experiences of those in adoptive and fostered care. Interestingly for those who have experience of long-term foster families, the parenting has been secure and many of the perceived difficulties relate to the requirement for local authorities and birth parents to be consulted on many decisions about the child. However these practical difficulties which can undermine the security of foster parenting can be addressed by reviewing the nature of fostering arrangements rather than driving parties towards the 'statutory guillotine'[2] of adoption. Recent research into tracing of birth parents reveals that the adopted person seeks to establish identity, not to challenge the integrity of the relationship with the adopters and their parenting[3]. In fact the desire not to challenge the adoptive relationship can act as an inhibitor to open searching for a birth parent[4].

The ethical balance

In the enthusiasm for secure, easy-to-understand adoption the ethics of it as a remedy, and as a process, are rarely examined[5]. Ethics require balancing of risks and benefits. In considering whether adoption is ethically appropriate in this new century, some thoughts on balances of transparency and abandonment, responsibilities and rights, autonomies and stereotypical assumptions, are offered.

Transparency and abandonment

Adoption procedure has promoted opaqueness[6] by putting barriers between birth families and adopters. The most blatant example of this is the freeing-for-adoption procedure, which creates a hiatus in parenthood in order to dissect the issue of severance of birth parentage where this is expected to be contested or problematic, from the positive establishment of new parentage by adoption. This opaqueness is a relic of the secrecy associated with adoption in the past, and of

1 *Adoption: A New Approach* (Cm 5017, Dec 2000) notes to ch 2.
2 New Zealand Law Commission *Adoption and Its Alternatives: A Different Approach and a New Framework (*Report no 65, Sept 2000) para 29.
3 J Feast and D Howe *Adoption, Search and Reunion: The Long Term Experiences of Adopted Adults* (March 2000) The Children's Society; and see Feast 'Comment: Adoption and Identity' [2000] Fam Law 287.
4 H Roche and A Perlesz 'A legitimate choice and voice: the experience of adult adoptees who have chosen not to search for their biological families' (2000) 24(2) Ad & Fos 8.
5 M Freundlich and R Phillips examine ethical issues internal to adoption in 'Ethical Issues in Adoption' (2000) 4(4) Ad & Fos 7.
6 On orders for access to information see K Barnett 'Adoption and Confidential Information' [1997] Fam Law 489.

the Chinese walls which local authorities were required to construct when considering plans for children. This disjointed process is both false and contrary to the interests of the child whose welfare will be best served by the sharing of knowledge and expertise in the planning and decision-making process. In child care practice, secrecy is breaking down and the freeing-for-adoption process has in some localities all but collapsed due to unpopularity, delay, and the difficulty of satisfying the welfare test in granting an order if there are no prospective adopters identified[1]. Proposals for shared decision-making about adoption involving birth families and prospective adopters have been aired for some years[2]. In America there is extensive literature, statute, experience and research into the practice of 'cooperative adoption'[3] which reveals the success of involvement in an open approach to adoption[4]. In New Zealand the practice of open adoption has been encouraged[5], and in reality in the United Kingdom many adopted children do maintain links with biological relatives[6]. Adoption law recognises that an order for contact can be made within the adoption process[7], but the instances in which this is done are rare, and the courts have stressed that the circumstances will be exceptional, warranting the continuation of contact for the child's interest rather than that of the relative[8].

In their recent extensive review of adoption law the Law Commission of New Zealand has proposed that there should be discussion of a 'parenting plan' by all interested parties before the court will make the appropriate order regulating parenting[9]. Furthermore that parenting plan would have to be lodged in court. It would deal with broad principles of parenting and contact (if any) rather than detail, and would not be justiciable, but disagreements over it could be referred to mediation[10]. The aim is to ensure that issues such as cultural heritage, genealogy, medical history and links with extended family are openly addressed and ownership of them accepted by those who will be parenting the child. This would

---

1 L Lambert, M Buist, J Tresiliotis and M Hill *Freeing Children in Adoption* (May 1989) Scottish Office Central Research Unit; N Lowe 'Freeing for Adoption – The Experience of the 1980s' 1990 JSWL 220.

2 For example K Wells and P Reshotko 'Cooperative Adoption: An Alternative to Independent Adoption' (1986) 65 *Child Welfare* 177; M Ryburn 'Openness in Adoption' (1990) 14(1) Ad & Fos 21; Lindley 'Adoption Law Review 1: Placement Orders: FRG's Proposals' [1994] Fam Law 326. Even the *Hurst Report* in 1954 at para 22 advocated openness in adoption.

3 For example M Rillera and S Kaplan 'Cooperative Adoption: A Handbook' (1985) Triadoption; J Etter 'Levels of Cooperation and Satisfaction in 56 Open Adoptions' (1993) 72 *Child Welfare* 257.

4 J Etter 'Levels of Cooperation and Satisfaction in 56 Open Adoptions' (1993) 72 *Child Welfare* 257; A Appell 'The Move Toward Legally Sanctioned Cooperative Adoption: Can it Survive the Uniform Adoption Act?' (1996) 30 *FLQ* 483. For a more cautious view see M Berry 'The Effects of Open Adoption on Biological and Adoptive Parents: The Arguments and the Evidence' (1993) 72 *Child Welfare* 257.

5 M Ryburn 'Openness in Adoption' (1990) 14(1) Ad & Fos 21; C Bridge 'Changing the nature of adoption: law reform in England and New Zealand' (1993) 13 *Legal Studies* 81.

6 J Fratter *Adoption with Contact* (1997) BAAF, London; M Ryburn 'Welfare and Justice in Post-Adoption Contact' [1997] Fam Law 28; D Casey and A Gibberd 'Adoption and Contact' [2001] Fam Law 39.

7 By virtue of a condition on the adoption order: Adoption Act 1976, s 12(6), Adoption (Scotland) Act 1978, s 12(6).

8 *Re C (A minor) (Adoption Order:Conditions)* [1988] 2 FLR 159; *Re T A Minor (Adoption: Contact Order)* [1995] 2 FLR 251; *K Petr* (unreported), discussed at (1994) 12 Fam Law Bull 2.

9 *Adoption and Its Alternatives: A Different Approach and a New Framework* (Report no 65, Sept 2000) para 106ff.

10 Mediation is commonly used in certain US states to manage co-operative adoption: see J Etter 'Levels of Cooperation and Satisfaction in 56 Open Adoptions' (1993) 72 *Child Welfare* 257; A Appell 'The Move Toward Legally Sanctioned Cooperative Adoption: Can it Survive the Uniform Adoption Act?' (1996) 30 FLQ 483.

give particular assistance in cross-cultural situations, a matter given considerable attention in the New Zealand report, but also of concern in the United Kingdom[1].

Critics might say that such a suggestion is idealistic, confusing and unworkable without unexpected goodwill on all parts. Of course there will be difficult cases, but within the relatively small number of adoption applications there are not sufficient numbers to justify the general existence of the brutally opaque and transplantative remedy of adoption. It is for those involved in organising the process to foster goodwill by a positive attitude to the joint process of planning for parenting. There is research evidence that this can work very effectively[2]. This planning would certainly help to break down the still image of abandonment, severance and assumption that child adoption brings to mind, which in itself is damaging for the child concerned. The positive image of security with the adopters is contrasted with a negative image of physical abandonment by the birth parent, adding to the 'legal' abandonment which adoption requires[3].

The trigger for some adoption plans is neglect or abuse by a natural parent. The decisions about looking after the child and in turn the decision to dispense with agreement of a birth parent focus on circumstances prevailing at the time, like a flip book of still photographs taken over a period in the child's life. The child's life is chaotic as a result, and stability, followed by permanency, is presumptively necessary[4]. But when the moving picture over that child's whole life is reviewed it might have very different story lines or endings. In law, are we happy to accept that if a child is orphaned after adoption the only person who cannot possibly have an interest to apply then to have a part in that child's life is the child's birth parent? The Romans in their wholly property-driven adoption model at least acknowledged that the process was fallible and might, in some circumstances, be undone.

Responsibilities and rights

When child care law in the United Kingdom moved towards the paramountcy of child welfare and the expression of parental responsibilities as a foundation for rights rather than vice versa, commentators spoke of the change of mind-set that this would require[5]. In the context of private law orders in family proceedings and in care proceedings that change of mind-set has been apparent. There is less evidence for this change in the context of adoption. Looking at literature on planning for adoption it is clear that care managers are encouraged to consider all alternatives before embarking on an adoption plan[6], but there is also research evidence that adoption is considered too late for young children who have been the subject of unsatisfactory or neglectful parenting[7].

1 PIU report, ch 2, box headed 'Key messages from research': *Adoption: A New Approach* (Cm 5017, Dec 2000) para 6.5; *Adoption: Procedure and Practice: A Guide for Adoption Agencies in Scotland* (2001) BAAF, London ch 2.

2 For example M Sykes 'Adoption with contact: a study of adoptive parents and the impact of continuing contact with the family of origin' (2000) 24(2) Ad & Fos 20.

3 M Ryburn 'Welfare and Justice in Post-Adoption Contact' [1997] Fam Law 28 at 36–37.

4 On our reliance upon assumptions rather than evidence concerning children, see C Piper 'Assumptions about children's best interest' (2000) 22 JSWFL 261.

5 For example C Sawyer 'Conflicting rights for children: Implementing welfare, autonomy and justice within family proceedings' (1999) 21 JSWFL 99.

6 For example *Adoption: Procedure and Practice: A Guide for Adoption Agencies in Scotland* (2001) BAAF, London ch 3.

7 PIU report, ch 3.

The proposed New Zealand model requires parenting plans to be considered by all parties, before a decision is made as to what will be best for the child from a spectrum of orders ranging from non-intervention, to a process akin to adoption. A process of this sort sets adoption in its proper place in child care law. It emphasises that adoption is not a separate process which is driven by adult needs rather than the child's needs. Interestingly the New Zealand Law Commission was attracted to the terms of the Children (Scotland) Act 1995 as a model of expression of this spectrum (although that Act does not include adoption as such in that spectrum, deferring to the separate regime in the Adoption (Scotland) Act 1978 where different tests and definitions apply).

Since the last round of legislation on child care in the United Kingdom the issue of rights has gained enormously in significance as a result of the incorporation into domestic law of the main elements of the European Convention on Human Rights[1]. That Convention was negotiated to restrict the encroachment upon fundamental human rights and freedoms such as had taken place during World War II. Whilst the United Kingdom ratified the Convention in 1951, little use was made of it in domestic courts. In their interpretation of legislation the English courts were quicker to have regard to the Convention[2] than the Scottish courts[3]. Breaches of Convention rights in cases emanating from the United Kingdom were noted by the European Court of Human Rights, and some of these had an effect on the secrecy prevailing then in family proceedings[4]. However the incorporation of Convention rights into domestic law and thus domestic proceedings allows the courts to have regard to those rights in making decisions on procedure and merits, and enables the higher courts to pronounce upon whether an act or omission of a public authority, including the courts or the legislature, complies with Convention rights.

Accordingly, in the context of adoption there is now the need to view Convention rights alongside the parental responsibilities and paramountcy of welfare[5]. Whilst the obvious focus of those rights is the child, the parent too has rights to family life, privacy and fair trial in adoption proceedings (including the pre-court stages of such proceedings). The right to a fair trial is absolute (although proportionality applies to the elements of that right set out in the Convention or identified in jurisprudence)[6] but the remaining rights are not absolute and processes which are designed to interfere with those rights on merit grounds are permitted[7]. However the process itself should ensure equality of arms[8]. In adoption procedures as they currently stand there is certainly not a transparent equality of arms. Access to material which informs decisions of adoption panels, preceded often by fostering panels, and courts is not available to all interested parties[9], which would include,

---

1 Human Rights Act 1998.

2 *R v Home Secretary, ex p Brind* [1991] AC 696.

3 *Kaur v Lord Advocate* 1981 SLT 322. It was eventually used first in an adoption case: *T Petr* 1997 SLT 724.

4 *McMichael v UK* (1995) 20 EHHR 205.

5 For a discussion of the impact of human rights legislation on the welfare principle, see J Herring 'The Human Rights Act and the welfare principle in family law – conflicting or complementary?' (1999) 11 CFLQ 223.

6 *Brown v Stott* [2001] 2 All ER 97; 2001 SC 43; 2001 HRLR 9.

7 As in *Soderback v Sweden* (2000) 29 EHRR 95; (1998) HRCD 958 (ECHR).

8 *Neumeister v Austria No 1* (1979–80) 1 EHRR 91; *Edwards v United Kingdom* (1993) 15 EHRR 417.

9 For a review of an open and inclusionary project, see S Pepys and J Dix 'Inviting applicants, birth parents and young people to attend adoption panel: How it works in practice' (2000) 24(4) Ad & Fos 40.

in its widest sense, all birth parents, persons claiming an interest in the future parenting of the child, and, not least, the child himself or herself. The right of a child over age 12 to consent to adoption in Scotland is an empty right if the child is not availed of the information that enables the right to be exercised. The same can be said of a birth parent who is not permitted to know what the adoption plans are for the child[1], for example whether this will involve the maintenance of birth family traditions or culture.

The right to family life[2] and to found a family[3] are by no means absolute. In deciding whether the right to family life has been breached the court must first consider what a family is, and views this largely as a matter of fact rather than law[4]. Accordingly there can be family life between parties who are unmarried[5] and their children[6] and between adults and children who have a genetic connection provided that is followed by residence or contact, the degree of which will affect whether there was family life[7]. The overt failure of adoption procedure to involve those who may have an interest in preserving family life with the child, unless that person meets the limited definition of 'parent' applying for the purposes of the Adoption legislation, must surely be open to challenge. So too must the process of freeing for adoption whereby the order for freeing intentionally dismantles a family (albeit an unsatisfactory family life) without replacing it *at that time* with another.

These examples illustrate the problems of the compatibility of adoption with human rights. It is not difficult to imagine that if there is a challenge on human rights grounds to an aspect of adoption, the traditional protective approach to the inherent 'goodness' of adoption would ensure that, at most, the procedure would be adjusted to render it overtly compatible. However, if one is to take a truly critical view of adoption, the incompatibilities with fundamental rights should add to the evidence against its continuation in its present form.

Autonomies and assumptions

As discussed in the first section of this chapter, there is a complex interaction of factors involved in the creation of security in the family setting which is to be the child's main source of parenting[8]. The child's autonomy is reflected in the requirement to have regard to the child's views. The autonomy of birth parents is reflected in the requirement to obtain parental agreement to adoption or to dispense with it if the parents are unmeritorious in their refusal or in conduct. The autonomy of de facto parents is not obvious, and it is often in a desire for that autonomy that an application for adoption is made. The adopter's autonomy originates in the power to apply. Autonomy is valued and acknowledged within the process but cannot determine it – of necessity there has to be a balance in which some of the preferred autonomy is relinquished or curtailed. The adoption process imposes the distribution of autonomies, but a preferable model would be

1 *Keegan v Ireland* (1994) 18 EHRR 342.
2 European Convention on Human Rights, art 8.
3 European Convention on Human Rights, art 12.
4 *K v UK* (1986) 50 DR 199.
5 *Berrehab v Netherlands* (1988) 11 EHRR 322.
6 *Johnston v Ireland* (1987) 9 EHRR 203.
7 *K v UK* (1986) 50 DR 199, *Kroon v Netherlands* (1995) 19 EHRR 263.
8 C Sawyer 'Conflicting rights for children: Implementing welfare, autonomy and justice within family proceedings' (1999) 21 JSWFL 99.

one which focused on negotiated adjustment, which has as its focus the welfare of the child, but acknowledges the imperatives of all of those who are linked to the child's origins and upbringing. An inclusive approach which emphasises the added value of a child's links with more than one family underlies the system of child care law, but is not evident at all in adoption.

The autonomy of a person providing parenting to apply for adoption is however curtailed by the definition of who may adopt. In both England and Scotland only a married couple or a single person may apply[1]. It has often been suggested that an unmarried couple who on the merits of application of the test for adoption are suitable, should be competent applicants[2], but this is not taken up in the Adoption and Children Bill. It has been acknowledged in recent years that an individual, albeit known to be living in a couple and intending to bring the child up in that household, is a competent adopter[3], but why does the law continue to prevent a cohabiting partner from joining in the application?

The answer seems to lie in stereotypes and an assumption that adoption must adhere to the stereotypical assumption of the 'family' as it emerges in the book of Genesis. It would be untenable then to create by the fiction of adoption a certificated adoptive family that could not be achieved by the presumptive parentage of a married couple or by single parent, regardless of the much increased natural incidence of parenting outwith marriage. We acknowledge that two married parents are better than one in the average step-parent adoption; even where the child has two known, living birth parents. Non-intervention is the norm in family proceedings in general, yet why are we so willing to intervene in such a dramatic way to realign families[4] but only in accordance with the historical family norm?

It is submitted that the way forward in recognising the diversity of families from those stereotypes is not to extend adoption to allow for applications to be made by unmarried couples. This would surely compound and prolong the static effect of adoption. Does the creation of ties with two unmarried persons by adoption justify the erasure of birth ties any more so than the current model of adoption? The only positive legal effect is to create extended rights of succession, to counteract the loss of rights of succession with birth family.

If the arguments in this chapter are accepted, succession stands alone as the legal factor justifying the retention of adoption orders, although it was one of the main stumbling blocks to its acceptance into the statute law of the United Kingdom[5]. That is perhaps unsurprising since it was the aim for which adoption was first conceived in ancient legal systems. It is clear however that adoption is no longer essential for the regulation of succession. Freedom of testation is now much more extensive in the United Kingdom than it was when adoption was

---

1 Adoption Act 1976, ss 14 and 15; Adoption (Scotland) Act 1978, ss 14 and 15.

2 M Ross 'Attitudes to Sexual Orientation in Adoption Law' (1997) 1 *Edin LR* 370; C Ball 'The White Paper, Adoption: A New Approach, A "curate's egg"' (2001) 25(1) Ad & Fos 6. See generally ch 7, below.

3 In *Re AB (Adoption: Joint Residence)* [1996] 1 FLR 27 the court could grant the order only in favour of one cohabitant but made a joint residence order. In *T Petr* 1997 SLT 724 the homosexual applicant was living with a partner, but on appeal against refusal of the adoption the court focused on the welfare test. See K Norrie 'Parental Pride, Adoption and the Gay Man' 1996 SLT (News) 321; M Ross 'Attitudes to Sexual Orientation in Adoption Law' (1997) 1 *Edin LR* 370.

4 J Masson, D Norbury and S Chatterton, *Mine, Yours or Ours? A study of step-parent adoption* (1983) HMSO in ch 9 question the future for step-parent adoption.

5 J Tresiliotis 'Adoption – evolution or revolution' written in 1995 and reproduced in M Hill and M Shaw (eds) *Signposts in Adoption* (1998) BAAF, London.

introduced into legislation, and inheritance is no longer linked to legitimacy. In any event laws governing succession are the correct means by which to regulate this, rather than creating legally fictitious families.

CONCLUSION

Adoption laws are a feature of the twentieth century. They are a mere three generations old, assuming a generation to be 25 years, roughly equal to the periodic reform of adoption law[1]. The range and flexibility of alternative orders now available bears no relation to the situation when adoption was introduced and in the intervening years. Yet, over that period adoption has continued in favour. Alternative orders are perceived to cause confusion or inhibit decision-making in relation to a child. Enhancing understanding, and training in how to access and use informal arrangements, with or without an order to regulate them, is crucial to the acceptance of alternatives. There is a current no-win situation where the attraction of alternatives *may* lead to the death of adoption, but perhaps adoption needs to be killed off to turn attention to the strengths of the alternatives.

The aim of the remedy that adoption was intended to be when introduced was to empower the child and secure parenting throughout childhood but also to enhance opportunities for identity and relationships in adulthood. At present adoption is too often sought in order to address inadequacies of parenting or untidiness of parenthood in the short term. The still image has grown in attraction to counteract difficult questions of whether an abusive, addicted or simply distant parent may in the future be an asset or liability to a child, physically or emotionally. But to airbrush out the objectively unpleasant or unreliable is to ignore and deny the importance of subjective influences upon identity and completeness. To impose a still image of post-adoptive harmony is to further undermine identity. The picture for any child, whether being parented by kin or non-kin, is a moving one, and any legal means of securing it must provide scope for editing and re-recording of imperatives. The images emerging through recent reviews make a strong case for security of family. To promise that security through the process of adoption is wholly unrealistic and unfair to children and adults. Adults owe it to children who require such security to bring our ideas up to date: to put away adoption with the sepia photographs typical of its statutory birth, and to join with the children in that vital present-day pursuit of making the video work.

1 C Ball 'The White Paper, Adoption: A New Approach, A "curate's egg"' (2001) 25(1) Ad & Fos 6.

6 Marriage and Cohabitation

Eric Clive

INTRODUCTION

This chapter is concerned with marriage and heterosexual cohabitation[1]. The focus is on questions of legal policy, within the sphere of private law rather than public law. Should a modern law regulate marriage and cohabitation and, if so, how? One way of approaching the issue is to ask what rules a modern civil code, perhaps a Scottish civil code or a European civil code[2], should contain on marriage and heterosexual cohabitation. This helps to draw attention to anomalous and discriminatory elements in the existing law which may be taken for granted, simply because they are there, but which would not deserve a place in a newly restructured law.

MARRIAGE

To regulate or not?

It would be logically and theoretically possible to say nothing about marriage in a modern civil code[3]. The justification would be that there is no strong public interest in the living arrangements or consensual sexual arrangements of competent adults. If two or more adult people choose to live together that is their concern. If they choose to have sexual intercourse together in private on a regular and more or less exclusive basis, or not to do so, that is also their concern.

There is an obvious public interest in the circumstances, including the nature of the relationships, in which people bring up children[4]. However, for the state to attempt to regulate natural child-bearing would give rise to such sensitive issues and such concerns about human rights that, beyond the area covered by the traditional laws on underage unions and incest, the theoretical public interest is not

1 Same sex relationships are dealt with in ch 7 below.

2 These are live issues. The author of this chapter is currently working on a scheme for a Scottish civil code or, perhaps more practicable, for a series of Acts restructuring branches of Scottish civil law. At the European level a lot of work has already been done on parts of a draft European civil code by a group under the leadership of Professor Christian von Bar of Osnabrück University. Family law is not, however, yet on the agenda of this group.

3 See E Clive 'Marriage: An Unnecessary Legal Concept?' in J Eekelaar and S Katy (eds) *Marriage and Cohabitation in Contemporary Societies* (1980) Butterworths, Toronto 71.

4 This public interest is clearly reflected in the laws on adoption, fostering and child-minding.

a practical one. In practical terms, therefore, if two adults choose to have a child together that must also be regarded as their concern.

Any public interest in regulating sexual conduct and conduct within intimate relationships can be met without creating and regulating a legal status of marriage. Potentially fertile sexual intercourse between closely related people can be regulated by the criminal law on incest. Potentially harmful sexual relations with young people can also be dealt with by the criminal law. Abusive conduct within intimate relationships can be dealt with without having a legal status of marriage. Rape and non-consensual sexual conduct generally can be dealt with by the criminal law. Assault and harassment, and similar types of injurious conduct, would also be dealt with primarily by the criminal law, as would theft and criminal damage to or interference with property. Those living on a long-term basis in a dwelling house with the permission of the owner or occupier could be protected against sudden eviction. The law on unjustified enrichment could be used to bring about fair results in cases where one party had gained at the expense of the other, without any legal cause or public policy justification, as a result of a relationship which had led to an economic imbalance. The protection and welfare of children could be dealt with by the criminal and civil laws, including laws on child support and aliment, without regard to whether the parents were married. The rules on intestate succession, and any other rules which give a preference to a spouse or surviving spouse, could use criteria based on strength and closeness of relationship, without using tests based on marriage or cohabitation as such. Various rules of public law, including rules of tax law and social security law, could concentrate on individuals rather than couples.

There would be advantages in such an approach. It would be more precisely directed at the actual problems[1]. There would be equality as between different types of living arrangements and relationships. Heterosexual couples would be treated in the same way regardless of whether or not they had gone through particular forms of ceremony. Same-sex couples, and three- or more-partner households, would be treated in the same way as heterosexual couples. All rules would be function-based rather than status-based. Choices of living arrangements would be less likely to be distorted by legal rules[2]. The law could be simplified quite considerably. There would not, for example, have to be any marriage law or any divorce law.

But, for all purposes other than speculative theory, we can forget this option for the time being. People expect their legal system to reflect their most important traditional views and customs. People would misunderstand the policy. To have no legal concept of marriage would not, of course, imply any devaluing of mutually supportive, lifelong, loving, cohabiting relationships or any assumption that, other things being equal, such relationships did not provide the best environment for bringing up children. It would not in any way restrict the freedom of

---

1 If a type of conduct or a type of problem can occur regardless of whether two people are married, a regulation expressed in terms of marriage is going to be an incomplete and unsatisfactory solution. This is the fundamental objection to the EU Council Regulation No 1347/2000 of May 2000 which regulates jurisdiction, choice of law and recognition and enforcement of judgments relating to the custody etc of children but only in the context of matrimonial proceedings. It is obvious that the same problems can arise outside matrimonial proceedings.

2 For example, incentives resulting from the law on income support to avoid a public commitment to living together as a couple would disappear.

churches and religious groups of all kinds to have their own rules and ceremonies on marriage for their own adherents. But this would not be understood. Many people would see the deliberate omission of rules on marriage and divorce from a new civil code as an attack on, or as a contemptuous dismissal of, traditional family and religious values. Politicians would not want to get into arguments on this point for no good reason.

There is also the European Convention on Human Rights. Article 12 provides that 'Men and women of marriageable age have the right to marry and to found a family, according to the national laws governing the exercise of this right'. The European Court on Human Rights has held that a Swiss law which had the effect of preventing certain people from marrying for a period of from one to three years after their divorce contravened this article[1]. It is probably safe to assume that a national law which precluded legal marriage altogether would also contravene it. Article 12 reflects the values of the 1940s. A more modern formulation might be framed in a different way. But, for the foreseeable future, art 12 exists in its traditional form and constitutes a barrier to radical reform.

For all practical purposes it can, therefore, be assumed that a modern civil code would include rules on marriage. There are functional advantages in having a legal concept of marriage. One is that it enables the law and the state to give its backing to a public commitment by the two parties to an important type of personal relationship – not the only important type of personal relationship but certainly one important type. Another advantage is that marriage provides a convenient pointer to certain legal results in situations where speed and certainty of decision-making are considered more important than just and refined solutions. The classic example is the law of intestate succession. In many cases 'Who is the surviving spouse?' provides the solution quickly and easily. A more refined question such as 'Who is the person whom the deceased would have wished to inherit?' might provide a better solution but only at the cost of delay, difficulty and dispute.

The extent to which marriage as a convenient pointer corresponds to marriage as an acceptable pointer depends to some extent on the availability and use of the law on divorce[2]. If broken marriages were not regularly tidied up by divorce there would be an unacceptably large number of cases where the legal spouse would not be the appropriate recipient of benefits or the appropriate subject of special rules. Divorces keep the concept of marriage healthy, just as wolves keep the herds of caribou healthy. The utility of marriage as a legal concept depends on the widespread use of divorce to dissolve broken marriages.

The fact that any civil code would contain rules on marriage does not, however, mean that there will not be a steady move towards a more functional approach to various legal problems. Policy makers are bound to ask 'If we need these rules for marriage why do we not also need them for similar situations outside marriage?' The recent history in Scotland of powers of arrest for breach of interdicts against abuse provides an instructive example. A change in the law in 1981 enabled powers of arrest to be attached to certain types of interdict to be known as 'matrimonial interdicts'[3]. The policy was to make interdicts against domestic violence or harassment more effective by enabling the police to arrest

1 *F v Switzerland* ECHR 18 Dec 1987 (Series A No 128) (10 EHRR 411).
2 It also depends to some extent on the frequency and nature of cohabitation outside marriage.
3 Matrimonial Homes (Family Protection) (Scotland) Act 1981, ss 14–17.

any person breaching the interdict. The benefit was intended primarily for spouses but was extended to a very limited class of cohabitants, defined as couples of opposite sex living together as husband and wife. It quickly became apparent that there were major gaps in the protection provided. Divorced women often needed protection and yet did not qualify. Not all heterosexual cohabitants qualified for protection and no same-sex partners did. In 1992 the Scottish Law Commission therefore recommended extensions[1]. These would have been useful but they still started from a status-based approach. The assumption was that the problem was one faced by spouses or ex-spouses and heterosexual cohabitants or former cohabitants. When the Justice and Home Affairs Committee of the new Scottish Parliament looked at this question in 1999 and heard evidence from different individuals and groups with experience of the problems, it concluded that the problem was quite general. The difficulty that an interdict against abuse might be ineffective if not backed up by a power of arrest was one faced by any person who had obtained such an interdict. The Committee therefore proposed a general, function-based approach. Anyone who had obtained an interdict against abuse should be able to apply for a power of arrest to be attached and the court should be able to attach such a power if satisfied that it was necessary to prevent abuse[2]. The Committee's proposal has now been implemented[3]. Within 20 years the policy had changed from a limited, status-based policy to a wide, function-based policy. There are other problems which would benefit from a similar development in thinking.

Definition

The traditional definition of marriage in terms of a union of one man and one woman, to the exclusion of all others, for life begs questions about the nature of the union[4] and is clearly inaccurate in relation to duration[5]. It also covers only monogamous marriages. From the strictly legal point of view the essence of marriage now is that it is a legal relationship between a man and a woman[6] who have made a commitment in a ceremony of an approved type, or in some other legally recognised way[7], to enter there and then into a relationship known as marriage and who have not subsequently been divorced. In most cases the relationship will be potentially cohabiting, potentially sexual, potentially child-producing and potentially lifelong, but these aspects are not essential. Two mentally competent 99-year-olds in separate nursing homes who could not cohabit, have

---

1 *Report on Family Law* (Scot Law Com no 135, 1992) paras 11.30–11.52.

2 *Proposal for a Protection from Abuse Bill,* (Scottish Parliament, Justice and Home Affairs Committee, 9th Report, 2000).

3 The Protection from Abuse (Scotland) Act 2001. The Bill for this act was the first to be promoted by a committee in the new Scottish Parliament.

4 For example, a business partnership is not a marriage even if it is between a man and a woman for the period of their joint lives and excludes the assumption of any additional partner.

5 Marriages need not be for life. Many are not.

6 This is the traditional view of marriage, reflected in the European Convention on Human Rights, art 12. See eg *Rees v United Kingdom* ECHR 17 Oct 1986 (Series A No 106) (9 EHRR 56); *Sheffield and Horsham v United Kingdom* ECHR 30 July 1998 (27 EHRR 163). It could, of course, change in the future.

7 These words are included to cover informal marriages such as the Scottish marriage by cohabitation with habit and repute or the American common law marriage.

sexual intercourse or produce children could enter into a valid marriage. A couple who had the firm intention to obtain a divorce if their relationship deteriorated significantly could marry. In most cases the commitment to marriage will involve a commitment not to have sexual intercourse with anyone other than the spouse (or spouses, in the case of a polygamous marriage) but this is not essential either. Two highly promiscuous people, who had no intention of changing their ways, could lawfully marry. So marriage might be defined as 'a subsisting legal relationship between a man and a woman who have gone through a legally approved marriage ceremony, or the legally recognised equivalent, with each other'.

This is insubstantial and circular[1] and it does not say anything about how long a marriage subsists. If you did not know what marriage normally was in a social sense you would not be much the wiser. Notwithstanding this, the definition does have advantages apart from accuracy. It is the formalistic nature of marriage as a legal concept which makes it useful for legal purposes. If you want to know whether a couple were married to each other at any time you do not need to ask potentially difficult questions about the factual nature of their relationship[2]. You just need to ask whether they got married and stayed married.

There is no need to define marriage for the purposes of a civil code and, given the rather vacuous nature of any reasonably accurate definition, it would probably be better not to attempt to do so. In the general part of a civil code, marriage could be given as an example of a legal relationship but that is probably as much as would be necessary or desirable from the point of view of definition.

Restrictions on marriage

Given that people can cohabit and have sexual relations if they wish to, subject to the laws on incest and underage sexual intercourse, there is little point nowadays in having extensive restrictions on who can marry each other. Nonetheless a few restrictions are justifiable.

If the main reason for having a legal concept of marriage at all is respect for a valued traditional institution with a long history and, for many people, powerful emotional and religious overtones, then it would clearly be politically difficult to depart from the traditional requirement that the parties must be of different sexes[3]. This is not to endorse discrimination on the ground of sexual orientation. Indeed there is great force in the argument that if the state recognises and regulates different-sex unions then it ought, as a matter of simple humanity and sound social policy, to recognise and regulate same-sex unions in an essentially similar way. There is value in supporting any public commitment by two people to a lifelong, intimate relationship having as its normal elements cohabitation, companionship and mutual support. It would be both just and convenient to use such a recognised relationship as a pointer to certain legal results in various

1 Marriage results from a marriage ceremony. A marriage ceremony is one where the parties agree to enter there and then into marriage. And so on.

2 Eg were they living together? For how long? Did they have children together? Did they have a sexual relationship together?

3 Note, however, that this formulation, rather than a formulation in terms of a man and a woman, would allow a true hermaphrodite (ie a person who is neither a man nor a woman) to marry anyone other than another hermaphrodite. At present the law is unjustifiably harsh on hermaphrodites.

situations. However, the better, and probably more acceptable[1], way of meeting this policy objective would seem to be by introducing registered partnerships for same-sex couples, as has been done in Denmark and other Scandinavian countries[2], rather than by diluting the traditional concept of marriage. Some traditional institutions can comfortably occupy a place in the law only so long as they are not exposed to excessively radical alteration.

At any rate, for reasons of practical politics, it will be assumed that a new civil code would require the parties to a marriage to be of different sexes.

There is also, for the same reason and for other reasons[3], little to be said in any traditionally monogamous country for departing from the rule that only those who are not already married can marry[4].

It would be necessary to have a minimum age for marriage – probably in the 16 to 18 years range – and to have a requirement of free consent to immediate marriage. Both are necessary to prevent abuse[5].

Some minimal restrictions on marriage between closely related persons, corresponding to the criminal law of incest, would also be justifiable for a mixture of reasons[6], not all convincing in themselves but adding up to a persuasive enough case for the purposes of practical politics. Such restrictions, however, are hard to justify in the case of relationships by affinity.

Formalities

Some legal systems allow only civil marriages. Others allow both civil and religious marriages. In the past some have allowed only religious marriages[7]. There are two important policy considerations. First, the law should respond to

1 For the debate in the US on this question see H Krause 'Marriage for the New Millennium: Heterosexual, Same Sex – Or Not at All' (2000) 34 *Fam LQ* 271–300; and M Dupuis 'The impact of culture, society and history on the legal process: an analysis of the legal status of same-sex relationships in the US and Denmark' (1995) *Int J L & Fam* 86–118.

2 See the Danish Registered Partnership Act 1989 (Act No 372 of 7 June 1989 as amended by Act No 821 of 19 December 1989, Act No 387 of 14 June 1995 and Act No 360 of 2 June 1999); the Swedish Registered Partnership (Family Law) Act 1994 (Act No 1994:1117 as amended by Act No 2000:374). I am indebted to Professor Svend Danielsen, Copenhagen, for making English translations of these Acts available. Norway and Iceland have followed the Danish approach. A Bill on the subject is before the Finnish Parliament. On the Danish Act see L Nielsen 'Family rights and the registered partnership in Denmark' (1990) *Int J L & Fam* 297–307 and M Broberg 'The registered partnership for same sex couples in Denmark' (1996) *Ch & Fam Q* 149–155.

3 To allow men to marry more than one wife at a time but not to allow women to marry more than one man at a time would be discriminatory and unfair. To allow both men and women to have two or more spouses at a time would be complicated and would lose some of the advantages of marriage as a pointer to appropriate legal results. There appears, in any event, to be no demand for any non-discriminatory loosening of the monogamy requirement.

4 We are talking here of the rules for marriage under the laws of the country concerned, not of the rules for recognition of marriages under the laws of other countries. Such rules should, in the interests of respect for existing relationships, recognise polygamous marriages validly entered into abroad.

5 See the Report by the Secretary General to the Commission on the Status of Women, *Consent to Marriage, Age of Marriage and Registration of Marriage* UN Doc E/CN6/356 (1959).

6 Genetics (but only a good reason in the case of potentially fertile unions), protection of the purity of family relationships (but do marriage rules really have much effect here?), promotion of wider links between families, respect for popular feelings and taboos.

7 So far as regular marriages were concerned this was the position in Scotland until the Marriage (Scotland) Act 1939 introduced civil marriages. The position before that was tolerable only because of the extensive use made of informal marriages by declaration of present consent.

people's needs and desires. Second, there must be an adequate opportunity for state control of entry into marriage, sufficient advance publicity often being an ingredient in such control. For both reasons it seems that to allow only religious marriages is not now an acceptable option. Many people who would want to marry are not religious. To allow only civil marriages would be a possible option, so long as there was freedom for people to supplement the civil ceremony with a religious ceremony (having no legal effect) if they so wished. But to allow both types of marriage, while retaining state control over who can celebrate religious marriages and requiring a marriage licence or the equivalent from the state authorities before any marriage ceremony can take place, seems the option most likely to meet people's wishes while respecting the need for state control. This option is likely to be more complicated to legislate for and to administer than an option allowing only civil ceremonies, because it would be necessary to have some system of identifying or registering authorised religious celebrants, but experience suggests that it can work well[1]. In effect the religious celebrant performs only the strictly ceremonial parts of the whole procedure.

Informal marriages

Most developed countries allow only formal marriages. Some states of the United States of America, however, continue to recognise common law marriages, which come into existence without any legal ceremony merely by virtue of cohabitation and presumed informal consent. Scotland still recognises marriages by cohabitation with habit and repute, which are very similar in nature to the American common law marriage.

In so far as the justification for legal regulation of marriage is respect for traditional family values it must be doubtful whether there is any case for informal marriages. The parties to such marriages have typically scorned or neglected any marriage ceremony and have simply drifted into a relationship. Worse, they have usually pretended to be married when they are not or have at least been guilty of dissimulation. These types of marriage are also difficult to justify in view of the functional justifications for legal marriage identified above – state support for a public commitment to the union and a clear, easily used pointer to certain legal results. Informal marriages involve no public or ceremonial commitment to a stable union. They provide no clear pointer to legal results in certain cases. There is usually great doubt as to their existence; litigation is usually necessary to settle the matter. Because they are initially unrecorded, parties can leave them and marry other people with little difficulty. The other party to the second marriage can then find that that marriage is void.

It seems clear that informal marriages have nothing in their favour as a means of getting married. They are a way, and not a particularly satisfactory way, of remedying certain injustices which might otherwise flow from cohabitation. If these injustices can be remedied by laws directed specifically at cohabitation then there would be no need for informal marriages. It was for these reasons that the Scottish Law Commission recommended the abolition of the Scottish

1 It has worked well in Scotland. There is no current demand for a change in the basis of the system. There is, however, some demand for a more liberal regime for non-religious marriages, allowing more opportunities, for example, for ceremonies in places other than a registrar's office.

marriage by cohabitation with habit and repute[1] – a recommendation which, unfortunately, the government has decided not to implement[2]. It may be supposed, however, that if marriage by cohabitation with habit and repute did not exist already, it would not now be introduced. There would be very good reasons for excluding any such marriages from, for example, a new European code of family law.

Rejection of the idea of informal marriages does not imply rejection of rules of evidence whereby the existence of a valid marriage may be presumed from the appearance of the status of husband and wife for a considerable time. Such rules are found in many legal systems and are clearly desirable.

Legal effects

It is quite common for civil codes to provide that spouses owe each other certain basic obligations, such as support, fidelity and adherence[3]. There may also be provisions about the basic rules on decision-making (for example, that the spouses take decisions concerning the family together) and on the spouses' obligation to contribute to family expenses. In any modern civil code it is clear that any specified rights and duties should be the same for both spouses. Such rules are not strictly necessary. However, they may serve a useful purpose in declaring the state's view of marriage as a mutually supportive relationship between equals. They may serve to banish older ideas of marriage as a male-dominated relationship, and would therefore be worth considering for inclusion in a modern civil code. For the non-monetary obligations of this nature it should perhaps be specifically provided that the only sanction is in matrimonial remedies such as divorce. An order for specific implement or performance would be inappropriate. To allow awards of damages would reintroduce some of the damaging allegations and counter-allegations of fault which many countries have been trying for some time to eliminate from the divorce law.

Judicial separation

Most legal systems with family law rules derived from canon law provide for, or once provided for, judicial separation, or separation from bed and board. Traditionally this is a remedy granted by a court ordaining and permitting the spouses to live apart but not severing the legal tie of marriage. Traditionally the grounds were cruelty or adultery. At one time the remedy made some sense. The parties were bound to live together. A court could terminate that obligation for cruelty or adultery. Allowing the innocent spouse to live apart enabled that spouse to claim aliment from the other without being met by the objection that support was available in the matrimonial home.

1 *Report on Family Law* (Scot Law Com no 135, 1992) para 7.9. The Commission pointed out that the law on this type of informal marriage can benefit those who have pretended to be married or who have allowed others to believe that they are married but does nothing for those who make no secret of the fact that they are cohabiting outside marriage.

2 *Parents and Children* (a white paper on Scottish Family Law published by the Scottish Executive in the year 2000) para 10.5. Most responses to the government's consultation on this question had favoured abolition but the government said that 'it did not wish to penalise those who wish to benefit from this form of marriage, however irregular it may be'. As there are only a few declarators of marriage by cohabitation with habit and repute a year the matter is not very important.

3 By adherence is meant an obligation to live together where possible or 'adhere' to each other.

Changes in the surrounding family law have now made the remedy of judicial separation a dubious one. The law of Scotland provides a good example of how the remedy has become unjustifiable as it stands. Spouses cannot now be obliged to live together[1]. They can separate when they want to, without the permission of a court. Aliment is available and a spouse who has good cause for living apart cannot be met with a claim that support is available in the matrimonial home[2]. Protective remedies in the form of exclusion orders are available to a spouse who wants to evict a violent spouse from the home[3]. So judicial separation has become an unnecessary remedy. A separate life, aliment and protection can be obtained without judicial separation.

Responding perhaps to an unarticulated impression that the nature of the remedy had changed, the legislature has made the grounds for judicial separation practically the same as the grounds for divorce[4]. So a person can obtain a decree of judicial separation, ordaining the other spouse to live apart, on the ground that the parties have been separated for five years. This makes no sense.

There is, however, a continuing view among certain religious groups that the remedy should be preserved as a sort of divorce for those who have religious objections to ordinary divorce. Whether there is any objective weight in this view is doubtful. Ordinary civil divorce is available to those of all religious persuasions or none. It is a civil remedy granted for civil purposes. All are free to regard it as having effects only in the civil sphere and as having no effects for religious purposes. Just as a church need not recognise civil marriage as having any effects for religious purposes, so it need not recognise civil divorce as having any effects for religious purposes. Indeed one wonders whether the religious support for judicial separation has been properly thought through. Suppose that the supporters of judicial separation had their wish and that all those who currently obtain divorces choose judicial separation instead. A large proportion of marriages would be socially meaningless. Marriage would not mean what it now means. It would be diminished as a legal and social institution. Thousands of married people would be living apart from their spouses. Many would enter into new sexual relationships and have children by new partners without being able to regularise their unions by marriage. The results would be damaging to what are widely regarded as traditional family values. Politically, however, the view of certain religious groups, however illogical and damaging it may be, could be sufficient to persuade politicians that it would be troublesome to abolish judicial separation at the present time[5].

If judicial separation is retained as a sort of lesser equivalent of divorce for those who object to divorce, and if the grounds are to be the same as the grounds for divorce, there is an argument for saying that various aspects of the remedy should be reconsidered and reformed. The very nature of the remedy might be reconsidered. It could be regarded as a declarator that the marriage has broken down but the parties do not want a divorce, rather than as a remedy which is

1 The action for adherence was abolished by the Law Reform (Husband and Wife) (Scotland) Act 1984, s 2(1) but by that time it had already been accepted for many decades that a decree of adherence would not be specifically enforced.

2 Family Law (Scotland) Act 1985, s 2(8).

3 See the Matrimonial Homes (Family Protection) (Scotland) Act 1981, s 4.

4 Divorce (Scotland) Act 1976, s 4.

5 The Scottish Executive has, for example, declined to follow the recommendation of the Scottish Law Commission that judicial separation should be abolished: *Parents and Children* (a white paper on Scottish Family Law published by the Scottish Executive in the year 2000) para 10.12.

intimately linked to the obligation to adhere and which makes no sense now that parties are free not to adhere if they so wish. Such a declarator could conceivably be useful for social purposes and for various legal purposes, such as income tax and social security. It would have to be decided in each context whether a judicial separation should have the same economic effects as a divorce. If, for example, a separated spouse retained pension rights as a spouse, it would be unacceptable to allow him or her to obtain rights in the other spouse's pension on the footing that the marriage had been dissolved.

So far as the civil law is concerned it is contrary to public policy to retain an unnecessary remedy which encourages parties to keep in existence legally a marriage which is not in existence socially. So the best course for a new civil code would be to have no provision for judicial separation. The next best course would be to have a form of judicial separation which made some sense.

Divorce

The term 'divorce' is used in different ways. Among lawyers it means the legal termination of the marriage as a legal relationship. Among lay people it is frequently used as an equivalent of marital breakdown. People say, for example, that divorce is bad for children when what they really mean is that marital breakdown is bad for children. Lawyers know that civil divorce has no necessary effects for religious purposes. Non-lawyers may be confused in this respect. There might therefore be something to be said in a new civil code for using a term which expressed the meaning of legal divorce more accurately – perhaps something like 'civil dissolution of marriage'. On the other hand 'divorce' is a well-known term which would no doubt continue to be used anyway and which is used in a number of international Conventions. For this reason a better approach would probably be to make clear the nature of divorce in the civil code itself by providing that divorce terminates the marriage for all legal purposes. To help religious groups make the position clear to their adherents it could readily be provided in the code that a civil divorce does not necessarily have any effect for religious purposes and that whether it does so or not depends on the rules of that religion[1].

In this chapter 'divorce' is used in the legal sense. It is a legal step, terminating a marriage legally and enabling the legal effects of a dead marriage to be tidied up. It has no necessary effect on living arrangements or personal relationships and, in most cases, will have no adverse effect on children, who may well be unaware that it has happened.

It is necessary to provide for divorce as a way of providing for the legal dissolution of marriages which have broken down in fact. Without the ready availability of divorce there would be thousands of marriages which were nothing more than legal shells bearing no relation to social reality. In such a situation, as noted above, the legal institution of marriage itself would rapidly fall into disrepute and become unusable for those purposes for which it is still legally useful. Divorce protects marriage. It is, paradoxically, most useful to those who believe most strongly in marriage. Those who do not care whether they live in cohabitation or marriage would not be too troubled if divorce were legally unavailable. If their first marriage broke down and they met somebody else they would just

1 This might make it easier to abolish judicial separation.

cohabit. Those who would be most troubled by the absence of divorce would be those who would be unwilling to cohabit outside marriage. It can therefore be safely assumed that any modern code which provides for marriage would also provide for divorce.

It is now generally accepted that divorce should be seen as a way of allowing broken marriages to be legally dissolved, at the request of at least one of the parties, rather than as a punishment for fault. Any law of divorce in a new family code would not be based on fault grounds as such.

There are three interesting questions. First, should the state be able to initiate divorce proceedings even if the parties do not? Second, should the basis of the divorce law be divorce on demand or divorce for breakdown? Third, if divorce for breakdown is a preferred option what should be regarded as an acceptable indication of breakdown?

If the state puts considerable effort into regulating marriage and if it confers certain benefits on the basis of marriage then, it might be asked, why should it not be able to seek the dissolution of marriages which are mere shams – for example marriages where the parties have not lived together for 20 years and have, for most of that time, been living with other people? It would not be illogical for the state to say 'Marriage is important. It is intended to be meaningful. It has legal effects. You are making a mockery of it. You do not deserve to be married. We cannot force you to live together but we can terminate your marriage.' Whether divorce at the instance of the state would be contrary to the European Convention on Human Rights is unclear. Perhaps the right to marry does not necessarily include the right to remain married in law while flouting the obligations of marriage in fact. The question is, however, unlikely to arise in practice. It would be politically unacceptable to have state representatives seeking to terminate people's marriages against their will. There is no need for it, no demand for it and no votes in it. If people suddenly stopped using the divorce law altogether a more proportionate response would be to reduce still further the legal effects of marriage.

Whether the basis of the divorce law should be divorce on demand or divorce for breakdown is more difficult. The strongest case for divorce on demand is where both parties want a divorce and present a joint request. Suppose, however, that they are still cohabiting happily and that their marriage has not broken down to any extent. They just want a divorce because they think it is more fashionable to live together while unmarried or because they have thought up a tax avoidance scheme which will work better if they are not married to each other. It is not at all clear that there is any public interest in acceding to such a request. Divorce on unilateral demand raises the same problem but also raises questions as to the interests of the party who does not want a divorce. Why should that party be divorced against his or her will if, let us suppose, the marriage is still functioning well? Divorce on the basis of breakdown seems sounder than divorce on demand.

If the ground of divorce is the breakdown of the marriage the most obvious, and in some respects the most refined, solution is to make the determination of breakdown a question to be determined on the evidence in each case. In practice such a solution could be made to work well if the requirements of proof were not too rigorous – if, for example, a statement by both parties, or a statement by one acquiesced in by the other, to the effect that the parties had not lived together for a certain period and believed their marriage to be irretrievably broken down, were accepted as sufficient evidence of breakdown. There would, however, be greater transparency in the law if some objective indicators of breakdown were recognised or required. The most obvious such indicator would be a period of separation. Clearly it should not be too long. It is important that divorce should be readily available to those whose marriages have in fact broken down and who want to tidy up the legal situation. Anything over a year would be suspect. A joint request for a divorce by the parties coupled with a statement that their marriage had broken down would also be a good indicator of breakdown, at least if there were a real risk of prosecution for perjury if the statement were knowingly false. It is also quite reasonable to regard certain factual situations, other than a period of separation, as good indicators of breakdown even if those situations involve fault. Fault and indications of breakdown are not incompatible – indeed rather the reverse. For example, it is a reasonable indication that a marriage has broken down if one of the parties wants a divorce because the other has taken up cohabitation with somebody else on an apparently long-term basis or has been violent or abusive to the applicant. There is no one answer to this question of appropriate indicators of breakdown and a whole range of solutions would work perfectly well.

If there is a reliable indication that the marriage has broken down then the main policy requirement is not to make divorce any more difficult, expensive or traumatic than necessary. No one is forcing anyone to seek a divorce. The starting point is that one party wants to terminate a legal relationship when the corresponding factual relationship has broken down. The factual termination has already occurred. Making divorce difficult or expensive does not save marriages any more than making funerals difficult or expensive saves lives. All the indications are, in any event, that people do not in fact seek divorce lightly, particularly if there are children. There is probably in practice no such thing as an easy divorce, whatever the law may say.

Nullity of marriage

It would be necessary in any civil code to make some provision for declarators of nullity of marriage or the equivalent. This is because parties to an invalid marriage should have a mechanism for resolving any doubts and cancelling any administrative or other indications that they are married. There is, however, no obvious need for any remedy of nullity going beyond those cases where the marriage is invalid from the beginning. In the civil law the appropriate way of dissolving a marriage which is valid but which has broken down is divorce. Some religions which disapprove of divorce may be tempted to use nullity in a wider way to achieve the same results as divorce. That is their privilege but there is no reason why this sort of consideration should be allowed to distort the civil law.

COHABITATION

The social phenomenon

It has in recent decades become increasingly common for heterosexual couples to live together in an intimate sexual relationship without marrying each other. The reasons for not marrying are various. At one time marriage was seen as a patriarchal institution enshrining ideas of male dominance. Even if that is no longer the case legally, old notions may persist. Often couples wish to have a trial period of cohabitation before getting married. Often they are simply not certain whether they wish to commit themselves to a lifelong union. Often one of them has had prior experience of the trouble and expense of divorce and does not want to repeat the experience[1]. There may, at any given time, be legal incentives to cohabit rather than marry[2]. The more common and acceptable cohabitation becomes, the more the onus of justification changes. People ask why they should marry rather than whether they should consider cohabitation without marriage[3]. Whatever the reasons, cohabitation has become common and normal.

To regulate or not

Cohabitation cannot be ignored by the legislator. Some regulation is essential. The only questions are what kind of regulation and how much. Many of the issues and arguments considered in this section apply equally to same-sex cohabitations. The reason for confining the discussion to heterosexual cohabitation is simply to avoid overlap with Professor Norrie's chapter in this book[4]. From the policy point of view there is a need to provide protection for same-sex cohabitants. Providing a form of registered partnership for same-sex couples would not be the complete answer. Many such couples would not register, just as many different-sex partners do not marry.

No negative regulation

Attempts have been made in the past to regulate sexual cohabitation by prohibiting sexual intercourse outside marriage. The pre-1707 Scottish Parliament tried to criminalise fornication[5] and open adultery[6] with, it seems, only limited success[7]. Indeed it has been claimed that open adultery is still in theory a criminal offence in Scotland[8] although it has long ceased to be prosecuted.

Until quite recently contracts between cohabitants have often been regarded as void on the ground of immorality[9].

The first stage in the legal response to the increasing occurrence and social acceptability of cohabitation ought to be the elimination of negative regulation. The minimum legal response to cohabitation in a tolerant society is the elimina-

1 Another illustration of the point made earlier – difficult and expensive divorce disfavours the institution of marriage.

2 For example, the social security benefits available to two single people may be greater than the benefits available to a married couple. Even if the social security law treats cohabiting couples as if married, it may be easier to disguise the fact of cohabitation than the fact of marriage.

3 See M Hibbs, C Barton and J Beswick 'Why Marry – Perceptions of the Affianced' 2001 Fam Law 197–207.

4 See Ch 7 below.

5 See the Act of 1567 (c 14) 'Anent the filthy vice of fornication'.

6 See the Act of 1551 (c 12) 'Anent open and incorrigible adulterers' and the Act of 1563 (c 10) 'Anent notour and manifest adultery'.

7 The Act of 1567 (c 14) 'Of adultery' provided 'That the Act for punishment of adultery be made so clear that the offenders delude not the law by the ambiguity thereof.' An Act of 1661 on Justices of the Peace (c 338) instructed justices to put into execution all Acts on fornication. The older Acts on fornication had to be 'ratified, renewed and revived' by the Act against Prophaneness of 1696 (c 31) and the Act against Profaneness of 1701 (c 12).

8 G Gordon *Criminal Law* (2nd edn, 1978) W Green, Edinburgh para 0-04.

9 Indeed the position is still not entirely clear in all countries. For Scottish law see *Report on Family Law* (Scot Law Com no 135, 1992) para 16.46 and for English law see Pawlowski 'Cohabitation Contracts – are they legal?' (1996) *NLJ* 1125–26.

tion of rules making it difficult or impossible for cohabitants to lead their own lives in a way which does no harm to anyone else and to regulate their own affairs in a way which suits them. To deny cohabitants the opportunity to regulate their own affairs as they wish would be patronising and indefensible.

Cohabitation contracts and other autonomous arrangements

If the ordinary law on contract is available to cohabitants and if, as is generally the case, the ordinary law on contract is flexible and adaptable to all situations (and not merely commercial situations or short-term situations)[1] then there is no obvious need for any special background law on cohabitation contracts[2].

Whether any cohabiting couple should have a cohabitation contract, and what should be in it, are matters for them. Some will not even consider the possibility. Cohabitation contracts are probably on the whole attractive only to those with, or likely to acquire, property. Many couples would consider it unwise or even potentially harmful to their relationship to attempt to regulate its future development or provide for its possible breakdown[3]. Even if these barriers are overcome, much will depend on the underlying law on cohabitation and on the contract. If the general law already provides necessary protections against economic exploitation as a result of cohabitation there may be less need for a cohabitation contract. An unfair contract could be worse than none at all. A rigid contract, making no allowance for potential changes in life situations, could also be worse than none at all.

Autonomous arrangements are not confined to cohabitation contracts. Property can be taken in joint names or transferred between the partners so as to achieve a running equality of assets. Insurance policies can be taken out. Wills can be made. Any enterprise carried on by both parties can be carried on in an ordinary commercial partnership.

The important point of legal policy for any new code is that there should be no legal barrier to the making by cohabitants of sensible contractual and similar arrangements[4]. Regulation cannot sensibly, however, be left to contractual arrangements alone. Many cohabiting people, including probably those most in need of protection, will not have contracts.

Children

Any legal discrimination against a child on the ground that the parents are or were cohabiting rather than married would be not only unfair and unjustifiable

1 There is no requirement of consideration or *causa* in Scottish contract law. Contracts are widely used for non-commercial purposes.

2 There is extensive literature on cohabitation contracts. See, for example, E Kingdom 'Cohabitation Contracts and the Democratization of Personal Relations' (2000) 8 *Fem LS* 5–27 and J Wightman 'Intimate Relationships, Relational Contract Theory and the Reach of Contract' (2000) 8 *Fem LS* 93–131.

3 The considerations are similar to those applying to ante-nuptial marriage contracts, on which see M Hibbs, C Barton and J Beswick 'Why Marry – Perceptions of the Affianced' (2001) *Fam Law* 197–207.

4 For this reason the Scottish Law Commission recommended that it should be made clear, for the avoidance of doubt, that a cohabitant had an insurable interest in the life of his or her partner and that certain special rules favouring life insurance policies on a spouse's life should be extended to cohabitants: *Report on Family Law* (Scot Law Com no 135, 1992) paras 16.41–16.45.

but also contrary to treaty obligations[1]. A more difficult question is whether cohabitants should be allowed to adopt jointly. If cohabitation were strictly defined for this purpose there could be good reasons for allowing such joint adoptions, given that there would be careful assessments of suitability in any case. The interests of children who might benefit from adoption would not be served by excluding from the outset all consideration of couples who might be excellent parents merely because they were not married to each other. A marriage ceremony is no guarantee of the stability of a relationship.

Guardianship of adults with incapacity

In legal systems where certain people have a preferential right to be appointed guardian of an adult with incapacity it makes sense to include the cohabiting partner in the list of such people. In countries such as Scotland[2], where there is no such preferential right and where a general test of suitability is used directly, this problem does not arise.

Prevention of abuse or unfairness in relation to welfare benefits

An early stage of the legal response to cohabitation is likely to be the extension of certain rules from marriage to cohabitation in order to prevent abuse or unfairness in the public law sphere[3]. Social welfare laws designed for family units rather than individuals must often, for example, treat cohabitation in the same way as marriage, if the law is not to be seen as manifestly unfair or open to abuse or both[4].

Providing protection

There are very strong reasons, and there may be strong political pressure, to apply protective laws, such as laws on domestic violence or occupancy rights in the family home, to cohabiting couples as well as married couples, and indeed more widely to anyone in need of protection. Experience suggests that there is likely to be little or no resistance to such protective measures even from those whose general stance is to seek to preserve the distinctiveness of marriage. It is difficult to argue that the protection of a legal institution should be achieved at the expense of innocent victims of violent or abusive conduct.

Rights and remedies in relation to third parties

If cohabitation is not unlawful, and if it is not even subject to social disapproval, it becomes increasingly difficult to discriminate against cohabitants in the availability of legal rights and remedies in relation to third parties, such as

---

1 See the UN Convention on the Rights of the Child, art 2 (Convention rights to be secured for each child within jurisdiction 'without discrimination of any kind, irrespective of the child's . . . birth or other status').

2 See the Adults with Incapacity (Scotland) Act 2000, s 59.

3 See, for example, the Social Security Act 1986, s 20; the Rent (Scotland) Act 1984, s 3 and Sch 1; and the Housing (Scotland) Act 1988, s 31(4).

4 It is beyond the scope of this discussion to ask whether social welfare rules should be designed for family units rather than for individuals.

the right of one party to recover damages for the wrongful death of the other[1] or the right of one cohabitant to be consulted if the other becomes mentally incapable[2].

Remedying economic imbalances arising from the cohabitation

Cohabitation of any length is likely to produce economic imbalances. In a relationship where everything is shared on a basis of trust and affection it can easily happen that, when things go wrong, one party ends up by accident with a much larger share of the joint assets or with an economic position which has been improved at the expense of the other party. In the absence of a legislative response to such situations it has been common for courts to seek to use various doctrines of the ordinary law, such as partnership, unjustified enrichment, implied contract or trust, to provide some relief. Such attempts, however ingenious, have rarely been totally satisfactory. Partnership, for example, may be limited to commercial relationships[3], and even where not so limited by the terms of the law, may have been designed with such relationships in mind. Unjustified enrichment does not cater well for situations where one party has provided another with benefits out of love or kindness in full knowledge of the fact that nothing is legally due[4]. Nor does it cater well for situations where one party has made economic sacrifices in the interests of the other or of the family without producing any actual enrichment. The invention of implied contracts or trusts is often pure fiction – a clothing of judicial legislation in terminology which looks respectable at first sight but is threadbare.

The same problems can arise in marriage. In any legal system it may be that solutions devised for marriage can be applied to cohabitation. In Scotland, for example, the Scottish Law Commission was able simply to recommend the extension to cohabitants of certain rules which enable the courts in dealing with divorce actions to make orders for the payment of capital sums or periodical allowances or for the transfer of property by one spouse to the other. The rules provide that in making any such order 'fair account should be taken of any economic advantage derived by either party from contributions by the other, and of any economic disadvantage suffered by either party in the interests of the other party or of the family'[5].

A special problem arises if one party is left with a child or children of the cohabitation to look after. Again this problem can arise after a marriage and the solution devised for marriage may be readily applicable to cohabitation[6]. General laws on child support may also provide a solution. If, for example, the

1 Available to a cohabitant in Scotland since 1982. See the Administration of Justice Act 1982, s 14(4), amending the Damages (Scotland) Act 1976, Sch 1.

2 See the Mental Health (Scotland) Act 1984, s 53(5) and the Adults with Incapacity (Scotland) Act 2000, s 87(1) (definition of nearest relative).

3 In the UK, for example, a partnership must be between persons 'carrying on a business in common with a view to profit': Partnership Act 1890, s 1.

4 It would be possible to adapt the law on unjustified enrichment so that it took account of the special features of certain intimate, long-standing relationships. In some respects this would be a better solution, because function-based and not linked to any particular status, than having special 'unjustified enrichment' type rules for spouses and cohabitants.

5 Family Law (Scotland) Act 1985, s 9(1)b).

6 See, for example, the Family Law (Scotland) Act 1985, s 9(1)(c) which provides that any economic burden of caring, after divorce, for a child of the marriage under the age of 16 years is to be shared fairly between the parties.

general law on child support provides that an absent parent must contribute not only to aliment for the child but also towards the support of the other parent so long as he or she has to give up work or incur extra expense in order to look after the child, then these rules will automatically provide a solution for the cohabitation situation[1].

Rights for surviving cohabitant

There is, or at least ought to be, nothing to prevent cohabitants from leaving wills in favour of each other. Subject to any laws on *legitim* or forced shares for children[2] such testamentary arrangements will be able to achieve the results desired by the testator, at least so far as the private law is concerned[3]. Many people, however, die without having made a will. The question of legal policy which arises for private law is whether the law should confer on a surviving cohabitant any rights to succeed on intestacy or any analogous rights. In so far as the law on intestacy attempts to provide for the deceased the results which he or she would probably have wished to provide for by will, there is a strong case for some provision for the surviving cohabitant[4]. There are two difficulties. First, there may be doubt about the facts of the cohabitation. How long did it last? What was its real nature? Second, there may be competing claimants, including a surviving spouse of the deceased or a former cohabitant who had provided support for many years only to be displaced by someone else in the period shortly before death. For these reasons there is something to be said for a solution whereby a surviving cohabitant does not have automatic rights of intestate succession but can apply to a court for a discretionary provision out of the deceased's estate[5]. The main advantage of such a scheme is its ability to take account of many different types of situation. Similar discretionary schemes have been in existence for many years in England and Wales and other Commonwealth countries. On the other hand, if cohabitations were strictly defined for this purpose, a law conferring fixed intestate succession rights would have the great advantage of avoiding the need for court applications.

Extending core rules of marriage to cohabitation

More difficulty arises when the question is whether to extend to cohabitants rules designed for the relations of spouses between themselves. The problem here is that if a couple have opted for cohabitation rather than marriage it seems objectionable to impose the core rules of marriage on them[6]. For example, it could be

1 See, for example, in the UK, the Child Support Act 1991, s 11 and Sch 1.

2 And subject also to any claims a surviving spouse of the deceased might have.

3 There may, however, be a need to consider whether any special inheritance tax exemptions or reliefs accorded to testamentary transfers to spouses should extend to similar transfers to cohabitants. See, for example, for the UK, the Inheritance Tax Act 1984, s 11 (transfers between spouses are exempt transfers).

4 The Scottish Law Commission had a public opinion survey carried out on this topic. The results strongly favoured intestate succession rights for the surviving cohabitant. See *Report on Family Law* (Scot Law Com no 135, 1992) paras 16.25–16.27. More recent surveys have confirmed this result. See *The Scotsman* 27 June 2001.

5 This was the solution recommended by the Scottish Law Commission in its *Report on Family Law* (Scot Law Com no 135, 1992) paras 16.25–16.37.

6 Strictly speaking, of course, only one party need opt for cohabitation. It takes two to marry.

difficult to justify extending to cohabitants the marital obligations of fidelity, support and adherence[1].

Definition of legally relevant cohabitation

The problem of definition of cohabitation is a difficult one[2]. It becomes particularly difficult if important fixed rights are conferred. There are various possible approaches.

One approach is to use the analogy of marriage and to define heterosexual cohabitation as the relationship which subsists between a man and a woman who are not married to each other but are cohabiting as if they were husband and wife. That, however, raises questions about what the essence of marital cohabitation is. It is also objectionable to some people precisely because it takes marriage as its model. None the less this is a popular and useful approach which avoids a number of difficulties. It could be useful to add that the partners must be of an age when they could marry, and not so closely related that they could not marry each other.

Another approach would be to define heterosexual cohabitation as the relationship which subsists between two people of different sexes, of marriageable age and not within the prohibited degrees of relationship, who are not married to each other but are cohabiting in an intimate, potentially sexual, stable relationship involving sharing of resources and mutual support. An advantage of this type of definition is that it could more easily and appropriately be adapted for same-sex couples.

The problem of stability or duration is difficult. Some legal effects are self-regulating in that the conditions for them will normally not be satisfied anyway until a cohabitation has lasted for some time. For example, it will normally take some time for economic imbalances due to a cohabitation to be produced, so that a law designed to redress such imbalances would not need to be linked to cohabitations of any particular duration. In relation to certain other legal effects it would be possible to dispense with any minimum duration and allow the matter to be determined retrospectively on the facts of each case. This could be done, for example, if the law allowed a surviving cohabitant to claim a discretionary provision on the death of the partner. Duration could simply be taken into account as one of the factors affecting the exercise of the discretion. In relation to certain other effects, such as fixed intestate succession rights (if they were to be conferred), it would be possible to lay down a minimum period of cohabitation of, say, two years before a cohabitation produced legal effects. It would also be possible, as has been done in Catalonia, Aragon and Navarra[3], to attach significant

1 Some modern laws on cohabitation do provide, however, for an obligation of maintenance so long as the cohabitation lasts. See, for example, the Catalonia Act 10/1998 of 15 July, art 26 concerning couples in stable unions.

2 See I D Willock 'Cohabitation: an Alternative Basis' 2000 *JR* 1-9.

3 In Catalonia by Act 10/1998 of 15 July on couples in stable unions, in Aragon by Act 6/1999, March 26 concerning unmarried stable couples and, in Navarra, by Act 6/2000, 3 July concerning legal equality for stable relationships. See Cantero 'The Catalan Family Code of 1998 and other Autonomous Region Laws on De Facto Unions' in *The International Survey of Family Law* (2001 edn) published on behalf of the International Society of Family Law pp 397–404. I am indebted to Dr Luis Arechederra of the University of Navarra, Pamplona, Professor Encarna Roca of the University of Barcelona, and to Dr Antoni Vaquer Aloy of the University of Lleida for information about these most interesting and progressive laws. In Catalonia the law has separate chapters, and different rules, for heterosexual and same-sex couples. In Aragon and Navarra the laws treat both types of couples in the same way.

legal effects to cohabitations if either they had lasted for a minimum period (two years) or the cohabiting couple had expressed in a public document their present intention of constituting a legally relevant cohabitation.

Another question is whether the definition of a cohabitation producing certain legal effects should apply only to couples where neither partner is already married. This could facilitate the resolution of certain questions. It could make it much easier, for example, to confer fixed succession rights on the surviving cohabitant and to give the same inheritance tax exemptions to transfers between cohabitants as apply to transfers between spouses. As, however, many cohabitations do involve at least one partner who is already married it might be thought unduly restrictive to confine some legal effects to couples both of whom are unmarried. A law redressing economic imbalances caused by the relationship should, for example, not be confined to such couples.

The only safe conclusion on the question of definition is probably that a functional approach would be best. Different definitions may be required for different purposes. In the key area of succession rights, for example, fixed intestate succession rights would require a more restrictive definition of cohabitation than a system of discretionary provision. Any extension of occupancy rights in the family home would probably also require a restrictive definition.

Registered partnerships

A number of countries have responded to the perceived needs of cohabiting couples by introducing registered partnerships. By registering, couples can qualify for many or most of the benefits and burdens of marriage. It seems clear that this cannot be regarded as an exclusive way of identifying those cohabitations where legal regulation is required. Many cohabiting couples would not register. Even the parties to unregistered cohabitations would need the range of legal protections discussed above. Whether it is necessary or desirable to introduce registered partnerships for couples of different sexes is a matter of debate.

In some countries registered partnerships have been made available to couples, whether they are of the same sex or of different sexes. The French law of 1999 instituting the *pacte civil de solidarité* allows cohabiting couples, whether of the same sex or of different sexes, to enter into a pact for organising their life in common[1]. There are restrictions on who can enter into a pact. The parties must be of full age and not too closely related. Neither of them must be married or already in such a pact. They must be cohabiting. The pact is entered into by a joint declaration made to the secretariat of the *tribunal d'instance* of the common domicile. It will be registered by the secretariat and then produces legal effects both for the parties and in relation to third parties. The parties, for example, owe each other mutual support and have solidary liability[2] to third parties for rent, household expenses and similar current expenditures of ordinary life. The pact should state the regime under which the couple's property is to be held. If it does not then any property acquired after the conclusion of the pact is deemed to be held jointly in equal shares. The non-entitled partner is given occupancy rights in the home if the other partner dies or deserts. The pact can be varied or ended by

1 Loi No 99–944 of 15 November 1999. See Steiner 'The spirit of the new French registered partnership law – promoting autonomy or weakening marriage?' (2000) *Ch & Fam LQ* 1-14.
2 Similar to joint and several liability.

mutual consent. Either partner can also repudiate it unilaterally. In either case there must be a writing registered with the clerk of the *tribunal d'instance* and in the case of a unilateral repudiation the dissolution takes place only after a delay of three months from the date of notification to the other partner. The pact is also ended by the death or marriage of either party.

Similar laws have been introduced in some other European countries although the legal effects of a registered partnership vary[1].

There is a strong argument, as noted above, for introducing registered partnerships for same-sex couples[2]. It is not so clear, however, that they are necessary for couples of different sexes. If such couples want to make a public commitment, to have their relationship registered and to have the full range of legal effects attributable to such unions, they have the option of marrying[3]. Under modern European marriage laws, marriage is no longer an unequal patriarchal union. The principle of the equality of the spouses is accepted. The legal effects of marriage are being progressively lightened and even where they are potentially heavy, as for example in countries with complicated matrimonial property regimes, the spouses can generally opt out of them. Conversely, in countries where the effects of marriage are not heavy and where, for example, the spouses keep their own property and are personally liable for their own debts, it is always possible and generally very easy in practice for spouses to opt into joint ownership and joint liability. Marriage can be adapted very easily to suit many different tastes. There does not seem to be any obvious need to provide registered partnerships for couples of different sexes, particularly if many of the same rules apply as for marriage. Indeed if different rules were to be proposed for same-sex partnerships on the grounds that these rules were more in tune with contemporary expectations, it would have to be asked why the basic marriage rules should not be reformed to bring them into line with what is perceived as being required today. Heterosexual couples who do not want to marry but who do want to record their commitment to each other and to help to resolve possible doubts about the nature of their relationship, particularly in its earlier stages, can record their commitment in a public document or draw up and register a cohabitation contract[4].

CONCLUSION

The dynamic nature of the law on marriage and cohabitation in the last 200 years or so is not in doubt. Two great stages of development can be identified.

In the first, which lasted from the middle of the 19th century until very recently, the struggle was:

1 Eg the Netherlands (Registered Partnerships Act 1998) and Belgium (*loi instaurant la cohabitation légale* of 23 November 1998).

2 As has been done in Denmark and other Scandinavian countries.

3 It was at least partly for the reason that marriage was available to heterosexual couples that the Danish law on registered partnerships was limited to partners of the same sex. There have apparently been no demands from heterosexual couples for an extension. I am grateful to Professor Svend Danielsen, who was the vice-chair of the commission which prepared the Danish Registered Partnership Act of 1989, for this information.

4 This is on the assumption that there is a suitable system for registering such private documents, as there is in Scotland in the Books of Council and Session.

- in relation to entry into marriage, to achieve legal equality between religions and adequate recognition for secular marriages;
- in relation to the legal effects of marriage, to achieve legal equality for the married woman;
- in relation to the dissolution of marriage, to achieve a humane divorce law based on breakdown rather than narrowly defined fault; and
- in relation to marriage and cohabitation, to achieve some protection against eviction from the home and domestic violence.

Most of these aims have been achieved to a large extent although improvements and refinements are still needed in some areas.

The second stage, which we are now in, is likely to be concerned with the extent to which, and the way in which, cohabitation, whether different-sex or same-sex or both, should be regulated. The debate on that issue is likely to feed back into marriage with the possibility of a more function-based approach being adopted to many problems.

7 Sexual Orientation and Family Law

Kenneth McK Norrie

INTRODUCTION

On 29 March 2000 the Scottish Parliament passed its fifth piece of legislation, the Adults with Incapacity (Scotland) Act 2000. One small provision tucked away in this important legislation amends the definition of 'nearest relative' in the Mental Health (Scotland) Act 1984, in order to include within that phrase members of conjugal same-sex couples[1]. The relative obscurity of this provision must not hide its import, for this is the first time that legislation anywhere in the United Kingdom has expressly and intentionally[2] given recognition, for civil law purposes, to the existence of same-sex family relationships.

The readiness with which the Scottish Parliament accepted the need for this provision reflects a fundamental shift in social and legal attitudes towards sexual orientation though, so far, this shift has manifested itself in only isolated and, some might say, relatively unimportant ways. Whether the cracks that have thus appeared in the heterosexist hegemony of contemporary family law will develop into a full-scale flood of equality and justice, leading to a recognition of the inherent dignity of gay men and lesbians and the domestic relationships they enter into or are part of, remains to be seen.

There is, however, little doubt that sexual orientation law is fast developing and, notwithstanding inevitable setbacks, is doing so in the right direction. This of course is a value-judgment, which would not meet with acceptance from those who cling to a belief in the inherent badness, or immorality, or social destructiveness, of homosexuality, but I think it is important to be entirely clear right at the beginning from what perspective this chapter is written. It will be the thrust of this chapter that sexual orientation, per se, is entirely irrelevant to all the issues that are encompassed within family law and that therefore the aim of policy-makers, legislators and judges should be to expunge from their thinking those assumptions, policies and rules which either discriminate directly against, or by refusing to recognise their existence or by assuming the

1 Adults with Incapacities (Scotland) Act 2000 (2000 asp 4), s 87(2).

2 There are other statutes, such as the (English) Rent Act 1977, the Rent (Scotland) Act 1984, the Children (Scotland) Act 1995 and the (English) Family Law Act 1996 in which concepts such as 'family' and 'household' are wide enough to allow the courts, if they are so minded, to include within their terms same-sex relationships: for a discussion from a Scottish perspective, see K Norrie 'We Are Family (Sometimes): Legal Recognition of Same-Sex Relationships After *Fitzpatrick*' (2000) 4 *Edin LR* 256 at pp 271–281.

unchallengeability of the heterosexist hegemony indirectly deny equal treatment to, gay men, lesbians and same-sex relationships[1]. Nor is equality enough. The aim of the law should be to ensure justice and that notion is, I perceive, wider than equality which is a prerequisite to but not definitional of justice. Justice in this context includes, as well as equal treatment, a recognition of the validity and moral legitimacy of gay and lesbian lifestyles and families, and of the inherent human dignity of gay and lesbian persons. Relationships gain legitimacy and dignity, and should thereby demand the law's respect, not by being sanctioned by the state or sanctified by a religious body, nor by having procreational potential, but through the mutuality of respect each member of a relationship shows, as manifested through acts of support and commitment. Judicial and legislative progress towards accepting the demands of justice is well underway in most western legal systems but it is not of course complete nor even yet at the stage at which it is unstoppable. It has hardly, if at all, started in much of the non-western world.

Steps towards recognition

Kees Waaldijk, in an important study of most of the legal systems in Europe[2], identifies what he calls a 'standard sequence of steps' that legal systems take in their developing legal recognition and regulation of same-sex sexual acts and same-sex relationships. The first step is the removal of the criminality of (male) homosexual acts[3] which existed in many legal systems for most of the 20th century[4] (though not, interestingly, for many years before that[5]). Decriminalisation occurred in England and Wales in 1967[6] and in Scotland in 1980[7]. Non-criminality is now widely seen in Europe as a definitional feature of a free

1 It is not the place here to explore the question of the cause or causes of homosexuality (or, indeed, heterosexuality). Anyone who doubts the profound irrelevance of that question is referred to B Macdougall *Queer Judgments: Homosexuality, Expression and the Courts in Canada* (2000) University of Toronto Press at pp 31–47.

2 See the self-described 'sketch' of his on-going work in 'Civil Developments: Patterns of Reform in the Legal Position of Same-Sex Partners in Europe' (2000) 17 *Rev Can Dr Fam* 62, expanding on earlier work, 'Standard Sequences in the Legal Recognition of Homosexuality – Europe's Past, Present and Future' (1994) 4 *Australasian Gay and Lesbian L J* 50.

3 Female homosexual acts were never criminal in Scotland or England or in any other European country, not because such acts were acceptable but because they were, to male legislators, inconceivable. The injustice to men of criminalising their activity found an odd reflection in the (different and, surely, lesser) injustice to women by their being rendered entirely invisible to the law.

4 Waaldijk points out the historically interesting, though largely unexplained, fact that criminalisation occurred in the great 19th-century empires of Britain, Russia, Austria and Germany, but did not occur in those countries such as France, the Netherlands, and the Iberian and Scandinavian countries which did not develop into empires or (in the case of Spain) had by then lost their imperial pretensions. It may be speculated that the militarism essential to hold together vast empires of disparate peoples placed such a high premium on both masculinity and high birth rates that sexual acts perceived as being inimical to either were seen as a threat to the state's ability to maintain its geopolitical position. To me this is a more convincing explanation than differences in religious moralities which, in an earlier age, would have been indistinguishable from political imperatives.

5 So for example in the United Kingdom while sodomy (same-sex or opposite-sex) was a common law crime, criminality (as opposed to moral opprobrium) was attached to all homosexual contact falling short of this only in 1885 with the Criminal Law Amendment Act of that year. For an early prosecution, see *Clark & Bendall v Stuart* (1886) 1 White 191.

6 Sexual Offences Act 1967, s 1

7 Criminal Justice (Scotland) Act 1980, s 80. See now Criminal Law Consolidation (Scotland) Act 1995, s 13, as amended by the Sexual Offences (Amendment) Act 2000, s 1 (UK).

and democratic society[1]; it is not yet perceived as such in many other countries, such as the United States. The second step, far less universal, is the enactment of non-discrimination legislation under which it becomes impermissible to discriminate against an individual on the ground of sexual orientation. The beneficiaries of this step are both men and women who may equally suffer individual discrimination in fact, irrespective of the criminal law's institutional discrimination. Such legislation exists, to a greater or lesser extent, in a number of countries[2], and in many countries where the legislature itself has failed to act, the courts have been able to fashion from existing provisions a principle of non-discrimination on the ground of sexual orientation[3]. The third step, which Waaldijk suggests is unlikely to be taken in any individual legal system without the taking of the first two steps, is for courts and legislatures to grant legal recognition and protection to the domestic relationships that gay men and lesbians enter into. Waaldijk, rationally but perhaps a touch optimistically, sees an internal logic in these steps which seems to make the progression inevitable. He says this:

> 'Once people engaging in homosexual activity are no longer seen as *criminals*, but instead as *citizens*, they can hardly be denied their civil rights, including their right not to be treated differently because of their (criminally irrelevant) sexual orientation. In this way the step of anti-discrimination not only follows, but builds on the step of decriminalisation. Similarly, the very idea of non-discrimination with regard to sexual orientation, simply demands that no one shall be disadvantaged by law because of the gender of the person he or she happens to love. In this way the links between the steps of decriminalisation, anti-discrimination, and partnership legislation are not

---

1 Within those countries that are signatories to the European Convention on Human Rights, decriminalisation was required after *Dudgeon v UK (No 1)* (1981) 3 EHRR 40; and *(No 2)* (1982) 3 EHRR 149. See also *Norris v Ireland* (1991) 13 EHRR 186 and *Modinos v Cyprus* (1993) 16 EHRR 485. In the USA, on the other hand, the Supreme Court held that it was not unconstitutional for states to criminalise a variety of homosexual sexual acts, collectively called, in that country, 'sodomy': *Bowers v Hardwick* 478 US 186, 92 L Ed 2d 140 (1986). Decriminalisation of 'sodomy' occurred in South Africa, unusually, as a result of, rather than as a precursor to, the enactment of anti-discrimination legislation: see *National Coalition for Gay and Lesbian Equality v Minister of Justice* 1998 (12) BCLR 1517, 1999 (1) SA 6.

2 See, for example, the New Zealand Human Rights Act 1993, s 21(1)(m) of which prohibits sexual orientation discrimination in specified circumstances such as employment, provision of services, and access to education; the South African Constitution, s 9(3) which prohibits sexual orientation discrimination in all circumstances (unless, under s 9(5), this can be shown to be fair); and the Northern Ireland Act 1998, s 75(1) which obliges public authorities in Northern Ireland to carry out their functions having regard to 'the need to promote equality of opportunity – (a) between persons of different . . . sexual orientation'.

3 In Canada, the Supreme Court held in *Vriend v Alberta* (1998) 156 DLR (4th) 385 that sexual orientation was a ground analogous to those expressly listed in the Canadian Charter of Rights and Freedoms, s 15 and that therefore it was unconstitutional for a province to omit sexual orientation discrimination from its non-discrimination provisions. In Europe, sexual orientation has been held to be implicitly included within the terms of the European Convention on Human Rights, art 14, with the result that it is an impermissible reason for discriminating in the application of the substantive rights contained in the European Convention: *da Silva Mouta v Portugal* 2001 Fam LR 2. On the other hand, the Inner House of the Court of Session refused to find that sexual orientation discrimination was included within the context of sex discrimination for the purposes of the Sex Discrimination Act 1975 (*MacDonald v Ministry of Defence* [2001] 1 All ER 620). This Act does not, of course, contain a general non-discrimination principle such as is found in the Canadian Charter or, to a more limited extent, the European Convention. Even within the terms of the 1975 Act that conclusion was not inevitable, as shown by the fact that one judge dissented (on the question of the correct comparator to adopt in a case of discrimination).

only sequential (in the European countries that have gone that far), but also morally and politically compelling'[1].

One might depart slightly from Waaldijk's analysis by splitting the final step of relationship recognition into two. The earlier and easier part of this step (which is often taken before the stage of introducing anti-discrimination legislation) is to give ad hoc recognition for a limited number of carefully delineated and, by and large, uncontroversial purposes – this is the stage that the Scottish Parliament has now reached – and the later and politically more dangerous part of the step is to grant recognition to same-sex relationships in all circumstances in which opposite-sex relationships are recognised by the law. Only a very few countries in the world have gone this far.

It is the purpose of this chapter to explore, first, the developing legal approach to same-sex relationships, primarily but not exclusively within the context of the law in the United Kingdom: it will be seen that legal systems across the world are responding, at an ever-quickening pace, to the social and moral changes in society which are leading to a rejection of the intolerance and even hatred to which gay men and lesbians, and same-sex couples, were commonly (and sometimes still are) subjected. The interesting questions which will then be addressed are (i) why is this happening, and (ii) what does this tell us about the nature and purpose of contemporary family law?

RECOGNITION: THE CURRENT SITUATION IN THE UNITED KINGDOM

Indirect recognition of same-sex relationships

Even before any explicit protections were extended to same-sex relationships, the law was being forced, if reluctantly, to acknowledge their existence and even to accept their validity. This occurred primarily in relation to disputes over children. It is one of the paradoxes of the law that while, as we will see, shielding children from homosexual influences has long been one of the main (though always spurious) arguments against the law legitimising same-sex relationships, and there are many provisions remaining in the law designed to make access to the status of 'parent' difficult for gay people[2], it was in child

1 K Waaldijk 'Civil Developments: Patterns of Reform in the Legal Position of Same-Sex Partners in Europe' (2000) 17 *Rev Can Dr Fam* at 86.

2 Adoption by couples is available only to married persons (Adoption (Scotland) Act 1978, s 14 and Adoption Act 1976 (England), s 14). Fostering of children by a same-sex couple is, in Scotland, prohibited (Fostering of Children (Scotland) Regulations 1996, SI 1996/3263 (S 253), r 12(4)). Pregnancy as a result of donated sperm will help some lesbians become 'parents' but their partners cannot adopt unless the birth parent gives up her rights, which would seldom be in the interests of the child and so seldom practically available (see *Re an Application by T* [1998] NZFLR 769); a parenting order after a surrogacy arrangement (which is likely to be used by male couples rather than female couples) is unavailable under the Human Fertilisation and Embryology Act 1990, s 30 since that order, like a joint adoption order, is available only to married couples (s 30(1)). And initial access by either a single woman (of whatever sexual orientation) or a lesbian couple to infertility treatment is, while not prohibited, certainly inhibited by HFEA 1990, s 13(5) which requires the provider of licensed infertility services to take account of the child's need for a 'father'. 'Father' in this and other provisions in the HFEA 1990 means a chromosomally male person: *X, Y and Z v UK* (1997) 24 EHRR 143.

law cases that judges first had to deal, in family law terms, with gay men and lesbians[1].

'Gay parenting is bad for children'

Originally, and unsurprisingly, judges tended to consider it axiomatic that it was against the welfare of children to be brought up by gay men or lesbians or to be exposed to gay or lesbian lifestyles. The assumptions inherent in such a view have been well exposed in the literature[2]. The beauty of an axiom, of course, is that it avoids the need for an explanation of the fears behind it. One could understand, without subscribing to, this assessment of welfare when the shadow of criminality hung over those bringing up children[3], but once that shadow was removed it became all the more essential to subject judicial fears to rational scrutiny. And as this happened, these fears have been revealed as chimerae.

Helen Reece[4] points out that until about the late 1970s the fear that children would be contaminated with homosexuality (ie would either be sexually abused or would become gay or lesbian themselves) was the main judicial concern lurking behind most of the decisions[5], but that since then the main concern has switched to the fear of the child being stigmatised and picked on and bullied as

1 Family law is not, however, the only area in which judicial fears for the safety of children manifest themselves. In *Saunders v Scottish National Camps Association* [1980] IRLR 174 an employment appeal tribunal upheld a decision of an industrial tribunal which refused to find unfair the dismissal of a man for being gay. They held that the industrial tribunal were entitled to find that a considerable proportion of employers would restrict the employment of homosexuals when required to work in proximity to children. The Court of Session found other reasons to uphold this wicked decision ([1981] IRLR 277) but they certainly did not distance themselves from these comments. The approach in *Saunders* is reflected in some jurisdictions' statutory law, such as some Australian states, where anti-discrimination provisions sometimes contain exceptions in relation to work involving children: see for example the Anti-Discrimination Act 1991 (QLD), s 28 and the Anti-Discrimination Act 1992 (NT), s 37.

2 See, in particular, S Boyd 'What is a "Normal" Family?' (1992) 55 MLR 269; 'Lesbian (and Gay) Custody Claims: What Difference Does Difference Make?' (1997) 15 *Can J Fam L* 131; H Reece 'Subverting the Stigmatisation Argument' (1996) 23 *J Law & Soc* 484; J Millbank 'Same-Sex Couples and Family Law', accessible at www.familycourt.gov.au/papers/html/millbank.html; Barton 'The Homosexual in the Family' [1996] *Fam Law* 626.

3 Though criminality was never an issue in the UK with lesbians, and it is gay women who remain much more likely than gay men to be bringing up children, the criminality attached to men certainly affected the social and judicial perception of women in same-sex relationships. In some jurisdictions in the US anti-sodomy legislation survives, and 'sodomy' is defined to mean all sexual activity except penile penetration of the vagina, with the result that lesbian sex is unlawful, and that fact has been used to deny lesbian women custody of their children: see, for example, *Bottoms v Bottoms* 444 SE 2d 276 (Va 1994).

4 H Reece 'Subverting the Stigmatisation Argument' (1996) 23 *J Law & Soc* 484.

5 See, for example, *Re D (An Infant) (Adoption: Parent's Consent)* [1977] AC 602 where Lord Wilberforce was unwilling to contemplate a gay man bringing up his child because of the risk that this 'may lead to severance from normal society, to psychological stress and unhappiness and possibly even to physical experiences which may scar them for life' (at 629). In *L & L* (1983) FLC 91-353 the High Court of Australia granted custody to a lesbian mother, but emphasised repeatedly that they were doing so because they were persuaded that she would 'not encourage the children to become homosexual'. In *JLP v DJP* 643 SC 2d 865 (Mo 1982) the Missouri court said this (in the face of expert testimony that homosexual child abuse was uncommon): 'Given the statistical incidence of homosexuality in the population . . . homosexual molestation is probably, on an absolute basis, more prevalent' (in other words, gay men are, self-evidently, more likely to abuse children than non-gay men). The court continued: 'Every trial judge . . . knows that the molestation of minor boys by adult males is not as uncommon as the psychological expert's testimony indicated' (in other words, it is within judicial knowledge that homosexual child abuse is more prevalent than the evidence presented to the court showed).

a result of a gay parent's sexuality. She suggests that the reason for this shift in approach was that the corruption argument was clearly judgmental (and unsustainable in the light of social and psychological research[1]) while the stigmatisation argument appears to be benignly neutral by focusing on the child itself, and more appropriate, therefore, for judicial expression. But she also points out that the risk of stigmatisation is, according to the research, as illusory as the risk of corruption. And Susan Boyd makes the powerful point that the stigmatisation argument 'allows one discriminatory act (homophobia in the community) to condone another (depriving lesbians and homosexual men of custody)'[2]. Yet the stigmatisation argument remains the preferred weapon of choice for judges seeking to deny gay parents residence of their children: because, Reece suggests, its very plausibility in theory dispenses with the need to prove it in reality.

This can be seen in a series of custody cases whose reasoning, from today's perspective, appears deeply flawed. In *Re P (A Minor) (Custody)*[3] a father sought to deprive a lesbian mother of custody while failing to offer the children a home himself – he argued that the children should be removed to local authority care. The Court of Appeal would not go that far but they did indicate that living in proximity to 'sexual deviance' could 'only be countenanced by the courts when it is driven to the conclusion' that there is no acceptable alternative. It was assumed, in other words, that living with a lesbian (or, presumably, a gay man) was the very last option (before local authority care) that ought to be considered. Eight years later the terminology of 'deviance' had been dropped, but in *B v B (Minors) (Custody, Care and Control)*[4] it was still assumed that the parent's homosexuality was a strongly negative factor in a custody dispute. In that case Judge Callman awarded custody to the lesbian mother, having found no evidence in the literature or research to support fears for the child's sexual orientation or for the risk of stigmatisation. However, he felt constrained to point out 'categorically' that it was important to distinguish between, on the one hand, lesbians 'who were private persons who did not believe in advertising their lesbianism' (like the mother in the present case)[5] and, on the other hand, 'militant lesbians who tried to convert others to their way of life'. Not only does the judge explicitly prefer gay women to remain within a heterosexually imposed realm of invisibility but, having in one part of his judgment dismissed reliance on unproveable fears based on stereotyping, he falls precisely into that trap when faced with the hypothetical militant proselytising lesbian. The implicit message is clear even from this case in which the lesbian mother was awarded custody: it would be bad

1 See in particular the important studies by Tasker and Golombok in the UK: 'Children Raised by Lesbian Mothers: The Empirical Evidence' (1991) *Fam L* 184; and 'Do Parents Influence the Sexual Orientation of their Children? Findings From a Longitudinal Study of Lesbian Families' (1996) 32 *Developmental Psychology* 3; and Patterson in the USA: 'Children of Lesbian and Gay Parents' (1992) 63 *Child Development* 1025. A wealth of research material has also been gathered together by McNeill 'The Lack of Differences Between Gay/Lesbian and Heterosexual Parents: A Review of the Literature' (1998) *National Journal of Sexual Orientation Law*, vol 4 issue 1, accessible at http://metalab.unc.edu/gaylaw/issue6/Mcneill.htm. Reece herself draws on an extensive array of this literature, not only to refute the corruption argument but to draw attention to some of the social benefits of gay parenting.

2 S Boyd, 'What is a "Normal" Family?' (1992) 55 *Mod LR* 269 at 274.

3 *Re P (A Minor) (Custody)* (1983) 4 FLR 401.

4 *B v B (Minors) (Custody, Care and Control)* [1991] *Fam Law* 176; [1991] 1 FLR 402.

5 This had been a concern also in *Re P* (A Minor) (Custody) (1983) 4 FLR 401, where Arnold P (at 404) clearly warmed to the mother because 'she is not one of those homosexuals who, as many do nowadays, flaunt their homosexuality'. Such flaunting of judicial heterosexuality is not uncommon.

for a child to grow up gay, which is of course the central flaw in the 'corruption/conversion/contamination' argument[1] which the judge purports to reject.

Lord Davidson in the Outer House of the Court of Session did not even distinguish between the 'good' (ie invisible) and the 'bad' (ie public) lesbian in *Early v Early*[2], when he removed an eight-year-old child from the mother who had always looked after him and awarded custody to his father, who had never looked after him and who had two convictions for child neglect[3]. The judge said that he was concerned about the fact that the child, living in a lesbian household, would have no male role models and might be teased at school. This case is remarkable in that the stigmatisation argument was deployed even while it was accepted (notice the 'might' at the end of the preceding sentence) that there was no evidence in the instant case that the fear had any basis in the reality of the life of the child whose future was being decided.

A rather different, but equally problematical, approach was adopted in the English decision of *C v C (A Minor) (Custody: Appeal)*[4]. Here Ward J had granted custody of a child to the mother, but was overruled for giving wholly inadequate weight to the fact that she had entered into a lesbian relationship. The Court of Appeal said that this fact would clearly have an effect on the child and that this had to be taken into account. The importance of that consideration turned on the issue of 'normality' and its – again self-evident – attractions. Glidewell LJ said:

> 'Despite the vast changes during the last 30 years or so in the attitudes of society to the institution of marriage, to sexual morality and to homosexual relationships, I regard it as axiomatic that the ideal environment for the upbringing of a child is the home of loving and sensible parents. When a marriage breaks down and that ideal cannot be attained and the court is called upon to decide which of two possible alternatives is then preferable for the child's welfare, its task is to choose the alternative which comes closest to that ideal'[5].

Leaving aside both the clumsy assumption that loving and sensible parents are always married and the fact that the axiom which founds the judge's reasoning is empirically unsubstantiated, the flaw in this approach is that it is unworkable in the absence of an evaluation of the factors that make any particular family form 'ideal'. Given that the family form of mother, father (married to each other) and child is not on offer, we cannot tell which is closer to that form if the options are either (i) mother, lesbian partner and child, or (ii) single father and child, without making a value-judgment on single parenthood, sexual orientation, and even male parenting. This lack of evaluation permits the judge to hide his negative assumptions about sexuality. Balcombe LJ held[6] that the judge had to choose which of the two available options 'can offer the nearest approach to [the] norm' but that approach is flawed for the same reason. The fact that one option is closer to the 'norm' than another is a matter of entirely neutral statistics. It is, for example, a departure from normality for a child to be brought up by a

1 Leaving aside entirely, as unworthy of comment, the assumptions (i) that conversion is possible and (ii) that attempts at conversion are ever actually made.

2 *Early v Early* 1989 SLT 114, affirmed 1990 SLT 221.

3 Both the Outer House and the Inner House judges denied that the mother's lesbianism was a decisive factor, but it is interesting to compare the minimal time both Lord Davidson and the Inner House spent worrying about the father's convictions with the time they spent worrying about the mother's lesbianism.

4 *C v C (A Minor) (Custody Appeal)* [1991] *Fam L* 175, [1991] 1 FLR 223.

5 *C v C (A Minor) (Custody Appeal)* [1991] 1 FLR at 228.

6 *C v C (A Minor) (Custody Appeal)* [1991] 1 FLR 223 at 231.

left-handed parent. But that tells us nothing about the child's welfare until we put a value on left-handedness or right-handedness. Only once a value is attributed (preferably founded on empirical evidence rather than assumptions and preconceptions) are we able to use it in the welfare balance – and a zero value such as would be attributed to left- or right-handedness renders the matter irrelevant to the application of the welfare test. It is likewise a departure from the norm (given that, statistically, there are fewer gay people than non-gay people) for a child to be brought up by a gay or lesbian parent, or for that matter by a single father, but these matters are in themselves irrelevant to the welfare test until such time as a value other than zero is attributed to them. It is entirely illegitimate ever to assume a negative (or, for that matter, a positive) value as 'axiomatic'.

'Gay parenting is bad . . . or is it?'

From about the mid-1990s, courts in the United Kingdom began to be more sanguine at the idea of gay and lesbian parenting, and at co-parenting by same-sex partners. In *Re H (A Minor) (Section 37 Direction)*[1] and *Re C (A Minor) (Residence Order: Lesbian Co-parents)*[2] joint residence orders were made in favour of lesbian couples one of whom had each, through donor insemination, given birth to a child. And in *G v F (Contact and Shared Residence: Applications for Leave)*[3] on the breakdown of the relationship between a lesbian couple the ex-co-parent was granted leave to make an application for contact and shared residence[4]. The watershed case in judicial attitudes in the United Kingdom to gay and lesbian parenting in the 1990s is the Scottish adoption case of *T Petitioner*[5] in which the Inner House of the Court of Session granted an adoption petition made by a gay man notwithstanding that he shared his life with a male partner who would take an active part in the upbringing of the child. The judge at first instance (Lord Gill) had refused to grant the adoption (notwithstanding that it was opposed by no one) on the basis that the fact that the petitioner was gay raised a 'fundamental question of principle'. The Inner House held that there was no such fundamental question and that the judge was wrong to base his decision on his own unsupported 'preconceptions about homosexuality'[6]. The importance of this decision lies in its rejection of the stereotyping to which gay men and lesbians had previously been judicially subjected[7]. It explicitly rejects the convenience of axiom which assumes without proof that gay or lesbian parents constitute some threat of harm to their children. Since *T Petitioner* and its English equivalent it

1 *Re H (A Minor) (Section 37 Direction)* [1993] *Fam Law* 205.

2 *Re C (A Minor) (Residence Order: Lesbian Co-parents)* [1994] *Fam LR* 468, [1994] *Practitioner's Child Law Bulletin* 95.

3 *G v F (Contact and Shared Residence: Applications for Leave)* [1998] 2 FLR 798.

4 For an unreported Scottish case involving a lesbian mother in which an ex-partner was held to have title to seek a s 11 order over a child, see *R v F*, discussed by J Fotheringham 1999 SLT (News) 337.

5 *T Petr* 1997 SLT 724. For comment, see K Norrie 'Parental Pride: Adoption and the Gay Man' 1996 SLT (News) 321, and M Ross 'Attitudes to Sexual Orientation in Adoption Law' (1997) 1 *Edin LR* 370.

6 *T Petr* 1997 SLT 724. Per Lord President Hope at 735L. The case was followed in England in *Re W (A Minor) (Adoption: Homosexual Adopter)* [1997] 3 All ER 620. See also *Re E (A Minor) (Adoption: Freeing Order)* [1995] 1 FLR 382 and the Canadian decision in *Re K and B* (1995) 125 DLR (4th) 653.

7 It is stereotyping that, for reasons most eloquently explained by Ackermann J in *National Coalition for Gay and Lesbian Equality v Minister for Home Affairs* 1999 (3) BCLR 280 at para 44, constitutes the most direct attack on the human dignity of gay men and lesbians. Stereotyping of human beings was the basis of Nazi philosophy.

ought not to be sufficient in a British court to raise the homosexuality of a parent or prospective parent and expect the court to assume some harm, though, of course, it always and rightly remains open to any party to lead evidence to show that a particular person constitutes a risk of harm to a particular child.

The approach exemplified by *T Petitioner* ought now to be regarded as entrenched in British constitutional law with the incorporation by the Human Rights Act 1998 of the European Convention on Human Rights and the requirement on domestic courts to follow the jurisprudence of the European Court of Human Rights[1]. That jurisprudence requires that discrimination in relation to the substantive rights contained in the Convention (including the right to respect for family life[2]) be permitted only when it has an objective and reasonable justification, that is to say when it has a legitimate aim, and when there is a reasonable relationship of proportionality between that legitimate aim and the means employed to achieve it[3]. The doctrine of proportionality requires an examination of the facts in each individual case and a rejection of stereotypical assumptions that might not be relevant in the particular circumstances before the court. In *da Silva Mouta v Portugal*[4] the European Court of Human Rights held that while the identification and protection of a child's welfare was clearly a legitimate aim, the means adopted to further that end, being a blanket discrimination against gay men and lesbians in residence disputes, was unjustified[5]. Discrimination on the basis of sexual orientation, it was held (for the first time, incidentally), came within the terms of The European Convention on Human Rights, art 14 and could not possibly be justified[6].

So, from a position in the 1980s in which the courts regarded same-sex relationships as 'deviance' from which children had to be protected, they are, at the turn of the 21st century, to be seen as in no way morally inferior to opposite-sex relationships, as an environment suitable for the bringing up of children[7]. Once that position has been reached, the way is open for same-sex relationships to attract in their own right, independently of children, legal recognition and protection.

1 Human Rights Act 1998, s 2. See I Karsten 'Atypical Families and the Human Rights Act: The Rights of Unmarried Fathers, Same-Sex Couples and Transsexuals' (1999) EHRLR 195.

2 European Convention on Human Rights, art 8(1). The European Court of Human Rights has not yet extended the right to family life to same-sex couples, but the House of Lords held that such a couple can be 'family' within the terms of domestic legislation (*Fitzpatrick v Sterling Housing Association* [1999] 4 All ER 707). The French *Conseil d'Etat* did, however, hold that same-sex couples come within 'family life' for the purposes of art 8 in *Prefet des Alpes Maritimes c M Marroussitch* 28 April 2000 (2000 *Pub L* 731) when it decided that deportation of a non-national in a stable and long-term relationship with a French person of the same sex was a disproportionate infringement of his art 8 right to family life.

3 *Marckx v Belgium* (1979) 2 EHRR 330 at para 33; *Inze v Austria* (1987) 10 EHRR 394, para 41; *Schmidt v Germany* (1994) 18 EHRR 513, para 24.

4 2001 Fam LR 2. See K Norrie 'Stay Standing if you Like Gay People' (2000) *SCOLAG* 34.

5 The extent to which this case can be used by members of same-sex couples to access other family law rights and liabilities in Scots and English law is explored in K Norrie 'Constitutional Challenges to Sexual Orientation Discrimination' (2000) 49 *ICLQ* 755.

6 The same constitutional entrenchment of protection from sexual orientation discrimination can be seen in *V v V* 1998 (4) SA 169 where the South African court founded upon the South African Constitution (and, interestingly, the United Nations Convention on the Rights of the Child) to reject a father's claim for sole custody on the basis that the mother's lesbian relationship might affect the children's sexual orientation. This decision renders the dreadful decision of *Van Rooyen v Van Rooyen* 1994 (2) SA 325 redundant.

7 There still remain, anomalously, statutory inhibitions on gay people accessing the status of 'parent' – see n 2 on p 154 above.

Direct recognition of same-sex relationships

Beyond the acceptance of same-sex relationships in so far as they involved children, the law in most jurisdictions until very recently simply ignored the fact that gay men and lesbians not only had sex with each other but also lived their lives together, undertook commitments towards each other and shared bonds of affection: these facts were of no concern to the law and carried no legal consequences. However, as the years passed from decriminalisation, and society's attitudes towards gay men and lesbians changed so that they came to be accepted in all walks of life – even at the highest levels of government – the issue moved from the private to the public, from the demand (now partially achieved[1]) to allow individuals a private (sex) life without state interference when that did not infringe on the rights of others, to the demand (still remote from achievement) to allow individuals to enter into unions bearing the full civic rights and responsibilities that attach to opposite-sex relationships. At first, such a demand met with uncomprehending resistance. Statute declared in 1988, famously and ungrammatically, that 'homosexuality' was a 'pretended family relationship'[2], and any government that passed such substantively meaningless[3] but symbolically malicious legislation was unlikely to enact other legislation conferring even the smallest degree of legitimacy on same-sex relationships. But governments, like walls, fall. Even before the eventual repeal (in Scotland) of the 1988 declaration, courts in the United Kingdom were able to fashion remedies out of the stuff of the common law which could be accessed by same-sex and opposite-sex couples alike, and even, in rare but significant situations, interpret the statutory law to apply to both types of couple.

In *Tilsley v Milligan*[4], for example, the House of Lords accepted the existence of a 'common intention constructive trust'[5] between two lesbians[6]: this is an (admittedly clumsy) way of providing for property readjustment on the break-up of a relationship. And in *Wayling v Jones*[7] the plaintiff successfully utilised the concept

1 Decriminalisation of gay male sexual acts has only partially fulfilled the demand for sexual equality. There is in the first place the (important) symbolism of language. The Criminal Law (Consolidation) (Scotland) Act 1995, s 13, which permits men to have sex with each other, permits what it describes as 'sodomy' and 'gross indecency' and 'shameless indecency': by this means the criminal law continues to constitute gay men (and by implication lesbians) as 'other': I make love, you have sex, he is grossly indecent. Second, sex between men remains more heavily regulated than sex between men and women (and far more regulated than sex between women), as is seen in Scotland by comparing the CL(C)(S)A 1995, s 13 with the earlier provisions in the same Act regulating (for purely protective reasons) non-gay sex. Third, we continue to see a preference shown for non-gay sex in, for example, the mental health legislation where the criminality of sexual acts with those of compromised understanding is much more tightly drawn for non-gay sex than for gay (male) sex – compare the Mental Health (Scotland) Act 1984, s 106 with CL(C)(S)A 1995, s 13(3).

2 Local Government Act 1986, s 2A, inserted by Local Government Act 1988, s 28; repealed (in Scotland) by the Ethical Standards in Public Life etc (Scotland) Act 2000 (asp 7), s 34.

3 See K Norrie 'Symbolic and Meaningless Legislation' (1988) 33 JLSS 310; and 'How to Promote Homosexuality: A Guide for Schools and Colleges' 1989 SCOLAG 74.

4 *Tilsley v Milligan* [1993] 3 All ER 65.

5 Developed in the domestic relations context by the House of Lords in *Pettitt v Pettitt* [1970] AC 777 and *Gissing v Gissing* [1971] AC 886. That the unmarried nature of the relationship is irrelevant was confirmed in *Grant v Edwards* [1986] Ch 638. For a discussion, see S Gardner 'Rethinking Family Property' (1993) 109 *LQR* 263 and J Mee, *The Property Rights of Cohabitees* (1999) Hart Publishing, Oxford.

6 See, to similar effect, the Canadian decision of *Anderson v Luomo* (1985) 14 DLR (4th) 749 and the New Zealand decision of *Hamilton v Jurgens* [1996] NZFLR 350.

7 *Wayling v Jones* [1995] 2 FLR 1029.

of proprietary estoppel to claim a portion of the estate of his deceased same-sex partner[1]. In neither of these cases, however, did the sexual orientation of the claimant, or the same-sex nature of their relationships, have much bearing on the issue, which was whether the common law doctrines involved applied in the particular circumstances of these cases[2]. All that can be taken from them is the dog (morality) that did not bark. Rather more significant is the case of *Fitzpatrick v Sterling Housing Association*[3] in which the House of Lords signals a more functionalist than formalist approach to family law. The plaintiff was the survivor of a same-sex couple, who sought to succeed to the tenancy held by his now-deceased partner on the basis that he was either the 'spouse' of the deceased tenant or a 'member of the tenant's family'. His claim to be a 'spouse' failed on the basis that the word is necessarily limited to a partner of the opposite sex, but he was successful in his claim to be a member of his partner's family. The majority in the House of Lords interpreted 'family' by looking at its function rather than at its form, with the important issue being how the relationship operates rather than its precise legal status. Though the technical effect of this decision was extremely limited, given that there are very few statutory benefits and liabilities accessed through the concept of 'family'[4], its symbolic importance is profound. A 'family' is a socially acceptable grouping of individuals and by accepting the concept of the gay family the House of Lords has conferred upon same-sex relationships a legitimacy (both social and legal) that they never had before. Further, in adopting a functionalist approach to determining which relationships are open to legal recognition and protection, the House of Lords is moving away from a status-based approach to family law in general. This is a matter to which we shall return.

Developments abroad

In 1999, as well as the non-constitutional decision of the House of Lords in *Fitzpatrick*, courts in three other English-speaking jurisdictions handed down judgments, the importance of which it is difficult to overstate, in cases in which the different treatment afforded same-sex and opposite-sex couples was directly, and successfully, challenged as being unconstitutional[5]. The Supreme Court of Canada held unconstitutional an Ontario provision[6] which provided

1 In the Australian case of *W v G* (1996) 20 Fam LR 49 (NSW) the doctrine of promissory estoppel was used by one ex-partner of a lesbian relationship against the other ex-partner to force the latter to contribute to the costs of bringing up the children born to the former during the course of the relationship. See J Millbank 'An Implied Promise to Parent: Lesbian Families, Litigation and *W v G*' (1996) 10 *Aust J Fam L* 112; R. Bailey-Harris 'Equity Still Child-Bearing in Australia?' (1997) 113 *LQR* 227.

2 The success of this approach depends, of course, on the existing legal environment and the legal materials available from which remedies can be fashioned. Scots law recognises constructive trusts and so property readjustment at the breakdown of a relationship might be possible in Scotland; proprietary estoppel and dependants' claims to succession do not exist in Scotland and a claim such as in *Wayling v Jones* [1995] 2 FLR 1029 could not be made here.

3 *Fitzpatrick v Sterling Housing Association* [1999] 4 All ER 707. For comment, see K Norrie 'We Are Family (Sometimes): Legal Recognition of Same-Sex Relationships After *Fitzpatrick*' (2000) 4 *Edin LR* 256; L Glennon '*Fitzpatrick v Sterling Housing Association*: An Endorsement of the Functional Family' (2000) 14 *Int J Law Pol & the Family* 226.

4 See K Norrie We Are Family (Sometimes): Legal Recognition of Same-Sex Relationships After *Fitzpatrick* 2000 4 *Edin LR* 256, at pp 271–276.

5 For a fuller discussion of these cases than is necessary here, see K Norrie 'Constitutional Challenges to Sexual Orientation Discrimination' (2000) 49 ICLQ 755.

6 The Ontario Family Law Act 1990, s 29(1).

for the awarding of financial readjustment on the break-up of both married relationships and unmarried but heterosexual relationships[1]; the Constitutional Court of South Africa held unconstitutional an immigration law[2] which allowed entry into South Africa of 'spouses' of South African citizens but excluded, through their inability to marry, the same-sex partners of such citizens[3]; and the Supreme Court of Vermont held it to be unconstitutionally discriminatory for the state to confer on married couples a whole raft of rights and responsibilities while not providing any means by which same-sex couples could access the same rights and responsibilities[4]. The most interesting feature about these three cases is the similarity in the arguments that the state in each used to justify the difference in treatment between same-sex and opposite-sex couples[5]. In secular societies which had long since decriminalised gay male sexual acts, and in which non-discrimination legislation was well-embedded, the states could not argue on the basis of the inherent 'wrongness' of same-sex relationships, though one is left with the impression, from the poverty of the arguments that were in fact advanced, that this was the underlying political stance. Predictably, the main justification put forward in all three cases was the need to protect children. This argument is illogical in those jurisdictions, like Vermont, which allow same-sex couples to adopt, and it was summarily dismissed as such there. But it is also illogical in any jurisdiction which countenances gay or lesbian people bringing up children, for this is an acceptance, as explained above, that children do not need to be protected from gayness per se. Another argument common to all three cases was that the exclusion of same-sex couples from legal recognition is necessary to protect the 'traditional' family. There is no substance to this argument either since the legal rights and liabilities of those entering into 'traditional' relationships are entirely unaffected by extending the rights and liabilities to others. In truth, those who claim to 'protect' the traditional family are seeking to preserve its special and preferred status[6], but since non-marital

1 *M v H* (1999) 171 DLR (4th) 577.

2 Aliens Control Act 96 of 1991.

3 *National Coalition for Gay and Lesbian Equality v Minister for Home Affairs* 1999 (3) BCLR 280. For comment, see R. Louw, 'Gay and Lesbian Partner Immigration and the Redefining of Family' (2000) 16 SAJHR 313; S. Motara, 'Making the Bill of Rights a Reality for Gay and Lesbian Couples' (2000) 16 SAJHR 344; de Vos 'Sexual Orientation and the Right to Equality in the South African Constitution' (2000) 117 SALJ 17; and Pantazis 'Lesbian and Gay Youth in Law' (2000) 117 SALJ 51.

4 *Baker v Vermont* 744 A2d 864 (1999).

5 See further, K Norrie 'Constitutional Challenges', n 5 on p 161 above, at 762–766.

6 In some countries marriage itself is given a special constitutionally preferred status. This is the case, for example, in Germany where the *Grundgesetz*, art 6 requires the state to give the institution of marriage 'special' (*besonderen*) protection. This has been interpreted to mean, for example, that in tax law married couples must be treated more favourably than single persons or unmarried couples: see D Hesselberger *Das Grundgesetz*, vol. II, pp 104–107. The European Convention on Human Rights, art 12 protects the 'right to marry' but while marriage for that purpose is the 'traditional' monogamous heterosexual union (see *Rees v UK* (1987) 9 EHRR 56 and *Cossey v UK* (1990) 13 EHRR 622) there is no implication that the state must give preferential treatment to such traditional unions as opposed to other unions, just as the right to found a family in the same article does not require the state to treat groupings of individuals better than individuals. Similarly, the limitation of ECHR, art 12 to 'traditional' unions does not inhibit the state conferring identical – or even, for that matter, greater – rights on other unions (otherwise we get the implausible result that those countries that have extended the consequences of marriage to cohabitants and registered partnerships are in breach of ECHR, art 12). Nor does the limitation of ECHR, art 12 to marriage as presently understood inhibit any state's right to vary its rules of entry: if the Netherlands is in breach of ECHR, art 12 by opening up marriage to same-sex couples then so too was the UK when it opened up marriage between ex-in-laws (Marriage (Prohibited Degrees of Relationship) Act 1986).

relationships have long been given some protection, the argument resolves into one of maintaining an institutional preference for heterosexuality and has little to do with 'family' as such.

Other legal systems have granted comprehensive statutory recognition of same-sex relationships to the extent of putting them in the same legal position as opposite-sex, though unmarried, couples. This is the case, for example, in New South Wales[1], New Zealand[2], in the Canadian provinces (following the decision of the Supreme Court of Canada in *M v H*[3]), and in the Spanish autonomous regions of Aragon and Catalonia[4]. Some jurisdictions have gone significantly further and created an institution for same-sex couples which has more or less all the legal consequences of the opposite-sex institution of marriage. Denmark, as is well known, was the first country in the world to do so, calling the institution (in English translation) 'Registered Partnerships'[5], and this lead has been followed by Iceland, Sweden, Norway[6] and the Netherlands[7]. France too has created an institution of registered cohabitation[8], open to same-sex and opposite-sex couples. As a result of the case of *Baker v Vermont*, the State of Vermont became the first in the United States to introduce a similar institution, called there 'civil unions'[9].

Marriage

So far, only one country in the world has taken what some see as the ultimate family law step and opened up its definition of marriage to include same-sex couples[10]. This occurred on 1 April 2001 in the Netherlands[11]. But claims by same-sex couples to access that institution have been made in many countries and are not new. As early as 1971 attempts were being made to persuade United States courts that statutes limiting marriage to opposite-sex couples were

---

1 See the Property (Relationships) Legislation Amendment Act 1999 (NSW), which amends the previously titled De Facto Relationships Act 1984 (now the Property (Relationships) Act 1984).

2 See the Property (Relationships) Amendment Act 2001, the Administration Amendment Act 2001 and the Family Protection Amendment Act 2001.

3 (1999) 171 DLR (4th) 577.

4 See E Roca 'Regulation of Same-Sex Partnerships from a Spanish Perspective' in M Maclean (ed) *Making Law for Families* (2000) Hart Publishing, Oxford at p 95 ff.

5 For a discussion of these provisions, see L Nielsen 'Family Rights and the "Registered Partnership in Denmark"' (1990) 4 *Int J Law & Fam* 297; M Broberg 'The Registered Partnership for Same-Sex Couples in Denmark' (1996) 8 *C & Fam L Q* 149. It should be noted that the rule described in these articles prohibiting registered partners from jointly adopting was removed in 1999.

6 See I Lund-Andersen 'Cohabitation and Registered Partnership in Scandanavia: The Legal Position of Homosexuals', in J Eekelaar & T Nhlapo (eds), *The Changing Family: Family Forms and Family Law* (1998) Hart Publishing, Oxford.

7 See W Schrama 'Registered Partnerships in the Netherlands' (1999) 13 *Int J Law Pol & the Fam* 315.

8 See C Martin and I Thery 'The PACS and Marriage and Cohabitation in France' (2001) 15 *Int J Law Pol & the Fam* 135.

9 Bill H847 (2000).

10 Marriage in every other jurisdiction is regarded as an institution ring-fencing heterosexual relationships. This is understood at common law (see *Corbett v Corbett (No 1)* [1970] 2 All ER 33 (England) and, to the same effect in South Africa, *W v W* 1976 (2) SA 308), under statute (see, in Scotland, the Marriage (Scotland) Act 1977, s 5(4)(e) and in England the Matrimonial Causes Act 1973, s 11(c)) and under European Human Rights Law (*Rees v UK* (1987) 9 EHRR 56; *Cossey v UK* (1990) 13 EHRR 622).

11 See K Waaldijk at http//ruljis.leidenuniv.nl/user/cwaaldij/www/NHR/news.htm.

unconstitutional.[1] These attempts were at that time uniformly unsuccessful, usually on the basis that marriage is an institution for procreation and the rearing of children[2]. More successful was the Hawaii case of *Baere v Levin*[3] in which the Hawaii Supreme Court held that the state had to produce compelling reasons why marriage should be limited to opposite-sex couples. When it was unable to do so[4], the way might have been open to same-sex marriage in that state, but for the fact that the legislature responded by changing the constitution of Hawaii[5]. In New Zealand an attempt was made in *Quilter v Attorney General*[6] to persuade the court that the Marriage Act 1955 was worded in gender-neutral terms and that it would be contrary to the New Zealand Bill of Rights Act 1990 to interpret it in such a way as excluded same-sex marriage. That attempt failed too. It would seem that constitutional challenges through the courts to the very definition of marriage are unlikely to be successful[7]. More successful, however, have been claims that it is discriminatory to deny same-sex couples some or all of the legal rights and liabilities that can be accessed by married couples: in other words claims to access the individual incidents of marriage, rather than the institution itself, are more likely to be successful. The interesting feature

1 See M Dupuis 'The Impact of Culture, Society and History on the Legal Process: An Analysis of the Legal Status of Same-Sex Relationships in the United States and Denmark' (1995) 9 *Int J L and the Fam* 86 at pp 88–95 for a discussion of the most important cases: *Baker v Nelson*, 191 NW 2d 185 (1971, Supreme Court of Minnesota); *Jones v Hallahan* 501 SW 2d 588 (1973, Court of Appeals of Kentucky); *Singer v Hara* 522 P2d 1187 (1974, Court of Appeals of Washington). In *Adams* v *Howerton* 673 F2D 1036 (9th Cir, 1982), unlike the other cases which sought to force the issuing of marriage licences, a marriage licence was actually issued to two men, but when legal recognition of the union was requested for practical purposes (in this case, immigration) the court refused. The main social policy which justified giving marriage protected status was stated to be procreation. *De Santo v Barnsley* 476 A2d 952 (1984) is interesting – a petition for divorce was raised by one man against another, the petitioner claiming that there existed a 'common law marriage' (which seems to be halfway between cohabitation and the Scottish concept of marriage by cohabitation with habit and repute) and claiming thereby financial provision. The petition was rejected on the basis that 'common law marriage' had to be identical, except in the lack of ceremony, to statutory marriage.

2 *Baker v Nelson* 191 NW2d 185 at 186; *Singer v Hara* 522 P2d 1187 at 1195.

3 852 P2d 44 (Hawaii, 1993). For analysis, see M Dupuis 'The Impact of Culture, Society and History on the Legal Process: An Analysis of the Legal Status of Same-Sex Relationships in the United States and Denmark' 1995 9 *Int JL and the Fam* 86 at pp 95–98.

4 *Baere v Miike* 910 P2d 112 (Hawaii 1996).

5 That change was retrospective: *Baere v Anderson* 9 Dec 1999 (unreported). The same occurred in Alaska after a case there called *Brause v Bureau of Vital Statistics* 1998 WL 88743. Around the same time as the Hawaii and Alaska cases, courts in the District of Columbia and New York State rejected marriage claims, on similar grounds to the earlier cases: see *Dean v District of Columbia* 653 A2d 307 (1995) and *Storrs v Holcomb* 168 Misc 2d 898 (1996).

6 [1998] 1 NZLR 523. For comment, see Butler 'Same-Sex Marriage and Freedom from Discrimination in New Zealand' [1998] Pub L 396.

7 This conclusion is not inevitable. The so-called 'traditional' definition of marriage is simply the one that is accepted by the law of any legal system at any particular point in its history, and that definition is not immutable. Not only do different countries define marriage differently (eg western countries normally define it as a monogamous union while some countries with a Muslim tradition define it to include polygamous unions) but single systems also change both their definitions (eg marriage was originally defined as a union for life, but that definition changed in Scotland in 1567 and in England in 1857 when divorce was introduced) and their rules for entry (eg the rules on a man marrying his deceased wife's mother were changed in the UK by the Marriage (Prohibited Degrees of Relationship) Act 1986, and the bar on inter-racial marriage in some states in the USA was declared unconstitutional in *Loving v Virginia* 388 US 1 (1967)).

about the Netherlands is that the marriage debate was played out – relatively uncontentiously[1] – in the legislature rather than the courts.

SEEKING MEANING

The narrative above shows that from about the mid-1990s on, there has been an ever-increasing movement throughout the western world towards the legal recognition of same-sex relationships, starting with ad hoc recognition in limited circumstances, through an equiperation with cohabiting opposite-sex couples, and culminating, in some countries, in the introduction of institutions which, in all but name, are legal marriages[2] and, in the Netherlands, is called marriage. How are we to explain this sudden explosion of judicial and legislative right-thinking? Part of the explanation must lie, of course, in the increased social acceptability and, vitally, social visibility of gay men and lesbians, and same-sex relationships, itself probably a consequence of decriminalisation, without which the environment of ignorance and distrust of 'other' could never truly dissipate. It is probably now not possible to separate out legal changes and social changes and to identify one as leading to the other – rather it is likely that they fed off and justified each other, but the catalyst for change, in either aspect, remains obscure. Waaldijk, in his study of the sequenced steps towards legal recognition taken in the European countries[3], explicitly locates the decriminalisation and anti-discrimination legislation, which occurred in Europe primarily in the late 1960s and in the early 1980s, within the context of the civil rights movements seeking equality and justice for racial minorities and, latterly, of a more current international human rights movement. Accessing this analogy is easy given that gay men and lesbians have little difficulty in pointing to a history of prejudice and discrimination; those who oppose them have substantial difficulty in distinguishing between race and sex discrimination (the moral and political arguments against which have long since been won[4]) and sexual orientation discrimination (the arguments in favour of which remain in the eyes of many – even those who disagree – within the bounds of morally and politically acceptable debate). Edwin Cameron, one of the most cerebral of writers on South African law[5], denies that it is possible so to distinguish the various forms of discrimination[6]. He points out that, historically, a variety of arguments were deployed in the effort to justify the oppression of women and blacks – there were naturalistic/biblical arguments (the bible says that women have a different place in society from men, so the law must say so too[7]); arguments concerning 'inherent' impediments (women have

1 Waaldijk, n 11 on p 164 above, makes the revealing point that the parliamentary debates were taken up mostly with concerns of whether Dutch same-sex marriages would be recognised abroad, and what would happen if one of the Royal Princes (or Princesses?) wanted to enter into such a marriage.

2 Though names are important in law. If benefits are given to 'spouses' and registered partnership is a separate institution from marriage, courts may choose, if they so desire (like the European Court of Justice in Case C-122/99P *D v Council* 31 May 2001), to limit spousal benefit to institutions called marriage.

3 See n 4 on p 152 above.

4 I accept that actual discrimination on these grounds continues to exist and that the law's response remains inadequate. But the point is that it is morally and politically unacceptable to argue in favour of such discrimination.

5 And now a judge of the Constitutional Court.

6 (1993) 110 SALJ 450 at 461–62.

7 The biblical arguments deployed in *Loving v Virginia* 388 US 1 (1967) to justify bars on inter-racial marriage are typical of such arguments which attempt to justify racial discrimination.

less judgment, and are weaker; blacks have less well-developed social and physical abilities); and arguments which sought to show that granting equality would change the existing order and would, therefore, be a precursor to social and moral disintegration. In the light of this historical analysis, Cameron offers this insight: 'It is striking how many of these arguments, now superseded in the case of women or blacks, are still employed against gays [sic] and lesbians'. The more sexual orientation discrimination is identified with race and sex discrimination, the less easy it is to justify it. There is cause to hope that this fact is being recognised at both a judicial and a legislative level. True it is that in some countries, such as Canada, South Africa and Vermont (and in the future, probably, the United Kingdom), the hand of the legislature has been (or will be) forced by the judiciary's interpretation of constitutional/human rights requirements. But this is not a universal truth and in many other countries, such as those European countries which have introduced registered partnerships, and Australian states like New South Wales and the ACT which have greatly enhanced the position of cohabitants and extended the definition thereof to include same-sex couples, the legislatures have, *ex proprio motu*, granted more and more rights and responsibilities to same-sex couples. In any case, constitutional development can become a tool of the judiciary only when advanced by the legislature. But it remains true that appropriate political will is a prerequisite to informed legislative change[1].

Political considerations

The change in political will leading to unexpected progress is, perhaps, most striking in South Africa. Ronald Louw suggests[2] that the granting of constitutional protection was arguably the most significant reason behind changed public attitudes towards gay men and lesbians. It has certainly been the factor which, in that country, has led to the most significant legal developments. But the question remains: where did the political impetus to grant constitutional protection come from? It is this question that is addressed by Carl Stychin, in a study of the political tactics adopted (with phenomenal success) by gay rights organisations in South Africa[3]. He reminds us of the unique situation in that country where it was the politically dominant regime that came to realise (with the realisation of its own utter unsustainability) the necessity, in a democratic society, for protection of minorities to be constitutionally entrenched. 'Moreover,' he adds, 'the political climate of South Africa remains one in which it is "politically incorrect" for mainstream constitutional players to oppose the granting of equality rights to a group which can claim a history of social exclusion'[4]. Yet there were countervailing considerations which made the ultimate victory in South Africa (which became the first country in the world explicitly to make sexual orientation

1 M Dupuis (above, n 1 at p 164) at 100 quotes the attorney in *Baere v Levin* 852 P2d 44 (Hawaii, 1993) pointing out the limitations to the legislative process in the absence of political will. 'If Martin Luther King had gone to the Alabama State Legislature for help, the schools would still be segregated today'.

2 R Louw 'Gay and Lesbian Partner Immigration and the Redefining of Family' (2000) 16 SAJHR 313 at 319.

3 C Stychin 'Constituting Sexuality: The Struggle for Sexual Orientation in the South Africa Bill of Rights' (1996) 23 *J Law and Soc* 455.

4 C Stychin 'Constituting Sexuality: The Struggle for Sexual Orientation in the South Africa Bill of Rights' (1996) 23 *J Law and Soc* 455 at p 461.

discrimination unconstitutional[1]) by no means certain. The strongly Calvinist tradition of the white community was reflected in the sexual conservatism of both the black and the Asian communities[2]; in addition, as Stychin notes, the incoming democratic government had greater priorities than gay law reform, including the dismantling of apartheid and the tackling of the economic injustices endemic throughout South African society. But in the end, the rhetoric of minority rights was simply too powerful to resist.

Though there are few countries in the world today in which such rhetoric is as irresistable as in South Africa, in the wider legal community (at least within the western world) it is exactly this rhetoric of rights that is, more and more, informing the manner in which legal claims are being made. John Dewar[3], writing on changes in family law in general, sees same-sex relationship recognition as symptomatic of an increased contractualisation of family relationships and of an increasing constitutionalisation, through international human rights instruments, which is being brought to bear on issues which traditional family law saw as entirely within the realms of private law. That constitutionalisation is even more apparent in the United Kingdom than Australia (from which perspective Dewar is primarily writing): the Human Rights Act 1998, the Scotland Act 1998 and the Northern Ireland Act 1998 are already resulting in court arguments being presented in a very different manner. They have clearly raised the rights-consciousness of both litigants and individuals who perceive that they are not being treated fairly by the law. 'Rights demand vindication', says Dewar:[4] they trump other considerations such as welfare, family privacy, parental authority, and even the traditional place of marriage. This constitutionalisation of rights overlaps with the increased contractualisation of families for, according to Dewar, rights by definition are individual and therefore their concern is not with the institution but with the individual's claims upon the institution: the right of non-discrimination, for example, is a direct challenge to the present definition of marriage. Dewar's thesis is to some extent vindicated by the fact that when the institution of marriage itself has been challenged by gay men and lesbians, the law (as was seen above) has been able to see off the challenges without much difficulty, but when the individual rights flowing from that institution are sought, as for example spousal support[5], succession rights[6], immigration rights[7], or even all the individual attributes of marriage[8], the law has been unable to resist the rationalist arguments and success has been extraordinary.

Political advancement is, of course, usually the result of pragmatism and compromise, and while increased recognition of same-sex relationships is broadly to

1 South African Constitution, s 9(3). Among the notable legal consequences of this provision were the striking down of the statute criminalising sodomy (*National Coalition for Gay and Lesbian Equality v Minister of Justice* 1998 (12) BCLR 1517, 1999 (1) SA 6) and the extension of marital rights to same-sex couples for immigration purposes (*National Coalition for Lesbian and Gay Equality v Minister for Home Affairs* 1999 (13) BCLR 280).

2 See, as an example of this conservatism translating into judicial decision, the case of *Van Rooyen v Van Rooyen* 1994 (2) SA 325, and its discussion by E. Bonthuys in 'Awarding Access and Custody to Homosexual Parents of Minor Children: A Discussion of *Van Rooyen v Van Rooyen*' (1994) 3 *Stellenbosch LR* 298.

3 J Dewar 'Family Law and its Discontents' (2000) 14 *Int J Law Pol and the Fam* 59.

4 J Dewar 'Family Law and its Discontents' (2000) 14 *Int J Law Pol and the Fam* 59 at p 72.

5 *M v H* (1999) 171 DLR (4th) 577.

6 *Fitzpatrick v Sterling Housing Association* [1999] 4 All ER 707.

7 *National Coalition for Gay and Lesbian Equality v Minister of Justice* 1998 (12) BCLR 1517.

8 *Baker v Vermont* 744 A2d 864 (1999).

be welcomed, there are dangers to the gay and lesbian community in accepting recognition on other people's terms – even when these are the only terms on offer. Stychin[1] makes a valid point when he says that the conservative rhetoric that gay and lesbian activists in South Africa adopted (such as that gayness is immutable and fixed at birth and that therefore gay people pose no threat to the general population in terms of conversion or promotion of their orientation) limits its own radical agenda by its acceptance of categorisations that might not reflect reality[2]. A similar argument to Stychin's is made in the American context by Nancy Polikoff[3]. She points out that the struggle for recognition of gay and lesbian relationships becomes more successful the more it denies its own social transformative agenda, and she draws an interesting analogy with the struggle for abortion law reform. That was originally argued on the basis of women's liberation and women's entitlement to sexual fulfilment, access to abortion being presented as part of a larger struggle to end male dominance; but access to abortion was only gained, and it seems can only be preserved, by adopting a much more conservative 'pro-choice' rhetoric which implies that abortion is an evil, though a necessary one. Her worry is that we get what we ask for – access to a necessary evil rather than the end of male dominance; access to an inherently gendered institution rather than the breakdown in all relationships which depend upon and are defined by gender-allocated roles. For this reason, it is all the more important that the tactics adopted by those seeking justice and equality for gay men and lesbians eschew the institutionalisation of relationships. This is a matter to which I shall return at the end of this chapter.

The privatisation of family law

Other writers suggest that the increased legal recognition of same-sex relationships is not a result of the constitutionalisation of family law (ie turning the subject into an aspect of public law) but exactly the reverse. Family law is, according to Susan Boyd[4], primarily concerned with the privatisation of social welfare and she suggests that the legal recognition of same-sex relationships must be seen in that light and perhaps even explained by that imperative. She points out[5] that the trite statement that the family is the basis of society is in fact founded on a privatisation model where the family is allocated the costs of producing and rearing children and of caring for dependent family members. Queer theorists, she argues, should resist the 'family' since it reflects heteronormativity where society is still, if to a lesser degree than before, structured around a norm whereby women assume greater responsibility than men for these caring roles,

1 C Stychin 'Constituting Sexuality: The Struggle for Sexual Orientation in the South Africa Bill of Rights' (1996) 23 *J Law and Soc* 455.

2 C Stychin also warns ((1996) 23 *J Law and Soc* 455 at p 464) that since sexual orientation protection can, like other protections, be removed from the Constitution, its very inclusion acts as a conservatising force, requiring gay men and lesbians to act moderately and reasonably in their future demands in order to consolidate their existing gains.

3 N Polikoff 'We Will Get What We Ask For: Why Legalising Gay and Lesbian Marriage Will Not "Dismantle the Legal Structure of Gender in Every Marriage"' (1993) 79 *Virg LR* 1535.

4 S Boyd 'Family, Law and Sexuality: Feminist Engagements' (1999) 8 *Soc & Leg Stud* 369; 'Best Friends or Spouses? Privatisation and Recognition of Lesbian Partnerships in *M v H*' (1996) 13 *Rev Ca Dr Fam* 321; and 'Expanding the "Family" in Family Law: Recent Ontario Proposals on Same-Sex Relationships' (1994) 7 *Can J Women and the Law* 545.

5 S Boyd (1999) 8 *Soc & Leg Stud* at 377.

which fact is itself both reflected and perpetuated in the labour market. In many areas of family law the state is stepping back[1] and encouraging individuals to seek private remedies rather than state ones: it is the public purse that is served by allowing same-sex couples to seek, for example, support from each other. Commenting on an earlier stage of *M v H*[2], in which the Supreme Court of Canada recognised a same-sex couple explicitly because (inter alia) to do otherwise would throw the cost of maintaining the applicant onto the public purse, Boyd says this:

> 'The more decisions such as *M v H*[3], which privatize responsibility for financial well-being, are applauded, the more the tide of shrinking public responsibility and expanded private responsibility is invited into our homes and families'[4].

There is a paradox here, of course, in that the law is pursuing (or at least drifting into) a right-wing model of society in which the role of the state is progressively diminished and individuals are encouraged to take more and more responsibility for themselves (leaving those unable to do so more and more vulnerable), while at the same time the right-wing tendency to sanctify the 'traditional' family is, together with religious arguments, the main source of opposition to equality and justice for gay men and lesbians.

Another Canadian writer, Claire Young[5], makes similar points to those made by Boyd but addresses in addition some unpalatable consequences to legal recognition of same-sex relationships. She points out that recognition in the tax and welfare regime might result in disadvantage overall, particularly in the case of low-income couples, where aggregation of income for means-tested benefits is presently avoided[6]. The benefits of recognition will go to those already economically advantaged and, given the gendered structures of property ownership and wealth creation that persist in all modern societies, that means that recognition is likely to benefit men at the expense of women. The gay male agenda which is driving reform may not, Young implies, reflect the needs of lesbian women. Boyd does not go quite this far, but she concludes that recognition is not about redistribution of wealth, either amongst the sexes, or amongst the different economic strata in society. She does not, of course, suggest that this is a reason to oppose recognition and her aim, I think, is simply to point out its limitations:

> 'my key concern, [she says[7]] is that lesbian/gay struggles for legal recognition of relationships, while clearly necessary, ought not to be seen as *sufficient* to achieve social equality across class, race and gender differences as they intersect with sexuality'.

---

1 An example is the no-order principle in child law.

2 *M v H* (1999) 171 DLR (4th) 577.

3 *M v H* (1999) 171 DLR (4th) 577.

4 S Boyd 'Best Friends or Spouses? Privatisation and Recognition of Lesbian Partnerships in *M v H* (1996) 3 *Rev Ca Dr Fam* 321 at p 338. (J Millbank, n 2 at p 155) above, at para 25, makes the same point in commenting on the Australian case of *W v G* (1996) 20 Fam LR 49 (NSW) where a lesbian used promissory estoppel to oblige her ex-partner to contribute to the costs of bringing up her children: 'It is possible that the imperative to hold Grace financially liable was not so much law's desire to validate a lesbian family as a somewhat more fiscal impulse to find a source of private support, whatever the gender of the source'.

5 C Young 'Taxing Times for Lesbians and Gay Men: Equality at What Cost?' (1994) 17 *Dalhousie LJ* 534–559.

6 Exactly the same position would occur in the UK if recognition occurs before tax law reform (which, in truth, is likely).

7 S Boyd 'Family Law and Sexuality: Feminist Engagements' (1999) 8 *Soc & Leg Stud* 369 at p 378.

If this is so, then the reform agenda which aims to rid the law of distinctions based on sexual orientation rather than on other grounds serves lesbians as well as it serves gay men and, in further answer to Young's concerns, recognition serves lesbians proportionately better than it serves gay men in parenting issues where, for entirely practical reasons, access is easier for women than for men. While the battles for recognition have been fought in primarily economic terms (spousal support, succession to tenancies, etc), it is submitted that the real point of these battles has been to achieve equality, justice and dignity for gay men and lesbians generally rather than economic advantages for individual pursuers. One can understand Susan Boyd's sardonic reaction to the success of *M v H*[1]: 'Oh good,' she tartly remarks, 'now we get to sue each other'[2]. But the point is that, other than in cases involving children, family law is by and large a system for redistributing property. Equality, justice and dignity are advanced if the same access to courts and to legal remedies is granted to gay as to non-gay people – and, crucially, if the same economic disadvantages as well as advantages are obtained. To put it crudely, equality requires taking the rough with the smooth[3].

The threat of assimilation

While most queer theorists and gay activists welcome the increasing legal recognition of same-sex relationships described above, many, as we have already seen, do not welcome all the possible implications. There is a particular resistance by some writers (myself included) to a strategy that seeks recognition through the medium of 'marriage'[4] because of the danger that institution poses of 'assimilation'. I have argued previously[5] that 'marriage' ought not to be the primary goal for gay activists since it is, inherently, a heterosexist institution which will respond to the needs and aspirations of the heterosexual majority rather than, where different, the needs and aspirations of gay men and lesbians. Nancy Polikoff[6] similarly argues against same-sex marriage on the ground that recognition of same-sex marriage will do nothing to challenge the present opposite-gendered characteristics of marriage, and she fears that the influence will in fact be the other way around, with same-sex couples facing social as well as legal pressure to conform to the heterosexual ideal. She points out that recognition of same-sex relationships, where it has occurred, tends to be accorded to those relationships which are closest in form to opposite-sex relationships, and which follow the normative rules evolved in that context[7]. Other writers too make

1 *M v H* (1999) 171 DLR (4th) 577.
2 S Boyd 'Best Friends or Spouses'? Privatisation and Recognition of Lesbian Partnerships in *M v H* (1996) 13 *Rev Can Dr Fam* at p 324.
3 Part at least of Boyd's worries ((1996) 13 *Rev Can Dr Fam* at p 337) is that the law seems to have been more ready to grant recognition when it saves the state money (eg spousal support) than when it might cost the state money (pensions and immigration).
4 The marriage debate is played out more vigorously in the USA than elsewhere, probably because the status has more significance (in the sense of many more legal consequences) there than it has elsewhere: see R Baird and S Rosenbaum (eds) *Same-Sex Marriage – the Moral and Legal Debate* (1997) Prometheus Books; and A Sullivan (ed) *Same-Sex Marriage – Pro and Con* (1997) Vintage Books.
5 'Marriage is for Heterosexuals: May the Rest of Us Be Saved from It' (2000) 12 *C & Fam L Q* 363.
6 N Polikoff 'We Will Get What We Ask For: Why Legalising Gay and Lesbian Marriage Will Not "Dismantle the Legal Structure of Gender in Every Marriage"' (1993) 79 *Virg LR* 1535.
7 *Fitzpatrick v Sterling Housing Association* [1999] 4 All ER 705 is a clear, but by no means the only, example illustrating this point.

similar points[1]. Katherine O'Donovan[2], for example, points out the paradox that both registered partnerships and increased recognition of cohabitation take (heterosexual) marriage as the unquestioned model to aspire to and she pertinently asks[3], what it is about 'marriage' that so attracts those, such as gay or lesbian couples, who are currently excluded. Her answer is that it is the mythology behind marriage that is being sought, its 'status as icon'[4], and, though she does not use this language, she warns gay men and lesbians against whoring after false gods. Eric Clive, many years ago, gave what remains one of the most convincing rationalist arguments why the law should withdraw from marriage, leaving it as a sacrament for those wishing religious approval, rather as baptism is, and conferring legal consequences on relationships for reasons other than the entry into the institution[5]. Yet, as O'Donovan[6] is at pains to point out, few people enter marriage for rationalist reasons[7]. It may well be difficult to resist the argument that justice requires equal access to even a flawed and mythologised institution, but it is not impossible. I suspect that true justice, cutting across sex, gender and orientation, requires the demythologising not only of marriage, but of the family itself. For the 'family' too, as a legal institution, carries assimilationist risks.

It has already been seen how legislative advancement, even short of marriage, has, by and large, been possible only by minimising the differences between same-sex and opposite-sex relationships. The same phenomenon can be seen in the strategies adopted by litigants seeking family rights less than marriage, whose success is more often than not founded upon the presentation of the same-sex couple as one emulating the heterosexist norm. Jenni Millbank[8] illustrates this point starkly with an Australian case[9] in which one member of a same-sex couple sought to be regarded as a 'spouse' of the other and resorted to arguing that he was the 'husband' because he took the 'active' or 'masculine' role in the relationship, as opposed to the 'effeminate or female-acting partner' who took the 'traditional female role'. The attempt to access relationship rights failed in this case and the queer theorist's response is equivocal. Millbank comments that 'as a litigative strategy it was oppressive not only to the diversity and originality of lesbian and gay relationships, positing them as mere mimics; it was also oppressive to gender equality within heterosexual relationships'. The fact that the litigative strategy of emphasising similarities has been largely successful obscures but does not subvert Millbank's point – that emulation of the most obvious features of opposite-sex relationships, which are not necessarily the most

1 See S Boyd (1996) 13 *Rev Can Dr Fam* 321, esp at p 326 and (1999) 8 *Soc & Leg Stud* 369 esp at p 379; and J Millbank "Which, then, Would be the 'Husband' and Which the 'Wife'?" Some Thoughts on Contesting the 'Family' in Court' (1996) 3 *Murdoch University Electronic Journal of Law* No 3: www.murdoch.edu.au/elaw/issues/v3n3/millbank.html; D Herman 'Are We Family? Lesbian Rights and Women's Liberation' (1990) 28 *Os H L J* 789; G Brodsky 'Paradise Lost, Paradox Revisited: The Implications of Familial Ideology for Feminist, Lesbian and Gay Engagement to Law' (1993) 31 *Os H L J* 589.

2 K O'Donovan 'Marriage: A Sacred or Profane Love Machine?' [1993] 1 *Fem Leg Stud* 75 at p 85.

3 K O'Donovan [1993] 1 *Fem Leg Stud* 75 at p 81.

4 K O'Donovan 'Marriage: A Sacred or Profane Love Machine?' [1995] 1 Fem Leg Stud 75 at p 86.

5 E Clive 'Marriage: An Unnecessary Legal Concept?' in J Eekelaar and S Katz (eds) *Marriage and Cohabitation in Contemporary Societies* (1980) Butterworths, London at pp 71–82.

6 K O'Donovan [1993] 1 *Fem Leg Stud* at pp 86–87.

7 Not that O'Donovan is disagreeing with Clive's basic premise: see her own review of books on cohabitation: 'Legal Marriage – Who Needs it?' (1984) 47 *Mod LR* 111.

8 Op. cit. at paras 16–17.

9 *Brown v Commissioner for Superannuation* (1995) 21 AAR 378.

attractive (eg inequality, dependency, dominance), tends to validate them. Not only is such an approach a direct threat to the queer world (for it has the effect of skewing the reality of individual relationships, by the imperative – for entirely understandable tactical reasons – of presenting to the world a facade of hetero-normativity within a homosexual environment), but it also ill-serves the straight world. For a less recognised but no less real danger in assimilation is that it denies access to what the queer has to offer to the straight – a practical illustration of the fact that diversity and originality is not destructive but is liberating. Equality, says Judge Sachs of the Constitutional Court of South Africa, demands not the suppression but rather the celebration of differences[1].

The underlying assumption, which it is certainly no part of my task here to challenge, is that the loss of a gay cultural identity[2] would impoverish society; in addition, there is the other danger that assimilation would simply shift the goal-posts for those relationships that are outwith the law's ken. Drawing gay and lesbian relationships within a family norm, as presently understood, would as Boyd points out 'draw lines between good homosexuals (middle-class, monogamous, double income) and bad homosexuals (gays who cruise the bars, baths and parks, and dykes who ride motorcycles topless)'[3]. Currently, except in limited circumstances, the law recognises and legitimises opposite-sex relationships only. If recognition is extended to same-sex relationships only in those circumstances in which they look, to all intents and purposes, to be identical to opposite-sex relationships except in the gender mix, then the law really has not progressed very far at all. It will continue to benefit long-term, stable, monogamous relationships in which the parties share a home and accept long-term emotional and financial obligations towards one another. But, those relationships which do not, or will not, fit into that norm (established by and for heterosexuals) will continue to be excluded for all purposes whether or not, for particular purposes, it would be fair, just and reasonable to include them[4]. And the law will continue to legitimise (and benefit) certain forms of family relationship while at the same time ignoring (and disadvantaging) others[5]. Boyd's point is that this

1 *National Coalition for Lesbian and Gay Equality v Minister of Justice* 1998 (12) BCLR 1517 at 1534, para 22.

2 Gay 'culture' is very much a late-20th century phenomenon and, by and large, is western in orientation. This highly modern development has little to do with the long history of same-sex sexual and emotional life-relationships (see J Boswell *The Marriage of Likeness: Same-Sex Unions in Pre-modern Europe* (1996) Fontana) and it seems likely that this now-distinctive culture evolved as a response to the criminalisation of gay male sexual acts in the late 19th century. The consequence of criminalisation was to create an underworld society in which like-minded individuals banded together not only for sexual fulfilment, but also for protection and support; their commonality of experience as 'other', as an excluded and despised minority, created a mindset from which developed common hopes, aspirations and experiences; their feelings of apartness motivated a search for stereotypically determined tastes in looks, dress, music – role-models, in other words. This is the stuff of which 'culture' is made.

3 S Boyd 'Best Friends or Spouses'? Privatisation and Recognition of Lesbian Partnerships in *M v H* (1996) 13 *Rev Can Dr Fam* 321 at p 326.

4 See further L Glennon '*Fitzpatrick v Sterling Housing Association*: An Endorsement of the Functional Family?' (2000) 14 *Int J Law Pol & the Family* 226, esp at p 240 ff, who is particularly concerned that platonic relationships are excluded from 'family' by *Fitzpatrick*. Interestingly, platonic relationships are included in the New South Wales legislation which extends recognition to same-sex relationships: see Property (Relationships) Act 1999 (NSW).

5 D Herman 'Are We Family? Lesbian Rights and Women's Liberation' (1990) 28 *Osgoode Hall LJ* 789 was one of the first to make this point when she said that validating same-sex couples who look like opposite-sex couples necessarily excludes other family modes, such as non-monogamous or non-cohabiting couples.

imperative comes not from the concept of 'family' but from capitalism itself, and she concludes that

> 'unless lesbian and gay efforts to achieve symbolic recognition of their families are accompanied by trenchant critiques of the limits of such recognition in delivering a redistribution of economic well-being, they will remain incomplete as political strategies, while they may simultaneously be the only *legal* strategies available'[1].

Recognition of same-sex relationships, she fears, is only likely on heterosexual terms, which challenges neither heteronormativity nor present socio-economic structures. It may be responded to this that it is not the purpose of same-sex relationship recognition to challenge capitalism, but it is, surely, its purpose to challenge heteronormativity, in the sense of questioning why one family structure should be preferred over another. And if heterosexuality as the identifier of rights and liabilities can be successfully challenged then the way is open to challenge other identifiers whose only justification lies in normativity, conformity, and history.

Family law as a Maineian movement

In 1861, Sir Henry Maine published his best-known work, *Ancient Law*, and there he argues[2] that the movement of legal systems from the primitive to the progressive has been uniform in one respect, that is to say by the gradual dissolution of family dependency and the growth of individual obligation in its place. 'The Individual', he says, 'is steadily substituted for the Family, as the unit of which civil laws take account'. The legal ties between people become progressively governed by contract, rather than by the reciprocity of rights and duties that make up family; and in his famous epigram Maine concludes that the movement from ancient to modern law can be characterised as a movement 'from *Status to Contract*'[3]. For over 100 years after these words were written, the family, as a source of rights and obligations, remained stubbornly a status-based institution. Automatic rights and liabilities, powers and responsibilities, continued to be drawn from status-defined institutions, most importantly marriage (for the domestic relations between adults) and legitimacy (for the domestic relations between adults and children). Marriage remains the primary source of automatic rights and duties between adults, and while legitimacy as a status has all but disappeared, it has been replaced by the (admittedly more acceptable but still problematical) status of parent. Succession rights, maintenance obligations, criminal and evidentiary immunities and all the other legally imposed consequences of family life remain by and large dependent on the status of marriage or parent.

However, the law of domestic relations in the United Kingdom is showing some evidence of escaping from the shackles of status, at least in respect of adult-adult relationships. The new constitutionalism introduced at the turn of the 21st century, with its emphasis on individuality, rationality and the need to identify the legitimate purpose behind the law, is likely to speed the process. As well as the tax and social security legislation, where it has long been in the state's (financial) interest to recognise non-marital conjugal cohabitation, there have been a

1 S Boyd 'Family Law and Sexuality: Feminist Engagements (1999) 8 *Soc & Leg Stud* 369 at p 381.

2 Maine *Ancient Law* (Everyman's Library edn, 1972) at p 99. For an examination of the influence of Maine and his works, see R Cocks 'Sir Henry Maine: 1822–1888' (1988) 8 *Leg Stud* 247. On Maine's views on 'Status', see G McCormack 'Status: Problems of Definition and Use' (1984) CLJ 361.

3 Maine *Ancient Law* (Everyman's Library edn, 1972) at p 100.

few statutory provisions extending rights and liabilities to non-marital couples, for sometimes the very purpose of the law would be subverted if it insisted on tying in legal consequences to status. A relatively early example of statutory recognition of non-marital relationships for this reason is found in the domestic violence legislation. The Matrimonial Homes (Family Protection) (Scotland) Act 1981 grants various forms of protection from domestic violence to the parties to a marriage, but since these protections (limited, be it admitted) can be accessed only when individuals can prove that their personal circumstances require it, there was no institutional need automatically to deny access to those who did not evidence the appropriate status. So the protections could be, and were, extended to the parties of non-marital (opposite-sex) couples. The following year the Administration of Justice Act 1982 amended the Damages (Scotland) Act 1976 and the (English) Fatal Accidents Act 1976 to include within the definition of 'relative' who could sue for negligently caused death of another, the survivor of a non-marital (opposite-sex) couple. Again such legislation, requiring as it does proof of negligence, never was based on status alone and there is no reason in practicality, therefore, to deny a claimant a right to prove the appropriate relationship at the same time as also proving the other elements necessary for the claim. Though in its terms the 1981 legislation is limited to opposite-sex couples, there is no rational basis upon which same-sex couples should be excluded from the protections contained therein and the 1981 Act is, for that reason, clearly incompatible with the European Convention on Human Rights. The Damages (Scotland) Act 1976 can, for reasons explored elsewhere[1], be reinterpreted consistently with the Convention so that same-sex couples can be brought within its terms. The law has, however, proved far more resistant to extending recognition of non-marital relationships to areas of the law in which proving status is all that is required to access a benefit (such as, for example, in the law of succession or of maintenance[2]).

Dewar[3], as we saw above, pointed out the opportunities for recognition of same-sex couples in this movement from status to individuality. He suggested that as we come to recognise rights inhering in individuals it is the individual who becomes the focus of the law's attention rather than the institutions they are part of and from which they derive status. This does, of course, come at a cost. Rebecca Bailey-Harris points out[4] that moving from status to individuality involves a movement from a system of absolute rules to one of discretionary or evaluative rules, and that this in turn involves a diminution in both predictability and, consequentially, the chances of extra-judicial settlement of disputes. However, if the end result is justice and equality for gay men and lesbians, as well as a more equitable approach to all family disputes, then it is suggested that this is a price well worth paying.

---

1 K Norrie 'Constitutional Challenges to Sexual Orientation Discrimination' (2000) 49 *ICLQ* at 776.
2 Scotland is unusual in the extent to which it ties in maintenance obligations to a legally determined status rather than a more factually determined factor such a dependency.
3 J Dewar 'Family Law and its Discontents' (2000) 14 *Int J Law Pol and the Fam* 59.
4 R Bailey-Harris 'Law and the Unmarried Couple – Oppression or Liberation?' (1996) 8 *C & Fam L Q* 137.

CONCLUSION

I promised to address two questions in this third part of this chapter: how to explain the sudden burgeoning of advances in legal recognition of same-sex relationships, and what that tells us about contemporary family law. The explanations, as we have seen, are primarily political and constitutional. What it tells us about family law is that the law is moving away from 'family' as a source of rights and liabilities. The logical end result of this movement would be the withering of any legal doctrine known as 'family law', as the individual aspects of property law, unjustified enrichment, obligations, and domestic violence law take on lives of their own. It is, admittedly, odd for a self-confessed family lawyer to regard this as a good thing, but there it is: for better or for worse, I do.

8 Domestic Abuse

Clare Connelly

This chapter examines the response of the legal system to domestic abuse by men against women and children. While it is recognised that many other forms of inter-relationship or familial abuse takes place, this chapter focuses on male violence against women, and the impact of that violence on, and the decisions that are made regarding, the care of children. It is argued that an inaccurate understanding of the causes and effects of abuse inform many of the decisions made in the legal process, which contribute to the poor response to domestic abuse. This chapter will reflect on some of the inadequacies in the legal system's response to domestic abuse and evaluate developments in other jurisdictions that are informing policy changes in Britain. The chapter ends with a case study of a woman's experience of domestic abuse and the legal response by both the civil and criminal courts to this abuse. This case study demonstrates that the legal system did not take the domestic abuse seriously and that it did not, at first instance, allow the woman's account of the abuse she had suffered to properly inform the decision in respect of child contact.

RESPONSES TO ABUSE OF WOMEN

The last thirty years has seen a period of some enlightenment in legal and government responses to violence against women. This is undoubtedly a direct result of the work by Women's Aid and other feminist campaigners who have moved this issue from the private untouchable realms of the home into the public and legal arena[1]. This movement into the public sphere is evident not only in the Scottish legal system but also on an international level[2] where the response to abuse against both women and children is changing[3].

---

1 R E Dobash and R Dobash *Women, Violence and Social Change* (1992) Routledge, London.

2 This is evidenced by the UN General Assembly which established domestic abuse as a human rights issue in the 1993 UN Declaration on the Elimination of Violence Against Women and the 1995 Beijing Fourth World Conference on Women which adopted a Global Platform for Action to improve the status of women worldwide, committing signatories to the development of plans to address violence against women.

3 The International Convention of the Rights of the Child imposes a duty on states to take all appropriate measures to protect a child from physical or mental violence, injury or abuse, negligent treatment, maltreatment or exploitation, including sexual abuse. See ch 19 of the Convention.

TERMINOLOGY

The use of terminology in this field is not unproblematic. While the term 'domestic violence' continues to be used to represent the abuse suffered by women, it has been suggested that 'domestic abuse' is a more appropriate term as it prevents merely focusing on physical violence to the exclusion of sexual and psychological abuse[1]. Other authors suggest that 'private violence'[2] is better to 'call into question the historical dichotomy between public and private, which so often excludes and hides the mistreatment of women and children both in and outside families'[3]. In this chapter, the term 'domestic abuse' will be used to represent physical, sexual and psychological abuse of women and children, while acknowledging that this abuse is by its nature 'private'.

MYTHS OF ABUSE

The legal response to abused women, whether in the criminal or civil context, is inadequate and has for a long time been informed by myths which focus on women as responsible for their abuse or play down the seriousness of that abuse. These myths include: 'She must deserve or provoke it'; 'She must enjoy it otherwise she'd leave'; 'It's just the odd domestic tiff. Everybody has arguments'; 'It's all caused by drink'; 'It only happens in problem families'; 'These men must be mentally ill'; 'Men who abuse were abused themselves as children'; 'It was a one-off. He's really sorry, and it won't happen again'; and 'Women should stay for the sake of the children. Children need a father'[4]. These myths have informed the attitudes of the law enforcement agencies and other legal personnel, for example prosecutors and judges, who are the decision-makers in the legal process. Perhaps the biggest myth is that domestic abuse is rare. Research studies reveal very high prevalence rates: domestic abuse comprises more than 25% of all reported violent crime in Britain[5]; one in nine women and over 5,000 children per year experience domestic violence[6]; and in an international context, it was estimated that between 25% and 60% of women suffered abuse, which was defined as only including physical abuse[7]. These and other prevalence statistics only represent part of the problem as women under-report domestic abuse.[8]

1 The Scottish partnership on Domestic Abuse, a multi-agency group formed in 1998 to set minimum levels of service and look at the needs of special groups, defined domestic abuse as gender-based abuse which can be perpetrated by partners, ex-partners or other family members and can include physical, sexual and mental/emotional abuse including verbal abuse, withholding money and other types of controlling behaviour.

2 M A Fineman, Preface in M A Fineman and R Mykituk *The Public Nature of Private Violence* (1994) Routledge, New York, p xi.

3 M A Fineman, Preface in M A Fineman and R Mykituk *The Public Nature of Private Violence* (1994) Routledge, New York, p xvii.

4 *Abused Women Myths and Reality* Edinburgh, Scottish Women's Aid.

5 R E Dobash and R Dobash *Women, Violence and Social Change* (1992) Routledge, London.

6 E A Stanko, D Crisp, C Hale and H Lucraft *Counting the Costs: Estimating the impact of Domestic Violence in the London Borough of Hackney* (1998) Crime Concern, London.

7 C McGee 'Children's experiences of domestic violence' (1997) *Child and Family Social Work* Vol 2, Part 1, p 13–23.

8 See L Kelly 'The Interconnectedness of domestic violence and child abuse: Challenges for research, policy and practice' in A Mullender and R Morley, (eds) *Children Living with Domestic Violence: Putting Men's Abuse of Women on the Child Care Agenda* (1994) Whiting and Birch London; M McWilliams and J McKiernan *Bringing it Out in the Open: Domestic Violence in Northern Ireland* (1993) HMSO Belfast.

DOMESTIC ABUSE AND THE CRIMINAL JUSTICE PROCESS

The misunderstanding of, and the failure to protect women from, domestic abuse is not unique to Scottish criminal law[1]. The changes that have occurred at policy level in Scotland are undoubtedly largely due to campaigns such as Zero Tolerance and the work of women's organisations, including Women's Aid. Each of these has played a part in highlighting the extent of domestic abuse, in influencing the Scottish Executive's examination of domestic abuse, and in bringing about changes in police policy. While such developments are welcomed, the response by the police and prosecutors to domestic abuse and the rules of criminal evidence and procedure still produce difficulties hindering an effective criminal justice response to this crime being delivered.

Police response to domestic abuse

The gate-keepers to law enforcement and sanction are the police. They have long been criticised for their failure to take domestic abuse seriously, their perception being that it was a 'private matter' and not 'real crime'. During the 1970s and 1980s this inadequate response was informed by the idea that domestic abuse was not serious, and was provoked and deserved[2]. When police did respond to 'domestics' they often attempted to reconcile and mediate between the parties, criminal charges were rarely brought and there was a prevalent view that it should be dealt with by social workers and the relevant legal response would be found in the civil courts[3].

Introduction of pro-arrest policies

A major change in policing in many jurisdictions has been the introduction of pro-arrest policies. In 1990, such policies were introduced in Scotland and England and Wales[4]. Where pro-arrest policies are in operation, an arrest should

---

1 See J Hanmer, J Radford and E Stanko (eds) *Women, Policing and Male Violence* (1989) Routledge, London; Women's Coalition Against Family Violence *Blood on whose hands?* (1994), Victoria; D G Dutton *The Domestic Assault of Women,* (1995) University of British Columbia Press, Vancouver; D G Dutton, The Criminal Justice Response to Wife Assault (1987) *Law and Human Behaviour* vol 11 pp 189–206; S Edwards, *Policing 'Domestic' Violence* (1989) Sage, London; N Z Hilton, *Legal Responses to Wife Assault,* (1993) Sage, California; A R Roberts, *Helping Battered Women,* (1996) Oxford University Press, Oxford; O J Zoomer, Policing Women Beating in the Netherlands, in J Hammer, J Radford and E Stanko (Eds), *Women, Policing and Male Violence,* (1989) Routledge, London.

2 See J Hanmer, J Radford and E Stanko (eds) *Women, Policing and Male Violence* (1989) Routledge London, p 18, and Women's Coalition Against family Violence *Blood on whose hands?* (1994) Victoria, p 72.

3 See R E Dobash and R Dobash *Women, Violence and Social Change* (1992) Routledge, London; R E Dobash and R P Dobash *Violence Against Wives: A Case Against Patriarchy* (1979) Free Press, New York; S Hatty *Male Violence and the Police: an Australian Experience* (1988) School of Social Work, University of New South Wales at p 179; S Edwards, *Policing 'Domestic' Violence* (1989) Sage, London; A Home 'Responding to domestic violence: A comparison of social workers' and police officer's interventions' (1991–1992), Vol 3, *Social Work and Social Sciences Review,* pp 150–162; and C Hoyle *Negotiating Domestic Violence; Police, Criminal Justice and Victims* (1998) Clarendon Press, Oxford, ch 1. S Hatty 'Policing and male violence in Australia' (1989) at p 106, and O J Zoomer 'Policing woman beating in the Netherlands', at p 143, both in J Hanmer, J Radford and E Stanko (1989) (eds.) *Women, Policing and Male Violence* Routledge, London.

4 The introduction of pro-arrest policies followed the issue of government circulars giving guidelines on police response to domestic violence. In Scotland, the Scottish Home and Health Department Police (CC) Circular No 3/1990, *Investigating of Complaints of Domestic Assault,* was issued in July 1990. This was similar to that issued in England and Wales by the Home Office, (Home Office Circular 60/1990, *Domestic Violence*).

occur where there is reasonable and probable evidence that an assault has occurred. Arrest is not mandatory and remains at the discretion of the attending police officers. The decision of these officers may be influenced by the circumstances at the scene of the incident and the woman's wishes regarding arrest. The inclusion of victim's choice in the application of pro-arrest policies is problematic. While on the one hand this may indicate that women's views are being taken into account by attending officers, it does not acknowledge the constraints within which women have to make these decisions.

Hoyle and Sanders, found that pro-arrest and prosecution policies assume that women who are subjected to abuse are conducive to 'free choice', that they are free agents and are able to make informed decisions regarding calling the police, arrest and prosecution[1]. The disempowering and coercive effect of the man's abuse is not tackled when these policies are applied unless a domestic violence officer, properly trained and resourced, is available to assist the woman. The role of domestic violence liaison officers in providing support and information is examined below.

Whose interests do pro-arrest policies serve?

The motivation of governments and police forces in introducing pro-arrest policies has been scrutinised. In England and Wales, the policy changes have been described as motivated by an attempt to re-establish police credibility, particularly in inner city areas where rioting and police abuses had damaged the police relationship with the community[2]. These responses have also been criticised for being part of a wider authoritarian right-wing approach in crime control which was not informed by feminist definitions, politics, research and did not include the provision of services[3].

In the United States, the introduction of pro-arrest policies and mandatory police training in dealing with domestic abuse incidents was partly motivated by an award of $2.3 million dollars in compensation to a woman, Tracey Thurman. The award was made on the grounds that the police had deprived her of her constitutional right to equal protection under the law and that they had been grossly negligent in their failure to protect her and her son from the violent acts of Charles Thurman. Tracey Thurman had a court order barring her abusive husband from assaulting her and had sought police protection over an eight-month period. On the occasion that resulted in the civil action, the police took 25 minutes to arrive at the scene and, on arrival, delayed in restraining Charles Thurman or removing the bloody knife he had in his hand. Charles Thurman continued to kick his wife in the head, face, and neck while she lay helpless on the ground. Tracey Thurman sustained life-threatening injuries, including multiple stab wounds to the chest, face and neck, fractured cervical vertebrae, damage to her spinal cord, partial paralysis below the neck, lacerations to her cheeks and mouth, loss of blood, scarring, shock and mental anguish[4].

---

1 C Hoyle and A Sanders, 'Police Response to Domestic Violence' (2000) 40 *Brit J Criminol*, pp 14–36.
2 R Morley and A Mullender, 'Hype or Hope? The Importation of Pro-arrest Policies and Batterers' Programmes from North America to Britain as Key Measures for Preventing Violence Against Women in the Home (1992) 6 *International Journal of Family Law*, at pp 265–288.
3 M Hester, L Kelly and J Radford *Women, Violence and Male Power*, (1996) Open University Press Buckingham, p 77.
4 A R Roberts *Helping Battered Women* (1996) Oxford University Press p 91.

The background against which some pro-arrest policies have been introduced was, therefore, not necessarily one that was motivated or informed by feminist concerns around appropriate policing of domestic abuse but was part of an attempt to re-establish the credibility of the police and to protect them from the payment of damages.

Domestic violence units and domestic violence liaison officers

Where pro-arrest policies have been introduced, they are often accompanied by the setting up of domestic violence units and/or specialised domestic violence liaison officers. The introduction of domestic violence liaison officers, particularly if accompanied by training of all operational officers to deal with domestic abuse incidents, has been reported as beneficial[1]. Difficulties arising from under-resourcing and the prioritising of responsibilities have, however, arisen. It is not clear whether the priority of these officers should be to secure a criminal prosecution, to adopt a co-ordinating role or to provide support and advocacy for victims[2]. If the role of advocate is prioritised, this may create a conflict of interest given the police role in the criminal justice process[3]. While agencies such as Women's Aid or Rape Crisis may be better suited to the role of advocate, they do not have the resources to provide this service.

Hoyle and Sanders found a variety of approaches being adopted by domestic violence liaison officers[4]. Although the level of support being provided to women varied amongst police officers, almost all of the women who had left violent relationships reported benefiting from the assistance of a domestic violence officer. Women reported that domestic violence officers provided emotional and practical support to pursue a prosecution and were able to inform women of the civil and criminal justice options available to them. Properly trained and resourced domestic violence officers can empower women and so provide an essential service, whereas inadequate resources may result in frustration and individuals leaving these posts[5].

Tracking and monitoring offenders

Tracking and monitoring of offenders has accompanied the introduction of pro-arrest policies. Forms of surveillance including CCTV and security systems have been installed in housing, and mobile phones and personal alarms are sometimes

1 The findings of Scottish fieldwork in this area are reported in K Goodall and H McKay *Police Classification and Responses to Domestic Violence Incidents* (1998) The Scottish Office Central Research Unit Edinburgh.

2 S Grace *Policing Domestic Violence in the 1990s* (1995) Home Office Research Study no 139 HMSO, London.

3 See R Morley and A Mullender 'Hype or Hope? The Importation of Pro-arrest Policies and Batterers' Programmes from North America to Britain as Key Measures for Preventing Violence Against Women in the Home' (1992) 6 *International Journal of Family Law*, 265–288, at pp 275–276.

4 C Hoyle and A Sanders 'Police Response to Domestic Violence' (2000) 40 *Brit J Criminol*, pp 14–36.

5 C Hoyle and A Sanders 'Police Response to Domestic Violence' (2000) 40 *Brit J Criminol*, pp 14–36, at p 31. In the area with the highest levels of victim satisfaction, more extensive support than had been envisaged by the Home Office was demanded by and provided to victims. As a result, the majority of the domestic violence officers spoke of stress. Within six months of the conclusion of the study, half of the domestic violence officers had left.

distributed[1]. Computerised domestic violence registers that aim to track offending against a particular woman and also offending by abusers against different women have been introduced in some areas. However, Plotnikoff and Woolfson's study of 42 of the 43 police forces in England and Wales found that forces lacked a systematic approach in recording incidents of domestic abuse and that as a consequence, information about previous incidents of abuse were not routinely passed on to responding officers[2].

Hanmer, Griffiths and Jerwood[3] monitored a graded response to domestic abuse incidents in the Killingbeck Division of West Yorkshire[4]. During the monitoring period the authors reported that police recording practices improved due to intensive follow-up and improved awareness amongst attending officers and control room staff[5]. They recommended introducing systems that allow accurate identification of repeat offences to be made, developing common definitions of 'domestic' amongst officers and the consistent use of identification codes. They suggested that attending officers should ask the victim about previous unreported assaults and that this information should form part of an effective police response.

Evaluations of pro-arrest policies

The effectiveness of pro-arrest policies has been scrutinised in some areas. A reduction in repeat violence is often used as the measure of success or to justify pro-arrest policies. The 'Minneapolis experiment' reported that arrest was the preferable police response to domestic abuse compared to advice/mediation or separation[6]. This study found that arrest combined with initial incarceration was the most effective response in reducing repeat offending in the six-month follow-up period. The methodology used in this study has, however, attracted criticism[7], and when it was replicated in two National Institute of Justice studies in Omaha, Nebraska and Charlotte, North Carolina, the results did not support the contention that mandatory or presumptive arrest policies had a deterrent effect on repeat offending[8].

Pro-arrest policies have, however, been positively evaluated elsewhere. In London, Ontario, the success of the pro-arrest policy has been attributed to the integrated multi-agency approach to domestic abuse which was present in this

1 See A R Roberts *Helping Battered Women* (1996) Oxford University Press at p 92 and Scottish Partnership on Domestic Violence, Current Initiatives in Scotland http://www.scotland.gov.uk/cru/documents/spda-04.asp.

2 J Plotnikoff and R Woolfson *Policing Domestic Violence : Effective Organisational Structures* (1998) Police Research Series Paper 100, Home Office, London.

3 J Hanmer, S Griffiths and D Jerwood *Arresting Evidence: Domestic Violence and Repeat Victimisation* (1999) Police Research Series Paper 104 Home Office, London.

4 This 'graded response' means that increase in incidents prompts an increase in activity by the police and other agencies.

5 Initial checks revealed that only 50% of attendances had appropriately been allocated a 'domestic code'; however, by the end of one year this had increased to 80%.

6 I W Sherman and R A Berk 'The specific deterrent effects of arrest for domestic assault' (1984) 49 *American Sociological Review*, pp 261–272.

7 See E S Buzawa and C G Buzawa *Domestic Violence: The Criminal Justice Response* (1990) Sage, Newbury Park, California.

8 For Omaha, Nebraska, see F W Dunford, D Huizinga and D S Elliot *The Omaha Domestic Violence Police Experiment, Final Report* (1989) National Institute of Justice and the City of Omaha; and for Charlotte, North Carolina, see J D Hirschel, I W Hutchison, C W Dean, J J Kelly and C E Pesackis *Charlotte Spouse Assault Replication Project: Final Report* (1991) National Institute of Justice.

area[1]. It is certainly the case that in Britain, the change in police response to domestic abuse has not always been integrated within a multi-agency response and has not been accompanied by much needed increases in funding for frontline agencies like Women's Aid or Rape Crisis.

Empowerment of women

The question of whether pro-arrest policies empower or disempower victims of domestic abuse is still being debated. Particular attention has been paid to whether they dissuade women from contacting the police. The factors favouring arrest include: immediate protection is provided for the woman by the action of removal; detention in custody may allow her to find a place of safety; pro-arrest policies indicate to attending police officers what their response to domestic abuse should be and such policies send a message to the abuser, the victim and the community that domestic abuse is a criminal justice matter. However, there are concerns that arrest may have negative effects for some communities. For example, arrest may threaten a woman's economic survival should her partner lose his job as a result and it is suggested that for members of ethnic minority groups, involvement with the police may raise concerns of racist abuse. Further, if arrest occurs in a vacuum without multi-agency support and protection, reprisals from an angry partner may further endanger the woman's safety[2].

It is not only the consequences of pro-arrest policies, but also the extent to which women can freely participate in decision-making on the question of arrest, that requires to be addressed if abused women are to be empowered. While changes in the police response to domestic abuse are welcome, a singular focus on arrest remains problematic. However, contact with domestic violence units and domestic violence officers, as a result of police involvement and an arrest taking place, can have a positive effect on empowering a woman to make decisions about abusive relationships.

Classification of abuse as a crime

The exercise of discretion in pro-arrest policies can be problematic. However, it should also be remembered that police attending an incident may be of the view that they are unable to arrest an abuser because his behaviour does not fall within the definition of a crime. Hatty found that the police response to women and children in Australia was dependent upon the woman appearing as 'deserving' of their protection and whether the circumstances of the incident matched their definition of a 'crime'[3].

In Scotland 'domestic abuse' is not a separate crime and the normal response is to charge the offender with breach of the peace, assault, vandalism or attempted

---

1 See P Jaffe, D Reitzel, E Hastings and G Austin *Wife Assault as a Crime: The Perspective of Victims and Police Officers on a Charging Policy in London, Ontario from 1980–1990: Final Report* (1991) London Family Court Clinic Inc, London, Ontario; P Jaffe, D A Wolfe, A Telford and G Austin 'The impact of police charges in incidents of wife abuse' (1986) *Journal of Family Violence,* 1(1) pp 37–49; and P Jaffe, E Hastings, D Reitzel and G Austin 'The Impact of Police Laying Charges in Hilton, NZ (ed) *Legal Responses to Wife Assault* (1993) Sage, London.

2 R Morley and A Mullender 'Hype or Hope? The Importation of Pro-arrest Policies and Batterers' Programmes from North America to Britain as Key Measures for Preventing Violence Against Women in the Home' (1992) 6 *International Journal of Family Law,* pp 265–288, at p 268.

3 S Hatty *Male Violence and the Police: an Australian Experience* (1988) School of Social Work, University of New South Wales.

murder. There are no national statistics revealing the prevalence of domestic abuse; however, a recent study by Strathclyde Police in Scotland does provide some insight. This study took the form of a 'Women's Safety Initiative' and was conducted between February and August 1998. During this time 4,439 incidents of domestic abuse were recorded. Of this number, the victims were women in 4,192 cases (94%), and men in 247 cases (6%). The domestic abuse incident was deemed to be a crime that could be established in less than half of all cases, n = 1,944 (43.8%). Of the remaining 2,495 incidents, 564 (12.7%) were identified as crimes that could not be established and an overwhelming 1,931 cases (43.5%) were identified as non-criminal incidents[1].

It is not clear why so many incidents were categorised as non-criminal. It cannot be discounted that attending police officers were exercising their powerful discretion and not categorising abusive behaviour as criminal conduct. This is particularly so given the extremely wide definition of breach of the peace which includes any disruptive, alarming or annoying behaviour[2]. If such discretion is being exercised, either consciously or unconsciously, then probable evidence that a crime has been committed will not be regarded as being present and any pro-arrest policy becomes futile.

This illustrates the concern that there is not necessarily a correlation between policy changes in police response to domestic abuse, for example pro-arrest policies developed at managerial level, and what is being implemented 'on the ground'[3]. The introduction of a specific offence of 'domestic abuse' will not address this problem; the name given to the crime committed becomes irrelevant if the attending police officers do not view the actions of the man as criminal and therefore not falling within the definition of any crime. The disparity between policy and action may be due to a lack of training or resources or it may be attributable to prevailing attitudes to domestic abuse.

Civil interdicts and arrest

An interdict (sometimes called an injunction in other jurisdictions) is a court order prohibiting a person from engaging in conduct that infringes the applicant's legal rights. Any person may apply for an interdict to protect them from an abuser. However, at the time of writing, an interdict with a power of arrest is only available where the parties are married or cohabiting[4]. Where an interdict is granted to provide protection from an abusive relationship, the conditions of the interdict may include for example not contacting or approaching the woman. Although it is the civil courts that grant interdicts, the breaching of an 'interdict with a power of arrest' is a criminal matter and is, therefore, dealt with by the police. An interdict with a power of arrest should, therefore, result in automatic arrest if the terms of the interdict are breached.

1 Strathclyde Police *Domestic Abuse Research Findings* (1999) distributed at Domestic Abuse Conference, Glasgow, May 1999.
2 The definition of this crime in Scotland can be found in *Wilson v Brown* 1982 SLT 361 at 362, col 2.
3 S Hatty *Male Violence and the Police: an Australian Experience* (1988) School of Social Work, University of New South Wales, at p 179.
4 Matrimonial Homes (Family Protection) (Scotland) Act 1981, s 14 and s 15(2). The Protection from Abuse (Scotland) Bill, (SP Bill 30), introduced 4 June 2001, proposes to entitle any individual who has obtained, or who is applying for, an interdict for the purpose of providing protection from abuse to apply to the court to have a power of arrest attached to the interdict. This includes divorced spouses, same-sex non-cohabitant partners, other family members such as parents or grandparents or neighbours of abusive people.

A Scottish study in Lothian and Borders Police Force in 1995 found that police officers often resented their lack of discretion when dealing with interdicts with a power of arrest[1]. This differs from pro-arrest policies that, as noted above, allow police a high level of discretion. The lack of discretion in relation to interdicts with a power of arrest is a result of operational guidelines issued by the Lord Advocate that 'arrest is expected in all but the most trivial of circumstances even where no offence other than a breach (of the interdict) has been committed'[2]. Officers interviewed felt that it was unfair that women would allow a man access to the home on some occasions, but on others demand that he be arrested. Interviews revealed that the officers viewed the interdict as placing a legal duty on the woman to do all that was in her power to keep her partner away from her. Some officers even expressed sympathy for the man on the grounds that he may not have read or understood the interdict[3]. Interdicts with a power of arrest were reported as being extremely unpopular and clearly led to both frustration and 'woman-blaming' by officers.

The existing provisions relating to interdicts with power of arrest may be extended by the Protection From Abuse (Scotland) Bill[4]. This Bill proposes that any individual be able to obtain an interdict with a power of arrest regardless of their relationship to the alleged abuser. In relation to police powers, it suggests that before carrying out an arrest, a police officer must have reasonable cause for suspecting that the interdict has been breached and that there is a risk of abuse or further abuse if the interdicted person is not arrested. These provisions, therefore, allow discretion to be exercised by the attending officers.

The Bill also contains provisions relating to the prosecution of those who breach interdicts. The Bill proposes that if the prosecutor decides not to proceed with a case against an arrested person, there must still be a hearing before a sheriff. At this hearing the sheriff can order further detention for up to two days, if satisfied an interdict has been breached and that there is a substantial risk of abuse or further abuse unless detention occurs. The sheriff cannot, however, insist that a prosecution be brought for breach of interdict. This new legislation may enable a wider body of people to apply for an interdict with a power of arrest. However, it does not curtail the discretionary decision-making of either the police or the procurator fiscal.

Prosecution

In Scotland, the procurator fiscal decides whether a case should be prosecuted, what charges should be brought and which court should hear the case. The decision to prosecute is based on whether the police report discloses a crime, whether there is sufficiency of evidence, whether the act is important enough to merit a prosecution and whether prosecution is in the public interest[5]. Apart from the

---

1 K Goodall and H McKay *Police Classification and Responses to Domestic Violence Incidents* (1998) The Scottish Office Central Research Unit, Edinburgh.

2 K Goodall and H McKay, *Police Classification and Responses to Domestic Violence Incidents* (1998) The Scottish Office Central Research Unit, Edinburgh p 16.

3 K Goodall and H McKay *Police Classification and Responses to Domestic Violence Incidents* (1998) The Scottish Office Central Research Unit, Edinburgh p 17.

4 This Bill was presented to the Scottish Parliament on 4 June 2001.

5 See A L Stewart *The Scottish Criminal Courts in Action* (2nd edn 1997), Butterworths, Edinburgh p 192; and S Moody and J Tombs *Prosecution In The Public Interest* (1992) Scottish Academic Press, Edinburgh p 56.

crimes of rape and murder, which can only be tried in the High Court of Justiciary, a decision on which court hears a case depends on the seriousness of the incident. The decision of the prosecutor not to proceed with a case cannot be reviewed or challenged by the public.

Prior to a decision on prosecution even being considered, a report requires to be made by the police. If an incident is not categorised by the attending police officers as a crime, it will not be processed further. In the Strathclyde Police 'Women's Safety Initiative', referred to above, of the 4,439 domestic abuse incidents that were reported to the police, only 1,339 (30.2%) resulted in reports being submitted to the procurator fiscal. No reports were submitted in 2,909 cases (65.5%)[1].

The decision to prosecute and the form the prosecution case takes, ie, the charges to be brought and both the court and the type of trial, depends initially on a report going from the police to the prosecutor and, thereafter, both the content of that report and the attitude of the prosecutor to the incident. The content of the report is therefore highly influential on how an incident is treated. Studies on the treatment of domestic abuse by prosecutors have shown that some view such incidents as matters outwith the criminal law whereas others regard such behaviour as criminal offences and feel they should be prosecuted whether or not the victim is prepared to co-operate[2].

Prosecution policies have been studied across jurisdictions and while there is not overwhelming evidence to suggest that domestic abuse is treated more leniently than other crimes, there is evidence that in offences where the victim knows the perpetrator, cases are less likely to be prosecuted, more likely to result in acquittal and, if convicted, more likely to result in a lenient sentence[3]. A review of Scottish cases found that domestic abuse cases were more likely to be assigned to the lower courts where sanctions are more lenient[4].

As part of their study of the prosecution service in Scotland, Moody and Tombs found that prosecutors, police and social workers responded to domestic abuse differently from other offences involving personal violence[5]. Some prosecutors perceived abused women as 'unreliable witnesses' who would refuse to co-operate with bringing their complaint to trial. While this perception is accurate in many cases, the criminal justice personnel did not appreciate that women feared suffering further abuse if they did support a prosecution. Studies have shown that even if a decision to prosecute is taken, it often resulted in a very short prison sentence or a fine that the woman may end up paying[6]. The incentives for women to participate in the criminal justice process were not there. It is not clear to what extent changes in prosecution policy or new forms of disposal have resolved women's concerns.

1 Strathclyde Police *Domestic Abuse Research Findings* (1999), distributed at Domestic Abuse Conference, Glasgow, May 1999.

2 S Moody and J Tombs *Prosecution In The Public Interest* (1992) Scottish Academic Press, Edinburgh, ch 4.

3 See D S Elliot 'Criminal justice procedures in family violence crimes' in L Ohlin and M Tonry (eds) *Family Violence* (1989) University of Chicago Press, Chicago; and D G Dutton 'The criminal justice response to wife assault' (1987) 11 *Law and Human Behaviour*, pp 189–206.

4 F Wasoff 'Legal protection from wife beating: The processing of domestic assaults by Scottish prosecutors and criminal courts' (1982) 10 *International Journal of the Sociology of Law*, pp 187–204.

5 S Moody and J Tombs *Prosecution In The Public Interest* (1982) Scottish Academic Press, Edinburgh ch 4.

6 R Morley and A Mullender 'Hype or Hope? The Importation of Pro-arrest Policies and Batterers' Programmes from North America to Britain as Key Measures for Preventing Violence Against Women in the Home' (1992) 6 *International Journal of Family Law*, pp 265–288.

While there is a suggestion that since the 1980s prosecution policies have become more responsive to domestic abuse and are able to protect victims while pursuing perpetrators, there is not substantial empirical evidence to support these claims. Decisions of prosecutors are not published and as noted above are not open to challenge by the complainer. There is a dearth of recent research in any jurisdiction which reveals how prosecutors are responding to domestic abuse.

Therapeutic disposals

A change in the criminal justice response which has been more closely monitored is the introduction of therapeutic disposals for abusive men who have offended and been convicted. While these studies do not reveal consistent results in respect of the effect of disposal on repeat offending, they do have a shared finding that it is essential that the man is prosecuted[1]. It has also been suggested that the introduction of more appropriate disposals would not only prevent recidivism but may also encourage women to report abuse and participate in the prosecution of an abuser[2]. Studies conducted in the United States of America found that the chances of the man assaulting his partner in the six-month period following prosecution were not affected by whether the disposal involved harsh punishment or rehabilitative treatment[3]. An evaluation of Scottish programmes for violent men found that women reported an additional violent act by their partner during the 12-month follow-up period in respect of 33% of the men participating in one of the rehabilitation programmes. This compared favourably to the 75% of the men who were subject to another type of sanction, for example fine, probation or prison[4]. These figures suggest that therapeutic disposals are more effective than traditional disposals in rehabilitating abusive men. However, further research in this area would be beneficial.

Rules of evidence

While policy changes may encourage prosecutors to proceed with cases and result in appropriate disposals being made available, the rules of evidence remain problematic. The requirement of corroboration in criminal trials in Scotland has prohibited the employment of alternative prosecution strategies where trials take place in the absence of the woman complainer. This is not possible in Scotland unless there are witnesses to the assault[5], or other corroborating

1 A review of USA evaluative studies is contained in D A Ford and M J Regoli 'The Criminal Prosecution of Wife Assaulters' in Hilton, NZ (ed) *Legal Responses to Wife Assault* (1993) Sage, London.

2 D A Ford and M J Regoli 'The Criminal Prosecution of Wife Assaulters' in Hilton, NZ (ed) *Legal Responses to Wife Assault* (1993) Sage, London.

3 D A Ford and M J Regoli 'The Criminal Prosecution of Wife Assaulters' in Hilton, NZ (ed) *Legal Responses to Wife Assault* (1993) Sage, London.

4 R Dobash, R E Dobash, K Cavanagh and R Lewis *Research Evaluation of Programmes for Violent Men* (1996) HMSO, Edinburgh.

5 Given the 'private' nature of domestic abuse it is unusual to have witnesses. The exception to this is children who are often present in the house and may hear and see the abuse taking place. Even when children are eyewitnesses their age and maturity may affect whether they are deemed by prosecutors to be suitable witnesses. If deemed suitable witnesses, the giving of evidence of this type clearly places a child in a very difficult position where they may feel conflicting loyalty towards both parents.

evidence, for example medical evidence of injuries. If the woman has told friends or relatives of the man's prior abuse towards her, the rules of evidence will not allow these accounts to be heard as corroborating evidence as they are deemed to be hearsay and not relevant to the charge. The hearsay rule provides that evidence or a statement made by a person otherwise than while giving oral evidence in Court is inadmissible as evidence of any stated fact[1].

The exception to this rule is in the case of 'professional' witnesses, for example a GP, who may be able to speak to prior reports of injuries under the guise that it is 'expert' and therefore opinion evidence that is being presented. Doctors can provide very valuable evidence relating to prior abuse that the woman has suffered. The disclosure of such abuse to a GP is not however automatic, perhaps because of shame or because the woman has not been allowed to seek medical assistance by the abuser. Evidence suggests that women may not always get the help they need from healthcare professionals[2] and in the study by McWilliams and McKiernan[3] only one third of the women who had told their GP about the abuse found their response helpful. It can be surmised that these women would be less likely to make further disclosures to their GP and this type of evidence may, therefore, not be available.

Evidence of prior abuse

Research findings indicate that women do not disclose domestic abuse and, therefore, there may not be witnesses who can speak to having been told of prior abuse. There are many reasons why abuse is kept private including: forgetting as a coping mechanism, fear of losing children[4], fear of not being believed, shame, pride, self-blame and lack of confidence[5]. This means that women who suffer a catalogue of violence often do not speak to their friends and family let alone professional agencies such as the police or social services.

Research indicates that women do not contact the police following the first instance of domestic abuse and that multiple abuses will have occurred before the police are contacted. A large scale survey conducted in Islington in 1992 revealed that women had only reported 28% of the assaults they had experienced[6]. If there are neither witnesses nor official records of the man's behaviour, it is likely to remain hidden from the police, prosecutor and sentencer. This will ultimately affect the offence(s) charged, whether or not bail is granted and any sentence imposed.

Even when there are previous convictions for similar abuse, in a trial these cannot be revealed to the judge or jury until the point of sentencing. Ironically,

1 Exceptions to the rule that hearsay evidence is inadmissable are contained in the Criminal Procedure (Scotland) Act 1995, ss 259–262.

2 J Pahl 'Health professionals and violence against women' in P Kingston and B Penhale (eds) *Family Violence and the Caring Professions* (1995) Macmillan, London.

3 M McWilliams and J McKiernan *Bringing it Out in the Open: Domestic Violence in Northern Ireland* (1993) HMSO, Belfast.

4 L Kelly 'The Interconnectedness of domestic violence and child abuse: Challenges for research, policy and practice' in A Mullender and R Morley (eds) *Children Living with Domestic Violence: Putting Men's Abuse of Women on the Child Care Agenda* (1994) Whiting and Birch, London. The fear of losing children is explored in more depth later in this chapter.

5 M McWilliams and J McKiernan *Bringing it Out in the Open: Domestic Violence in Northern Ireland* (1993) HMSO, Belfast.

6 Cited in G Hague and E Malos *Domestic Violence Action for Change* (1993) New Clarion Press, Cheltenham, pp 65–66.

although a lack of evidence of prior abuse is problematic, even where such evidence is available it can hinder rather than help a prosecution. Myths around domestic abuse including that it is provoked, deserved, or reasonable, inform judges' and juries' interpretation of the woman's account of her abuse. Presenting evidence of a long history of abuse may result in juries and judges viewing the abuse as less serious because it was tolerated. Consequently, the woman's account may be viewed as exaggerated and her credibility affected. In the case study that follows, the sheriff asked of the woman 'if the violence was that bad, why didn't you leave?'. This question was posed even though the woman had been seriously assaulted following separation. The sheriff also concluded that the woman had exaggerated the violence she had suffered.

The adversarial process

As the law and legal process involves an exchange of narratives in the context of a courtroom, it is usually the case that the more successful of the competing accounts presented by both sides in a legal dispute is the one which appeals to a dominant or shared stereotype. It is this account that is afforded the label 'truthful' and acceptable to the party deciding the facts. Fineman suggests that 'law is most effective when it tracks societal norms and values about which there is strong agreement. Therefore, it is no surprise that law incorporates dominant stereotypes and replicates existing ingrained inequalities'[1]. The particular difficulty with domestic abuse is that the associated stereotypes have such wide effect, influencing as they do the response of police and prosecutors to domestic abuse and decisions around child contact and residence should a woman decide to leave the abuser.

EFFECTS OF ABUSE ON CHILDREN

Children are often the invisible victims of domestic abuse and their role as secondary victims of their mother's abuse has only recently been recognised. Even if not a direct recipient of physical injuries, a child who witnesses domestic abuse is still a victim of that abuse by their experience[2]. Trauma, fear and an increased risk of behavioural problems can be the result[3]. The authors of one study have even gone so far as to assert that there are only two routes for children or adolescents dealing with being the recipient or witness of abuse, namely suicide or

1 M A Fineman Preface in M A Fineman and R Mykituk *The Public Nature of Private Violence* (1994) Routledge, New York, p xvi.

2 The witnessing of violence against their mothers has been shown to have psychological and developmental effects on children. See H H Hughes 'Psychological and behavioural correlates of family violence in child witnesses and victims' (1987) 58 *American Journal of Orthopsychiatry*, pp 77–90. This negative psychological impact of wife abuse on both women and their children is clearly cross-cultural, evidenced by the findings of an empirical study of Chinese women and their children; C So-Kum Tang, 'Psychological Impact of Wife Abuse, Experience of Chinese Women and Their Children' 1997 12 *Journal of Interpersonal Violence*, no 3 466–478.

3 J W Fantuzzo, L M DePaola, L Lambert, T Martino, G Anderson and S Sutton 'Effects of interparental violence on the psychological adjustment and competencies of young children' (1991) 59 *Journal of Consulting and Clinical Psychology*, pp 258–265; H M Hughes and S J Barad Psychological functioning of children in a battered women's shelter: A preliminary investigation (1983) 53 *American Journal of Orthopsychiatry*, pp 525–531.

homicide[1]. In their study, Kashni and Allan found high rates of prior family violence in respect of juveniles who committed intra-familial homicide and that the homicide frequently followed an unsuccessful suicide attempt and was viewed as an effort to escape from the family violence[2]. Much of the research on the effects of domestic abuse on children is problematic as it tends to be conducted within a refuge setting, focuses on restricted questions, results in there being an over-representation of lower socio-economic classes and does not properly explore the effect of race, status, frequency of violence and the children's exposure to it[3]. Children in shelters may not only have witnessed extremes of spousal violence but may also be traumatised by the fact that they are in a refuge[4]. Nevertheless, a review of the literature does indicate that living with domestic abuse does impact on children's welfare and that there is a significant overlap with child abuse[5].

Children are also the direct victims of domestic abuse and may be assaulted if present during a domestic violence incident. Such assaults can occur when children attempt to intervene to stop the violence and protect their mother. A Yorkshire study found that children do intervene when their mother is being attacked and if children did not try to protect their mothers, it was usually because they were too young[6].

The link between domestic abuse and child abuse

Research findings show that child abuse occurs disproportionately in homes where domestic abuse also occurs[7]. While studies in this area have examined whether abused mothers have abused children[8], an alternative methodology analysed the hospital records of the mothers of children who had been registered on the suspicion of child abuse in a metropolitan area of the United States of America over a twelve-month period[9]. These hospital records did not contain the

1 J H Kashani and W D Allan *The Impact of Family Violence on Children and Adolescents* (1998) Sage, Thousand Oaks, California.

2 J H Kashani and W D Allan *The Impact of Family Violence on Children and Adolescents* (1998) Sage, Thousand Oaks, California.

3 R Morley and A Mullender 'Domestic Violence and Children: What do we Know From Research' in A Mullender and R Morley (eds) *Children Living with Domestic Violence* (1994) Whiting and Birch, London.

4 J W Fantuzzo, L M DePaola, L Lambert, T Martino, G Anderson and S Sutton 'Effects of inter-parental violence on the psychological adjustment and competencies of young children (1991) 59 *Journal of Consulting and Clinical Psychology*, pp 258–265.

5 R Morley and A Mullender 'Domestic Violence and Children: What do we Know From Research' in A Mullender and R Morley (eds) *Children Living with Domestic Violence* (1994) Whiting and Birch, London.

6 J Hanmer *Women, Violence and Crime Prevention: a Study of Changes in Policy and Practices in West Yorkshire* (1990) (Violence, Abuse and Gender Relations Unit Research Paper no 1 1990), Department of Applied Social Studies, University of Bradford, Bradford, p 26.

7 R J Wright, R O Wright and N E Isaac 'Response to battered mothers in the paediatric emergency department: a call for an interdisciplinary approach to family violence' *Paediatrics* 99 (1997) pp 186–192; E K Suh and E M Abel 'The impact of spousal violence on the children of the abused' (1990) 4 *Journal of Independent Social Work*, pp 27–34.

8 For example, L H Bowker, M Arbitell and J R McFerron 'On the relationship between wife beating and child abuse' in K Yllo and M Bograd (eds) *Feminist Perspectives on Wife Abuse* (1988) Sage, Newbury Park, California.

9 E Stark and A Flitcraft 'Woman battering, child abuse and social hereditary: what is the relationship?' in N Johnson (ed) *Marital Violence* (1985) Routledge and Kegan Paul, London; E Stark and A Flitcraft 'Women and children at risk: a feminist perspective on child abuse (1988) 18 *International Journal of Health Services*, (1), pp 97–118.

individual's account of the abuse they had suffered and may, therefore, only present a partial picture. The records revealed that 45% of the 116 mothers with registered children had a medical history that indicated their partners had assaulted them. An additional 5% did not contain enough evidence to indicate if violence had occurred; however, their records suggested a history of 'marital conflict'[1]. Children were twice as likely to have been registered for physical abuse where there was a history of their mothers having been abused and their fathers were more than three times as likely to be their abuser. These children were more likely to be removed from their home than those registered children whose mothers were not also the victims of abuse[2].

The limited United Kingdom and Irish research that has been conducted reflects the United States findings. A study by social services found that at least one third of children on the Child Protection Register had mothers who were experiencing domestic abuse in the home[3]. An Irish study found that 28% of women who had used refuge accommodation reported that their children had also been severely beaten by their partner[4]. A Scottish study of 20 women whose children had been part of the child protection system as a result of being sexually abused by the mother's partner, all reported that they had been subjected to domestic abuse and only three reported that this did not involve physical violence[5].

Parental homicide

An extreme effect of domestic abuse for children arises when one parent kills another. This effectively leaves the child parentless, as one parent is dead and the other will be in custody or hospital. From 1983 to 1992, between 42% and 49% of all female homicide victims in England and Wales were killed by their current or former partners or lovers. For most years during that period, about one fifth of all homicide victims were women killed by male partners or lovers[6]. High proportions of these women are likely to have had children. For the same period, between 7% and 11% of male victims were killed by their current or former partners or lovers[7]. The latter figure does not reveal the extent to which these homicides resulted from actions of self-defence or if they were provoked by the man's violence. When men kill their partners it generally follows a history and pattern of violence, whereas women tend to kill following years of suffering violent abuse[8]. The loss of a parent in such circumstances is inevitably traumatic and

1 E Stark and A Flitcraft 'Women and children at risk: a feminist perspective on child abuse' (1988) 18 *International Journal of Health Services*, (1), pp 97–118 at p 104.
2 E Stark and A Flitcraft 'Women and children at risk: a feminist perspective on child abuse' (1988) 18 *International Journal of Health Services*, (1), pp 97–118 at pp 105–106.
3 M O'Hara 'Child protection and domestic violence: changing policy and practice' *The Links Between Domestic Violence and Child Abuse: Developing Services* (1993) London Borough of Hackney, p 20.
4 M Casey *Domestic Violence Against Women* (1987) Dublin Federation of Refuges.
5 J Forman 'Is There a Correlation Between Child Sexual Abuse and Domestic Violence? An Exploratory Study of the Links Between Child Sexual Abuse and Domestic Violence in a Sample of Intrafamilial Child Sexual Abuse Cases' (1995) Women's Support Project, Glasgow.
6 *Criminal Statistics: England and Wales 1992* (1993) HMSO, London, pp 78–79, Table 4.4.
7 *Criminal Statistics: England and Wales 1992* (1993) HMSO, London, pp 78–79, Table 4.4.
8 A Browne *When Battered Women Kill* (1987) Free Press, New York, p 10; and C P Ewing *Battered Women Who Kill: Psychological Self Defense as Legal Justification* (1987) D C Heath & Co, Lexington, Massachusetts, p 23.

research findings indicate that the witnessing of the homicide, or being in the home at the time of the homicide or observation of the aftermath, commonly results in the development of the symptoms or the full syndrome of post-traumatic stress disorder[1]. Dealing with such bereavement can be problematic as the child may have conflicting emotions of loss together with horror and shame. They may also be placed under media pressure and attract stigma due to their experience[2].

Police response to children

Whereas in the past children were not regarded as victims unless they were direct recipients of abuse, police forces now recognise their legal obligation to respond to children in such situations. In Scotland this response has taken the form of reporting the presence of children to a superior officer and/or the Reporter to the Children's Panel. In cases where a child is present in the home during the domestic abuse incident and there are concerns for the physical or emotional well-being of the child, a report should be made to the Reporter to the Children's Panel who will decide on whether the statutory grounds for referral to the panel are fulfilled[3]. This decision obviously relies on a value judgement being made by the attending officer and is discretionary. In England and Wales, Plotnikoff and Woolfson found that domestic violence officers exercised their own judgement as to whether or not social workers should be informed of the presence of children in homes where a domestic violence incident had been reported. The criterion for referral was seldom incorporated into inter-agency agreements and child protection and domestic violence agencies' responses were rarely integrated[4].

The change in police response in Scotland is cautiously welcomed as it suggests that the connection between domestic abuse of women and the abuse of their children has been formally recognised. There is also a multi-agency working group drafting the protocol for this intervention; however, their guidelines are not yet public[5]. It is important that this recognition of the effects of abuse on

1 D Black and T Kaplan 'Father kills mother: Issues and problems encountered by a child psychiatric team' (1988) 153 *British Journal of Psychiatry*, pp 624–630; R S Pynoos and K Nader 'Children's exposure to violence and traumatic death' (1990) 20 *Psychiatric Annals*, pp 334–344.

2 D Black and T Kaplan 'Father kills mother: Issues and problems encountered by a child psychiatric team' (1988) 153 *British Journal of Psychiatry*, pp 624–630.

3 The provisions for the protection and supervision of children are found in the Children (Scotland) Act 1995, s 52, which replaces the Social Work (Scotland) Act 1968, s 32. This section states that the reporter should refer a child to, and arrange for, a hearing if satisfied that there is a prima facie case that at least one of the s 52 'grounds of referral' is satisfied and that the child is in need of compulsory supervision which includes measures for protection, guidance or control of the child. There are 12 grounds for referral in s 52 including where the child is likely to suffer unnecessarily or to be impaired seriously in his health and development due to lack of parental care and where a member of the household is a Sch 1 offender (sex offender) or has been convicted of an incest offence. The consequences of the grounds of referral either being accepted or established are a supervision requirement either within the family or it may involve the removal of the child to be cared for elsewhere. For more information see A B Wilkinson and K Norrie *The Law Relating to Parent and Child in Scotland* (1999) W. Green, Edinburgh, ch 19.

4 J Plotnikoff and R Woolfson *Policing Domestic Violence: Effective Organisational Structures* (1998) (Police Research Series Paper 100) Home Office, London. As the Children's Panel and, therefore, the Reporter do not exist in England and Wales, the appropriate course of action there is to contact the local social work department.

5 This information was provided by the Women's Support Project in Glasgow. The partners involved in drafting the protocol are police, Reporter to the Children's Panel and social work.

children does not result in women or children being further penalised for the man's abuse. Research findings from the United States of America and England suggest that this has been the consequence of introducing similar policy.

Child protection and domestic violence services

The growing awareness in the United States of the connection between domestic abuse and child abuse has resulted in tension and occasional clashes between child protection services and domestic violence services. This occurs when domestic abuse becomes public and the child protection and domestic violence services are involved. If the mother is viewed by the child protection services as being unable or unwilling to protect her children from further abuse, the child will be removed to a place of safety. This decision is made not on the basis of whether the mother was responsible for past abuse but whether she is able to protect the child from future abuse. The mother may also be prosecuted with the abuser for child abuse if it is deemed that she was reasonably capable of protecting her child but failed to do so[1].

It is evident from such responses that while the man's abuse has not been prevented, the woman and the child are being penalised. The threat of removal of children may result in women pretending they can protect their children. Fear of removal is one of the reasons that both women and children do not tell social services about domestic abuse[2]. Two-thirds of women who participated in a recent study in Coventry were either threatened with the removal of their children, or had their children removed, by social services[3]. A better response to domestic abuse than removal of children, is to provide advocacy and protection for the woman from the abuser which will in turn protect children from domestic abuse[4].

MORE MYTHS

A prevailing myth in relation to women who are abused is that the abuse will stop if they leave their violent partner. There are many reasons why women stay in abusive relationships, including their children and for economic reasons. It is clear that women do leave abusive relationships and it appears that the process of leaving can be a long and painful one. The act of leaving does not necessarily result in the woman or her children being safe from abuse. A study by Harris and Grace found that the single largest category of rapists were ex-partners[5]. In a famous direction to the jury in a case where a woman had killed her abusive partner the judge said in relation to the provocative effect of his violence:

---

1 C Wilson 'Are Battered Women Responsible for Protection of their Children in Domestic Violence Cases' (1998) 13 *Journal of Interpersonal Violence*, No 2, pp 289–293 at p 292.

2 C McGee *Childhood Experiences of Domestic Violence* (2000) Jessica Kingsley Publishers, London, ch 6.

3 C Humphreys *Social Work, Domestic Violence and Child Protection: Challenging Practice* (2000) Policy Press, Bristol.

4 E Stark and A Flitcraft 'Women and children at risk: a feminist perspective on child abuse' (1988) 18 *International Journal of Health Services*, (1), pp 97–118; and L H Bowker, M Arbitell and J R McFerron 'On the relationship between wife beating and child abuse' in K Yllo and M Bograd, (eds) *Feminist Perspectives on Wife Abuse* (1988) Sage, Newbury Park, California.

5 See J Harris and S Grace *A Question of Evidence?* (1999) Home Office, London.

> 'Now there is evidence before you that the deceased was a drunkard . . . that he was a bully, that he assaulted his wife from time to time and that he made her life a misery. But, hundreds, indeed thousands of wives in this country, unfortunately, suffer this fate. The remedy of divorce or judicial separation or factual separation is available to end this torment.'[1]

The 'torment' is not necessarily brought to an end by separation[2]. It is acknowledged that women are at the greatest risk from their abusive partners when they are attempting to leave or seek help[3] and as the case study in this chapter suggests, even post-separation abuse continues to be responded to less effectively than stranger abuse. Post-separation violence or 'separation assault' is an attempt by the abuser to regain control and power over the woman and to punish her for ending the relationship. Separation assault is not unusual and in numerous cases has resulted in the woman's death[4]. Figures for England and Wales indicate that 30% of the women killed by their husbands were no longer living with the man at the time of their death[5].

Neither the prevalence of post-separation abuse, nor the impact on children of witnessing abuse, is understood or appropriately responded to by the legal system in relation to decisions on contact and residence. The perpetration of the myth that separation will lead to safety is untrue and reinforces the 'women-blaming' approach often adopted in relation to male abuse, namely that women are responsible both for causing the abuse and for stopping it. The fear that women experience when they leave an abuser is due to the abuse suffered and often because the abuser has told the woman that he will find her and harm her if she leaves[6]. The figures stated above illustrate the high numbers of men who carry out this threat. Men will go to great lengths to find their partners and have used contact with their children as a means to continue abusing their former partner[7].

DECISION OF RESIDENCE AND CONTACT

In many jurisdictions decisions in relation to parental responsibilities or rights are decided on the basis of the welfare or 'best interests' of the child principle[8].

1 *HM Advocate v Greig* (May 1979, unreported), High Ct Edinburgh. Cited in C H W Gane and C N Stoddart *A Casebook On Scottish Criminal Law* (1991) W. Green / Sweet & Maxwell, Edinburgh, p 527.

2 See L R Keenan 'Domestic Violence And Custody Litigation: The Need For Statutory Reform' 1985, 13 *Hofstra Law Review*, 407–441, at pp 421–422.

3 E Pence *The Justice System's Response to Domestic Assault Cases: a Guide for Policy Development* (1989) Minnesota Program Development Inc, Duluth, Minnesota, at p 345; and A Browne and K R Williams 'Exploring the effect of resource availability and the likelihood of female-precipitated homicides' 23 *Law and Society Review*, (1), pp 75–94.

4 See M R Mahoney 'Legal Images of Battered Women: Redefining the Issue of Separation' (1991) *90 Michigan Law Review* pp 1–94, at pp 65–66; and A Jones *Next Time She'll Be Dead* (1994) Beacon Press, Boston, pp 149–152.

5 S Edwards *Policing 'Domestic' Violence* (1989) Sage, London, at p 200.

6 A Browne *When Battered Women Kill* (1987) Free Press, New York, at p 115.

7 M Hester, J Humphries, et al, 'Domestic Violence and Child Contact' in A Mullender and R Morley *Children Living with Domestic Violence: Putting Men's Abuse of Women on the Child Care Agenda* (1994) Whiting & Birch, London.

8 In Scotland this principle is contained in the Children (Scotland) Act 1995, s 11(7) and in England and Wales in the Children Act 1989, s 1. Although the provisions differ, the spirit of the legislation is similar in both jurisdictions.

This includes court decisions in respect of contact with or residence of the children. The definition of the welfare or 'best interests' of the child principle is not exact: however, the House of Lords has interpreted it as

> 'a process whereby, when all the relevant facts, relationships, claims and wishes of parents, risks, choices and other circumstances are taken into account and weighed, the course to be followed will be that which is most in the interests of the child's welfare as that term now has to be understood'[1].

This definition is not particularly helpful. However, case law suggests that the test includes the emotional and physical well being of the child, the age and sex of the child and the characteristics of the parent[2].

Both of the Children Acts in Scotland, and England and Wales were deemed to be significant pieces of child legislation which introduced a child-centred approach and were anticipated to replace the previous adversarial system with one which was more child-friendly. In practice, however, the 'welfare principle' embodied in the legislation is viewed by some writers as having been translated into the patriarchal belief that the best interests of children are delivered by retaining paternal control through continuing contact with the father, regardless of whether he is an abuser[3]. The inadequate response by the courts to applications for contact or residence is viewed as having been exacerbated rather than abated by these respective Children Acts. As predicted by feminists, the content and application of this legislation is compromising the safety of women and children[4].

Contact

As the mother usually has actual possession of any children it is normally fathers, either married or unmarried, who will raise an action for contact. While the motivation in doing so may be because the father wishes to have contact with the child, abusive men may also be motivated by a desire to retain control over an ex-partner. The process for any individual who intends to oppose residence or contact is traumatic. For an abused woman, however, it may also be dangerous as the courts may reveal her new address to the abusive partner. Radford et al, following their survey of 130 abused parents (129 mothers and 1 father) report that the provisions to ensure the safety of the abused partner during court proceedings are inadequate. Thirty-eight of the 121 parents involved in court proceedings were exposed to more violence when the abuser learned their address as a result of the contact case going to court[5].

---

1 Per Lord MacDermott in *J v C* [1970] AC 668, at 710–711.

2 A review of the Scottish case law in this area is found in A B Wilkinson and K Norrie *The Law Relating to Parent and Child in Scotland* (1999) W Green, Edinburgh, ch 9; and L Edwards and A Griffiths *Family Law* (1997) W Green, Edinburgh, pp 106–123. The English legislation includes a 'welfare checklist' in the Children Act 1989, s 1.

3 L Harne and J Radford 'Reinstating Patriarchy: The Politics of the Family and the New Legislation in A Mullender and R Morle (eds) *Children Living with Domestic Violence: Putting Men's Abuse of Women on the Child Care Agenda* (1994) Whiting & Birch, London.

4 M Hester, J Humphries et al, 'Domestic Violence and Child Contact' in A Mullender and R Morley (eds) *Children Living with Domestic Violence: Putting Men's Abuse of Women on the Child Care Agenda* (1994) Whiting & Birch, London.

5 L Radford, S Sayers and Aid for Mothers Involved in Contact Action *Unreasonable Fears?* (1999) Women's Aid Federation of England, Bristol, at p 19.

If women oppose actions by abusive fathers for contact or residence, professionals often believe that she is using her children to avenge her ex-partner. Radford et al, report that 20% of parents who had cases heard in court were advised by their solicitor not to mention domestic violence; 9% were advised not to mention abuse of the child; and domestic violence was not mentioned in almost half of the welfare reports prepared[1]. Women are being discouraged from mentioning abuse while at the same time being encouraged to agree informally to contact[2].

Contact and evidence of prior abuse

Evidence of prior abuse may be excluded from court hearings on the ground that it is irrelevant; however, when such evidence is admitted the court has ultimate discretion whether to be influenced by it[3]. Reference to prior abuse is sometimes classified as exaggerated and something which is now in the past[4]. Radford et al, found that even where there were substantial convictions for violence, courts sometimes exercised their discretion and awarded contact[5]. In their study, almost half of the 130 respondents had injunctions against their partner to prevent violence and one in five of the abusive partners had criminal convictions for violence against their partner[6]. The contact application was opposed by 64% of the abused parents. There were a number of reasons for this, including concerns that their children would be subjected to physical violence (49%), neglect (47%), or sexual abuse (27%). Parents were also concerned for their own safety, should contact be granted, and 38% feared that their ex-partner would kill them[7]. Of those surveyed 75% reported that the court did not consider the violence they had suffered sufficient cause to refuse contact even though 95% of these people had experienced a history of violence that indicated a risk of homicide. In 75% of cases the application by the abusive partner for contact was granted. Contact resulted in further abuse of the individual and their children for 92% of parents[8].

Are abusive men suitable role models?

The question as to whether abusive men are suitable carers or appropriate role models for children does not appear to be considered by the courts. Hester et al,

1 L Radford, S Sayers, and Aid for Mothers Involved in Contact Action *Unreasonable Fears?* (1999) Women's Aid Federation of England, Bristol, at p 23.
2 L Radford, S Sayers, and Aid for Mothers Involved in Contact Action *Unreasonable Fears?* (1999) Women's Aid Federation of England, Bristol, at p 23.
3 The difficulties encountered in proving domestic abuse in criminal trials are shared in the civil courts. The woman's credibility can be damaged if she is the only person giving evidence about the abuse she has suffered. The courts and associated professionals often view such evidence as motivated by grievances against the man and may doubt the truthfulness of the evidence.
4 M Hester, J Humphries et al 'Domestic Violence and Child Contact' in A Mullender and R Morley (eds) *Children Living with Domestic Violence: Putting Men's Abuse of Women on the Child Care Agenda* (1994) Whiting & Birch, London, at p 108.
5 L Radford, S Sayers, and Aid for Mothers Involved in Contact Action *Unreasonable Fears?* (1999) Women's Aid Federation of England, Bristol, pp 25–26.
6 L Radford, S Sayers, and Aid for Mothers Involved in Contact Action *Unreasonable Fears?* (1999) Women's Aid Federation of England, Bristol, at p 13.
7 L Radford, S Sayers, and Aid for Mothers Involved in Contact Action *Unreasonable Fears?* (1999) Women's Aid Federation of England, App 1, table 4 at p 39.
8 L Radford, S Sayers, and Aid for Mothers Involved in Contact Action *Unreasonable Fears?* (1999) Women's Aid Federation of England, p 19.

refer to 'bizarre' instances where contact has been awarded, including where the father had been convicted of abusing step-children, where the father had been convicted of the attempted murder of the mother of his children, and where the father had been convicted of the manslaughter of the mother of his children[1].

Views of the child

The Children Acts provide that the court shall, as far as practicable, have regard to the views of the child, taking account of the child's age and maturity. In the Scottish provisions, a child aged 12 or more is presumed to be mature enough to form a view. Children under 12 can also express views if deemed mature enough[2]. A similar obligation is embodied in the English and Welsh provisions[3]. Apart from the fact that ascertaining children's views is highly complex and time-consuming, research has shown that professionals involved in court actions relating to contact did not even talk to children[4]. The torn loyalties of children who may or may not wish to see an abusive father may not be resolved by these provisions. It is also not clear from the legislation exactly how much weight must or should be given to children's wishes and whether professionals are in a position to assess what is in 'their best interests'[5].

Does contact result in further abuse?

The award of contact by the court may expose the mother and children to more trauma and violence. Despite the fact that children have been shown to be at risk during contact visits where there is a history of domestic abuse, court decisions do not always reflect this. Radford et al found that courts did not adequately assess the safety risks to women and children when contact orders were granted to violent men and as a consequence, two out of three of the parents and 76% of children who had been physically abused by the violent parent were further abused as a result of contact being granted[6]. Contact orders have been used as a further means to abuse women physically, sexually or verbally; children have also been abducted under these orders, or hand-over arrangements not adhered to[7]. They may also expose children to the risk of sexual and violent abuse, neglect from inadequate parenting and witnessing or being implicated in further violence and abuse of their mother[8]. Contact centres are not viewed as offering

1 M Hester, J Humphries et al 'Domestic Violence and Child Contact' in A Mullender and R Morley *Children Living with Domestic Violence: Putting Men's Abuse of Women on the Child Care Agenda* (1994) Whiting & Birch, London p 107.

2 Children (Scotland) Act 1995, s 11(10).

3 Children Act 1989, s 1(3)(a).

4 M Hester, J Humphries et al 'Domestic Violence and Child Contact' in A Mullender and R Morley *Children Living with Domestic Violence: Putting Men's Abuse of Women on the Child Care Agenda* (1994) Whiting & Birch, London, at pp 115–117; and ch 1 above.

5 M Hester, J Humphries et al, 'Domestic Violence and Child Contact' in A Mullender and R Morley, *Children Living with Domestic Violence: Putting Men's Abuse of Women on the Child Care Agenda* (1994) Whiting & Birch, London p 116.

6 L Radford, S Sayers, and Aid for Mothers Involved in Contact Action *Unreasonable Fears?* (1999) Women's Aid Federation of England, Bristol, pp 19–21.

7 M Hester and L Radford 'Domestic Violence and Access Arrangements for Children in Denmark and Britain' 1992, 1 *Journal of Social Welfare and Family Law*, pp 57–70, at p 61.

8 M Hester, J Humphries et al, 'Domestic Violence and Child Contact' in A Mullender and R Morley *Children Living with Domestic Violence: Putting Men's Abuse of Women on the Child Care Agenda* (1994) Whiting & Birch, London p 106.

permanent protection to women and children. They are only a temporary arrangement until unsupervised access can be granted[1].

LEGAL CHANGE

There is some evidence of change in the English courts. In the case of *Re L; V; M; and H (A child) (Contact: Domestic Violence)*[2], the refusal of the application by each father for direct contact against a background of domestic violence was confirmed on appeal. While this case recognises that there is a presumption in favour of contact it notes that where there are allegations of domestic violence in relation to a contact application the effects of that violence must be considered. This includes the conduct of both parties towards each other and towards the children, the effect of the violence on the children and on the residential parent, and the motivation of the parent seeking contact. Evidence of domestic violence is not viewed as a prima facie bar to contact but must be weighed against the application of the welfare principle and the positive impact for the child should contact be granted. Walker LJ notes[3] that judges and advisers alike *may* have undermined the effect of children being exposed to domestic violence. He emphasises that domestic violence is not to be elevated to a special category that should lead to a presumption against contact; rather, it is one highly material factor amongst many which may offset the assumption in favour of contact when applying the welfare principle and the welfare checklist contained in the Children Act 1989, s 1(1) and (3). While this judgment goes some way to address concerns expressed in this chapter, it does not recognise the difficulties of proving prior abuse in court, nor does it guarantee that the existing discretionary assessment of such abuse will be replaced by a more vigorous and accurate approach.

Positive changes are also found in other jurisdictions. For example, in the United States of America there is a rebuttable presumption that children should stay with a non-abusive parent in a place that they choose. In New Zealand, a rebuttable presumption exists that residence orders will not be granted to violent parents and there will only be unsupervised access if the court is satisfied that the child will be safe[4].

These changes cannot address all of the concerns which have been referred to above. Clearly, further changes in decision-making around contact and residence are required. Fundamental requirements are that women and children are listened to and believed, and that children's accounts of violence or expressions of not wishing to see their father are not viewed as being manipulated by the mother and therefore irrelevant[5].

1 M Hester, J Humphries et al 'Domestic Violence and Child Contact' in A Mullender and R Morley (eds) *Children Living with Domestic Violence: Putting Men's Abuse of Women on the Child Care Agenda* (1984) Whiting & Birch, London.
2 *Re L; V; M; and H (A Child) (Contact: Domestic Violence)* [2000] 2 FLR 334.
3 *Re L; V; M; and H (A Child) (Contact: Domestic Violence)* [2000] 2 FLR 334 at 371.
4 Radford et al *Unreasonable Fears?* (1999) Women's Aid Federation of England, Bristol.
5 M Hester, J Humphries et al 'Domestic Violence and Child Contact' in A Mullender and R Morley (eds) *Children Living with Domestic Violence: Putting Men's Abuse of Women on the Child Care Agenda* (1994) Whiting & Birch, London, at p 116.

CASE STUDY

This case study has been included to illustrate the inadequate legal response to one woman and her children who were subjected to domestic abuse. It refers to two court cases: one criminal arising from an attack on the woman, Donna, by her ex-partner, Ron, and his subsequent civil action for contact with his daughter. Scottish Law governed both Court actions but neither case has been reported in the law reports[1].

Donna married Ron in April 1992. She had a daughter Alison from a previous marriage. Her relationship with Ron was a good one until shortly after they were married. Two days after their wedding Ron assaulted Donna for the first time. (It is not unusual for violence only to occur in a relationship after marriage or another similar event which cements the relationship.) Violence continued throughout the marriage and also while Donna was pregnant and after the birth of her daughter Flora in February 1994. The violence suffered by Donna was witnessed by her older daughter, Alison.

Donna and Ron separated in February 1995 and in June 1995 Donna moved with her two daughters to a flat. She continued to work and support her two daughters while Ron failed to contribute any financial support. His parents retained contact with the child Flora while Ron only saw her on two occasions and was out of the country for periods of time when no one knew where he was. Ron had an alcohol problem and had on occasion attempted to remove the child Flora while under the influence of alcohol.

Donna withheld her address from Ron as she feared attack. During their relationship Ron had told her on numerous occasions that if she left him he would find her and harm her. She had an agreement with his parents that they would not disclose her whereabouts to him. Her flat was secured by numerous locks on the front door due to fear of an attack from Ron.

In the early hours of 9 November 1995, Ron climbed scaffolding that was erected outside Donna's first floor flat. He smashed a window and climbed into the living room where he assaulted Donna in front of Alison and Flora. During what was a very violent assault Ron was strangling Donna. She was losing consciousness when neighbours finally managed to kick in her front door and restrain Ron until the police arrived[2]. A number of police officers were present however, the only female officer remained stationed downstairs at the building entrance[3]. While the male officers interviewed Ron in one room, Donna and the two girls were in the other room of the small flat.

Donna was wearing her nightdress which was now covered in Ron's blood and her daughters, aged 11 years and 21 months respectively, were extremely distressed. Her neighbours, whom she did not know well, continued to be present during the initial questioning by the police. Ron was taken into custody and the police asked if Donna wished to attend hospital. She could not attend

1 The information provided here was obtained during an interview with the woman and from a copy of the sheriff's written decision in the court action for contact. The names of all parties have been changed.

2 The neighbours had great difficulty getting through the front door due to the large number of locks. These locks had been put on the door because of Donna's fear that Ron would find her flat and attempt to gain entry. This additional security could have cost Donna her life.

3 As only one female officer was present at the scene of the crime she should have been present in the flat.

hospital as there was no one to leave her children with and she required to clear up the glass and blood and have the broken window repaired.

Ron appeared in court later on 9 November, was refused bail and was remanded in custody. Later that day Donna received the decree of her divorce from Ron. Ron subsequently appealed against the refusal of bail and was awarded bail four days later. Aware that Ron had been liberated, Donna lived in constant fear of future attacks. Alarm systems were installed in both her house and car.

Donna made contact with the police to find out which charges were to be brought against Ron. She was told that the charge would be breach of the peace and that the case would be heard in the district court[1]. Donna did not consider this to reflect the severity of the assault or the circumstances within which it was committed. She contacted the Woman and Child Unit at Clydebank Police Station and spoke with a police officer who agreed that the charges did not reflect the seriousness of the assault that had occurred. She tried many times to speak to the prosecutor who was marking the case[2] and only by her persistence did the prosecutor agree to speak to Donna's lawyer. Following this conversation the case was marked as an assault to be heard in the sheriff court[3].

Donna was an educated, articulate, middle-class woman who worked as a university lecturer and was used to dealing with authority. In an interview I conducted with Donna, she admitted that putting pressure on the prosecutor to have the seriousness of the charge increased was not easy. The importance of police reports and prosecutors' discretion is highlighted in this case. If Donna had not previously been married to her attacker there is no possibility the accused would have been charged with breach of the peace or that the case would have been marked to be heard in the district court. The levels of violence together with the fact that the attacker overcame the security of the house would have more likely resulted in a charge of attempted murder.

When Ron's trial finally came around in December 1995 he pled guilty. Sentence was deferred for six months for Ron to be of good behaviour whereupon he was admonished at Glasgow Sheriff Court[4].

Ron subsequently raised an action for contact with his daughter Flora. In the time period between the assault and the action being raised, Donna did not allow Ron or his parents contact with the children. She was of the view that Ron's parents had revealed her address to Ron prior to the assault. During the subsequent contact hearing Ron's father admitted to having revealed Donna's address to Ron.

The sheriff granted contact to Ron following a six-day proof ending in June 1998[5]. The sheriff principal overturned this decision on appeal. However, the

1 This is the lowest criminal court in Scotland where the sentencing powers of a lay justice were, at that time, restricted to 60 days imprisonment or a fine of £2,500. Alternatively, if a stipendiary magistrate was presiding in the court a sentence of 3 months imprisonment or a fine of £5,000 could be imposed.

2 Marking involves a prosecutor deciding which charges should be brought and which court should hear the case. These decisions will be based on the police report and affect the sentencing powers of the court should the accused be convicted.

3 Assault is a more serious charge than breach of the peace and the sheriff court is a higher court, therefore, the seriousness of the charge had been increased by this change. As it is not competent to add charges to a complaint it is assumed that in this case the original charge was not proceeded upon and a new charge of assault was brought against Ron.

4 An admonishment results in the person having a previous conviction for the offence. However, there is no punishment.

5 This case is unreported.

sheriff's judgment reveals a profound misunderstanding of issues of domestic violence and how this may affect children.

The sheriff found that it was in the best interests of Flora that she had contact with Ron and stated that this contact should be under the supervision of Ron's parents. In the judgment the sheriff is intensely critical of Donna, while Ron is described as 'a bit of an adventurer who would inevitably be an interesting father to a child. He has sailed boats abroad and is presently engaged in organising a transatlantic sponsored rowing expedition'. The sheriff did not accept that Ron was an alcoholic but said that he might have a drink problem due to the four drink/driving offences he had committed, only three of which Ron could recall. The sheriff accepted his proposition that there had only been two incidents of violence between the parties, including the November 1995 incident, and rejected the evidence of Donna and her daughter Alison that there had been a history of violence involving a large number of assaults. All research supports the accuracy of Donna's account of violent incidents becoming more regular and increasing in severity over time. The sheriff even refers to Ron being in a very emotional state between February and November 1995 and states that this was exacerbated by Donna's refusal to allow him access to the child Flora except on her terms. This is presented almost as an excuse for Ron's attack on Donna.

Further reference was made to the best interests of Flora being met by granting contact, particularly under the supervision of grandparents who were felt to have the child's best interests at heart. This is despite the fact that the grandfather had admitted in court to revealing Donna's address to Ron.

The judgment demonstrates the sheriff's ignorance of the effects of domestic abuse on children. It is of some concern that she chose to ignore evidence of a psychologist who was of the view that granting contact to Ron would have a negative effect on both of the children. Alison gave evidence during the court hearing. Even though the contact application did not relate to her she had witnessed Ron's violence on several occasions and feared for her sister Flora's safety should contact be granted. During her evidence Alison described her loathing of Ron. The sheriff dismissed her concerns out of hand, saying that 'her fears about the pursuer [Ron] were exaggerated' and that Donna's considerable antagonism towards Ron and his family had influenced Alison. Alison was not shielded when she gave evidence that included talking about the violence by Ron towards Donna which she had witnessed. During Alison's evidence Ron turned to face her, laughed and generally intimidated this 11-year-old child. At no point did the sheriff intervene and address his behaviour.

The description by the sheriff of the two parties in her judgment reveals a profound misunderstanding of domestic abuse. Describing Ron, she states: 'the evidence disclosed that when sober he was charming, personable and pleasant'. Of the defender, Donna, she states

> '(she) impressed me as an intelligent, articulate lady who undoubtedly and understandably feels very aggrieved at the pursuer's conduct towards her during their marriage. She has in my view a strong personality. There is no doubt she has suffered some violence and abuse at the hands of the pursuer and there is no doubt that she experienced an extremely distressing incident in November 1995. I was of the view however that she exaggerated the pursuer's conduct although there can in my view be no excuse for violence towards a spouse to any degree'.

This reluctance to accept Donna's account of events or take her fears seriously is further reinforced in the way the court hearing was conducted. Donna gave evidence for five hours. Most of this examination was not done by Ron's solicitor but instead directly by the sheriff whose questions included: 'If the violence was that bad why didn't you leave?' This question was asked even though Donna had left and was the victim of a very serious attack after leaving.

The extent to which this sheriff erred in both her decision and judgment is reflected in the fact that the sheriff principal overturned her decision following an appeal which only lasted a couple of hours. What is not clear is if this case is unique or an example of common practice. There is not adequate evidence available to enable an assessment as to how such cases are being dealt with in the main. Anecdotal evidence does suggest that profound misunderstandings of domestic abuse still informs decisions in the criminal justice system and the civil courts, in relation to criminalisation of conduct and decisions on contact and residence.

CONCLUSION

This chapter has outlined both the failings and the improvements in the criminal justice response to domestic abuse. Given the failings, an important question is whether the legal process is the best forum within which to tackle abuse. The criminalisation of domestic abuse should result in it being brought into the public forum and responded to as a problem within society rather than a private dispute between individuals.

Recent work has suggested that the criminal justice process is capable of responding to domestic abuse. However, the adoption of policies that both empower the victim and deal with the offender's behaviour is necessary. Hoyle and Sanders suggest that empowerment requires pro-arrest policies, conditions to be attached to bail to prevent further abuse, domestic violence officers available to liase with the victim during the period of arrest and bail, and that the domestic violence officer and the victim should assess the victim's needs and desires in relation to the abuse[1]. They suggest that rehabilitation programmes are also required but suggest that these could be available in the context of restorative justice and diversion from prosecution[2]. The difficulty with diversion programmes is that they may lessen the criminal sanction associated with such behaviour and in the case of domestic abuse may serve to undermine the seriousness of that abuse. Such an approach may be best suited where a prosecution is deemed problematic due to lack of evidence. But where a successful prosecution is possible, it would be preferable if rehabilitation programmes were used as a disposal following conviction.

Lewis et al, suggest that a criminal justice response that prioritises process as well as outcome is capable of responding to domestic abuse[3]. They suggest that the incorporation of surveillance and control (through arrest and prosecution)

---

1 C Hoyle and A Sanders, 'Police Response to Domestic Violence' (2000) 40 *Brit J Criminol*, pp 14–36, at p 31.

2 C Hoyle and A Sanders 'Police Response to Domestic Violence' (2000) 40 *Brit J Criminol*, pp 14–36, at p 33.

3 R Lewis, R E Dobash, R P Dobash and K Cavanagh 'Laws Progessive Potential: The Value of Engagement with the Law for Domestic Violence' (2001) 10 *Social & Legal Studies*, (1), pp 105–130.

and rehabilitation of both actions and beliefs has the best prospects of eliminating abuse. This, combined with wider efforts to change attitudes, is essential[1].

This chapter has indicated that appropriate responses to domestic violence are lacking in both the civil and criminal legal contexts. Research findings and knowledge of those working in this field should inform any changes. Where there are gaps in knowledge, and there are many, more research is required. The full effects of domestic abuse must be examined as a holistic picture and not discrete problems which are deemed to arise in isolation. The assistance women require to end abusive relationships, the appropriate legal response to abusive men and the decisions regarding contact and residence with children following separation must be informed by the facts of abusive relationships and not the myths.

Government responses in the United Kingdom whether they be from the Scottish Partnership on Domestic Violence or the Home Office should focus on male violence as the problem and not on women's responsibility to control or end this violence. The importance of correctly identifying where the problems lie and who is responsible is illustrated by the 1999 Home Office and Women's Unit initiative 'Living Without Fear'[2]. This document's stated aim is 'to combat violence against women'. It records that two women are killed by their current or former partner every week; that one in four women experience domestic violence at some stage in her life; that domestic violence starts and/or escalates during pregnancy and that women aged between 16 and 29 are at the greatest risk of experiencing domestic violence[3]. As Jones notes, these statistics are all about male violence yet men are not mentioned. She suggests that a re-wording which reads, 'Every week two men kill a current or former partner' would have more meaning and stop the perpetuated denial of men's responsibility for their own actions[4].

The rhetoric of policy documents like, 'Living Without Fear' is futile without real funding for frontline agencies and changes in attitude in law enforcement and service-providing personnel. The Scottish Executive has committed £18.3 million to domestic abuse. However, it is clear that refuge and other frontline service provision is still grossly under-funded. Scottish Women's Aid indicated that it needs a higher level of secure core funding if it is to meet the demand for refuge places[5]. In England and Wales, the government has undertaken an increase of £6.3 million in the grant to Victim Support and a pledge of £6 million to be made available to future projects within the Home Office Crime Reduction Strategy[6]. However, this does not compare with what is needed or what is already provided by way of 'free' labour by volunteers in Women's Aid and Rape Crisis[7]. The levels

---

1 R Lewis, R E Dobash, R P Dobash and K Cavanagh 'Law's Progessive Potential: The Value of Engagement with the Law for Domestic Violence' (2001) 10 *Social & Legal Studies* (1), pp 105–130, at p 124

2 *Living Without Fear* (1999) Women's Unit, Cabinet Office, London.

3 *Living Without Fear* (1999) Women's Unit, Cabinet Office, London p 7.

4 H Jones 'Kind Words and Compromises' 1999/2000 *Trouble & Strife* (Winter) pp 17–21.

5 In 1999 Scottish Women's Aid was forced to find alternative accommodation for 3,215 women and 4,318 children due to a lack of refuge places: *Guardian* Tuesday, 5 December 2000.

6 *Living Without Fear* (1999) Women's Unit, Cabinet Office, London.

7 H Jones 'Kind Words and Compromises' 1999/2000 *Trouble & Strife* (Winter) pp 17–21, at p 18. Jones notes that the overall budget of the Crime Reduction Strategy is £250 million and that at least £60 million, 10 times that committed to the Living Without Fear initiative, will be spent on burglary. She estimates that women volunteer 2,340,000 hours of unpaid work annually to Women's Aid and Rape Crisis. If this work was paid at £5 per hour the cost would be £11,700,000.

of government-funding in the United Kingdom compare poorly with those in the United States of America where the Violence Against Women Act 1999 secured $120 million for direct domestic abuse services and $75 million for rape and sexual assault services rising respectively to $260 million and $100 million in 2002.

The placing of domestic abuse and wider issues of violence against women on the political and therefore public agenda is clearly progress. The challenge to government and legal personnel is to ensure that mistakes of the past or those experienced in other jurisdictions are not duplicated in the implementation of policies intended to tackle domestic abuse.

9 Process Notes: Mediation in Family Disputes

Jane Scoular

INTRODUCTION

Alternative dispute resolution has been described by Simon Roberts as 'a fugitive label attached to a range of disparate and contradictory, but entangled, projects'[1]. The phrase not only encompasses a number of practices such as mediation, mini-trial and conciliation (which are typically outlined in textbooks and 'how-to' guides in the area) but rather extends beyond its application as an organising term for discrete identifiable techniques. Research reveals that one's perspective and disciplinary approach radically alter what meanings are evoked, suggesting that alternative dispute resolution is the site of multiple and contested meanings. For the pioneers and those who continue to work in the area it may be an activity and philosophy which is 'self-consciously directed toward facilitating the escape of disputants from lawyer domination'[2]. Yet for another group of practitioners it may appear as an extension of legal practice or as a supplement to court processes[3]. Further, by broadening the field of inquiry out from a myopic focus on courts into a wider study of disputes, the term can be seen to encompass 'key issues for socio-legal scholars: norms and ideology, power, rhetoric and oratory, personhood and agency, morality, meaning, and interpretation'[4]. As Silbey and Sarat note, 'Alternative dispute resolution is part of a continuing contest over the dominance of the courts in the apparatus of state law'[5].

This chapter attempts to engage with these mutiple meanings in an attempt first to sketch the arrival of mediation into recent legal and policy frames, and then to focus more particularly on the trajectory of mediation in family disputes. The claim that such practices are 'alternate' to law is questioned, as family

1 S Roberts 'Alternative Dispute Resolution and Civil Justice: An Unresolved Relationship' [(1993)] MLR Vol 56, 452 at p 452.

2 M Palmer and S Roberts *Dispute Processes: ADR and the Primary Forms of Decision Making* Butterworths, London, at p 2.

3 M Palmer and S Roberts *Dispute Processes: ADR and the Primary Forms of Decision Making* Butterworths, London p 2.

4 L Mulcahy 'The Devil and the Deep Blue Sea? A Critique of the Ability of Community Mediation to Suppress and Facilitate Participation in Civil Life' (2000) 27(1) *J Law & Soc.*, 27(1) 133, referring to P Caplan 'Anthropology and the Study of Disputes' in P Caplan (ed) *Understanding Disputes: The Politics of Argument* (1995) Berg, Oxford.

5 S Silbey and A Sarat 'Dispute Processing in Law and Legal Scholarship: From Institutional Critique to the Reconstruction of the Juridical Subject' [1989] *Denver Law Review* 437 at p 440.

mediation is revealed to be reliant upon legal institutions and dependent on legal norms and sanctions[1]. This is not to deny its distinctive features but to highlight the simultaneous interdependence and oscillation between mediation, legal discourse and lawyering. This, it will be argued, has produced a blurring which carries with it serious implications for the protection of legal rights and also for the ethical practice of mediation. This assimilation must be resisted, it is argued, and can be achieved by a 'reigning in' of both disciplines. In pursuance of this, the chapter concludes by advocating the need for sustained ethical reflection to re-capture and re-affirm the ethical difference of mediation. Such a project requires a recognition of the 'discursive construction of ethics'[2] rather than the application of static concepts to a process in which ethical norms are negotiated and created. In light of this, the chapter ends by re-figuring the standard ethical norms of autonomy and neutrality in a way that recognises their dynamic quality and is sensitive to the critiques of informal justice and the cultural specificity of many of its norms[3].

ALTERNATIVE DISPUTE RESOLUTION?

The historical mapping of alternative dispute resolution is a complex project and is increasingly so, the wider one's lens is set. It is impossible to properly understand the area fully without first acknowledging the contingency of our current understandings of dispute resolution. Anthropological, historical and social-science research reveals the commonplace fixation with courts as places where law is made and disputes settled, to be myopic and empirically flawed.

Historically, in the common-law world at least, mediation, in contrast to adjudication, can be seen to have a much longer tradition. Indeed it is a practice which continues as a primary means of dispute resolution in non-western cultures[4]. As Palmer and Roberts note, 'If the time-scale is expanded sufficiently then even in the common law world we may see that state-sponsored adjudication is the real novelty'[5]. It is only in relatively recent times that a strong-centralised nation state emerged in the west, and in support of this form of government there emerged legal codes, norms which were administered by a system of courts and 'serviced' by the emergence of lawyers as 'a specialised service profession'[6,7].

---

1 M Galanter 'Compared to What? Assessing the Quality of Dispute Resolution' 1989 *Denver University Law Review* Vol 66, xiii.

2 L Cooks and C Hale 'The Construction of Ethics in Mediation' (1994) 12(1) *Mediation Quarterly*, 55, 57. This will be elaborated on in the final section of this chapter.

3 S N Shah-Kazemi 'Cross-Cultural Mediation: A Critical View of the Dynamics of Culture in Family Disputes' (2000) *Int Journal of Law, Policy and the Family* 302.

4 S N Shah-Kazemi 'Cross Cultural Mediation: A Critical View of the Dynamics of Culture in Family Disputes' (2000) *Int Journal of Law, Policy and the Family* 302.

5 M Palmer and S Roberts *Dispute Processes: ADR and the Primary Forms of Decision Making* Butterworths, London p 48.

6 S Roberts 'Family Mediation in the New Millennium' in S Cretney (ed) *Family Law: Essays for the New Millennium* (2000) Family Law: Jordan Publishing, p 33.

7 Roman law has a much longer tradition of adjudication but alternative forms would have continued alongside. J Thomas *Textbook of Roman Law* (1976) North Holland Publishing, Amsterdam, New York, Oxford.

Alternative to what?

And yet even this is to present a simplified and polarised picture of disputing. What is alternative about these apparent 'new' methods is seen to be their distinction from formal court-based procedures of litigation and adjudication. However, this by no means describes the way in which 'justice' is administered in the west. The centrality of 'authoritative third-party determination' can be seen from many portrayals of law, the structure of legal education and theories of adjudication, which still dominate jursiprudential inquiry[1]. Yet, the sheer practical impossibility of 'adjudication for all' means that lawyer-negotiations in pursuance of settlement is the oil that keeps the engine running. As Palmer and Roberts succinctly illustrate:

> 'This is a culture in which government-sponsored adjudication is found in combination with a dominant legal profession which claims monopoly control over dispute management, using litigation in a distinctive way as the vehicle for pursuing strategies of late settlement'[2].

'Alternative' when used in this context may be seen to give a misleading, one-dimensional impression of disputing when in fact what emerges is more of a continuum of processes – from adjudication at one extreme to bilateral negotiation and avoidance at the other[3].

There are further problems with this terminology. Alternative dispute resolution instantly gives the impression of a discrete range of practices, neatly occupying a space outside the present legal order. Yet, such a separation is difficult to sustain both conceptually and empirically. Whatever the aspirations of those who practise and promote alternative dispute resolution, they are, as Galanter argues, 'not located in autonomous institutions that operate independently of the norms and the sanction of the legal system. Instead alternative dispute resolution is typically situated near legal institutions and dependent on legal norms and sanctions'[4]. The difficulty on an empirical level is that in the present context, legal institutions, practitioners and scholars have been embroiled in various ways in the recent ascent of alternative methods in the west.

This interdependence can be seen if we consider the three distinct 'movements' that have shaped the current configuration of alternative dispute resolution as it is currently practised and debated in policy fields and in academic literature[5]:

Access to Justice

The access to justice movement emerged in the 1960s and 1970s with the aim of 'relieving legal poverty', defined by Cappalletti and Garth as 'the incapacity of

---

1 S Roberts 'Family Mediation in the New Millennium' in S Cretney (ed) *Family Law: Essays for the New Millennium* (2000) Family Law: Jordan Publishing, p 33.

2 M Palmer and S Roberts *Dispute Processes: ADR and the Primary Forms of Decision Making* Butterworths, London p 1.

3 F Sander 'Alternative Dispute Resolution in the United States: An Overview in Justice for a Generation' Papers for the 1985 London Meeting of the American Bar Association, (1985) West Publishing Co St Paul, Minn.

4 M Galanter 'Compared to What? Assessing the Quality of Dispute Resolution' 1989 66 *Denver ULR* xiii.

5 M Palmer and S Roberts *Dispute Processes: ADR and the Primary Forms of Decision Making* Butterworths, London pp 2–3 and later developed in ch 2. This account is indebted to the structured and nuanced historical accounts offered in this text and in Simon Roberts' further writings.

many people to make full use of the law and its institutions'[1]. In raising awareness of the social and economic barriers which hindered many citizens' access to legal institutions and the prohibitive costs and delays associated with adjudication, concerns which remain prevalent today, informality was often cast as an attractive alternative, alongside reform of the legal system itself[2].

Alternative dispute resolution

Such concerns provided fertile ground for an emergent alternative dispute resolution movement which formed in the 1970s in the United States and soon after in the United Kingdom[3]. In contrast to the access to justice movement, the focus was not on improving the efficiency of the formal structures but rather in looking to alternative ways of conceptualising and processing disputes. Legal scholarship in this area was greatly influenced by anthropological and ethnographic studies[4] which offered a more expansive view of conflict in contrast to the prevailing focus of disputes which narrowed them into formal legal confines[5]. As Palmer and Roberts note, 'a growing comparative awareness prompted expansive reflection on 'complementary' and 'alternative' arrangements at home' and this gave rise to 'a range of disparate experimental procedures sharing the common label of 'alternative dispute resolution' ... which moved into space previously occupied by lawyer negotiations and adjudication'[6]. The proliferation of techniques was accompanied by an increasing disciplinary specialism and this subsequently prompted the emergence of an independent profession, 'offering institutionalised support for party negotiations away from the surveillance and control of the legal profession'[7]. This idea of a new profession entirely separate from legal professionals is perhaps misleading as the activities of lawyers and indeed courts did not remain unaffected by such changes. Indeed the third factor, which has influenced the present juncture of dispute resolution, is, rather paradoxically, the fact that the expansion in alternative methods has been accompanied by their increasing institutionalisation.

1 M Cappalletti and B G Garth *Access to Justice , Volume 1* (1978) Sijthoff and Noorrdhoff, Milan p 26.

2 M Palmer and S Roberts *Dispute Processes: ADR and the Primary Forms of Decision Making* Butterworths, London p 26.

3 To describe this as a social movement is to recognise, as with all social movements, that it represents the crystallisation of a number of factors and interests of its constituent parts.

4 K Llewellyn and E A Hoebel *The Cheyenne Way: Conflicts and Case Law: Conflicts and Case law in Primitive Jurisprdence* (1941) University of Oklahoma Press, Oklahoma; M Gluckman *The Judicial Process Among the Barotse Of Northern Rhodesia* (1955) Manchester University Press; P Gulliver *Social Control in An African Society, A Study of the Arusha, Agricultural Masai of Northern Tanganyika* (1963) Boston University Press; *Neighbours and Networks: The Idiom of Kinship in Social Action Among the Nadendeuli of Tanzania* (1971) University of California Press; *Disputes and Negotiations: A Cross-Cultural Perspective* Academic Press, London, New York.

5 This led to strain on legal methodology and many scholars began to harness relevant social science techniques; M Palmer and S Roberts *Dispute Processes: ADR and the Primary Forms of Decision Making* Butterworths, London at p 2, refer to Richard Abel's work as being groundbreaking in this respect: R Abel (ed) *The Politics of Informal Justice Vol 1: The American Experience* (1982) Academic Press, New York.

6 M Palmer and S Roberts *Dispute Processes: ADR and the Primary Forms of Decision Making* Butterworths, London p 45.

7 M Palmer and S Roberts *Dispute Processes: ADR and the Primary Forms of Decision Making* Butterworths, London p 60.

Institutionalisation

It is possible to consider that the increasing reflection on disputing engendered by the access to justice and alternative dispute resolution movements initiated a sort of 'self-evaluation' in the legal profession and its institutions. The less naïve, however, may offer a contrasting view that lawyers were responding to increased competition by introducing new dispute management techniques in order to be able to offer, or certainly market, an increased range of services. Such expansions saw 'attempts to co-opt mediation, presenting it as part of legal practice'[1]. In addition civil justice reform at this time focused primarily on the 'principle' of efficiency and saw an increasing role for courts in assisting and encouraging settlement as a means to control costs and better manage disputes. Roberts describes the creation of new 'procedures on the threshold of the courts which the parties are required to traverse before they can get to adjudication'[2]. This heralded increased judicial activity at the pre-trial stage, where the 'court may orchestrate further attempts at bilateral negotiation, refer the parties to outside mediation, or direct attempts at mediation by court personnel'[3]. The effect of such reforms then is that methods previously considered to be 'alternative' now 'appear as part of the judicial repertoire of dispute management'[4].

These attempts to find more efficient methods to manage civil justice are not in any sense novel – as Palmer and Roberts argue, it has been widely recognised that in most, if not all, societies which have developed states and courts, 'there is a perpetual oscillation between adjudicatory-based mechanisms and values and on the other hand pressures to settle disputes in a less formal or 'alternative' manner'[5]. This 'recurrent dialectic between legality and its alternatives'[6] is brilliantly outlined by Nader. She argues that this history is even more complex than a simple oscillation between these two polar opposites: 'even within a particular political and economic context there are pressures at work that mean the cycle comes to rest at a place that is necessarily different from its starting point'[7]. Applying this to the context of family disputes, the oscillation between the formal and informal can be seen to be constant with various 'events' producing a shifting of emphasis in one direction and another. In the section which follows I will outline the effects of the oscillation between family mediation, legal discourse and lawyers and the way in which certain events have impacted on the area to produce a position in which there is a significant blurring of the roles of professions in the area of family disputes.

1 M Palmer and S Roberts *Dispute Processes: ADR and the Primary Forms of Decision Making* Butterworths, London p 3. It would be fair to say that both factors are present then and now.

2 S Roberts 'Alternative Dispute Resolution and Civil Justice: An Unresolved Relationship' (1993) 56 MLR 452 at p 458.

3 M Palmer and S Roberts *Dispute Processes: ADR and the Primary Forms of Decision Making* Butterworths, London p 48.

4 S Roberts 'Alternative Dispute Resolution and Civil Justice: An Unresolved Relationship' (1993) 56 MLR 452 at p 458. He argues further that the involvement of judges in case management and in negotiations themselves is 'radically transforming our understandings of what a court is': S Roberts 'Alternative Dispute Resolution and Civil Justice: An Unresolved Relationship' (1993) 56 MLR 452 at p 461.

5 M Palmer and S Roberts *Dispute Processes: ADR and the Primary Forms of Decision Making* Butterworths, London at p 49.

6 L Nader 'The Recurrent Dialectic Between Legality and its Alternatives: The Limits of Binary Thinking' (1986) *University of Pennsylvania Law Review*, Vol 136, p 62.

7 M Palmer and S Roberts *Dispute Processes: ADR and the Primary Forms of Decision Making* Butterworths, London p 50.

THE TRAJECTORY OF MEDIATION IN FAMILY DISPUTES[1]

Family mediation – an emerging profession

The development of family mediation in the United Kingdom has been chronicled in more depth elsewhere[2] and what follows is a rather plotted history for the purposes of later discussion.

The growth of family mediation, both north and south of the border, displays a common pattern, beginning with the initial creation of mediation services in the not-for-profit sector[3]. This is then followed by expansion and the many resultant services being brought under umbrella organisations of Family Mediation Scotland[4] and the National Association of Family Mediation[5] respectively, who co-ordinate activities in relation to entry, training, professional standards and accreditation. Further centralisation of these activities has recently taken place with the creation in 1997 of the United Kingdom College of Family Mediators, an over-arching body to which all main family mediation providers subscribe[6].

An attempt to describe the activity of family mediators is fraught with difficulty and initial definitions will be subject to more in-depth analysis later. The initial mediation services grew from a belief that they could offer a different form of dispute resolution to separating parents and their children, distinct from the legal model which assumed (and assumes) an unrivalled position in the area[7]. The initial mediators came from counselling and social work backgrounds, yet the discipline that emerges, as Walker notes, is distinctive from such practices[8]. What does emerges, in simplest terms, is a practice directed towards facilitating joint decision-making through party negotiations. Fuller describes 'the central quality of mediation [as] its capacity to reorientate the parties toward each other, not by imposing rules on them, but by helping them to achieve a new and shared perception of their relationship'[9]. It contrasts to adjudication in that mediators facilitate rather than impose a decision. In contrast to the partisan who offers advice and represents one party's interests,

> 'The skill of the mediator lies in facilitating the crucial exchanges of accurate and constructive information that lead through adjustments of expectations and preferences to greater understanding, coordination, and order, and eventually to the settlement of the dispute. This kind of expertise, involving as it does no authority to impose an out-

1 This term is taken from S Roberts 'Family Mediation in the New Millennium' in S Cretney (ed) *Family Law: Essays for the New Millennium* (2000) Family Law: Jordan Publishing, p 38.
2 T Fisher (ed) *Family Conciliation in the UK: Policy and Practice* (1990) Family Law, Bristol.
3 Fisher identifies the first services as those established in Bristol and SE London in late 1970s. The first service in Scotland was established in Lothian in 1984. Services in Grampian, Central, Tayside and Strathclyde were established three years later and twelve regional services now operate in Scotland, under the umbrella organisation Family Mediation Scotland.
4 FMS operates twelve independent regional family mediation services and their mediators are drawn from a range of relevant professional backgrounds.
5 *Roberts* (2000) p 36.
6 *Roberts* (2000) p 36.
7 This can be seen by the primary categorisation of divorce as a 'legal' event.
8 *Walker* (1996), p 59, referring to her earlier work with colleagues: Walker, McCarthy and Timms *Mediation: the Making and Remaking of Co-operative Relationships* (1994) University of Newcastle Upon Tyne, Relate Centre for Family Studies.
9 L Fuller 'Mediation: It's Forms and Functions' (1971) 44 *Southern California Law Review*, 305 at p 325.

> come or to give advice, determines the unique, even paradoxical, nature of the professional relationship of the mediator with the parties'[1].

By moving away from viewing disputes as 'discrete, bounded up and pathological episodes, generated by rule-breach'[2], it becomes possible to characterise disputes in a different way – as a failure in communication, a difference in values or a struggle for resources. Other distinctive features of this process are said to be that decision-making authority lies with the participants, participation is voluntary, and that the process is confidential, impartial as to outcomes and flexible to meet the varying needs of individual disputants'[3].

In offering a comprehensive definition or in categorising the activity of mediators in this field it is important to acknowledge that there are a number of different approaches to the role. As Walker notes, 'the ad hoc development of mediation resulted in differing ideologies, a multiplicity of practices, and a distinct tension between principles embodied in the law and the theoretical perspectives of social welfare'[4]. The principal divergence in opinion today is around 'facilitative' and 'evaluative' approaches to mediation:

> 'The facilitative mediator believes it is inappropriate for the mediator to give his opinion, for at least two reasons. First, such opinions might impair the appearance impartiality and thereby interfere with the mediator ability to function. Second, the mediator might not know enough – about the details of the case or the relevant law, practices or technology – to give an informed opinion'[5].

For the present purposes it is fair to say that a minimalist facilitative approach constitutes the underpinning approach of mediation offered by the family mediation services in the not-for-profit sector[6]. This is in contrast to the much more active evaluative mediator, typically found in the private sector and those who mediate alongside their primary professional positions:

> 'The evaluative mediator assumes that the participant wants and needs the mediator to provide some direction as to the appropriate grounds for settlement – based on law, industry practice or technology. She also assumes that the mediator is qualified to give such direction by virtue of her experience, training and objectivity'[7].

As Roberts notes, 'there is not yet a general consensus as to the scope and boundaries of what might be appropriate in support of party negotiations'[8].

The practice of mediation, and informal justice generally, is not without its critics. While many of the advocates of informal processes, such as mediation, view this development as deprofessionalising an important realm of social interaction and as providing greater opportunity for popular participation in handling disputes, there are also commentators who raise concern over the

---

1 M Roberts 'Systems or Selves: Some Ethical issues in Family Meditation' (1992) 10 Mediation Quarterly 3, 4 at p 7.

2 M Palmer and S Roberts *Dispute Processes: ADR and the Primary Forms of Decision Making* Butterworths, London at p 7.

3 *Walker* (1996) p 54.

4 *Walker* (1996) p 53.

5 L Riskin 'Mediator Orientations, Strategies and Techniques' (1994) 12(9) *Alternatives*, 111.

6 S Roberts 'Alternative Dispute Resolution and Civil Justice: An Unresolved Relationship' (1993) 56 MLR 452 at p 456.

7 L Riskin 'Mediator Orientations, Strategies and Techniques' (1994) 12(9) *Alternatives*, p 111.

8 S Roberts 'Alternative Dispute Resolution and Civil Justice: An Unresolved Relationship' (1993) 56 MLR 452 at p 456.

issues of power imbalance[1], the compromising of legal rights[2] and extension of social control[3]. These issues will be considered in more depth in the later sections of the chapter.

Lawyers, law and mediation

In the opening part of this chapter I warned that the use of the term 'alternative' gave a false impression of an activity which occupied a space outside legal discourse and the legal profession. This caution certainly applies in the family sphere where lawyers have been far from motionless in light of increasing competition and direct state sponsorship and promotion.

As family mediation started to expand it was joined by parallel activities in both the courts and in the legal profession. Roberts recounts that the first mediation services in England were accompanied by court sponsorship[4] and a number of local initiatives in which district court judges encouraged settlement through early stage appointments[5]. Building on these activities, family law was encompassed in the far-reaching reforms in the civil justice system, initiated by Lord Woolf[6] and the subsequent Civil Procedure Rules 1998[7] which as Roberts notes, 'leaves settlement and litigation deliberately entangled'[8]. More specifically, if one looks to the membership of the Family Law Associations of Scotland, and England and Wales, there was a noticeable rise in the number of lawyers specialising in family law and broadening their skill base to include child welfare[9]. Assisted by the Bar and the Law Society's sponsorship of alternative dispute in the 1990s, there were even a noticeable number of solicitors training as mediators[10], and their number now form established professional groupings: Solicitors in Mediation in England, and Comprehensive Accredited Lawyer Mediators in Scotland.

Institutionalisation

The Scots position reveals a much smaller degree of institutionalisation of mediation than that which has taken place, albeit temporarily, south of the border. Compulsory attendance at mediation as a prerequisite to legal aid was considered but rejected in Improving Scottish Family Law[11]. The recent White Paper

1 T Grillo 'The Mediation Alternative: Process Dangers for Women (1991) Yale LJ 100, 1545 and see p 220 below.
2 O Fiss 'Against Settlement' (1984) Yale LJ 93, 1073.
3 R Abel 'The Politics of Informal Justice, Volume 1: The American Experience, New York, Academic Press. See Introduction in particular.
4 S Roberts 'Family Mediation in the New Millennium' in S Cretney (ed) *Family Law: Essays for the New Millennium* (2000) Family Law: Jordan Publishing, p 35; G M Partimer 'Bristol In-Court Conciliation Procedure' (1981) *Law and Society Gazette*, Feb 25.
5 S Roberts 'Family Mediation in the New Millennium' in S Cretney (ed) *Family Law: Essays for the New Millennium* (2000) Family Law: Jordan Publishing, p 34.
6 Lord Woolf *Access to Justice: Final Report to the Lord Chancellor on the Civil Justice System of England and Wales* (1996) HMSO, London.
7 Civil Procedure Rules 1998, SI 1998/3132.
8 S Roberts 'Family Mediation in the New Millennium' in S Cretney (ed) *Family Law: Essays for the New Millennium* (2000) Family Law: Jordan Publishing, p 34.
9 The rise in the number of female lawyers is also a factor: M King, ''Being Sensible': Images and Practices of the New Family Lawyers' (1999) 28(2) *J of Social Policy* 249 p 250.
10 In 1996 the Solicitors Family Law Association membership had increased by 75%.
11 http://www.Scotland.gov.uk/library/documents-w8/158L-04-htm.

Parents and Children[1] resisted such a move once again and instead opted to increase direct funding of services. This means that mediation services have been able to co-exist with legal services without too much governmental pressure. Court referrals were introduced by the Sheriff Court Ordinary Cause Rules, r 33.22[2], which empowers sheriffs to refer parties to a mediation service.

In England and Wales the scene is much more involved. The political reluctance to support fully the abrogation of a fault-based divorce law saw compromises placed in the Family Law Act 1996, Pt II which offered no fault but only with compulsory information meetings and compulsory mediation for couples seeking legal aid[3]. Unusually this legislation was piloted before implementation and the results of the research into the pilots has recently been published. Information sessions were introduced by the Family Law Act 1996, s 8 and their stated aim was to help 'save saveable marriages' by encouraging parties to use counselling and to direct parties to mediation if salvage was not possible in an effort to reduce costs and divert couples from the adversarial system – and lawyer negotiations were included in this categorisation. Research carried out by the Centre for Family Studies under the leadership of Janet Walker reported only limited referral to such agencies and rather paradoxically many parties left even more determined to commence divorce proceedings[4]. Interviews revealed that separating couples did not appreciate the information on marriage-saving, which many had attempted before filing for divorce, and would prefer processes to be more tailored to their rather than politicians' needs.

Research was also commissioned by the Legal Services Commission from a team led by Gwynn Davis, to evaluate the implementation of the mediation component of the Family Law Act 1996 and this work was able to assess the impact of the implementation of the notorious s 29 which compelled legal aid recipients to attend an initial mediation meeting[5]. The research considered the cost-effectiveness of mediation in contrast to lawyers' services and assessed clients' views of each process[6]. The findings revealed no reduction in cost after a rather complex application of multi-variate analysis[7]. In evaluating the relative benefits of each process, the research admirably moved away from a wholly legal-centric measurement of success which would involve looking at settlement rates as the sole outcome. Rather the research also included questions which asked participants in what ways the processes made things better. The response revealed a high level of satisfaction from consumers of both services, although lawyers attracted more support across hard and soft measures[8].

This method, while much more responsive to indicators which mediators value, remains somewhat limited in that asking a single party their view of how

1 http://www.Scotland.gov.uk/justice/family law/pac-00-asp.

2 OCR r 33.22.

3 For a discussion of how the Law Commission's proposals for no-fault divorce and the subsequent Family Law Bill became mangled, see V MacCallum 'Fault lines rock Act' (2001) *Law Society Gazette*, 1 Feb, 26 at p 27.

4 http://www.open.gov.uk/lcd/family/fla/flapt2.htm dated 16 January 2001.

5 The mandatory requirement to attend a mediation meeting not only conflicted with the voluntary nature of the process but also with individuals' rights to legal services.

6 A full account of the research objectives and findings can be found at the news section of the LSC website: http://www.legalservices.gov.uk. G Davis, S Finch and R Fitzgerald 'Mediation and Legal Services – The Client Speaks' [2001] *Fam Law* February, 111.

7 G Bevan, G Davis and P Fenn 'Can Mediation Reduce Expenditure on Lawyers?' [2001] *Fam Law* March, 186.

8 I have some reservations as to these results which I will discuss more fully below.

well *their* partisan understood *their* position and comparing this with a party's view of a mediator whose understanding and effectiveness is not wholly directed at that singular party but between parties, is not comparing like with like and is likely to lead to a less favourable individual result for mediators[1]. Yet one cannot overlook the positive benefit partisans are seen to bring to individuals. Partisanship remains important for parties who 'feel they lack the resources, the knowledge or the authority to achieve what they believe to be a fair outcome'[2].

The result of the evaluations of these pilots does not as the government had hoped show mediation to be a cheaper alternative, nor does it seem to be a service which can replace partisanship. Yet as I will discuss in detail below, this is not the way in which mediation should be presented. It is not an alternative to legal advice but rather provides a different way to resolve disputes. This research shows that mediation is not an antidote to the problems of funding which are not easily remedied or the difficulties of 'managing' divorce. Many have been critical of the government's casting of mediation as a panacea for 'alleged ills of the adversarial process'[3] and this should include mediators themselves, who must be concerned that politics have been played with their profession. What is clear from the researchers' conclusions is that mediation needs to be free to establish itself on its own and that this does not require maligning lawyers' work.

Before considering the ways in which mediation should develop, it is also necessary to consider the blurring of roles which has taken place as mediation, and legal negotiation interact and compete for their position in the shadow of the law.

Dangerous liaisons: the problems of assimilation

The 'entanglement' of litigation and settlement created by judges being drawn into a managerial role[4] has not been without its critics, paralleling critiques of mediators' involvement in what are considered to be legal spheres[5]. The principal concern is that judicial involvement in settlement threatens to compromise the integrity of adjudication. Roberts talks of meanings being blurred:

> 'The beauty of adjudication, if we can call it that, is that we know unambiguously what we are experiencing – the imposed decision of an authoritative superior. That clarity is lost once courts begin to involve themselves in the sponsorship of settlement'[6].

The presence of mediation in courts, staffed by court personnel, and even court referrals, alters the meaning of mediation. It becomes an adjunct to adjudication, 'less an affair of joint-decision making and more a means of lubricating third-party decision … In "in-court" mediation control is taken back by third parties despite any illusion that it is handed over to the parties themselves'[7].

---

1 This limitation is understandable, as evaluating mediation and lawyer negotiations is not a simple task and much more work needs to be done on methodology in this field.

2 G Davis, S Finch and R Fitzgerald 'Mediation and Legal Services – The Client Speaks' [2001] *Fam Law* February, 114.

3 S Day Sclater 'The Limits of Mediation' [1995] *Fam Law* 494.

4 S Roberts 'Alternative Dispute Resolution and Civil Justice: An Unresolved Relationship' (1993) 56 MLR 452 at p 461; see M Zander 'The Government's plans on civil justice' (1998) *MLR*, 61(3), 382; 'The Woolf Report: forwards or backwards for the new Lord Chancellor?' (1997) *CJQ*, 16, 208.

5 O Fiss 'Against Settlement' (1984) *Yale LJ*, Vol 93, 1073.

6 S Roberts 'Alternative Dispute Resolution and Civil Justice: An Unresolved Relationship' (1993) 56 MLR 452 at p 462.

7 S Roberts 'Alternative Dispute Resolution and Civil Justice: An Unresolved Relationship' (1993) 56 MLR 452 at p 556.

Concern has also been raised over lawyers' involvement in this area as mediation is developed as an auxiliary practice in many firms[1]. Roberts first questions the compatibility of such distinct roles[2]. He sees a 'considerable gulf between the conduct of partisan advisory and representative roles and the delicate, complex task of orchestrating negotiations'[3]. This also raises ethical problems in that parties' identification of mediators with their established legal roles necessarily changes the dynamics, and perhaps even the accuracy of the term 'mediation'.

This criticism is not levelled at lawyers alone as members of many other professional groups have taken up mediation. This increasing range of interventions which operate under the generic label of 'mediation' results in a lack of clarity. As Roberts notes,

> 'As long as established professional groups are successful in holding themselves out as providing mediation – accountants, family therapists, lawyers and social workers are already seeking to do so – the core component in the promised intervention is likely to remain submerged'[4].

There have also been more subtle changes, picked up by empirical research, which reflect the way in which practitioners have in general responded to this 'conciliatory-charged' atmosphere.

The work of Michael King is important in outlining this change[5]. His findings are generally supported by other research[6] including a recent study by Myers and Wasoff in Scotland[7].

'Responsive and defensive' lawyering[8]

King's research focuses on the way in which 'a new spirit of family law', confirmed[9] by the Children Act 1989, has been translated into practice. The Act

1 S Roberts 'Alternative Dispute Resolution and Civil Justice: An Unresolved Relationship' (1993) 56 MLR 452 at p 463.

2 S Roberts 'Alternative Dispute Resolution and Civil Justice: An Unresolved Relationship' (1993) 56 MLR 452 at p 457.

3 S Roberts 'Alternative Dispute Resolution and Civil Justice: An Unresolved Relationship' (1993) 56 MLR 452 at p 466. Roberts notes: 'It remains unclear whether it is feasible to shift back and forward between these two roles, even if it is understood that no intervener may exercise more than one role in a particular dispute.'

4 S Roberts 'Alternative Dispute Resolution and Civil Justice: An Unresolved Relationship' (1993) 56 MLR 452 at p 457.

5 M King 'Being Sensible': Images and Practices of the New Family Lawyers (1999) 28(2) *J of Social Policy* p 249.

6 B Neale and C Smart '"Good" and "Bad" Lawyers? Struggling in the Shadow of the Law' (1997) 19 *JSWFL* 377.

7 This is research which has previously been criticised by the present author: see J Scoular and C Irvine 'Meeting in the Middle: A Review of Myers and Wasoff's study of solicitors' and mediators' divorce practice' Scottish Executive Central Research Unit, 2001 SLT (News) 125. Myers and Wasoff replied in F Myers and F Wasoff 'Meeting in the middle: a reply to Scoular and Irvine' 2001 SLT (News) 128. The primary concern expressed was that due to the research method employed, the defining characteristics of mediation are lost. Nevertheless, the research offers a great deal of information and analysis which greatly contributes to the field, an appreciation of which should have been reflected in the earlier review. Importantly this research offers very important data on the way in which mediators and family lawyers view their roles and the image of the 'conciliatory lawyer' lends weight to King's assertion that roles are being blurred.

8 S Roberts 'Family Mediation in the New Millennium' in S Cretney (ed) *Family Law: Essays for the New Millennium* (2000) Family Law: Jordan Publishing, p 35.

9 I say 'confirmed' rather than 'introduced' as the legal reforms do not exist in a vacuum and were responding to changes in society and the professional practice which it in turn influences.

abolishes custody in favour of responsibility shared by parents and states that the courts are only obliged to make an order where it considers that it would be better for the child that the order be made than that none should be made at all. This important provision is mirrored in the Children (Scotland) Act 1995[1].

Wide statutory discretion makes it problematic for lawyers to predict with any real certainty the possible outcomes of a case in order to advise clients appropriately. This is even more so in context of the Children Acts, when all lawyers can predict with certainty is that 'the court will not wish to make many decisions unless absolutely necessary'[2]. As King notes, 'this judicial reluctance (encouraged by the Children Act), tends to emphasise the value of lawyers in setting boundaries negotiations of solutions, "smoothing over" or "cooling down" the conflict between parents'.

This has created a change in the lawyering role, as King explains:

> 'Given that the law itself provides only the most general guidelines on how separating and divorcing parents should conduct themselves, the divorce lawyer, responding to their clients' grievances and demands about their children, must draw from extra legal sources these principles of behaviour for the guidance of separating and divorcing parents'[3].

This, King notes, leads to the creation of a makeshift normative framework which extends beyond legal principles and includes 'a distillation of the knowledge established by child welfare experts and their research studies'[4]. This framework contains the recognised maxims: children come first, contact with both parents is beneficial to children, conflict is bad for them, and parties should co-operate to sort out their problems and should co-operate. This assists lawyers who, rather than dismiss their clients' interests, 'reformulate them in terms of their legal interests,' that is 'to be co-operative, reasonable and sharing in the eyes of the law'[5]. King concludes that 'parents who keep within the boundaries of this normative framework are seen by solicitors as acting with "commonsense" and "being reasonable" and "sensible"'[6] and in this way solicitors are able to regain their role in advising on, albeit reconstructed, legal norms.

Irreconcilable differences

King's earlier work with Christine Piper identifies a tension between the need to prioritise the welfare of children as legislation now prescribes, and the on-going commitment to clients' interests, which are both demanded of the partisan family lawyer[7]. This creates a tension, according to King, arising from the contrasting

---

1 *Porchetta v Porchetta* 1986 SLT 105, followed by *Sanderson v McManus* 1997 SC (HL55) but see *White v White* 2001 SLT 485.
2 M King 'Being Sensible': Images and Practices of the New Family Lawyers (1999) 28(2) *J of Social Policy* 249 at p 254.
3 M King 'Being Sensible': Images and Practices of the New Family Lawyers (1999) 28(2) *J of Social Policy* 249 at p 255.
4 M King 'Being Sensible': Images and Practices of the New Family Lawyers (1999) 28(2) *J of Social Policy* 249 at p 255.
5 B Neale and C Smart '"Good" and "Bad" Lawyers? Struggling in the Shadow of the Law' (1997) 19 *JSWFL* p 390.
6 M King 'Being Sensible': Images and Practices of the New Family Lawyers (1999) 28(2) *J of Social Policy* 249 at p 255.
7 M King and C Piper *How the Law Thinks About Children* (2nd edn, 1995) Arena, Aldershot.

ideologies of welfare (which requires maximising the good of others) and justice (defined as the good of the individual)[1].

That the law would assign such contrasting values cannot be viewed as an aberration: far from it. It is the only way in which positivist law is able to accommodate the plurality of norms that exists in society. Dewar calls this the 'Normal Chaos of Family Law', meaning not that family law does not have a normative content, but rather that this consists of 'a plurality of legal norms stemming from two different, and perhaps inconsistent, ways of characterising legal obligations between family members'[2]. Yet how successful this incorporation can be is called into question by King, using autopoietic theory[3] which describes law and welfare as closed, self-referring systems of communication. Any effective merging is precluded as the discursive boundaries of each system are impermeable. While recognising that external information (ie welfare considerations) may influence the content of law, this information is inevitably colonised by law and reproduced in its own code of lawful/unlawful[4].

The effects of blurring

King reports that a modification of the partisan role was felt by clients who wished solicitors to advance and secure their interests but found 'solicitors are often unwilling to meet fully their ... expectations'[5]. Lawyers were not relinquishing their partisan approach completely; it was particularly stressed as necessary when dealing with a partner who was 'unreasonable'. Nor were they 'abandoning all attempts at to achieve justice for their client in favour of child welfare objectives'[6]. Rather justice was reconstructed, according to King. 'Justice' was modified to accommodate norms of child welfare and 'injustice' moved away from representing unfairness to one or other of the parents, but related instead to the deleterious effects on children of unreasonable, selfish or foolish parental behaviour[7]. Gwynn Davis agrees that certain stereotyping of both problem and solution emerges in this context as lawyers have little time or skills to get to grips with the parent–child relationship as they press towards their goal of settlement. He does say, however, that although 'partisanship may be muted, it remains an essential feature'[8].

This adaptation of role can be seen as an attempt to respond not only to the increasing demands of modern legalism[9] but also to counter the elevation of

1 M King 'Being Sensible': Images and Practices of the New Family Lawyers (1999) 28(2) *J of Social Policy* 249 at p 252 referring to B Neale and C Smart '"Good" and "Bad" Lawyers? Struggling in the Shadow of the Law' (1997) 19 *JSWFL* p 380.

2 J Dewar 'The Normal Chaos of Family Life' (1998) *MLR*, 467 at p 469.

3 G Teubner 'How the law thinks: Towards a constructivist epistemology of law' (1989) 23(9) *Law and Soc Rev*, 727.

4 This approach is not without its critics. Adrian James argues that effective decision-making in the legal field necessitates the integration of these perspectives: A James 'An open or shut case. Law as an autopoietic system', 19(2) J Law & Soc, 271.

5 M King 'Being Sensible': Images and Practices of the New Family Lawyers (1999) 28(2) *J of Social Policy* 249 at p 263.

6 M King 'Being Sensible': Images and Practices of the New Family Lawyers (1999) 28(2) *J of Social Policy* 249 at p 267.

7 M King 'Being Sensible': Images and Practices of the New Family Lawyers (1999) 28(2) *J of Social Policy* 249 at p 267.

8 G Davis 'Love in a Cold Climate' in S Cretney, (ed) *Children Law at the Millenium* (2000) Family Law, Jordan Publishing.

9 An area of law that extensively incorporates materials or information from other disciplines: M Galanter, 'Law Abounding: Legalisation around the North Atlantic' (1992) 55 *MLR*, 1.

mediation in family law, which has seen solicitors altering their practices to respond to this increasing competition. This is an understandable response from a professional group, as King comments:

> 'Altering their colours in response to changes in the particular environment in which they find themselves operating ... may well be [a] ... survival and self-preservation strategy which professionals adopt to promote themselves and defend themselves against external threats'[1].

However, as Eekelaar notes, 'the central justification for lawyers' involvement in family disputes, namely the protection of individual interests within a framework of rights, may be compromised and undermined'[2] in this process. It is important to recognise that it is not just law that is compromised in this exchange but also the distinctive features of mediation. As Roberts observes,

> 'If the beauty of mediation is seen to be that it leaves responsibility for decision-making in the hands of the parties themselves, this feature is inevitably diluted or lost altogether as the process is moved in ideological terms, in terms of the intrusion of specialist personnel, even in terms of space, 'nearer to the law'. The strength of the mediator lies in his identification with the values of joint-decision making, agreement and compromise, and in his neutral posture at a point adjacent to the parties themselves. To link family mediation to the world of law will arguably sap the vitality of both'[3].

Mediation as adjunct

If we consider the space mediation occupies and the meanings assigned to it in this context, it becomes clear that it is not only law and legal values that are compromised by this increasing assimilation. If we recognise that lawyers' primary goal is settlement then it becomes clear that mediation in this context risks becoming an adjunct of this. In King's research, solicitors are shown to act as gate-keepers to mediation and describe their reasons for referring to parties 'as a stage in a strategic operation' the object of which is settlement. Framed in this way the dispute remains under the management of a solicitor who views success on its ability to resolve 'the dispute' in ways that were acceptable to their client'[4]. In this context support for mediation was not seen in terms of its broad objectives of facilitating communications between people and fostering co-operation. In fact, Walker's research even reveals that there is a view, shared by a large section of the legal profession, that considers, '... if only all lawyers would adopt a conciliatory approach when dealing with matrimonial issues, mediators as a distinct professional group would be unnecessary'[5].

I don't intend to lay blame at the door of lawyers who have often been parodied in an effort to distinguish mediation from negotiation and partisanship.

1 *King* p 253 refers to T Parsons 'Professions' in the *International Encyclopaedia of Social Science* (1968) New York, pp 536-46, T L Johnson *Professions and Power* (1972) Macmillan, London; M Douglas *Risk and Blame: Essays in Cultural Theory* (1994) Routledge, London.

2 G Davis 'Love in a Cold Climate' in S Cretney (ed) *Children Law at the Millenium* (2000) Family Law, Jordan Publishing p 137, referring to J Eekelaar 'Family Law: Keeping us "on message"' (1999) *Child and Family Law Quarterly*, vol II, no 4, 387.

3 S Roberts 'Mediation in Family Disputes' (1983) 46 *MLR* 537, p 555.

4 M King 'Being Sensible': Images and Practices of the New Family Lawyers (1999) 28(2) *J of Social Policy* 249 at p 259.

5 *Walker* (1996), p 67, referring to the earlier study: P McCarthy and J Walker 'Mediation and Divorce Law Reform – The lawyers' view' (1995) *Family Law*, July, vol 25, pp 361–364.

Rather I aim to illustrate that the oscillation between the two disciplines has inevitably resulted in a blurring of the edges which need to be defined.

The effect of this blurring makes it clear that we need a better clarification of the interface between mediation and law. What we have at present is in danger of appearing as a convenient compromise which risks sapping the vitality of both discourses[1]. This resembles, rather ironically, a compromise created by a zero-sum negotiation. This is the phrase used to describe the meeting-in-middle or compromise arrived at as a result of lawyer or 'shadow of the law' negotiations, which meets halfway rather than attempts to break out of a positional mode to effect a creative, mutually beneficial solution. The problem of zero-sum negotiation in the context of the present overlapping of mediation and legal practice is articulated by Menkel-Meadow[2]:

> 'For me the conceptual "compromise" is as dangerous as the compromise in negotiation, by blunting what the parties really require and by meeting in the middle that may not accurately reflect the appropriate or actual choices which are both available and best for a wide range of parties and lawyers'[3].

It is necessary then to sharpen these blurred edges in order to state clearly the basis for complementary services in this area of dispute resolution. Fiscal restrictions in addition to the concerns raised above will necessitate a dovetailing of services[4]. For mediation not to be absorbed into the legal system it is necessary that it be sufficiently differentiated from settlement and lawyer negotiations in a meaningful and respectful way.

Mediation has been described as a practice in search of a theory[5] and too much discussion of what is distinctive about this process is based on 'out-of-hand dismissal of the legal process'[6]. Indeed mediation's failure to command an agreed theoretical framework, as Walker observes, has meant that mediators have not been provided with explanatory models that inform their practice and enable them 'to take account of research findings which require practice to be revised and modified'[7]. Rifkin also notes that mediators have 'no theoretical paradigm within which to make shifts' and that many of the recommendations of researchers are ignored or met with cynicism[8].

To capture the distinctiveness of mediation we need to go beyond what is currently found in codes of ethics which have proliferated due to the emerging regulatory framework in the area. Fixing certain core values in codes at this relatively early stage, without reflection, may prove folly. Morris sees it as vital that 'tensions should not be resolved but maintained, in order to provide an environ-

---

1 S Roberts 'Mediation in Family Disputes (1983) 46 *MLR* 537, 556–56.

2 C Menkel-Meadow 'Towards Another View of Legal Negotiation: The Structure of Problem Solving' (1984) *ULA L Rev* 754.

3 C Menkel-Meadow 'Lawyer Negotiations: Theories and Realities – What We Learn From Mediation' (1993) *MLR* 361 at p 367.

4 *Walker* (1996) p 69.

5 A Taylor 'A General Theory of Divorce Mediation' in J Folberg and A Milne (eds) *Divorce Mediation: Theory and Practice* (1988) The Guilford Press, New York.

6 J Eekelaar 'Family Justice: Ideal or Illusion? Family Law and Communitarian Values' (1995) 48 *Current Legal Problems*, Pt 2, p 191.

7 *Walker* (1997) p 64. This may be an overstatement as work has and is taking place on key issues such as domestic violence and cultural awareness in mediation circles which does attempt to translate research into meaningful practice. It is also likely to be monitored with quality assurance-check.

8 J Rifkin 'The Practitioner's Dilemma' in J P Folger and T S Jones (eds) *New Directions in Mediation: Communication, Research and Perspectives* (1994) Sage, Thousand Oaks, California.

ment conducive for both studying and grappling with the issues'[1]. Bearing this in mind I intend to critically examine the core values of mediation – encompassing neutrality, fairness and autonomy[2]. By offering different perspectives on what seem to be, and indeed are often portrayed as, relatively straightforward concepts, I hope to generate debate on the extremely complex issues involved in constructing an ethical framework for a dynamic process.

THE DISCURSIVE CONSTRUCTION OF ETHICS

Recognition of the dynamic nature of mediation and the role that the parties play in constructing ethics in the process itself means that conventional *a priori* ethical conceptualisation is not germane to this context. Cooks and Hale argue that the discursive construction of mediation should be at the centre of any attempt to define a set of ethics. This term refers to the interactions and communicative challenges that define the process of mediation for the parties. Parties go to mediation with what could be termed an ethical problem which each perceives as right and the introduction of a non-partisan mediator begins the process of transforming these positions in a way so as to conform with an ethical framework both can subscribe to[3]. As Cooks and Hale argue, rather than apply ethics to a generalised picture, we have to consider 'how the ethics, justice and fairness are created within a situated discourse'[4]. This ties in with a post-modern theory of justice as espoused by Drucilla Cornell who maintains that justice is not an end, something that can be achieved, but rather is something to be struggled for[5]. In the same way mediation cannot be defined only as a process in which individuals discover the correct way of interpreting the other's meanings or achieving mutual understanding. This focus on an end product does not take into account the ongoing nature of negotiated understanding. Cooks and Hale conclude, 'Rather mediation should be examined as a process with possibilities for co-ordinating the various meanings that humans give to their lives'[6].

Cultural hegemony

Before moving into a detailed examination of neutrality and autonomy, it should first be recognised that, as Shah-Kazemi argues, 'mediation is susceptible to the spectre of cultural hegemony'[7], particularly in its preference for a neutral outsider, and its culturally specific constructions of autonomy and self-determination.

Gulliver notes that the construction of the mediator as an impartial and sometimes 'neutral' intervener is a strong Western stereotype and is one which

1 C Morris 'The Trusted Mediator: Ethics and Interaction in Action in J Macfarlane (ed) Rethinking Disputes: The Mediation Alternative (1997) Cavendish, London p 344.
2 It becomes clear from this discussion that the two concepts overlap to some extent.
3 C Morris 'The Trusted Mediator: Ethics and Interaction in Action in J Macfarlane (ed) Rethinking Disputes: The Mediation Alternative (1997) Cavendish, London p 302.
4 L Cooks and C Hale 'The Construction of Ethics in Mediation' (1994) 12(1) *Mediation Quarterly* 55 at p 56.
5 D Cornell *Philosophy of the Limit* (1992) Routledge, New York pp 117–169.
6 L Cooks and C Hale 'The Construction of Ethics in Mediation' (1994) 12(1) *Mediation Quarterly* 55 at p 57.
7 S N Shah-Kazemi 'Cross Cultural Mediation: A Critical View of the Dynamics of Culture in Family Disputes' (2000) *Int J of Law Policy and the Family* 302 at p 303.

remains dominant in professional mediator groupings in the West[1]. If we consider the dynamics of mediation which involves engaging with and transforming the parties' ethical and normative framework, then as Shah-Kazemi rightly argues:

> 'The process of negotiation and *a fortiori*, mediation does not and cannot be situated in a cultural or normative vacuum; the disputants view of the world, their cultural identities, their universe of meaning invariably and indelibly shapes the dispute management process'[2].

This requires a mediator who understands, if not shares', cultural values, some of which are not fully encapsulated in the liberal model[3].

LeBaron Duryea, whose research focused on Aboriginal peoples in North America, also argues that the individualistic approach to conflict evidenced in western thinking is not mirrored by those from more collectivist cultures:

> '. . . the individualist approach to ethics dominant in Western societies is not reflected in the ethics of many non-Western societies, where ethical values may reflect loyalty to family, religious or cultural values. Codes of ethics developed for mediators in the West implicitly incorporate dominant Western views of both conflict and ethics. In pluralistic societies, this unexamined approach to the framing of mediator ethics may not be realistic in the long-term'[4].

An awareness of this cultural hegemony further confirms the need to move away from static concepts. Theorising which recognises the discursive construction of mediator ethics is better able to support a plurality of values[5].

Re-figuring neutrality

The unfeasibility of mediation's claim to neutrality is constant in critiques[6]. Indeed it is ironic that a process whose identity is often so reliant on being alternative to law has fixed on a concept which law itself has found so difficult to sustain. It is certainly the case that the neutrality, if we understand this to mean that the mediator is unbiased, is not only impossible to achieve but risks being unethical in that such an approach would fail to recognise power differentials between parties.

It is most likely the case that the idea of neutrality was to found upon in order to distinguish mediators' activities from those of judges and partisans. Yet a number of studies have shown that neutrality gives a misleading impression as

---

1 *Gulliver* (1979) p 212. He points out that the 'truly disinterested, impartial mediator is rather rare' and often appears as a representative of a community to which both disputing parties belong, whether through political, spatial, familial connection: *Gulliver* p 214.

2 S N Shah-Kazemi 'Cross Cultural Mediation: A Critical View of the Dynamics of Culture in Family Disputes' (2000) *Int J of Law Policy and the Family* 302 at p 303.

3 Vibha Pankaj's research on the subject of mediation for minority ethnic families in Scotland reveals the need for culturally sensitive modification of ethics and working practices: V Pankaj *Family Mediation Services for Minority Ethnic Families in Scotland* (2000) Scottish Executive CRU, Edinburgh.

4 C Morris 'The Trusted Mediator: Ethics and Interaction in Action in J Macfarlane (ed) *Rethinking Disputes: The Mediation Alternative* (1997) Cavendish Publishing, London, p 308.

5 This will also assist more effective mediation intevention as 'The perceptions that parties have of the dispute, and the choices open for the way forward, are to a high degree delineated by the ethical and normative framework within which the parties operate' *Shah-Kazemi* p 318.

6 J Rifkin, J Millen and S Cobb 'Towards a New Discourse for Mediation: A Critique of Neutrality' (1991) 9(2) *Mediation Quarterly* 151.

mediators are far from passive in the process. Conversational analysis reveals active intervention by mediators in 'shaping communication towards settlement seeking and away from polarised and conflictual positions'[1]. Dingwall and Greatbach's work demonstrates that by setting the order of speech, time allocation and in re-framing parties' narratives mediators display a 'selective facilitation' which influences both process and outcome[2]. This 'sophisticated strategy' may, as Myers and Wasoff note, point to the expertise of mediators but is nevertheless an activity which 'comes into conflict with the core values of the service'[3].

Before abandoning the concept it is important to consider the work of Rifkin, Millen and Cobb[4] who support the aforementioned critique but also offer a more sophisticated ethical discourse that more accurately captures the practice of mediation. They offer a two-pronged definition of 'neutrality' which encompasses:

1. Impartiality which refers to 'the ability of the mediator to maintain an unbiased relationship with the disputants' which mediators utilise to 'make clear that they are present simply to listen and not to influence the disputants' explication of the case'[5].
2. 'Equidistance' which identifies the ability of the mediator to assist the disputants in expressing their 'side' of the case. Thus, mediators will temporarily align themselves with parties to support each party. By performing this they are able to support each party in a 'symmetrical' way.

It is clear that both versions of neutrality are incompatible. The first as outlined above is not supported by research into mediation activity or indeed any examination of the skills mediators train in and practise. By contrast, neutrality when viewed as a balancing activity, much more accurately describes mediation which while certainly not a neutral activity is one which very much attempts to ensure equality in the process.

The limits of balancing

The limits of this discursive balancing must also inform the ethical practice of mediation. Power dynamics created by gender differences form the most common critique of informal processes in the family sphere. At its most extreme, the problematisation of women's position in such processes warns that face-to-face negotiation in cases involving domestic violence can further reify and

1 *Walker* (1997) p 74. See the work of S Cobb and J Rifkin 'Neutrality as a Discursive Practice: The Construction and Transformation of Narratives in Community Mediation' in S Silbey and A Sarat (eds) 11 *Studies in Law, Politics and Society* (1991)JAI Press, Greenwich, Conn; S Cobb and J Rifkin, 'Practice and Paradox: Deconstructing neutrality in mediation' (1991) 16(1) *Law & Social Inquiry* 35.

2 R Dingwall ' Empowerment or Enforcement? Some Questions About Power and Control in Divorce Mediation' in R Dingwall and J Eekelaar (eds) *Divorce Mediation and the Legal Process* (1988) Oxford University Press, Oxford.

3 *Myers and Wasoff* ch 6 p 2.

4 J Rifkin, J Millen and S Cobb 'Towards a New Discourse for Mediation: A Critique of Neutrality' (1991) 9(2) *Mediation Quarterly* 151 at p 151.

5 J Rifkin, J Millen and S Cobb 'Towards a New Discourse for Mediation: A Critique of Neutrality' (1991) 9(2) *Mediation Quarterly* 151 at p 154.

privatise abuse[1]. I do not intend to review this debate – it should surely be beyond doubt that given the prevalence of domestic violence in society[2] and our increasing awareness of its dynamics, it is not appropriate to negotiate in an informal setting without the protection of legal rights and partisans. As Menkel-Meadow argues, 'These important political and legal concerns must be 'part of the calculus of what should be negotiated and by recognising that some things are simply not negotiable'[3].

The recognition of the limits of mediator balancing require an understanding of the different ways in which both mediation and legal processes are able to empower individuals. As Myers and Wasoff note, 'participation is not the only basis for the empowerment of the parties to a dispute, and participation does not necessarily lead to empowerment for all'[4]. Partisanship can offer valuable support[5] in the form of 'professional representation by a knowledgeable and powerful advocate who is better able, through skill, training and experience, than the party to articulate and advance their case'[6].

Interest-based mediation, on the other hand, has an ability to transform power. As Chornenki oberves:

> 'When joint efforts take place, the parties do exercise power, but not as influence or control. Instead they are engaged in the power of the collective, here referred to as 'power-with' ... As opposed to having power over a person ... when power-with occurs, one can observe ... the aims, processes, methods, or behaviour that create order, stability and unity of direction'[7].

It is important to note its limitations, as Chornenki notes, as this is not an activity a mediator magically performs:

> 'Power-with is not something a mediator can foster or create without the assistance of the parties and the flaw in a great deal of mediation promotion and description is that it can create the impression that the process, and/or the mediator, are able unilaterally to bring about (through technique, skill, good judgment, intuition) the kinds of conditions that will lead to an elegant, economical and efficient solution'[8].

---

1 The work of Astor in Australia is very influential: H Astor, 'Mediation in Disputes Involving Violence Against Women: Recent Australian Developments' (1998) *Fam Med* Vol 82 p 18. Work in the US includes C Bohmer and M Ray 'Effects of different dispute resolution methods on women and children after divorce' (1994) *Fam L Q* Vol 28 p 223; T Grillo 'The Mediation Alternative: Process Dangers for Women' (1991) *Yale L J* 100, 1545. In Scotland a study by Jane Lewis which found that in 1/4 of mediation cases were known by the mediation service to have involved some violence, but that generally mediators did not assume that mediation should not take place if there had been a history of abuse: J Lewis *The Role of Mediation in Family Disputes in Scotland* (Legal Studies Research Findings no 23) at p 54. This mirrors findings in England and Wales from M Hester and L Radford *Domestic Violence and Child Contact in England and Denmark* (1996) Policy Press/ Joseph Rowentree Foundation; Hester, Pearson and Radford *Domestic Violence: A national survey of court welfare and voluntary sector mediation practice* (1997) Policy Press.

2 And indeed threatening and abusive behaviour often continues into separation.

3 C Menkel-Meadow 'Lawyer Negotiations: Theories and Realities – What We Learn From Mediation' (1993) *MLR* 361 at p 368.

4 *Myers & Wasoff* Ch 6 p 4.

5 As evidenced by the research of *Davis et al.*

6 *Myers & Wasoff* Ch 6 p 4.

7 G Chornenki 'Mediating Commercial Disputes: Exchanging "Power Over" for "Power With" in J Macfarlane (ed) Rethinking Disputes: The Mediation Alternative (1997) Cavendish, London, p 164.

8 G Chornenki 'Mediating Commercial Disputes: Exchanging "Power Over" for "Power With" in J Macfarlane (ed) Rethinking Disputes: The Mediation Alternative (1997) Cavendish, London, p 166.

AUTONOMY

The prioritisation of parties' autonomy is evident from the vast majority of literature concerning the subject which stresses that mediation is a consensual process that assists parties in reaching self-determined resolutions to their disputes.

A debate in the early 1990s sought to clarify this position as there had been, prior to this time, a strand of mediation practice which adopted a particular therapeutic approach called 'systems theory' which viewed families as a unit whose properties and pathologies transcend the individuals involved[1]. In an exchange of views on the matter, Marion Roberts dismissed this approach as having no place in mediation as it elevated a professional's view of a family's pathologies at the expense of the individual's own perceptions[2]. Autonomy, she posits, is clearly central to mediation:

> 'Decision-making capacity is what defines this standard of adulthood. The realization of the parties' authority through their own control over decision-making is what distinguishes mediation from other forms of intervention, for example, adjudication. The issue of autonomy and its location with the parties themselves is absolutely central to mediation'[3].

Yet autonomy which envisages independent, free-standing, rights-bearing individuals is much closer to the legal model which mediation is distinguished from. This has led some to align mediation with those discourses which have critiqued liberalism as failing to recognise the effects of community on the construction of the subject.

Autonomy versus communitarianism

The possibility and desirability of autonomous objectivity has also been challenged 'by those whose ethical theories contemplate interdependent communities whose members have mutually reciprocal responsibilities'[4]. Communitarian philosophy, which stresses the importance of seeing the individual through their interconnectedness within the community, rather than through their abstractedness from each other, would appear an ideal theory for mediation to embrace.

Bush for example describes the importance of recognition in mediation: 'evoking recognition is itself an accomplishment of enormous value: the value of escaping our alienated isolation and rediscovering our common humanity, even in the midst of bitter division'[5]. Indeed the family has been portrayed by one of the most prominent communitarian theorists, Roberto Unger, as the ideal that this political movement aspires to[6].

Understandably, feminists have been wary of this portrayal of the family[7]. While this is a site for mutual fulfilment, obligation, love and interconnectedness

---

1 M Roberts 'Systems or Selves: Some Ethical Issues in Family Mediation' (1992) 10 *Mediation Quarterly* Vol 3, 4.
2 M Roberts 'Systems or Selves': Some Ethical Issues in Family Mediation' (1992) 10 *Mediation Quarterly* Vol 3, 4 at pp 7–8.
3 *Roberts* M p 5.
4 C Morris 'The Trusted Mediator: Ethics and Interaction in Action' in J Macfarlane (ed) *Rethinking Disputes: The Mediation Alternative* (1997) Cavendish, London p 329.
5 *Bush* p 270.
6 R Unger *Critical Legal Studies Movement* (1986) Harvard University Press, Cambridge, Mass 1975.
7 For a detailed examination of this area see E Frazer and N Lacey *The Politics of the Community: A Feminist Critique of the Liberal-Communitarian Debate* (1993) Harvester, Hemel Hempstead.

it has also been shown to be a site of violence, imposed dependence and economic oppression. The problem is, as Iris Marion Young points out[1], that the ideal of community exhibits a totalising impulse that denies difference in its insistence that interdependence only be achieved at the expense of autonomy. Such homogeneity of values is not useful for modern communities that display a plurality of norms. Merry's work in the area of community mediation, for example, warns that community mediation programmes have been transplanted from the very different context and ideals of pastoral societies (homogeneous groupings, with similar value-base which can be used to settle disputes) to the 'heterogeneous, transient, anonymous, and morally diverse American city whose citizens believe they possess legal rights and should be protected by the courts'[2].

Embracing communitarianism wholeheartedly is a dangerous course for family mediation to follow also. Mediations focusing on parents making mutual decisions may seem to fit easily within the communitarian framework. However, adopting an ethical theory which denies the importance of rights or parties' individual interests, would simply confirm the fears that informal justice compromises legal rights and suppresses difference[3].

Autonomy versus Ethic of Care

It is not surprising that Carol Gilligan's work is frequently referred to in this context[4]. In an 'Ethic of Care[5]' Gilligan's research revealed that men and women display a different ethical outlook, with men generally prioritising justice, rights and autonomy and women the values of connection, care and intimacy[6]. She then contends that authoritative ethical frameworks such as law promote 'male' values at the expense of 'female' values and argues developed ethical should incorporate an appreciation of both[7]. In the mediation context, Williams argues that mediators must be sensitive to these distinctions in moral language. This will enable them to better understand the norms that will govern an agreement as well as being better able to 'facilitate parties' development of solutions that

1 I Young 'The ideal of community and the politics of difference' (1986) 12 *Social Theory and Practice*, 1. Young also points out that mutuality or intersubjectivity is philosophically impossible as it presupposes that a subject can know himself or herself and express that knowledge accurately and unambiguously to others to enable sharing to take place. As Kristeva notes, 'Any individual subject is a play of differences that cannot be comprehended' 1977.

2 S E Merry 'The Social Organization of Mediation in Non-industrial Societies: Implications for Community Justice in America' in R Abel (ed) *The Politics of Informal Justice, Vol 2 Comparative Studies*, (1982) Academic Press, New York, London p 20.

3 This includes the interests of children which are often conflated with adult interests: see at ch 1 above. It is hoped that the increasing use of child consultants may offer an increased opportunity for the children's voices to be heard in this context.

4 B Williams 'Implications of Gilligan for Divorce Mediation: Speculative Applications' (1994) 12(2) *Mediation Quarterly* 101.

5 C Gilligan *In a Different Voice: Psychological Theory and Women's Development* (1982) Harvard University Press, Cambridge, Mass.

6 She recognises that both sexes speak in terms of 'rights' and 'care' but that preferences demonstrated in her study are gendered. For a fuller discussion of this debate in the context of feminist legal theory see J Scoular 'Feminist Jurisprudence' in S Jackson and J Jones *Contemporary Feminist Theories* (1998) Edinburgh University Press, Edinburgh.

7 This idea has been the subject of Deborah Tannen's work which analyses the way in which men and women communicate and confirms these findings: D Tannen *You Just Don't Understand: Women and Men in Conversation* (1990) William Morrow and Co, New York. It may also have influenced the rather reductive and clichéd *Men Are From Mars* J Gray (1992) Harper Collins.

reflect the perspectives of both justice and care, rights and responsibilities'[1]. While I would agree with this, the disadvantage of adopting Gilligan's theory uncritically is that it identifies sex, sexuality and gender identity as fixed. In so doing it 'reinforces conventional stereotypes of the feminine by the current gender structure and potentially constrains women and men in their fashioning of their individual lives'[2].

Autonomy and difference

The way in which mediation will best be able to advocate its difference and offer an alternative to legal discourse is in the way it, as a process, is able to recognise the standpoint of the 'concrete other'[3]. This means that parties with concrete histories, identities and emotions are given space to explore and negotiate their post-separation or divorce identities and arrangements. In assuming this standpoint, parties are able to abstract from their commonality without compromising their difference.

This contrasts with legal discourse where individuals are required to speak according to a vocabulary of rights which are held by individuals in the abstract sense. Respect for difference will only be paid (if it is recognised at all) to what Seyla Benhabib describes as the 'generalized other'.

The standpoint of the 'generalised other' requires us to view each and every individual as a rational being entitled to the same rights and duties we would want to ascribe ourselves. In assuming the standpoint, we abstract from the individuality and concrete identity of the other. We assume that the other, like ourselves, is a being who has concrete needs, desires and affects, but that what constitutes his or her moral dignity is not what differentiates us from each other, but rather what we as speaking and acting rational agents have in common. In contemporary moral psychology and moral theory, it is the viewpoint of the 'generalised other' that predominates as it permits moral theory (and as a result legal theory) to be universal. 'Universalistic theory neglects such everyday interactional morality and assumes that the public standpoint of justice, and our quasi-public personalities as right-bearing individuals, are the centre of moral theory'[4].

As King's work demonstrates, even when moving away from an overtly legal standard the normative framework solicitors have constructed is inevitably generalised into what is considered reasonable/ unreasonable. While mediator influence is also able to have a generalising influence, mediation by its very nature is more able to give parties space to consider their concrete differences and mutual interests. What we need to do now is consider when public norms must interrupt private ordering while respecting the space it creates for individuals to fashion their own solutions to their concrete situations.

In a society where inequality is widespread, a greater reliance on public norms may be necessary. Given that the parties in family mediation are largely heterosexual couples and given the social and material inequality that continues to

1 C Morris 'The Trusted Mediator: Ethics and Interaction in Action in J Macfarlane (ed) *Rethinking Disputes: The Mediation Alternative* (1997) Cavendish, London p 316.
2 D Cornell *The Imaginary Domain* (1995) Routledge, New York.
3 S Benhabib 'The Generalized and Concrete Other: Towards a Feminist Critique of Substantialist Universalism' (1986) *Praxis International*, vol 5 no 4, 402.
4 S Benhabib 'The Generalized and Concrete Other: Towards a Feminist Critique of Substantialist Universalism' (1986) *Praxis International*, vol 5 no 4, 402.

characterise this relationship, then mediation must not promise to offer a substitute for legal advice, rights, partisanship and structural equality. It can, however, offer support and space to those who are able and willing to reconfigure their concrete identities and family relationships. This offers a more limited role for mediation than that envisaged by policy-makers and proponents in recent years, yet it is no less important. An ethically informed theory and practice of mediation, promises to accommodate a more diverse range of interests as well as rights and to recognise and promote a variety of perspectives. The challenge is to ensure that the material and structural inequalities, which still very much characterise family life, are balanced alongside the quest for situated justice.

Index